All That Glitters

All That Glitters:

Country Music
in America

Edited by

George H. Lewis

Bowling Green State University Popular Press
Bowling Green, Ohio 43403

Popular Music Series
B. Lee Cooper, General Editor

Copyright © 1993 by Bowling Green State University Popular Press

Library of Congress Catalogue Card No.: 92-74544

ISBN: 0-87972-573-7 Clothbound
     0-87972-574-5 Paperback

Cover design by Gary Dumm
From an idea by George H. Lewis

Dedication

This book is dedicated to Steve, who, in his too-short life, wrote the perfect country and western song many times over; and to Norman, who never did decide if Hank Snow or Kris Kristofferson was the best country singer who ever lived.

The lyrics of life, as they knew them, will never die.

Also to Rhiannon, whose young life is, already, such a sweet song.

"Oh, the crowd will always love you...."

Contents

Introduction

Crude with a tang of the Indian wilderness, strong with the strength of the mountains, yet, in a way, mellowed with the flavor of Chaucer's time—surely this is folk-song of a high order. May it not one day give birth to a music that shall take a high place among the world's great schools of expression?

The Spirit of the Mountains
Emma B. Miles, 1905

I

It was cold that Tuesday night in Nashville, and the Exit In was nearly deserted. Although December had not yet arrived, it had snowed—was still snowing lightly—and the streets of Music City were white and quiet. On this night in 1973, I sat with Steve Goodman, who was drinking bourbon and working on something he called the ultimate country and western song. Steve had already gotten prison, mama, pickup trucks and trains into it. He was working hard on rain and lost love.

On stage, the singer began a tune that had been a hit for him nine years before. Steve stopped talking and listened, his dark eyes glowing. "Damn!" he finally said. "That guy's *so* good! You know his stuff?"

I nodded, but Steve had turned back to the singer. "It's the touch," he said softly, as if in a dream. "With the great ones, it's in the touch."

The Touch is something you recognize when you hear it. Hank Williams' cry as he moaned the blues, the high lonesome sound of Bill Monroe's bluegrass, or the manic rush of Carl Perkins' rock-a-billy classic, "Dixie Fried." It's also present in the work of contemporary artists. Listen to Randy Travis' quiet despair in "Diggin' Up Bones," the weary desolation of Emmylou Harris' "Boulder To Birmingham," or the bright bluegrass fiddle of Alison Krauss on her "Too Late To Cry" album.

The Touch is talent, but it is also connectedness—an awareness of and linkage to, the deep country roots of the music. Indeed, fiddling and singing were present at the time the first settlements were made in the New World. Nick Tosches, in *Country*, writes of John Laydon, a pioneer of Jamestown who, in the 1630s, played his fiddle like "a Man wilde by Fever," as his friend Nathaniel Powell wrote in his diary. And the October 7, 1737 issue of the *Virginia Gazette* contained an announcement of fiddling and singing competitions to be held as part of the year's St. Andrew's Day festivities:

1

2 All That Glitters

That a Violin be played for by 20 Fiddlers, and to be given to him that shall be adjudged to play the best. No person to have the Liberty of playing unless he brings a Fiddle with him. After the prize is won, they are all to play together, and each a different Tune; and to be treated by the Company.

That a Cuire of Ballads be sung for, by a number of Songsters; the best Songster to have the Prize, and all of them to have Liquor sufficient to clear their Wind-Pipes.

Blacks in America, from the earliest days, were also adept at playing the fiddle. In 1779, the *Virginia Gazette* ran a notice concerning Harry, a runaway slave, who was "very fond of playing the fiddle, and is an artful cunning fellow." Lydia Parrish wrote in *Slave Songs of the Georgia Sea Islands* that the fiddle, although sinful, was the favored instrument of Southern blacks. Butch Cage, the black fiddler who recorded early in this century, remembered hearing old black fiddlers in Mississippi performing songs now associated with white fiddling and bluegrass, in the late 1800s— songs like "Arkansas Traveler" and "Old Wagoner."

The first known recording of country music was accomplished in 1922, when fiddlers Henry C. Gilliland and A.C. ("Eck") Robertson, fresh from a Confederate reunion in Richmond, wound up in New York City, knocking on RCA Victor's studio door, demanding to be recorded. Whether from shock and anxiety (the two of them were dressed as a cowboy and a rebel sharpshooter and had clearly slept for more than one night in these clothes), or just to get rid of them, the engineers agreed. Robertson's solo of "Sally Gooden" and their duet, "Arkansas Traveler," was released by RCA in April 1923.

Then, in 1927, in a former hat factory in Bristol, Virginia, Ralph Peer recorded Jimmie Rodgers, and the Carter Family. Peer was attracted to Rodgers because he "was an individualist. He had his own style." Rodgers' unique style was, to a great extent, derived as much from American black music, which he grew up around and loved, as it was by the Southern white country tradition. The Carter Family, on the other hand, was Appalachian harmony so sweet that, when Peer heard Sara sing her first notes, he knew "it was going to be wonderful." Wonderful it was. And the rest, as they say, is history.

II

I just recently played at a spot in Levonia, Georgia, a town of about 1,500. The park's out on the side of a mountain, has a creek running through it. People that run it are country people. They're fine people. And when I left they gave me a dog. And I took it with me. I've been wonderin' what the Nugget will give me when I leave.

Mel Tillis, playing the Golden Nugget, Las Vegas, Nevada

Modern country music, as I term it, began as America moved out of the shadows of World War II and into the quiet promise of the 1950s. Regional country musics of the 1930s and 1940s were consolidating in Nashville in what was soon to become the country radio and recording center of America. As the new medium of television lured the best shows from radio, country (and rock and roll) music moved in to fill the vacuum. A nationally based "sound"—or at least a consensus of musical attitude as to how to approach and create a hit country song—was developing, along with major artists who defined this sound with their trailblazing musical work.

This book is a look at modern country music in America, from its "roots" in the early 1950s to the musical crossroads it stands upon today. In these pages, writers examine aspects of the music as diverse as the creation of country "culture" in the honkytonk; the development of the Nashville music industry; the influence of regional scenes, like Austin; and why country music singers are similar to the English romantic poets.

These themes, and many others, are analyzed from various perspectives—historians, sociologists, musicologists, folklorists, anthropologists, ethnographers, communications specialists, journalists, national media critics and others are all represented in these pages. Taken together, these diverse views of country begin to suggest what a fascinating and multi-faceted phenomenon this music is and how central it is to contemporary American popular culture.

There are several major issues that wind their way through these diverse essays—issues that are not confined to a study of country music, but are central to most cultural studies. Here I identify ten of these issues, posing them as questions that the various authors in these pages address with respect to country music.

1. *Authenticity.* Can a musical form that is mass produced and distributed be thought of as "authentic," and, if so, who defines it as such?

2. *Creativity.* To what extent is the creativity of an individual artist compromised by his/her need to work within the impersonal cultural industry system, which defines music as "product" instead of "art?"

3. *Regional Influences.* To what extent has country music been influenced by regionally popular songs and styles—and has this sort of influence disappeared in modern, commercial versions of the music?

4. *Southernization.* Is country music really southern music? If so, what does its national popularity say about America as a whole? If not, can specific, non-southern influences be identified?

5. *Traditionalism.* To what extent can country artists, by returning to traditional roots in their music, regain the immediacy and vitality many feel the genre once had—or to what extent does such an effort produce only second rate, modern day copies of earlier sounds? (ie, you can't go home again...)

6. *Pop Borrowing.* Is experimentation and borrowing from other pop forms a legitimate form of creativity for country artists, or are the major and important artists likely to be those who stick to traditional forms?

7. *Meaning.* What does country music mean to its listeners? Do they uncritically accept and absorb lyrics from Nashville, or—especially in taverns and honky tonks—do audience members *interact* with the music to create their own meanings?

8. *Contradictions.* To what extent are there contradictions evidenced in the messages of country songs? Do these contradictions have to do with the position of the country audience in the American socio-economic class structure and/or do they reflect contradictions in American values themselves?

9. *Socialization.* To what extent do country music lyrics reflect and reinforce traditional role relationships in the country audience? Has this changed at all, as new country artists—especially women—gain power and autonomy in the industry by virtue of their strong record sales?

10. *Academic Interest.* If country music is the music of choice of the American white working class, and if it is important to this group and others in anchoring meaning in their lives, why have so few liberal academics taken it seriously for study?

III

The book is divided topically into seven sections. Each section has a brief introduction and overview of major themes and issues discussed in the essays of the section. Each introduction concludes with a short "Playlist" of country music that is relevant and topical to the issues raised in the section. Each musical piece is identified by artist, album title and recording company. Although most of these recordings are still in print, a few may have to be located in specialty stores that deal with folk, country and bluegrass music. But there are a surprising number of such stores (and mail order houses) around the country. Check around locally and you are sure to find a lead.

Taken together, these "Playlists" offer a fine introduction to modern American country music, though—linked to the specific essays as they are—the recordings are not meant to be totally definitive of the larger body of modern country music, nor should they be taken as a list of the "best" of country music. They do, however, offer a way to move from the written words of these pages into the music itself.

In closing, I'd like to mention a few individuals who have helped, especially, in making this project a reality: Steve Thompson, who invited me to give a paper on country music at the 1988 American Anthropological Association Meeting in Phoenix and at whose session (and the party afterwards) the idea of this book sparked to life; Katie Stewart and Joli Jensen, who both not only contributed wonderful essays themselves, but also suggested further leads that evolved into fine pieces as well; Paul Kingsbury of Nashville's Country Music Foundation and Paul Wells of Middle Tennessee State's Center for Popular Music, whose research on my behalf and generosity in allowing me reprint permissions greatly enhanced the depth and scope of the book; and Pat

Browne, of the Popular Press, who has had faith in the project from the start.

George H. Lewis,
Stockton, California
October, 1992

References

The following seven books are essential sources for anyone interested in reading further in the area of American country music. They are all highly recommended.

Dorothy Horstman. *Sing Your Heart Out, Country Boy, Revised Edition.* Nashville, Tennessee: Country Music Foundation Press, 1986. This is the revised version of a classic work, in which Ms. Horstman interviews song writers as to how they developed specific songs, and also includes the lyrics of these songs in the text.

Paul Kingsbury (editor). *Country: The Music and The Musicians.* New York: Abbeville Press, 1988. This collection of essays covers country music from its beginning to 1985. The book includes many rare and wonderful photographs, taken from private collections and from the archives of the Country Music Foundation.

Bill C. Malone. *Country Music, U.S.A.*, Second Edition. Austin: U of Texas P, 1985. Although scholars argue with Malone about minor points here and there, this book is generally considered the definitive history of American country music.

Jimmie N. Rogers. *The Country Music Message: Revisited.* Fayetteville: U of Arkansas P, 1989. A communication theorist takes a look at what country songs say, and teases out the messages contained in the music.

Neil V. Rosenberg. *Bluegrass: A History.* Urbana: U of Illinois P, 1985. Quite simply, the best book on bluegrass music and, as some have described it, the best book on *any* form of popular music yet written.

Irwin Stambler and Grulun Landon. *The Encyclopedia of Folk, Country and Western.* New York: St. Martin's, 1984. This is a standard reference work and, although a bit weak on pre-1950 regional artists, includes a number of important figures from the folk and folk/rock circles that many mainstream country sources overlook (or ignore).

6 All That Glitters

Nick Tosches. *Country: Living Legends and Dying Metaphors In America's Biggest Music.* New York: Scribner's, 1985. This book, described by critic Greil Marcus as "a superbly detailed assault on everything country music honors as most holy, and a loving, scabrous portrait of what *is* most holy," is must reading. There is no book on popular music of any kind quite like it.

Lighting Up The Purple Sky:
Roots of Modern Country

The roots of modern country music are sunk deep in post World War II America, a time of great shifts and changes in the social fabric of the country. For many, the psychic upheavals of war were followed by the social upheavals of the new era. The city (and its suburbs) became the focal point of America, and migration to these cities, easier credit (and the things it purchased), and the baby boom became new realities to which the culture had to adjust.

Country music reflected the new concerns and ambivalences of its audience, from songs like Roy Acuff's "Wreck On The Highway—" which depicted the new secular order, high on alcohol, and racing down a dark rain-stained road toward death—to the spring-water pure music of Bill Monroe—a resurrection of the traditional musical forms of the past.

It was at this time that country music—to a great extent a collection of loosely connected regional styles—began to develop, in Nashville, a critical mass artistically. Although it can be argued—and correctly so—that major influences on modern country include artists other than those found here, it would be difficult not to recognize the import of Bill Monroe, Hank Williams, Patsy Cline and (yes) Elvis Presley as central architects of this "new" national music.

Robert Cantwell argues, in "Mimesis in Bill Monroe's Bluegrass Music" that his music was a successful solution to the problem of marketing a rural and traditional music to the new national public audience that increasingly was defining rural music as backward, comic and embarrassing in nature. Bluegrass, Cantwell feels, presented traditional music without self-parody, and thus paved the way for the commercial acceptance of this style of music as a serious musical form. Monroe's success has opened the doors for traditional performers as diverse as Flatt and Scruggs, Norman Blake, The New Grass Revival, The Whites, Ricky Scaggs and Alison Krauss.

Richard Leppert and George Lipsitz, in "Age, the Body and Experience in the Music of Hank Williams" see Williams "standing at a crossroads in history, at a fundamental turning point for relationships between men and women, white and black, capital and labor" in the post-war era. They point to the fact that Hank Williams brought a tremendous range of diverse musical genres to play in his music, while at the same time articulating the "blasted hopes and repressed desires" of the country audience. Hank Willaims "wrote the lives" of the post-war audience and reinvested country music with everyday meaning, as have

7

singer/songwriters who have followed in his larger-than-life footsteps—artists such as George Jones, Merle Haggard, Rodney Crowell, Dwight Yoakum and even his own son, Hank Williams, Jr.

Patsy Cline's hits had the background vocals and instrumentation of the developing "Nashville sound" of the early 1950s, as Joli Jensen points out in "Patsy Cline: Musical Negotiation and the Nashville Sound" Her songs became popular because of radio airplay in the newly defined radio-record environment of Nashville. Ironically, this "commercial, yet country" sound was something that Cline fought *against* in her career, as she preferred the traditional sound of country to that which was replacing it and which she so successfully helped to define. She was always a rebel, as Jensen shows. A woman in a male dominated business, she opened many doors for the female singers who followed her and have helped define modern country—people such as Loretta Lynn, Dolly Parton, Emmylou Harris, Reba McIntyre and Rosanne Cash.

Elvis Presley's fusion of black and white music was a pop phase of inter-actions between black and white musicians in the American south that goes back at least to the early part of the 17th century, as Bill C. Malone explains in "Elvis, Country Music and the South." White country musicians, from Jimmie Rodgers to the present, have demonstrated a continuing fascination with black sounds, songs, styles and images. Presley took this fascination and made it popular far beyond the traditional boundaries of country music. In so doing, he underscored the black/white musical mix of modern country, as well as being the central figure in the creation of "rockabilly" as a country style early in his career. As Malone points out, Presley also, years later, paved the way for the Rhinestone Cowboy crooner, the MOR artist who could play Vegas lounges and cross records over onto the adult easy listening radio play lists—singers such as Glen Campbell, T.G. Sheppard, Ronnie McDowell and Kenny Rogers.

Playlist

Bill Monroe	Bill Monroe and the Bluegrass Boys 1950-1958	Bear Family
Hank Williams	I'm So Lonesome I Could Cry	Polydor
Hank Williams	I Won't Be Home No More	Polydor
Patsy Cline	The Patsy Cline Story (2 vols)	Decca/MCA
Elvis Presley	The Sun Sessions	RCA
Various Artists	Hillbilly Music...Thank God! (Vol 1)	Capitol

Mimesis in Bill Monroe's Bluegrass Music

Robert Cantwell

The morality of art consists in the perfect use of an imperfect medium.

Oscar Wilde

What is now widely called bluegrass music, which reached its maturity in Bill Monroe's band on the Grand Ole Opry in the mid 1940s, offered a successful solution to the practical problem of marketing an essentially rural, old-fashioned and traditional music to public audiences increasingly unresponsive to the old-fashioned music except as parody, or burlesque, modes of self-consciousness which for twenty years had been generally encouraged in rural performers by radio and recording entrepreneurs. But it was a practical problem with moral implications: to preserve in the marketplace without self-parody a form not originally or inherently commercial was symbolically to affirm the essential dignity of the way of life from which that music had come and of which it was the expression—a way of life whose erosion by social and economic change had a vivid illustration in the evolution of the Grand Old Opry, which by the 1940s had acquired network status and a national reputation and had relegated the genuinely rural and traditional musician to the background (Malone 72).

By interposing himself between a public audience and a string-band whose music has a traditional character and by cultivating intensively the essential features of that music so that a more remote audience might more readily discern them, Bill Monroe negotiates the meeting of one phase of culture and another and makes of that negotiative or mediating process an aesthetic third dimension which is in effect mimetic: just as we make moral inferences about a dramatic character on the basis of his actions, so do we make moral inferences about the musician according to his management of his materials. "I think you can watch people," Monroe says, "any kind of work they do in the way of music, and tell pretty well through their life what they've gone through, if you watch it close enough."[1] A musical performance is potentially, then, a kind of dramatic action, "mimetic" in the sense that the musician "represents" or "figures forth" a character in action who is, whatever his

Reprinted with permission from the *Journal of Popular Culture*, Volume 13:2 (Fall 1979), pp. 209-220.

relation to actuality, essentially a fiction.

But the power of a musical instrument, style or kind to "figure forth" is colored by a complex burden of historical, social and cultural associations from which our response to music can never be entirely separated. It is plausible, I think, that a self-conscious traditional musician, for whom the range of those associations is not controlled by formal convention, as it is in classical performance, might expand his field of artistic choice to include them, establishing, in effect, his own conventions and creating an expanded art which includes both musical and dramatic elements. That Bill Monroe has in fact done so is powerfully suggested by the widely imitated and rigorously consistent pattern of his stage performance, over which he appears to exercise almost complete control. It is also suggested, I think, by a certain disproportion in his reputation among those who have seen him perform as contrasted to those audiences, primarily urban, who have only heard him on record. I suspect that the intense allegiance Monroe inspires as a performer, though obviously a tribute to the power of his music, testifies also to those features of his art which cannot be conveyed on a phonograph record.

The complex effects of Bill Monroe's performance are difficult to describe; but its more obvious features have frequently been noted. Monroe himself is a striking figure—dashing and patrician, presenting that peculiar clarity of image one associates with public, particularly political figures. While offstage he might easily be mistaken for some popular rural evangelist or Southern senator, on-stage he is, perhaps, the prosperous and genteel Kentucky planter of the recent past. By whatever subtle means one represents himself to the world—Bill refers to it as "the way a man carries himself"—he conveys the impression of a profound natural dignity which seems to have arisen from the habit of reflection upon matters of principle. However one interprets the message of his person, it is clear that the sheer amplitude of that message places him in a sensory foreground to which the Bluegrass Boys provide a background; the consequence of this arrangement is a three-dimensional acoustic and pictorial space which resonates socially and morally to the intellectual and physical activity of the musicians.

Aristotle likes the pleasure we take in mimesis to the pleasure of learning: "This," the artist has affirmed, "is that" (Chapter IV). In the later stages of a mimetic art, as its audience grasps the laws of the evolving mode, the artist may struggle to conceal himself, conferring an apparently independent life upon his subject; but at the outset he must persistently intercede, offering his own imagination as a medium through which an otherwise indefinite idea might be resolved. He is, in other words, a teacher, and his art has scholarly overtones

If you study music deep enough, old time music, why you get to learn what's good for it and what's not good for it. You just can't play it now and not pay any attention to it and do that. You've got to be thinking about it, maybe when you're working doing other things; you've got to keep your mind on that music and really get deep in it. I think I've studied old time music deeper than anybody in the country.... (Rinzler)

American Popular Music

The relationship an audience perceives between Monroe and his band, in whom his music is both represented and embodied, might be compared, albeit imperfectly, to the relationship between, say, a Lomax or Seeger who has brought a folk musician out of the field to the attention of an urban or intellectual audience. The important difference is that for Monroe, the relationship is the subject matter of a dramatic art which symbolically emphasizes the voluntary reintegration of the mediating figure, in what might be called an act of condescension, with the life he has economically, socially and artistically transcended but in which his imagination is rooted and to which, therefore, he must periodically return in art.

That a moral inference might be made about Monroe on the strength of this act of condescension—I use the term in its primary sense—I think its obvious, and however we might describe that inference, it is certainly the moral foundation of bluegrass music. Monroe's art—his sensitive interpretation of old-time music, his intellectual grasp of the social implications of representing that music to a contemporary audience—demands that the mastery of it, within certain limits of course, include mastery over the style, range and originality of his musicians; and because his four musicians, the Bluegrass Boys, are also a tiny community of men, Monroe's governance of them has the appearance of, and often is in fact, the exercise of moral authority. To the force of such authority in him much of his audience is highly responsive, and it provokes metaphors such as the "father" of bluegrass music, or more extravagantly, the "master" of it: a term whose religious thrust is, I think, lost on no one.

Urban audiences unfamiliar with bluegrass music will sometimes naively suppose that the Bluegrass Boys are not professional musicians and would no doubt feel betrayed to discover that in spite of testimony to the contrary, Kenny Baker, Monroe's superb fiddler, is not a coal-miner, though he has mined coal. This is a sure sign of the success of the fiction, which, like many fictions, modifies reality only slightly, but with a precision that accomplishes a thorough separation from it. Bill Monroe's sidemen are in fact never anything less than experienced and expert—almost without exception the best in bluegrass; in order to play in Monroe's band a musician must have complete command not only of Monroe's material and of the heavily syncopated, driving rhythms typical of his music, but of the delicate economy of expression which, it seems, a bluegrass musician can learn from Bill Monroe alone and whose purpose, I think, is to promote an overall unanimity or singularity of effect. "Nobody can say they play bluegrass," reports former Bluegrass Boy Bob Black, "until they play it with Monroe" (Hollobaugh 31).

12 All That Glitters

What is important for us, though, is that Monroe's paternal role becomes in performance a subject of dramatic representation. In harmony singing Monroe will carefully modulate his powerful voice to the voices of the others; often he will move among individual members of the band during instrumental breaks, or drop behind them to observe the whole, taking care that his own variations on the melody—he calls it "getting the most out of a tune"—do not duplicate any of theirs. Occasionally he will address his mandolin directly to a banjo or guitar picker who has fallen off the pace. "Monroe knows what everybody's doing at all times," Black continues. "He has a thousand ears under that hat" (Hollobaugh 31). At times one cannot help but feel that were Monroe to relax his grip upon the operations of the band for an instant the entire phenomenon would dissolve before our eyes.

Among many young musicians Bill Monroe is notorious for his insistence upon wholesale good-looks and good grooming in the members of his band; the figurative sons or disciples of the father of bluegrass, of course can be no less. Monroe's sovereignty over them—and from this one must partially exclude fiddler Kenny Baker, who as a kind of right-hand man in the management of Monroe's ten thousand acres of music is intermediate between Monroe and the rest—is implied by the poker-faced expressions of the members, whose immediate audience is, of course, Monroe himself, whose approval for various reasons they wish to solicit; the actual audience, whatever its ethnic character, often seems to arouse terror in them. That a band member should address the audience directly, except by Bill's implicit invitation in an instrumental break, or in any other way call special attention to himself, is unusual and unseemly. The membership of the Bluegrass Boys is, moreover, constantly in flux, and in recent years many of the Bluegrass Boys have been boys in the literal sense: young enough to be Monroe's sons or even grandsons. This flux has been explained in various ways: Bill wishes to populate the field with musicians trained in his style; or he does not pay them enough; or he becomes quickly dissatisfied with them; or they with to throw off his yoke. Perhaps all are true. But the formal explanation is that young and newly professional musicians remain in that psychological and aesthetic background which mimetically the music requires; their individual excellence seems somehow to attach to Monroe, as a son's to a father's.

The acoustic instruments upon which Bill insists—banjo and fiddle especially—quite obviously belong, moreover, to the parochial or even domestic background of the music. They are historically connected to a species of Southern music which predates the Civil War and in the popular imagination are emblematic of both the region and the period—Bill calls them "antiques" even if one happens to have been manufactured yesterday in Tokyo. The systematic structure of bluegrass admits each of them in turn into the public or secular foreground, where, as Bill's own remarks suggest, they are played in a fashion that somehow captures the essence of the old-time styles and of the special character of the instruments themselves. We must have, for example, the characteristic tolling of the five-string banjo, the bass runs of the guitar and the rhetorical wail of the fiddle constantly before us[2] To thus sharpen or amplify the auditory texture of traditional styles by devices peculiar to bluegrass and not, strictly speaking, traditional, transforms the instruments—If I may offer a conjecture—into representations of themselves. In presenting the particular music of his instrument the musician is at the same time representing it as a class or kind. "This," the banjo-player seems to affirm, "is the banjo." And "This," says the fiddler, "is the fiddle." The vigorously compressed vocal phrasing of bluegrass, too, which draws sentences on into dense parcels of words, seems designed to represent an impassioned mode of speech, particularly Southern speech, through the emotional contour of song; its heavily accented pattern of emphasis reflects the singer's effort to preserve the phonetic integrity of the phrase within the constraints imposed by rhythm and melody. Bluegrass singers call this "singing with feeling," a style which often resembles pulpit oratory with its intense conviction and unnerving directness of address. To that intensity lyric is usually subordinate—as, indeed, it is in the churchhouse, where the preacher's message is always and ever the same.

If Bill Monroe did not actually invent this style, he certainly consolidated it for bluegrass. Lord and Parry long ago pointed out that illiterate epic singers think of language in phrases and word-groups, not as discrete words for which they lack an alphabetic image (25). Bill Monroe, of course, is not illiterate; but his speaking voice has the lovely melodic quality typical of semi-literate or illiterate speech, and he reads with a sub-vocal movement of the lips[3]

For his accompanying instrument, Monroe has chosen the most anomalous of all, the mandolin, which among the many stringed instruments that have passed from traditional into commercial music has most stubbornly resisted such a transformation (how may electric mandolins are there in Nashville?) and whose role even in traditional music was a modest one. It is Bill Monroe's tirelessly inventive, aggressive, blues-influenced style alone that has brought it into prominence. For the mandolin, like the banjo, cannot readily produce tones perfect enough to qualify it for the fine arts—not, at least, as we have come to know them. No formal techniques are available which will arouse in the mandolin the intensity and brilliance of the violin; nor are further technical improvements likely to give the banjo the resonance of the guitar or the nimbleness of a mechanically more sophisticated stringed instrument such as the harpsichord. Consequently the emotional impact of the mandolin or banjo is the issue of the musician's struggle to advance ideas sufficiently complex to draw the instrument out of its background of associations—but not at the expense of that background. The predominantly urban practice of confining oneself to melodic elaboration becomes swiftly tiresome; what distinguishes the great bluegrass musician is the subtlety of rhythm and depth of tone that joins idea to association in a single transcendent effect, upon an instrument which in spite of its many charms is not inherently subtle or deep.

Generally speaking then, the bluegrass style emphasizes the tension between the imagination of the musician and the available means of expressing it, a tension which implies that in playing his old-fashioned folk instrument with the expressiveness, energy and drive necessary to move a public audience, the musician has made the best possible use of limited resources. He has made a little go a long way. In this resourcefulness an alert observer will detect the agrarian ethic of strict economy with which the national ideals of self-sufficiency and independence are often associated. This is perhaps why Bill Monroe and other bluegrass musicians insist that bluegrass is the only true "country" music; the insight is a moral one, not sociological or historical. One cannot help but note the yawning gulf between Monroe's music and the country-western music of Nashville, which, with its electric instruments and ostentatious costumes implies a repudiation of the rural ethic—or perhaps a Saturday-night holiday from it. We might somewhat speculatively extend the principle and suggest that the vocal tension characteristic of bluegrass and other folk-singing styles, like the sexual repression with which Alan Lomax has associated it, reflects underlying economic conditions, particularly conditions of scarcity. The rich, full operatic voice and the mellow, ingratiating voice of a jazz singer, have little place in bluegrass; rather the singer must sing against the restrictions imposed by high pitches, or, ideally, through some natural flaw—a faint hoarseness such as Ralph Stanley's. Earl Taylor can sing, it appears, without opening his mouth—or if he must through one side of it only.

One final note on the mandolin: Monroe is in possession of many fine antique mandolins, including at least one exceedingly rare Gibson F-5 in mint condition conspicuously autographed by Lloyd Loar, the designer of the delicately carved, scroll-cornered flatback mandolin now chiefly identified, through Monroe's influence, with bluegrass music. There is little doubt that of the many mandolins available to Monroe many sound as good at least as the battered and mutilated instrument he chooses to play on stage, the most important attribute of which is that it is *his* mandolin. As he plays, the unmistakable relish and pride, his eyes fixed on the fingerboard, the instrument thrust forward or held up where we can see it, he actually seems to be *teaching us how to play it* ; nor can we help but wonder that Bill has somehow got this broken down old thing freshly arrived from the attic to work, and in so doing has, like Aladdin rubbing the ancient lamp, evoked the spirit of a lapsed existence which imaginatively we long for.

Which brings me to the actual subject matter of Monroe's music. The process of sharpening or amplification in bluegrass has parallels in other art forms which are recapitulations, reconstitution's or summaries of obsolescent styles or kinds. In literature we find analogies in renaissance recreations of ancient epic and romance; in music we find them, perhaps, in the development of chamber music and fugue out of sixteenth-century antecedents. Often such recreations, deliberately or not, are parodies of the original: because parody ridicules by exaggerating what attaches to the object by association, and caricature through disproportion, a distorted or superficial conception of one's model will appear to ridicule it. In country music we have parody in blackened teeth and bib overalls, and caricature in excessively high pitches, accelerated tempos, or fake southern drawls. Monroe's music, however, is a kind of caricature without ridicule; it seems to strike at what is fundamental or seminal, has theoretical force and amounts to a generalization or type: which is simply to say, perhaps, that bluegrass is what Monroe calls "the old southern sound"—a distillation or purification of southern string-band music. As such it is highly abstract, with an enormous capacity to absorb subject matter and may as easily provide an occasion for technical innovation as become a repository of traditional songs or commercial and sentimental songs composed along traditional lines. The *impulse* to purify, however, to invite the imaginative leap of which we have been speaking, as well as the impulse to accept it, is not abstract; it is antiquarian and even reactionary: the characteristic modes of the romance imagination. I use the term "romance" loosely to refer to all those kinds of art which employ rigorous formal conventions as a device for containing the free and spontaneous play of the imagination, spontaneity being, as psychoanalysis recognizes, the mode of expression most congenial to the unconscious mind. Thus defined, the term refers not only to those kinds of poetry, music and painting normally called romantic, but to many popular and folk arts, including the folktale and the ballad. Usually associated with the remote, the exotic, or the antique, romance contemplates a human action in an idealized natural setting at a distance sufficient to discover its typical or perennial patterns, or what are often called archetypes or myths. To place its subject matter at a suitable distance, romance will typically interpose some mediating agent through whom the audience must apprehend the matter second-hand.

Nelly Dean, the dramatized narrator of Bronte's *Wuthering Heights* , is such an agent, as is the mysterious cabalist whom Coleridge invents to annotate his *Rime of the Ancient Mariner* Northrop Frye describes the romantic world ("Specific" 303ff) as one "idealized by reverie" in which good and evil are sharply discriminated; characters in romance consequently may "expand into psychological archetypes" so that we find in hero, heroine and villain figures upon whom, in Jung's terms, *libido, anima* and shadow might readily be projected: thus the romanticism of most popular literature, with the "suggestion of allegory...constantly creeping in around its fringes." With its reliance upon the understructure of the individual psyche, Frye goes on, romance "radiates a glow of subjective intensity" which inclines toward the "tragic emotions of passion and fury" from which "something nihilistic and untamable" is likely to escape. The social affinities of romance, he adds, with its "grave idealizing of heroism and purity," are with—think of Byron—the aristocracy.

In these sense, I think, bluegrass is romantic. The grave idealism and subjective intensity are everywhere apparent in bluegrass and in the personalities of bluegrass musicians, as is the untamable thing that howls like a banshee in some of the more acute and concentrated efforts of bluegrass tenor singers. In the singer himself we have a hero, in the *persona* of the solitary pilgrim reminiscent of Bunyan's folk allegory, or, closer to home, of the disconsolate rambler touring the nightscape of honky-tonk and tavern; in a more carefree spirit he may become the yodeling cowpoke of the Western plains. Our heroine is a maiden descended nearly without modification from the ballad tradition and bound up with an indefinite longing for lost places and times:

> Oh in dreams I see my darling
> In a gingham dress she looked so sweet;
> Oh I long for old Kentucky
> And my darling once more to meet. (Monroe)

But the grown woman in bluegrass lovesongs is far more likely to betray than to love you; she partakes of an evil expressed mutually in songs of romance shattered by infidelity as of households broken up by death—the severing of human ties, particularly family ties with their foundation in sexual love. Rarely do we meet the Prince of Death face-to-face—but we do meet him. His profoundest expression echoes the Christian imagination at its most primitive, as in "The Little girl and the Dreadful Snakes": I ran as fast I could through the dark and dreary wood/But I reached our darling girl too late (Price). Evil has a more effete expression, too, in a landscape inherited from the 19th-century bourgeois preoccupation with the grave—dreary and funereal, sometimes in bluegrass vaguely associated with city streets, in which the disoriented soul, whose symbol is often an orphaned child, confronts an earthly existence from which all light has withdrawn to the ineffable glory beyond, itself accessible only through death.

Altogether, of course, these themes represent the immediate background of bluegrass, which includes Anglo-Irish folk tradition, evangelical religion, turn-of-the century popular songs, rural blues and the beginnings of the country-western motif, which through Jimmie Rodgers exercised strong influence on Monroe. But what is more to the point, perhaps, is the material which bluegrass does *not* absorb from its background or from other kinds of music: it largely rejects the trivializing or antiseptic treatments of love common in popular music, for example, while at the same time rejecting the sexual innuendo of the blues; from country-western music it rejects the tendency to treat the contemporary social, political or domestic problems. There are telling exceptions, of course: John Prine's "Paradise," which is about strip-mining in eastern Kentucky, joined the bluegrass repertoire almost at once. Though its themes may occasionally range into the northern urban present, the thematic center of bluegrass remains the southern rural past, especially the mountain past, which since the days of Cecil Sharp has been a subject for romantic contemplation. And if the affinities of romance, finally, are aristocratic, then Bill Monroe, costumed as a prosperous southern landowner, offers to his audience an image cleansed of vulgarity in which it can identify a social and economic ideal: "someone they can look up to," Monroe says, "a gentleman."

Like the peasant balladeers who saw the outlines of human passion in the lives of their betters, and those aristocrats who for the same reason idealized the rustic or pastoral life, Bill Monroe has translated social distance into aesthetic distance, particularly the vast social distances which are the stuff of romance. In doing so, of course, he objectifies himself—the image we behold in Bill Monroe is beyond us whatever our social status; it is beyond us the way sculpture is beyond us. But, like a Byzantine icon, it is an image that stares back at its beholder. By placing himself imaginatively on an aristocratic plane, Monroe climbs to a prospect from which he can contemplate his own life and by extension the entire way of life his own represents, at a distance. "Way down in the Blue Ridge Mountains..." "Back in the hills of old Kentucky..." The narrator of these lines has been figuratively expelled from the world of which he sings, so that in Monroe's music, subject matter and the manner of its representation meet in the fact of exile. The three-dimensional configuration of the bluegrass band, the tension between musician and instrument, and the distance between the singer and subject—in this interplay resides, I think, a single unitary purpose.

If bluegrass is somehow romantic, with the romantic emphasis upon the simplicity as well as the extremity of human experience, perhaps we can describe with some precision, at the risk of seeming a bit fanciful, what species of the many possible romantic effects bluegrass attempts to produce. I've tried to suggest that if in a mimetic art moral inferences can be made on the basis of a human action, then the bluegrass style, with its antique instruments, its vigorously syncopated phrasing and tonsil-busting pitches, is an ordeal designed to challenge, and in challenging expose the artist's intellectual, imaginative and moral resources. All serious music, of course, presents such a challenge; but bluegrass exploits it for mimetic ends. No doubt we admire Itzhak Perlman and may make certain moral inferences about him on the basis of his playing—indeed, since we suppose that such qualities as imagination and intelligence manifest themselves in any violinist's performance, we *must* make such inferences. But *that* we do is peripheral to his art. Perlman's aim is to join our souls to the soul of the composer, Monroe's to set forth a moral ideal. Perlman's relationship to the composer's text, which can be said to be held in common by its typical audience, somewhat resembles the relationship between, say, an epic singer and his materials, which are traditional and communal. Thus, surprisingly, the art of classical music, with respect at least to the relationship among composer, performer and audience is much more like a traditional art than is Monroe's music, which, though it calls upon traditional materials, is essentially original and individual (Kellogg 55-56).

We should conclude then by considering Monroe's astonishing voice, which has been compared to everything from a railroad whistle to a bowl of fresh cream. Its power, like unto a jet-engine, is obvious to anyone; not so obvious, perhaps, is its delicacy and lustre: "Bill's got a pearl in his voice," Ralph Stanley says. According to Bill Keith, the well-known chromatic banjo-player who traveled with the Bluegrass Boys in the 1960s, Monroe in riding from show to show would attempt to sing the songs of one performance a half-tone higher for the next. This is not high singing for its own sake; rather it is an effort to preserve the morally-grounded tension between the vocal powers and the demands the singer makes upon them. Where that tension is lost, in singers for whom high notes pose no difficulty, though the broader mimetic effect of the style may remain in force, its *moral* dimension is lost. Were this not the case bluegrass music would be dominated by eunuchs or sopranos or both. Moreover to sing *above* one's range—to sing, that is, where the only feature of the voice still under control is pitch, which cannot properly be called singing at all, is to invite an uncomplimentary inference. "If you sing *too* high," Bill says, "people'll say, 'Now that man's used bad judgment'." *Judgment* Bill Monroe's judgment consists in knowing, among other things, at what point in his vocal range on a given day or evening a song can be attacked to produce a certain emotional effect popularly called "the high lonesome sound"—and if that should happen to be in B-flat, well then, let the fiddler, who would no doubt prefer to play in A, play in B-flat. For the "high, lonesome sound" occurs only at the apex of an arc which describes the line of equilibrium between vocal force and what might be called vocal flavor or value.

What is the "high, lonesome sound"? I wonder if it is not a musical equivalent of that characteristically romantic effect produced by the conjunction of beauty and terror called the Sublime. Certain of our romantic art comes to mind, such as the painting of the Hudson River School, which by miniaturizing the human figure isolates it in a landscape of immense proportion and ineffable detail, an image whose poignancy consists in our recognition that the painter has placed us at a distance from our subject so vast that our powers of observation have been in effect supernaturally expanded. This recognition is accompanied, I think, by a sensation of exile and solitude, which by virtue of the union of the emotions of isolation and expansion arouses a powerful conviction of intellectual or spiritual growth measured by the headlong fall of the eye into an impossibly remote vanishing point. The scale of the earth has been expanded, and there is no foreground; we have the giddy sensation of being held aloft by an invisible support—nor will the painter allow us to look down at our feet. By taxing the powers of perception to the limits of what pleasure can be taken in beauty, the sublime intensifies the painful disproportion between what we can imagine—and thus desire—and what we can actually possess.

What the romantic painter achieved pictorially, Monroe achieves musically: though I hesitate here to make too sharp a distinction between auditory and visual experience. Auditory impressions are seldom unaccompanied by some phantom and fugitive visual interpolation, and since in human perception kinesthesia is the norm, we are justified, I think, in attempting to understand one sense in terms of another.

In the psychic universe through which the romantic imagination moves— again I follow Frye (*The Secular*)—heights, and, if the metaphorical extension will be permitted, high-pitched sounds are perennially associated with intellect and spirit, with moral purity and ultimately with the divine. All organic processes, including thought and feeling, establish sensation in and are traditionally identified with various points in the body; the highest operations of the mind seem to take place (of course I know this only by report) *above* the top of the head: "I know I have read a poem," says Emily Dickinson, "when I feel as if the top of my head has been blown off." Moreover the figures we apply to high-pitched sounds—sharp, keen, pure, piercing and the like—are generally the same ones we apply to wit, intelligence and moral sensitivity. In the kinesthetic sensorium, the high-pitched note for which the jazz trumpeter or bluegrass singer has exchanged his soul moves us toward a point at the center of experience, a point without dimensions and therefore out of time that organizes attention and sharply resolves the will. Visually that point is literally a vanishing point—it flings the singer back into the distant hills from which he came, miniaturizes him, as it were, freeing him from imperfections and placing him in a field of immensities which for a fleeting moment of psychic unity— what might be called a momentary arrest of thought—we grasp; but *from which we must depart.*

It is the way Bill Monroe conducts himself on this rarified plane of high notes that his mimetic genius shines forth most brilliantly. Other singers, perhaps, can reach their vocal *premium mobile,* and do it with ease, precision and grace. But Bill Monroe, one might say, does it bravely—leaping, not climbing, not clinging by the fingernails but standing solidly upon two feet— only for a moment, but long enough to breathe the air and plant a flag. Nor, having arrived, will he depart carelessly or in haste; rather he soars away like an eagle, imitating, in certain absolute performances such as "Good-bye Old Pal" or "Muleskinner Blues," the natural decline of receding sounds—the Doppler effect—and thus provoking an inestimable sensation of loss that to which, according to the momentum of musical expectation, we have become deeply committed. The emotion is bereavement, and we find an expression of it in the pearl in Bill's voice to which Ralph Stanley referred: a vocal image which I myself have heard only in the voices of certain elderly people and in voices, especially children's, struggling to hold back tears.

And *that's* what makes us feel lonesome.

One wonders if bluegrass music is not the complex response of an inspired hill-country musician who early in a professional career found himself behind a proscenium arch in the vast, dark spaces of a public auditorium, with a sea of impersonal faces spread out before him—wonders, especially, when one recalls that Bill Monroe has been visually impaired all his life. In giving birth to bluegrass, Monroe must somehow have redefined his relationship to his inheritance of traditional music, must have expanded his awareness, perhaps, as I have suggested, under the influence of a crisis at once practical, social and psychological, sufficiently to make of those cultural boundaries which formerly enclosed him a formal design which is the content of a newly-formulated and more abstract medium. The simple presence of formal design suggests visualization: hence the usefulness of a visual analogy. In some respects bluegrass seems an auditory exploration of terrestrial space; the very name implies it. In his singing and playing Monroe generates a hypothetical perspective which does away with the actual setting—auditorium, nightclub, park—and establishes an imaginative landscape, sunlit, boundless and green, of which the band—itself a neat and compelling picture—is the center and source.

Bluegrass is not more than 50 years old. But it essentially captures a richly variegated and more ancient world of traditional and popular music— "ancient tones," in Monroe's phrase—which would otherwise have been forgotten, whose sources are commingled with the sources of our national life. As a coherent ensemble style, bluegrass provides the basis for what could conceivably become, with further refinement, a native classical music; indeed in Bill Monroe's band at least it is already a classical art. Though its implied tense is the past, it discovers our humanity in retrieving from the past facts of imagination that are immune to time and change.

Notes

[1]Quoted in Rinzler's notes. I should like to acknowledge at once a sweeping and profound debt to Ralph Rinzler, who has made a more intimate acquaintance with Bill Monroe possible for me and whose deep understanding of and enthusiasm for Monroe has helped me better to appreciate his genius. All of Monroe's remarks quoted here are taken from conversations between 15 and 18 April 1977, a four-day period during which Rinzler and I traveled with Monroe's band.

[2]Suggested to me by Bill in an interview on 17 April 1977.

[3]I observed this while traveling with Monroe in April.

[4]The opening lines of the refrains of Monroe's "Little Georgia Rose" and "On My Way Back to the Old Home," respectively.

Works Cited

Aristotle. Poetics Chapter IV.

Frye, Northrup. The Secular Scripture: *A Study of the Structure of Romance*. Cambridge: Harvard UP 1976.

_____."Specific Continuous Forms." *Anatomy of Criticism* Princeton: Princeton UP 1957. 303ff.

Hollobaugh, Dix. "Iowan Bob Black Grazes on Nashville's Bluegrass." *Des Moines Sunday Register* Picture 19 Sept. 1976: 31.

Kellogg, Robert. "Oral Literature." *New Lit. History 5* (1973-74): 55-56.

Lomax, Alan. *Folk Song Style and Culture*. New York: American Society for the Advancement of Science 1968.

Lord, Albert B. *The Singer of Tales*. New York: Harvard UP 1960.

Malone, Bill. *Country Music U.S.A.: A Fifty-year History*. Austin: U of Texas P, 1968.

Monroe, Bill. "Rose of Old Kentucky." BMI.

Price, Albert. "The Little Girl and the Dreadful Snake." BMI.

Rinzler, Ralph. "The High Lonesome Sound of Bill Monroe and His Bluegrass Boys," MCA-110 [formerly Decca DL7-47801].

Age, the Body and Experience
in the Music of Hank Williams

Richard Leppert and George Lipsitz

He was so ordinary he merges with the crowd in my memory. (Mrs. Lilly McGill, teacher, Georgiana, Alabama, on her former pupil, Hank Williams.)

Houston Baker locates the blues at the crossroads of lack and desire, at the place where the hurts of history encounter determined resistance from people who know they are entitled to something better (Baker 7, 150). Like the blues singers from whom he learned so much, Hank Williams (1923 to 1953) spent a lot of time at that particular intersection. There he met others whose own struggles informed and shaped his music. Williams' voice expressed the contradictions of his historical moment—post Second World War America—a time when diverse currents of resistance to class, race and gender oppressions flowed together to form a contradictory, but nonetheless real, unity of opposites. Standing at a crossroads in history, at a fundamental turning point for relationships between men and women, whites and blacks, capital and labour, Williams' songs about heartbreak and failed personal relations identified the body and the psyche as crucial terrains of political struggle in the post-war era.

Hank Williams was an extraordinary artist, a songwriter with a gift for concise yet powerful expression and a singer with exceptional phrasing and drama. Yet we miss the point if we view Williams solely as an individual genius who rose above the crowd; the real story of Hank Williams is how he remained part of the crowd by letting its diverse currents flow through him. His extraordinary popularity, his success at introducing country music to new audiences and his influence on an astonishingly diverse range of popular musical artists and genres all stem from Williams' ability to understand and articulate the blasted hopes and repressed desires of his audience.

Above all, Hank Williams understood that the profound changes in American family life during the 1930s and 1940s had ushered in a new era, fundamentally altering old categories of age, gender and romance. His songs soared to popularity in the early 1950s, a time often hailed as the 'golden age' of the family (May, *Homeword* ; Mintz and Kellogg). Yet Williams' narratives exuded a fatalism and despair about personal relationships. They resisted romantic optimism and also avoided the kinds of closure and transcendence

Reprinted from *Popular Music* Vol. 1, 3 (1990) 259-274, by permission of Cambridge University Press and the authors.

historically associated with male subjectivity. In this way, they expressed what Tania Modleski has described as a refusal to be oedipalised (Modleski 74), and what Fred Pfeil calls the "deoedipalisation of American society" (Pfeil 395-6).[1]

This is not to argue that Hank Williams found his way to an emancipatory political programme or even to a cultural vision completely free from dominant constructions of gender, sexuality and romance. Far from it. But it is to claim that Williams' music and lyrics represented a significant refusal to accept dominant cultural narratives and that they gave voice to potentials for resistance that remain important to this day. People can be imprisoned by cultural stories as easily as by iron bars and stone walls. Indeed, the core insight of contemporary cultural studies has been the understanding that people are more frequently contained within cultural narratives than within jail cells. In this context, all refusals are important because they represent a challenge to the prisons of mind and spirit that repress emancipatory hopes. Our exploration of the music of Hank Williams focuses on the ways in which he gave an individual voice to collective fears and hopes about the body, romance, gender roles and the family. We wish to locate these issues variously in the site/sight of his physical body, his voice, his lyrics and his music.

Age and Historicisation of the Body

Hank Williams began his career as a child prodigy and ended it as a still young man who appeared years older than his age. At thirteen, he won an 'amateur hour' contest in Montgomery, Alabama with a song protesting against the conditions facing labourers for the federal Works Progress Administration. Williams' singing and songwriting immediately earned him a spot as 'The Singing Kid' on a local radio show featuring 'Dad' Cryswell and his band (Caress 25). But his first recording session did not come until 11 December 1946 and he attained his first hit record in 1947 (Kingsbury and Axelrod 247). His last recording session occurred on 23 September 1952, slightly more than three months before his death in the early morning hours of 1 January 1953. Thus his career as a country singer spanned only six years, beginning when he was twenty-three and ending with his death at twenty-nine. Despite Williams' short life and the relative brevity of his career, among the more striking aspects of his work as a lyricist, composer and performer were the multiple and complex encodings of both age and experience as played out on the ground of the individual human body, both physically and psychically. Significantly, he located his work within a context that invariably posited that body not in the transcendence of timeless/universal humanism, but in the history of rural southern poor and working class America in the mid-twentieth century.

The concept of youth is largely taken as a 'natural'—and not constructed—category in American middle-class culture today. But in the early post-war years (especially among the rural poor) the concept had little bearing on life as it was lived, as Williams' own typical experience as a child labourer illustrates. To be young was essentially to be an even less reliable wage slave than one's parents, in a setting when obtaining work at all ages was a necessity for survival. Hank Williams lived out his short life within this larger reality; he lived out his decade as an 'official' of-age adult under still more complex circumstances, during a decade of traumatic post-war change in America in general and in the rural south in particular. In this respect, his experience paralleled that of a generation of young men—and women— who came of age during the war (where, in the field, a twenty-six year-old might commonly be referred to as the Old Man) and who confronted the jolting realities of an atomic peace immediately re-defined in terms of Cold War and economic upheaval, massive migrations from the land to the emerging suburbs and changing prescriptions for family life and for relations among races, classes and genders.

Hank Williams was heard as 'authentic' at a time when authenticity was a prime determinate in the success of in-person and radio performers. (Like other country singers of his time, Williams never pulled back from the live-performance circuit; audiences were built and maintained by visual contact and live radio, without which recording careers could not develop, and "in his prime, Hank was doing two hundred one-nighters a year" [Koon 88; see also 93].) There are several interlocking reasons why this is so, among which the 'age' of the experiences his lyrics described and the 'age' of his voice were special importance. At a more immediate—and pre-musical—level, his appearance played a part as well.

At twenty-three, as at twenty-nine, Williams was a chronologically young man long past youth indeed, a man who seemingly never experienced youth as was borne out by his physical appearance. At six feet in height he was not especially tall, but his thin body (140 lbs), and the hats he perpetually wore (to cover his thinning hair about which he was sensitive [Williams 144]), made him look taller: he stood out. Toward the end of his life he was haggard, gaunt, physically wrecked. He began drinking by the time he was eleven (Williams 15), a habit he continued with few interruptions for the rest of his life, compounded by drug use in his later years (amphetamines and Seconal, the sedative chloral hydrate and morphine). He had a form of spina bifida which exacerbated his chronic back pain and, near the end, hepatitis and a heart condition; and he suffered from malnutrition—when drinking heavily he did not eat, sometimes for days on end (Williams 175, 205, 207; Koon 50). His body could never properly fill out his expensive tailor-made suits (evident even in the posed publicity shots).

The appearance of Williams' body marked the urgency of age as a central category in his work, especially in a culture where increasingly prescriptive post-war expectations of bodily behavioural propriety were being forged. It was well known that Hank Williams lived his life on the edge. His music masked none of it. His songs about failed love followed closely the dismal history of his marriages—and his innumerable one-night stands—just as his obsession with death and repentance (of which more follows) confirmed that he knew the price he was paying both in this life and, unless he was careful, likewise the next. Williams referred to himself as 'ole Hank' both on the air and in private.[2]

Audiences were by no means amused by or even tolerant of his most drunken performances, especially when he failed to remember lyrics (Williams 180). His increasingly debilitating alcoholism culminated in his being thrown off the Grand Ole Opry in 1952 (Williams 172-3, 191, 196-8); his trips to sanitariums for drying out 'became almost routine' (Williams 194). Nevertheless, audiences "loved Hank partly *because* of his problems," according to Frank Page, associated with Shreveport's KWKH Louisiana Hayride (Williams 198).[3] For those who saw his live performances, drunk or sober, his physical vulnerability was both obvious and affecting. In body he confounded the model of the self-reliant, self-contained in-shape and battle-tested post-war male ("He'd come slopping and slouching out on stage, limp as a dishrag" [Williams 140 quoting Montgomery Advertiser columnist Allen Rankin]).

Hank Williams' lyrics and music, like his physical appearance, reflect age and the historicisation of the body in love songs and gospel numbers alike. In the first instance, his subjects invariably exude a spoken or unspoken history. His upbeat love songs ("If You'll be a Baby to Me") characteristically refer to a rural timelessness, a pastoral imagery that pulls back from post-war futurism ("I can plow and milk the cow [You] keep the homefires burnin' ") but which, by recalling agrarian cyclical chronology, confront the sense of the real (not imagined) loss of that way of life.[4] To be sure, images of the man in the field and the woman in the kitchen correspond roughly to the Levittown ideal of suburban social organisation, but only to an urban/suburbanite. The rural reality encoded here is one of shared labours: the woman is not kept cosy by her man's work; she is a labourer as well. She heats her cookstove with wood and coal, and she does the wash with her bare knuckles. In this way Williams' lyrics, built on traditional domestic rural social organisation, incorporate simultaneously an ancient and recent past that his listeners clearly recognised, that most had lived or were still living, but which they also knew was ending in favour of a future that was profoundly uncertain. In this regard, Williams when he sang about love, voiced more than the desire for partnership: he voiced the pain of loss for a way of life that could already be described with the anxiety of ending.

As regards gospel, the fact that a young man in the 1940s might sing of Jesus (and in 20 percent of his repertory [Koon 81]) is not in itself particularly surprising, at least in the rural south, though the numbers of Williams' gospel tunes may be unusual (some were recorded under his own name, others under the pseudonym of his alter-ego Luke the Drifter). In many respects a tune like "How Can You Refuse Him Now?" is quite an ordinary, even conventional piece of white gospel. But in other ways, this song and others like it exceed conventions. Unlike contemporaneous southern black gospel, his tunes are seldom upbeat; neither musically nor lyrically do they convincingly encode happiness, let alone ecstasy. Instead, they fixate on death (as in "We're Getting Closer to the Grave Each Day," recorded when he was twenty-six and "Mother is Gone") and on death rituals ("The Funeral"; in this instance that of a black child).[5] Williams' religious lyrics speak to life's suffering and failures, often without recourse to the promise of an afterlife. As such they tend to exceed and politically subvert the generic passivity encoded especially into much white gospel music. (The musical and performative vitality of black gospel, by contrast, acts to undercut the otherworldly fixation of the lyrics, re-establishing the physical present, as well as the spiritual future, in the lives of believers.) That is, once the hope of afterlife is pushed aside, the terrain that matters is located in the concrete personal and social body, not in the abstract soul. Thus even in "I Saw the Light," perhaps his best known gospel song—but certainly not his best—the most Williams can offer for accepting Jesus fails to exceed this life, as it vaguely conjures up the rather tired imagery of smiling in the face of adversity (as the phrase now runs: "Don't worry, be happy"). The text proffers consolation, and consolation is the only reward; the reserve with which Williams sings the words only confirms the limits of hope offered, all the more given his 'biological' youth from which conventional 'idealism' and future directedness are already stripped.

"Men with Broken Hearts," a Luke the Drifter (non-gospel) recitation (recorded 21 December 1950), locates the terrain of failure in particularly dismal (and unrelenting) fashion, calling forth rhetorically to God at the end, but without hope for redress. The text speaks of defeat in the metaphor of men's broken bodies—stooped shoulders, heads "bowed low," vacantly staring eyes— walking allegories of what Williams calls 'living death', relief from which can only come via death itself.

At the level of an unconscious politics lies the gesture of recognition that to have failed in this life is to have failed: it carries its own punishment and there is nothing more beyond it, or at least nothing no one can safely predict. In "We're Getting Closer to the Grave Each Day," Williams reiterates the theology of Christ's redemptive death and, to be sure, he makes passing reference to the Judgement Day. But the image that incessantly repeats is that of the approach to the grave. In "How Can You Refuse Him Now?" the image of Christ crucified is not that of the redeemer, but of a man suffering. It is His suffering that should trigger our response, not our own fear of death or a hope for afterlife. Christ, in essence, becomes one of us, a man in trouble.

Hank Williams' singing voice registers differently from his [FM!-] radio-perfect speaking voice. There is an aura of careworn exhaustion even in his quasi-upbeat tunes. Thus in the 56-second fragment "If You'll Be a Baby (to Me)," a lyric essentially proposing marriage, Williams does not sound like a teenager in love, nor even a twenty-year-old. There is no sense of passionate sensuality in either the words or the voice. There is instead a textual promise of peace ("no quarrellin' ") and vocal—explicitly timbral—expression of hope for refuge. That is, the putative subject of the tune has all the naivete of uncomplicated first-love-and-family aspirations ("I'll be your baby/And I don't mean maybe"), but Williams' voice encodes something more complex. The delivery is subdued, the words slightly swallowed, the overall acoustical effect establishing associations less of first love than of trying-once-more. It is a voice of knowing, not anticipating, confined to a narrow range (a major sixth), middle register (the high note is A below middle C) and a middling dynamic. The enthusiasm presumed by the lyrics is undercut by the doubtfulness of the delivery.

In "A House Without Love is Not a Home," the narrative plays off a long-time relationship now failed, its imagery repeatedly referring to the passage of time and loss. The timbral difference from Williams' deep, resonant speaking voice is striking. The voice is thin—and, characteristically, his pitch wavers on held notes, especially in the upper half of his narrow register. It is a voice lacking certainty—but gaining thereby in credibility. The melodic structure produces a different effect from that of "If You'll Be a Baby (to Me)." In the earlier tune, Williams' upper register is not called upon and most of the intervallic relationships are seconds, apart from the major/minor thirds and a single perfect fourth. In "A House Without Love" the range extends over a tenth (to E above middle C), and the tune is largely constructed around the interval of a fourth: that is, it is far more disjointed, providing the opportunity/necessity for him to connect the two pitches of the interval with a slurred slide (in instances where the interval is falling, as the majority of them do). And though, to be sure, this is a musical gesture characteristic to much country music, it is a musical practice—outside country music—more commonly located in the singing of women than men. Combined with the other vocal features we have described, it registers uncertainty, vulnerability and—given the lyrics—the sorts of failure that only age can produce.

Both tunes are in the key of C and neither uses any chromatic inflection: the melodies are musically straightforward, 'guileless'. Indeed, Williams characteristically keeps melodic, rhythmic and harmonic surprises to a minimum—the arch-shape of his melodies is sufficiently predictable that committing the tunes to memory is easily accomplished on one or two hearings. All of this affects the reception of Williams' music. Taken together, the appeal is that of a boy-man; the musical vocabulary encodes a simplicity on the verge of the child-like; contrarily, the voice is marked by uncertain age. The contradiction results in the ambiguity and complexity of audience reactions, especially when combined with his physical performance image. He is to be mothered, but also to be erotically loved and above all to be heard as one's own: a capsulised history of a self-consciously regionally-ghettoised people.

If we look at Williams' gospel tunes, the same features are found ("We're Getting Closer to the Grave Each Day," "How Can You Refuse Him Now?"); indeed, the distinctions between these two primary genres of his work are few.[6] Notable among them are the frequent shift from the duple time characteristic of the secular tunes to a lilting 3/4 in gospel; in the religious tunes, he uses a more pronounced slur-slide on downward moving intervals; and here too the famous vocal 'tear' (as in both weeping and pulling apart) appears: the voice momentarily breaks, in a convention of pathos which Williams perfected (this device occurs repeatedly in "We're Getting Closer to the Grave Each Day").

There was a considerable rift between Williams' deep, resonant speaking voice and the thinner, more nasal, crooning quality of his singing, a rift notably widened by the accompanying change in his physical appearance when, from standing before the microphone conversing, he shifted into song: "It was like a charge of electricity had gone through him" (Williams 140). (Between songs Williams enjoyed folksy bantering with his audiences; indeed such contacts were conventional in gigs and radio shows alike. And many Luke the Drifter bits were essentially monologues with musical accompaniment.) Minnie Pearl was struck by his stage presence from the first time she encountered it: "He had a real animal magnetism. He destroyed the women in the audience" (Williams 144)[7] He knew how to use his body; hunching forward into the mike, "He'd close his eyes and swing one of those big long legs, and the place would go wild" (Williams 145)[8] He played on a sexuality that was exciting precisely because of the contradictions it contained. Minnie Pearl suggests that Williams appealed to women's maternal instincts. Others suggest a far more sensual dimension, though both reflected his true character—a womaniser nevertheless dominated by his strong mother. This contradiction engenders an ambiguity of a simultaneously exciting but politically dangerous sort. It constitutes a partially masked refusal to adhere to standards of propriety established for a post-war culture of re-domestication, a culture built on self-contradictory and increasingly complex erotic economies of controlled role-playing. Williams— like Elvis soon after him—marked with his bodily gestures a language of difference and demand, just as one might expect (or hope for) in the young— thereby accounting for the insistence then, as now, that youth be tightly controlled, especially physically. Yet his speaking and singing voices also referenced acoustics culturally characteristic of middle age and beyond, just as his love songs consistently dealt with the failures of middle age and his gospel tunes with death. In sound and sight alike, he encompassed the experiences of life's full range of contradictions, hopes and failures for a society which unquestionably recognised in him both what they loved and hated of themselves.

Gender Difference and Social Class:
Identity by Alienation

America as a social and political organization is committed to a cheerful view of life.

(Film critic Robert Warshow)

That's just it, Minnie, there ain't no light.

(Hank Williams to Minnie Pearl)

Kent Blaser points out that forty-five of Williams' fifty most important songs deal with relationships between men and women, and that fifteen of these complain about being abandoned by one's partner (Blaser 23). From "Lovesick Blues" to "Your Cheatin' Heart," his most popular songs articulate loneliness, frustration and despair as necessary parts of the search for love. This pessimism made a break with the traditional romantic optimism of popular music as crafted in Tin Pan Alley, but in the context of post-Second World War America it held special significance.

After the Second World War, Americans married earlier and in greater numbers and had more children than had been true in the past. This extraordinary increase in marriages and births brought with it an unprecedented focus on the family by both private capital and the state. The nuclear family emerged as the primary social unit, a unit whose true home was the suburban shopping mall (Leo 31), and everything from the Cold War to the growth of suburbs to increases in private debt and consumer spending drew justification from uncritical celebrations of the nuclear family and heterosexual romance (May, "Explosive" 155). In that context, Hank Williams' fatalism and existential despair rebuked dominant social narratives and spoke directly to the internal psychic wounds generated by the gap between lived experience and an ideology that promised universal bliss through the emergence of romance and the family as unchallenged centres of personal life.

Hank Williams' own life experience allowed him precious few illusions about the nuclear family, and in that respect he exemplified a broader social and historical experience. The Great Depression of the 1930s had underminded both the theory and the practice of the nuclear family. Unemployed fathers deserted their families in large numbers; by 1940 1,500,000 married women lived apart from their husbands. Many families formed extended households by moving in with relatives, but in the mid-1930s an estimated 200,000 vagrant children roamed the country. Women and children once again entered the workforce in large numbers, and their earning power undercut the previously unchallenged authority of male breadwinners (Mintz and Kellogg 137-8). Mobilisation for the Second World War accelerated these trends. During the war, six million women workers entered high-paying production jobs in industry. Sixteen million Americans left their homes to join the armed forces and another fifteen million travelled to new jobs in war production centres. Under these conditions, old ties of family and community broke down, and Americans experimented with new gender and family roles (Mintz and Kellogg 155).

Hank Williams' family life reflected these larger social trends. His father had suffered shell shock in combat during the First World War and, after a series of short-term jobs in the late 1920s, was committed in 1930 to the Veterans Administration Hospital in Biloxi, Mississippi where he stayed ten years. Thus for most of the time between his sixth and sixteenth birthday, Hank Williams was raised by his mother and his sister. His mother assumed an awesome presence in his life and career, supporting her children with her own labour during the hard years of the Great Depression and managing her son's entry into show business. Like many working class children, he also spent considerable time with relatives outside his nuclear family, living for a year when he was six with his cousin J.C. in Monroe County, Alabama, so that J.C.'s sister could go to school in Georgiana by living with Hank's mother and sister (Caress 12). Lilly Williams moved her family to Montgomery in 1937 when Hank was fourteen, and she ran a boarding house there that exposed her son to yet another extended household.

There was little in Hank Williams' personal experience that conformed with the reigning cultural optimism about the nuclear family. He started dating Audrey Mae Sheppard, a married woman with a daughter at home and a husband overseas, in 1942. Sheppard's father threatened to kill Hank over the relationship, and when Hank first brought Audrey home to meet his mother, Lilly asked "Where'd you get this whore?," a comment that provoked a fistfight between mother and son (Caress 35-6, 38). In a culture that increasingly lauded motherhood in the abstract while imposing ever-greater burdens on it in practice, not every son could use the words Hank Williams employed to speak about his mother to Minnie Pearl, "Minnie, there ain't nobody in the world I'd rather have alongside me in a fight than my mama with a broken beer bottle in her hand" (Pearl 213). Hank married Audrey in 1944 before a Justice of the Peace in a Texaco station in Andalusia, Alabama, but the marriage was illegal because it came too soon after Audrey's separation from her husband to satisfy the requirements of Alabama law (Koon 19). Hank and Audrey were divorced in 1948, but reconciled after the birth of their son Randall Hank (Hank Williams, Jr) in 1949 (Koon 29-30). The tempestuous relationship led to another divorce, and his remarriage (in 1952) to Billie Jean Eshlimar (who had been abandoned by her first husband) led to constant bickering among Williams, his mother and both his wives (Caress 189).

Biographer Jay Caress locates the roots of Williams' personal problems in the singer's distance from the experience of a nuclear family, arguing that Williams "never made the normal psychological transfer from what psychologists call dependent mother love to assertive, independent (father emulating) mother love" (12). Yet Hank Williams' experiences with strong-willed and competent women left him with a deep respect for women and a powerful desire for connection to them. His 'failure' to make the oedipal break led him to remain in dialogue with all of the significant women in his life, and led him away form the dominant 'heroic' image of masculinity.

In an age when cultural voices ranging form the masculinist rhetoric of Mickey Spillane novels and John Wayne films to the conformist and paternalistic pressures of outer-directed corporate culture to the hedonistic appeals of *Playboy* magazine all encouraged men to widen the distance between themselves and women, Williams presented a masculine voice that longed for reconnection with the feminine, that refused the oedipality of the dominant culture in favour of an almost pre-oedipal craving for intimacy, pleasure and reconnection with women (Modleski 72-9). Of course, even this refusal could be channelled into the kind of flight from the family and responsibility that Barbara Ehrenreich describes as an important factor in sexualising and engendering male consumer desire in the 1950s (Ehrenreich). The pre-oedipal stage might be seen as the perfect model for the needy narcissism vital to consumer desire. As Fred Pfeil explains, "the increasing number of de-Oedipalized middle-class male subjects, even ostensibly politically progressive ones, in no way guarantees any decrease in their fear of and hostility toward women" (Pfeil 396). But the rise of a de-oedipalised subjectivity does constitute the body and psyche as sites for political meaning, and it also evidences a kind of subjectivity that seeks connection rather than separation, that disconnects ego and identity from hatred of a (proximate) mother and identification with a (distant) father. Collective social problems can never be solved by purely individual responses, but individual predispositions can often disclose contradictions and interruptions in dominant ideology that prefigure the sites where resistance might emerge. In Hank Williams' case, resistance to the oedipal narrative reveals structural weaknesses within the idealised nuclear family and its promises of happiness, as well as the existence of a popular desire for something better.

Hank Williams not only refused a narrowly oedipal definition of masculinity, but in fact he spent most of his life as a fugitive from nearly any stable identity. As a child he attached himself to black street singers Rufus Payne (known as Tee Tot) and Connie McKee (known as Big Day) who became his first strong adult male role models. Before deciding on a life as a musician, he tried out for the rodeo, and while working as a shipfitter's helper in Mobile, Alabama took a secret trip to Portland, Oregon in 1944 to try his luck in the Kaiser shipyard in that city. Even after achieving stardom, he went to work under the pseudonym Herman P. Willis for Dallas nightclub owner (and later assassin of Lee Harvey Oswald) Jack Ruby (Koon 34). As a young musician, he formed a country and western bank with "Indian Joe" Hatcher on lead guitar and "Mexican Charlie" Mayes on fiddle. He adopted the pseudonym "Luke the Drifter" for a series of recitations and repeated the 'drifting' theme by naming his band of Alabama-born musicians the "Drifting Cowboys" (Caress 20, 22, 26, 17; Koon 34). While on tour with his band, he loved to listen to baseball games on the car radio, but had no favourite team (Williams 135). He sang religious hymns to his audiences, but lived a decidedly non-religious life.⁹ This refusal to accept any permanent identity also characterized Williams' view of class which he interpreted through the frame of gender. As Dorothy Hortsman notes,

> The farmers and labourers who made up the original market for country music were for the most part dirt-poor, bypassed by the American dream and the means of achieving it. Burdened with poor land, a poor economy, and hostile natural forces beyond their control, many felt they were, indeed 'born to lose'..A tragic love affair, then, is the final insult—and perhaps the focus for economic and social frustrations it would be unmanly to admit. (Horstman 140)

Country musicians in general, and Hank Williams in particular, locate the politics of gender on the terrain of social class difference, but less on the overt ground of society and its institutions than on the privatised body, particularly its psyche. In the process, Williams gives sight to the unseen, especially in love song laments about infidelity and failed relationships.

Marital cheating was a taboo subject in country music recordings prior to the social upheavals of the 1940s, so that Hank Williams' "Your Cheatin' Heart," among the classics of the genre (recorded in his last session—23 September 1952—together with another tune of the same sort, "Take These Chains from My Heart" and two others), was a type of song having a very short history. When Williams wrote these tunes, their subject rang true, not as repetitious or timeless commentaries, but as expressions of profound and shattering change. They caught on precisely because he was able to locate the societal in the most personal and private terrain of sexual love. It was not that infidelity never occurred in the rural south prior to Williams' generation; it was rather that infidelity was admitted for the first time among the expressible catalogue of failures. By inscribing the rising stakes of societal suffering in infidelity, by locating that suffering in the psyche, he undercut the final refuge for resistance. The soul of the privatised body could no longer be separated, refuge-like, from the larger social economy: cheating songs confirmed devolutionary change.[10]

Similarly, songs of unrequited love ("I'm So Lonesome I Could Cry"; "Cold, Cold Heart"), though excluding the sin of adultery, preserve the political essentials of songs about cheating, even if they accomplish their politics of emotion in a slightly different fashion. By emphasising a love that is never responded to, as opposed to a love that once was but is now lost, unrequited love songs fundamentally account for an equally defeating—if not necessarily worse—sort of failure: the inability to find love in the first place, to love but not be loved in return, to be rejected. It is in songs of unrequited love that of the work Hank Williams approaches black music most directly, and where it crosses gender lines into emotional ground more commonly occupied by women, and notably by women who are black (e.g. Billie Holiday, Nina Simone). As Billie Holiday, dying, gravel-voiced, movingly—and pathetically—sang in "Glad to Be Unhappy," one of her last recorded songs, when someone you adore fails to love you back, "It's a pleasure to be sad."

The emotional intensity that Billie Holiday accorded to this topic,[11] via her vocal/timbral inscription of failure (as well as by the words), bears a distinct similarity to that achieved by Hank Williams, though musically by quite different means. The difference can be stated quite simply: the musical and cultural traditions that would allow a black woman to produce this lament generally affect men in a quite dissimilar way. For a man to utter similar sentiments, in this society, reflects a more extreme degree of failure and frustration. The fact that Williams wrote and sang such tunes, in other words, produces effect by collapsing the distinction not only between genders, but between races as well (southern whites, after all, heard blues music). Not only with subject matter, but also with what might be termed the politics of timbre, an acoustic solidarity is implicitly forged: between genders, between the races and among the poor. Black audiences recognised the elements of their own culture in Williams' music and in large numbers attended the Louisiana Hayride when he was on the the bill.[12] Blues singer B.B. King remembers paying special attention to the songs by Hank Williams that he heard on the radio while working on a Mississippi plantation because:

> Like Hank Williams, man, when he wrote 'Cold, Cold Heart,' tunes like that, that carried me right back to my same old blues about 'don't answer the door' and all that kind of stuff. 'Cause this is a guy hurting. He's hurting from inside. And 'Your Cheating Heart', many things of this sort are just to me another form of blues sung by other people. (Redd 97)

The sound of a white man's voice singing about these subjects, hence crossing gender and racial boundaries, inscribes a socio-cultural disruption of the most encompassing finality, at precisely the instant that it offers the specifically *acoustic* opportunity to establish a relationship of resistance with another socially alienated group.

Finally, even in tunes of courtship or proposal, like "If You'll Be a Baby (to Me)," conventional romantic love is not part of the equation;[13] instead there is an offer of a partnership for mutually-supporting labour, and the extent of the male singer's love is promised in terms of the work appropriate to her that he's willing to shoulder: if she cooks, he'll plow and *even* do the churning. He loves her and considers doing 'women's' work a gesture of his devotion.[14] This may not be in the depoliticised tradition of romantic love, but it *is* romantic love of the most meaningful and committed sort. It openly recognises the mutuality of marital labour and the urge to take on more than what society conventionally identifies as the man's share. (It is arguable that, under these conditions, what otherwise passes for romantic love might flourish past the stages of passion characterising young relationships.) Lyrics of this sort are all the more striking given the national phenomenon in the early post-war years of a return to 'traditional' pre-war gender divisions, articulated especially in the domestication of the suburb with its removal of women from the labour force, as well as in a broad range of popular cultural expressions built upon the assumption of innate antagonisms between men and women, ranging from commercial television programmes and film noir motion pictures to the lyrics of most popular songs.

Yet for all his shifting subjectivities, a remarkable consistency characterises Williams' voice, and that consistency is connected to his class and regional identity. There is no discernible difference between his earliest recordings and his last, and the same holds for his unsophisticated, elementary, essentially three-chord guitar strumming. The voice is common, untrained. The delivery is inevitably straightforward, without pretense, without acrobatics or tricks—unless one counts the country-conventional vocal 'tear' mentioned earlier. The upper range, which Williams uses to good effect in producing acoustic tension, is thin and often strained, the latter quality exacerbated by a notable and fast vibrato; the low and middle range is both rich and firm, like his speaking voice. Together these variant timbres produce a comfort in the latter, inevitably undercut by the vulnerability of that comfort in the former. Moreover, he typically gives accentual and dynamic emphasis to his high voice, that is, to that part of his range that semiotically undercuts the culturally coded paternal assuredness of the deeper male sounds.

Williams' slightly nasal twang is especially obvious in the higher register—the locus of tension—thus most evident in precisely in the acoustic space that best identifies pain and its politics. The country twang, in other words, locates him as one of his listeners' own, a man who shared their experiences. Nasality in other circumstances provides the southern rural poor with subcultural/community identity, like any other accentual or dialectical effect. But in extra-regional popular culture (notably the movies, often in grotesquely exaggerated burlesques like *Ma and Pa Kettle*, and in later television shows like *Beverly Hillbillies*) that effect becomes a weapon for derision, a fact never lost on any poor person. Hank Williams exploited that sound in a timbral expression of class and regional solidarity, though to be sure he was not unique in this regard. To similar, if more obvious, purpose is his swallowing of word endings at phrase ends ("quarrellin'," "churnin' "), and regional pronounciations ("yer" for "your" and so on). In his Luke the Drifter recitation "Beyond the Sunset" (recorded 10 January 1950), he tells of a man's vigilant loyalty to a woman preceding him in death; it is his memory of her that gives him the strenth to go on. The recitation depends on an implicit understanding of the uses of memory as regards its connection to history, issues that go far beyond the narrower topic of this small piece. As "Beyond the Sunset" has it: "Memory is a gift from God that death cannot destroy." The politics embedded here grow from the fact that Williams recognised less that songs are social constructions and more that society itself is constructed by the songs we sing, the stories we tell and the *sounds* we voice in the narration.

Everybody's Lonesome for Somebody

I'm so lonesome I could cry. (Hank Williams lyric)

What prepares men [*sic*] for totalitarian domination in the non-totalitarian world is the fact that loneliness, once a borderline experience usually suffered in certain marginal social conditions like old age, has become an everyday experience of the ever-growing masses of our century. (Hannah Arendt in *The Origins of Totalitarianism*

Goodbye Hank Williams, my old friend, I didn't know you but I've been the places you've been. (Tim Hardin lyric)
Hank Williams you wrote my life. (Moe Bandy lyric)

The extraordinary popularity of Hank Williams' songs in the late 1940s and early 1950s played a crucial role in transforming country music from a regional and class-bound genre to a staple of mass popular culture. Along with related developments in popular speech, dress and dance, the rise to national prominence of country music reflected the emergence of a prestige from below in which cultural hybrids emanating from intersections of race, class and gender articulated a new basis for American commercial culture.

Class, race and gender all contributed to the grounding of Williams' music in oppositional cultures and practices. His songs resonated with the materials memory forged in previous popular struggles against hierarchy and exploitation. But as a creation of a distinct historical moment, he added a new element to the historic struggle for the good life. In an age of renewed racism, he created a music that underscored the connections between whites and blacks. At a time of upward mobility and cultural assimilation for much of the working class, he affirmed his standpoint as a worker and an ordinary citizen. In an age of resurgent patriarchy, he lamented the schisms between men and women, resisted the dominant oedipal narrative and sought closer connections to women. Finally, he foregrounded existential despair in an age of exuberant and uncritical 'progress', countering ubiquitous romantic invocations of the superiority of the nuclear family with honest words and deep emotions drawn from the hurts of history and the experiences of everyday life. As modern life became increasingly characterised by 'the policing of families' as part of capital's project to colonise the psyche and the body, Williams constituted his own voice and body as sites of resistance. Millions of fans could feel that he 'wrote their lives', because even when they did not know him, they could feel that he knew the places they had been.

Notes

[1]We use psychoanalytic language here as a shorthand way of describing our culture's dominant narratives about the construction of subjectivity, not because we believe in any innate or transcendent human personality.

[2]See the examples quoted by Williams' second wife Billy Jean in Horstman 194.

[3]His chronic back problem, for example, was explained on a pre-recorded-for-broadcast apology that Williams produced from his hospital bed when he had to miss a December 1951 appearance in Baltimore. It is reproduced as the final cut on *Hank Williams: I Won't Be Home No More (June 1952-September 1952)*, Polydor 833-752-1 Y-2, volume 8, and the last, of Polydor's comprehensive, retrospective series of Williams' recordings.

[4]The loss of home through the upheavals of war and migration are a recurrent theme in Southern culture beginning with the Civil War and become more intense after each of this century's two world wars. One price paid for migration was guilt for not remaining to "share the common burden." See Horstman 3-5.

[5]See further Hume 94-6, "Dead Kids and Country Music."

[6]The other genres being the Luke accompanied monologues and the occasional novelty songs like the slightly bizarre "Indian" love song "Kaw Liga" or the famous "Jambalaya."

[7]On Williams' securing of women following show dates, see *ibid.*, p. 164. Nor was his stage presence effective only on women: "He quickly became the favorite act on a military entertainment entourage to Europe in 1951. [Moreover, on] a celebrity-studded touring show known as the Hadacol Caravan he upstaged such luminaries as Jack Benny, Milton Berle, and Bob Hope, and eventually took over the closing spot." (Blaser 17, n. 18) For details of the Caravan tour, see Williams 150-5; Koon 36, 38.

[8]Cf. Frank Page: "He was just electrifying on stage..He had the people in the palm of his hands from the moment he walked out there." (*ibid.* 74) See also Koon 28.

[9]His contradictory relationship to religion is encapsulated in what is probably an apocryphal story about a young fan who admitted to not being a 'God-fearing boy', and found Hank piping up "Don't let it trouble you none. I ain't afraid of God, either" (Caress 81-2). Koon quotes the very authoritative Bob Pinson as saying that the Shestack interview, from which this story is taken, is "all fiction; it never happened" (Koon 94). Yet the quotation seems to capture correctly something about Williams' view of religion. Roger M. Williams notes, "Hank, after his childhood, never demonstrated an interest in organized religion. But he had flashes of intense personal feeling about spiritual matters,

which led to some of the finest songs he ever wrote. Further, he knew that 'sacred songs' always find a ready market in country music" (Williams 57).

[10]Inevitably, in the upheaval of a wartime society, with women working, husbands and wives separated, easy social and geographical mobility, and honky tonks no longer populated exclusively by women of easy virtue, country writers began to flirt with, then to address directly, the subject of cheating (Horstman 182; see also Hume 84-5).

[11]See also the work of Nina Simone, ten years Hank Williams' junior, for example, on her live album, *Little Girl Blue*, especially "He Needs Me (He doesn't know it but he needs me)."

It is worth noting the correspondences and, especially, the differences between Hank Williams' songs of failed love and some of the early recordings of Patsy Cline (all songs written by others, whereas Williams mostly performed his own material). "If I Could Only Stay Asleep" moves slowly, underscoring the sense of loss inscribed by a vocal line repeatedly leaping to high notes only to slide back as if in defeat. "I'm Blue Again" registers the vocal 'tear'—perfected by Williams—to help mark a text entirely about loss, but this effect (and others) acts in contrast to the tempo, oddly upbeat, and to Cline's vocal delivery which breathes an air of confidence seriously undercutting the text's defeatism. Indeed, time and again in Cline's work, discrepancies occur between the putative subjects of the lyrics and her delivery of them. Among the reasons Patsy Cline is such an exciting singer is that, like Hank Williams, she pushed hard against the margins of musical conventions—stretching semiotic possibilities, introducing contradictions and unexpected tensions and, in particular, refusing to be bound by conventional expectations of vocal delivery located in gender distinction. Thus whereas Williams voices a feminine identity, meditating traditional masculine vocal qualities, Patsy Cline voices a masculine identity, notably by mediating the passivity that tunes of loss commonly inscribe lyrically and often musically. The loss of a man may be getting her down, so her words go, but she won't be down for long, so her voice encodes. She subscribes to the potential joys of men and women relating to each other but she refuses (not textually but vocally) to be overwhelmed by the absence or failure of the experience. It is very difficult to listen to "I've Loved and Lost Again" and really believe that the pain will be permanent. She will be up and dancing soon, playing a profoundly (vocally) liberated role: her vocal-gutteral growls on "Gotta Lot of Rhythm (In My Soul)," a thoroughly upbeat number, echo an effect heard commonly in early rock 'n' roll singers (both male and female).

[12]On these shows Williams typically included one or two Luke the Drifter recitations that specifically addressed black subjects, such as "The Funeral." This recitation, to the accompaniment of Hammond organ and steel guitar (recorded 10 January 1950), tells of the narrator, a white man, coming upon a humble country church and witnessing the funeral service for a black child. To be sure, Williams repeats racial stereotypes and dialogue embedded in southern racism (the child is described as having "curly hair, protruding lips; the black preacher's speech includes 'sho'nough"); on the other hand, Williams in effect absents himself as narrator almost from the start, giving sole voice to the preacher whose sermon he repeats at length. That is, a white man takes a pew to witness a funeral and thereafter tells his story: he tells his (primarily white) audience that he has learned something from what he describes as the "wisdom and ignorance of a crushed, undying race." (See Williams 74-5.) Hank Williams' own

funeral, held in Montgomery auditorium, included about two hundred blacks—seated in the segregated balcony—among the three thousand mourners who managed to squeeze inside; moreover, the music was provided in part by a black quartet, the Southwind Singers, in addition to various white country music luminaries (see Koon 54).

[13]Indeed, romantic love is generally in short supply in the country music of Williams' day, precisely because it could have had little ring of credibility in the circumstances of its hearers. See Horstman 119.

[14]Occasionally Williams confronted the politics of class more directly; perhaps the best example is "A Mansion on the Hill" (recorded 7 November 1947). Audrey Williams has said that (Chicago, urban-bred) Fred Rose gave Hank the title and sent him off to see what he could do with it. The result was an explicit articulation of high-low class hierarchy invited by Rose's title—the lyrics employ a binary opposition between the mansion on a hill and the narrator's cabin in a valley. (See Horstman 165)

Works Cited

Baker, H. Blues, *Ideology, and Afro-American Literature: A Vernacular Theory.* Chicago: Univ. of Chicago P, 1976.

Blaser, K. " 'Pictures from Life's Other Side': Hank Williams, country music, and popular culture in America." *The South Atlantic Quarterly* 84 (1985) (1): 12-26

Caress, J. *Hank Williams: Country Music's Tragic King.* New York: Stein and Day 1979.

Ehrenreich, B. *The Hearts of Men: American Dreams and the Flight from Commitment.* Garden City, NY: Anchor Press/Doubleday 1984.

Horstman, D. *Sing Your Heart Out, Country Boy.* New York: Dutton. 1975.

Hume, M. *You're So Cold I'm Turnin' Blue: Martha Hume's Guide to the Greatest Country Music.* New York: Penguin 1982.

Kingsbury, P. and Axelrod, A., eds. *Country: The Music and the Musicians. Pickers, Slickers, Cheatin' Hearts & Superstars.* New York: Abbeville P 1988.

Koon, G. *Hank Williams: A Bio-Bibliography.* Westport, CT: Greenwood P 1983.

Leo, J. "The familialism of man in American television melodrama." *The South Atlantic Quarterly,* 88 (1) (1988):31-51

May, E.T. *Homeward Bound.* New York: 1988.

_____ "Explosive issues: sex, women, and the bomb." *Recasting America.* Ed. L. May. Chicago: U of Chicago P 1989. 154-70.

Mintz, S. and Kellogg, S. *Domestic Revolutions.* New York Free P 1988.

Modleski, T. "Film theory's detour." *Screen,* 23 (5) (1982): 72-9

Pearl, M., with Dew, J. *Minnie Pearl: An Autobiography.* New York: Simon and Schuster Television 1980.

Pfeil, F. "Postmodernism as a `structure of feeling'." *Marxism and the Interpretation of Culture,* ed. L. Grossberg and C. Nelson Champaign: Univ of Illinois P pp. 381-405

Redd, L. *Rock is Rhythm and Blues.* East Lansing:Michigan State UP 1974.

Williams, R.M. *Sing a Sad Song: The Life of Hank Williams.* 2nd ed. Urbana: U of Illinois P 1981.

Patsy Cline, Musical Negotiation, and the Nashville Sound

Joli Jensen

Patsy Cline's performance career began in the mid 1940s and ended with her death in 1963. She began recording in Nashville in 1955 and became a member of the Opry in 1960. Her hit records crossed over into the pop charts, yet she was considered, and considered herself to be, a country star. Her rise to fame involved performing on radio and television broadcasts and in honky-tonks, clubs and talent shows.

She had several big hits, including "Walkin' After Midnight," "I Fall to Pieces," "Crazy" and "Sweet Dreams." They became popular in the new 1950s and 1960s radio-record environment; their success depended on pop radio play. They had the instrumentation and background vocals that characterize the Nashville Sound, and many credit her with demonstrating its potential. Yet she consistently fought the pop styling that brought her success—her voice may have been smooth, rich and "pop" sounding, but she considered herself to be a country singer and resented being forced into recording slower, more melodic material.

While Patsy Cline is not a typical performer, she is still an excellent vantage point from which to explore the nature of the country music business in Nashville in the 1950s. Virtually all her recording sessions are available on record. Memories of specific sessions are surprisingly clear and consistent. Her unwillingness to sing in the pop style suited to her voice and the times sparked explicit disagreements and audible stylistic mixtures. Her temper helped make these stylistic disagreements memorable for her producer and sidemen. This, combined with the telling and retelling of Patsy Cline stories and the impressive musical memory of professional musicians has made it possible to reconstruct the atmosphere of her recording sessions and to develop a deeper understanding of the negotiational definitions involved in her career and the shaping of her recordings.[1]

Biography

Patsy Cline was born September 8, 1932 in Winchester, Virginia.[2] One resident described Winchester as a "tired old Blue Ridge town," run by "the handfull of people who have always owned most of it" (Bageant). She was born when her mother was sixteen on what has been described as the wrong side of the tracks.

Her name then was Virginia Patterson Hensley, and she was stage struck.

An early photograph shows sixteen year old Patsy dressed up for an amateur show wearing high heels and short shorts—she had been performing in such talent shows since she was four. When she was sixteen her father left the family, and Patsy quit school and began working at a local drug store. She also set out to become regionally known. She walked into a local radio station and told the the announcer (and bandleader) Jim McCoy that she could sing. He says that he was impressed by her nerve and her voice and that she soon was singing on his live Saturday morning radio broadcasts. At about this time, she also made a trip to Nashville, with her mother and sister. She apparently sang on Roy Acuff's WSM show and several other shows, but she did not stay for more than a few days. As the story goes, they ran out of money and spent their last night in Nashville sleeping on benches in the park.

Still living in Winchester, she began playing with a locally popular band, Bill Peer and the Melody Playboys. Peer was well-known and liked in the community; Patsy's relationship with him was the beginning of the gossip and scandal that followed her the rest of her life.

The band played taverns, dancehalls, clubs, lodges, drive-ins and parks—the places that keep local bands in business. They played country music in a rousing, honkytonk style, with Patsy fronting them as a rough, sexy, yodeling vocalist. She apparently loved to perform for crowds and was able to give as good as she got in the jukejoints and honkytonks that made up the majority of the band's jobs.

As happens, word gets around when someone with talent and style is becoming popular. Patsy was also developing a reputation as a hell-raiser. She was coming to the attention of several people who would be important to her career throughout the 1950s—Connie B. Gay, the "impresario" of country music in the Washington DC area, the staff of the Arthur Godfrey Talent Scouts show in New York, Ernest Tubb on the Opry and Bill McCall, owner of a small Nashville record label, Four Star.

Patsy signed a recording contract with Bill McCall late in 1954. Four Star was one of the small companies that sprang up in Nashville in the mid 1950s to capitalize on the confusing but booming music business. Four Star signed performers and licensed material, but then leased recording and distribution rights to larger, more established companies like Decca. From 1954-1961 Patsy was locked into a contractual arrangement that limited her to recording Four Star material. From the beginning, her sessions were directed by Decca A & R man Owen Bradley, one of the most prominent figures in the development of the Nashville Sound. Until 1960, he had to choose songs from the catalog that McCall provided. Only one of those songs, a pop-styled number called "Walkin' After Midnight" ever became widely popular.

Patsy lived in Winchester, commuting to Nashville for recording sessions until 1960, when she moved there with her second husband Charlie Dick. In the mid 1950s she became one of the stable of country performers managed by Connie B. Gay.[3] He owned three country music radio stations and twenty-two television shows in the Washington area and contracted out performers on a *per diem* basis. Patsy was a regular cast member (with Jimmy Dean) on his Town &

Country Jamboree in 1956, wearing sexy, midriff-baring cowgirl outfits. She appeared on numerous musical variety shows, both on television and on radio. She was eventually "let go" by Gay because her unreliability, rebelliousness and drinking had gotten out of hand.

Still under contract with Four Star, but without a hit record, she appeared on the Arthur Godfrey Talent Scouts show, one of the most popular television shows of the time. She was convinced, after much heated discussion, to perform the pop styled song she had recently recorded, "Walkin' After Midnight." It was a big success, going to #17 on the pop charts and #3 on the country charts, after its televised performance. Patsy continued for several months as a regular on the show and also began touring and making appearances on the live country music circuit based in Nashville. In 1957 she signed on with road show promoter X. Cosse, who also represented Ferlin Husky, another "crossover" country artist. An album of Four Star material was released in the spring of 1958 and sold reasonably well on the country market.

In later 1959 she signed with the National Artists Bureau and appeared on syndicated television shows like Ozark Jubilee. In 1960 she was finally released from her Four Star contract and signed on with Decca. She moved to Nashville and her first Decca release—"I Fall To Pieces"—was a crossover hit. She signed on with the Opry late that year. From then on she was an Opry "star," appearing at least three weekends a month, going on Opry package tours to places like Carnegie Hall and the Hollywood Bowl, recording frequently, with her records doing well in both markets. She moved to a bigger house, bought a mink coat and generally reveled in her success. She was seriously injured in a 1961 car accident and suffered severe facial lacerations as well as several broken bones. Her hospital stay, and return to the Opry stage on crutches, received a lot of favorable publicity. She began to wear heavier makeup and wigs after the accident, to cover the facial scars. She kept a grueling schedule of live appearances and was killed with two other Opry performers and her manager, flying back from a Kansas City benefit performance.

The outline of Patsy's career includes many of the characteristics of the country music business in the 1950s. Her early performance career was in small clubs and honkytonks. She used radio and then television to become regionally known. In order to become successful, her records had to succeed in both the pop and country markets. She valued her country identity and connections and maintained them in spite of her "pop" success.

Her allegiance was to the Opry based definitions of country music, yet her later recordings and performance style are pure Music Row—the smooth, sophisticated "countrypolitan sound."

While her career embodies many of the basic characteristics of commercial country music during the period, certain aspects of her life set her apart. Her temperament and habits, her unusually rich and expressive voice, the problems of being a honkytonk angel in a business that portrays women performers as saintly and pure, shaped her career. These aspects will not be directly discussed, although they are taken into account. The focus of the rest of this essay is on the country-pop tension as it played itself out in her career, the content, style and atmosphere of her recordings and the connection her career had to the rest of the country music business of the time.

Country vs. Pop

Patsy Cline defined herself as a country singer, and her Nashville career was shaped by her unwillingness to adopt a pop sound and image. The continuing irony of her career was that her pop styled material was what made her widely successful, while her country material had appeal mainly on the Opry and live shows. Patsy desperately wanted success, and yet she balked at achieving it by crossing over into the pop record market. By tracing these tensions in her career, I hope to make clear the reality and tenacity of the country-pop distinction, a distinction that dominated the 1950s and continues to be refigured today.

Winchester, Virginia was, and still is, a town that is clearly divided along class and status lines. The rich people live on the hill, in large houses hidden by trees. Patsy grew up in a rundown section of town, surrounded by factories and warehouses. Patsy's early performance experience was with "hillbilly bands," dressed in western garb, playing roadhouses. Her personal style and demeanour reflected this early experience—she was rough talking, sexually aggressive and deeply ambitious.

If her mother is to be believed, "from the time she was about ten, Patsy was living, eating and sleeping country music. I know she never wanted anything so badly as to be a star on the Grand Ole Opry" (Nassour 37). Clearly Patsy was someone from a lower class background, with very little education, who learned to deal with the world in taverns and roadhouses. Her world was shaped and reflected by country music. She wanted to be a star, but was unwilling to shed the "hillbilly" image that she was told was preventing her from success.

Many of the rural-urban tensions of honkytonk songs are clear in her career. In the early 1960s, when things were really taking off for her, she bought a mink coat, a new car, and had a house built that included a bathroom with real gold sprinkled into the marble. It was the height of uptown, but she considered herself, still, to be just an "ole Va. gal" (Cline).

This self-definition is clear in a rare tape of a performance in Atlanta where she tells the audience about her recent Carnegie Hall appearance with the Opry cast.[4] In a warm, familiar voice, with a thick accent, she tells them how out of place she felt ("Talk about a hen out of a coop!") and how thrilled she was that a real princess, the Princess of Persia, had complimented her on her singing. She opened the set with "Come On In," and between songs kidded with the band in a casual, country style ("Let's see what damage we can do to this one, boys").

The story of "Come On In" has a certain irony. It is a rousing country tune that celebrates the warmth of folks back home who "love you as their own." It was her standard opening number, one that embodies, clearly, idealized communal values. Yet, ironically, Patsy was deeply disliked by many in Winchester. She was booed at least twice when she returned there after moving to Nashville

(McCoy). She was met with active hostility by people in her home town who did not approve of her, yet she continued to sing about, and celebrate, the mythic image of a warm, supportive community.

The Opry cast acts out that mythic image. When Patsy was hospitalized in 1961, she was surprised and touched by the cards, flowers and visits from Opry cast members. Her own generosity and willingness to help friends is frequently commented on—it is as if she attempted to create on her own the warmth and trust that was supposed to be there, in the country music world. It was a warmth and trust she apparently never experienced in Winchester.

One of the symbols of country music that Patsy clung to was the stylized cowgirl outfits she wore in her early career. She fought hard to continue to wear them on the Connie B. Gay television shows, and later on the Arthur Godfrey Talent Scouts show. She had to be convinced, over and over, that her fringed and sequined outfits were not appropriate for the shows. She would be asked to wear the demure cotton frocks popular at the time for "girl singers."

Her persona was tough, brassy and honkytonk. According to a fellow performer, "I first met her when I joined the Town & Country Jamboree in 1956. She came on strong and I said to myself, 'Who is the woman?' My first impression of her, all decked out in a cowgirl outfit—hat, boots, shirt with sequins and rhinestones—the works—was that she was a tough lady, and she was" (Nassour 98).

The brassy country image was not what they wanted on television in New York. Patsy did not like what was happening to her as a regular on the show:

> She was being leaned toward pop, and Patsy wanted country. Patsy bugged (them) to let her wear some of the western outfits her mother had made. But they kept saying no. Patsy was most unhappy and they could tell. Finally, because Patsy was driving them crazy, Arthur relented and agreed to do a show with a western theme....They wore white western everything. (Nassour 133)

The battle over clothing is intertwined with the battle over material, arrangements and vocal styling. Patsy's voice was exceptional and suited to a range of material. She was vocally flexible enough to sing several different musical genres, but was personally unwilling to follow her voice. According to Bradley:

> When Patsy and I first started working together, she didn't have her own style—sometimes she sounded like Kitty Wells, other times like Patti Page. (Gantry 64)

That she was able to sound pop made her commercially interesting to Nashville's recording industry, but Bradley had to work carefully with her, because she would often refuse to do songs that she felt were pop songs.

Her first big hit, "Walkin' After Midnight," was written by pop song writer Donn Hecht, also under contract to Four Stars' Bill McCall. He recalls that McCall played him one of her tapes, saying that he'd "spent a fortune releasing her and she's bombed out every time." When McCall asked Hecht for his opinion for why that was, Hecht remembers saying "That's easy, she's not a country singer at all." McCall disagreed with Hecht's assessment, saying that Patsy, like other country singers, had a "tear" in her voice. He asked Hecht to find an apprpriate song for her voice, and Hecht says he looked through old song sheets, coming up with:

> a yellowed lead-sheet of a song nobody ever wanted called "Walkin' After Midnight," originally written for Kay Starr. Her A&R department, for some reason, wouldn't let Kay record it. It was pure B-flat blues and, with Patsy's voice still surging through my brain, I put the two together.

When Patsy heard the song, she hated it. She said, "But that's nothing but a little ole pop song," according to Hecht, who countered with, "And you're nothing but a little ole pop singer who lives in the country." She eventually agreed to record it only if a song she liked ("Poor Man's Roses") was on the flip side (Hecht 44).

The same feelings against the song surfaced for the Godfrey performance, when she had to be convinced to sing "Midnight" over her strenuous assertion that she was *not* a pop singer. When she sang it, and the audience went wild, applauding for more, she chose to do a hard country follow-up—Hank Williams' "Your Cheatin' Heart" (Nassour 127).

Eventually, the success of her smoother material, combined with the increasing acceptance of the Nashville Sound, seems to have soothed her strident rejection of pop styled material. She always called herself a country performer, but began, in the early 1960s, to wear cocktail dresses on the Opry stage, and there are pictures of her on a Vegas date wearing a long black sequinned gown. Fellow crossover performer Faron Young believed that:

> She realized that she could be a lot more commercial and be hotter copy without a hayseed image. She left that country girl look in those western outfits behind and opted for a slicker appearance in dresses and high fashion gowns. From the way I saw it, and I told her, she had the potential to become a Kay Starr or Patti Page. (Nassour 329)

What is clear from the country-pop tensions in Patsy Cline's career is that it mattered a lot to her that she be defined as a country singer. It fulfilled a life long dream of success, and it also identified her with a specific set of values. In other words, generic tensions really count—one of these tensions would have existed, were choice of musical genre merely a matter of aesthetic preference, or based purely in commercial self-interest.

For Patsy, to go pop was to abandon an identity and a connection to her background, beliefs, experience. She refused to do it, over and over. But the music business was struggling with the same tensions, and she was eventually able to become part of the resolution of them, by singing smooth, arranged material, while calling herself, and believing herself to be, a country performer.

She was on the Opry, she was on the charts, she talked like a hillbilly and sang like a torch singer, she started out wearing cowgirl outfits and ended up wearing gowns. She was able to stay country because country was redefined and she was careful to stay within that definition. Today (interestingly) these distinctions have been refigured, and Pasty Cline represents "classic" or "traditional" country performance.

Recordings

Patsy Cline's definition of herself, as a performer, can be traced through her recording sessions on Music Row. Listening to tapes from her sessions in order[5] is a compelling illustration of the uncertainties of the times and the limits of her Four Star contract. It also reveals an unfocused search for something that would "work," and the coalescing of a professional, orchestrated sound that, eventually, did.

Few of Patsy's early songs have stood the test of time. The mediocrity of the Four Star catalog, combined with the uncertainty of the times, and Patsy's style, resulted in an uncomfortable mix of material. The Four Star material combines different musical genres—country ballad, swing, rockabilly, popular and pop-novelty, rhythm and blues, sacred—in the same sessions and sometimes in the same song. Few of these songs appear on the "best of" albums released since her death.

The Four Star material, taken as a whole, reveals much about the problems of making good songs when the material is limited, commercial music is in transition, the songs aren't successful and the performer is uncertain. Patsy's singing, while distinctive and often appealing, is severely hampered by the lyrics, the arrangements and her unwillingness to give up the style she learned fronting small tavern bands. Her phrasing reflects the beat, and her vocal tricks are extremely predictable; she modulates up, or growls, or croons, in the same way, in the same places, again and again. While there are songs that hint of her future style, most of her renditions are neither moving nor memorable.

This makes "I Fall to Pieces" all the more amazing. On this song, recorded in her first Decca session, she lets her voice float, while the guitar counterpoints her expressive phrasing.[6] It is sudden and dramatic display of vocal ease and one that continues in various degrees for the rest of her Decca sessions.

For the first time, melodic and emotional material was being matched with a relaxed, expressive, personal voice. This is the combination that appears in "I Fall to Pieces," and its success ensured its continued use.

The discovery of the power of this softer, more emotive style did not eliminate all the elements of her earlier recordings. Arrangements still vary in style, but not nearly as dramatically, and while Patsy still insisted on country stylistic markers like growling, yodelling and belting out endings, she was frequently convinced to try a smoother style.

The beat has softened considerably in the later tunes, and the arrangements are smoother and more subtle. Patsy's voice is relaxed and confident, and she takes risks—pauses, breathes, sighs, drawn out words—that add emotional power to the lyrics. It is as if she suddenly believed, as Bradley suggests, that she didn't have to use the tricks she'd developed to impress live audiences, she could, instead, simply out-sing everyone.

What marks the Decca sessions is the juxtaposition of traditional country with purely popular material. Songs like "Your Cheatin' Heart," "Faded Love,"[7] "San Antonio Rose" and "Blue Moon of Kentucky" contrast with pop standards like "True Love," "You Made Me Love You," "Always" and "Love Letters in the Sand." These songs represent either end of the country-pop continuum; most of her later songs fall into middle ground—"hurting" songs with the smooth arrangement that was becoming known as the Nashville Sound.

It is difficult to fully explain the quality and power of Patsy's later work. It is more than a wider vocal range, fewer tricks, more expressive phrasing. Friends say that she was also more relaxed, confident, sure of herself as a recording artist as her songs became more successful in both markets. Bradley attributes much of the change to "knowing who you are," finding an identity as a performer.

Patsy's identity was tied up with the redefinition of country music as the Nashville Sound. The sidemen on most of her Decca sessions were Floyd Cramer on piano, Buddy Harmon on drums, Bob Moore on bass, Grady Martin, Ray Edenton, Hank Garland and Harold Bradley on guitar, the Jordanaires on vocal backup. These are the session musicians celebrated as the reason for the Sound's success—Patsy's development of an identity as a recording artist coincided with Nashville's development of a commercially successful sound.

Sessions

Patsy's ambivalence about smoother material, as well as aspects of her relationship to Bradley and the Jordanaires, is well illustrated by Ray Walker's story of the session where they recorded "I Fall to Pieces."

> Patsy was scared. She was quite an artist on stage, and she had done pretty well with the western-swing type uptempo music. She had never sung a song like 'I Fall to Pieces' before, and she didn't consider herself that kind of a singer.
>
> The first time she did the ending, she came up on the tag, went up an octave, and actually sang a little faster. It just floored me. I stopped right in the middle of the ooohs and aaahs or whatever we were doing, and she looked over and said, 'What's wrong, Ray?' I said, 'Is that the way you're going to end the song?' She said, 'Well, Owen wanted me to end it by slowing down and taking the last line out, but I feel safer going up and really belting out the ending.' I said, 'Patsy, this is not a belt out song. You had me practically in tears, and then all of a sudden the clowns walk in.' She said, 'Well, okay,' and went back, and things really smoothed out. She got lower and lower and so gutsy. She had us spellbound.
>
> When 'I Fall to Pieces' got the reaction it did, they brought her right back into the studio to do an album. She came in saying 'The record's making noise, it's making noise, I can't believe it,' and she hugged me and said, 'And they're all talking about that ending.'

The success of "I Fall to Pieces" did much to convince Patsy that "her sound" was a more melodic one. Still, she was uncomfortable if she was labeled a pop singer. Harlan Howard recalls her reaction to his song "When I Get Through You":

> It was kind of a teenybopper song, the lyrics were aimed at young girls, high school kids. Patsy recorded the heck out of it, but she was a little embarassed because it was not your conventional 'Your Cheatin' Heart' kind of country ballad. They put it out with a Justin Tubb ballad on the back side, and I used to get mad at Patsy, because she'd go on the Opry, and she'd sing the ballad, she'd plug the B side. She felt that she might be betraying her country fans. She was quite concerned with her fans, and not letting them down, and them not putting her down.

This concern with "not being put down" is only one aspect of Patsy's complex personality. She described herself as a "hellcat," and her temperament was part of her reputation in the business. Gordon Stoker recalls that "she felt like she had to fight constantly to keep her head above water. And she did, she fought, she died fighting. She was a fighter right down to the end."

Walker suggests that "her nervousness, her arguing and her temperament made those songs. She really wanted to do what the song called for, but she was so afraid that a song with a beat wouldn't sell. I think that she was fighting that change, and by fighting that change, and by fighting her own fears, she put a certain depth in her singing."

As she overcame her fears, he continues, and began to cooperate more with Bradley, "she found out that there was nothing to fear and nothing to be ashamed of, and she started singing songs that her heart felt. She started singing them with a positive conviction, because they were really nothing but a remake of her life."

Patsy's relationship with Owen Bradley was a special one, based on mutual respect but marked by intense arguments over material and arrangements. Harlan Howard says, "They were real close, it was a father-daughter type thing. When they got in a disagreement they'd argue and cuss and debate, but they'd always resolve it." Walker remembers, "Patsy was very vociferous about what she wanted to do, and Owen would just say, softly, 'Well now Patsy'." Howard remembers a frequent compromise over material during the sessions: "Owen would say, 'Well you do these two, but then you do these two over here, and we'll see which one turns out to be a hit'." Bradley's choice would be the softer, melodic material, Patsy's would be the harder country songs.

When Bradley talks about the differences between Patsy's earlier and later material, he is quite candid about the problems they had.

> In retrospect, we had a girl with a good strong voice, she could really sing, but she was not a Kitty Wells or a Jean Shephard, she was not like some other girl singers. She felt that if she was going to compete, she had to do those kinds of songs. One of the problems we had is that, if you don't get played alot you don't know who you are. If you're a little bit this, and a little bit that, then you're really nobody. Now if you listen to the early songs we did, we were a big flop as long as we tried to do everybody else's thing. When we tried to do Patsy's thing, when we found *our* thing, we figured out who

we were. It isn't that we were so smart, we sort of lucked onto it. I can't say I was that smart; if I had been, I'm sure I would have done it alot sooner.

The Business

An interesting aspect of Patsy Cline's career is the way she was promoted as a performer. Fan magazines, just developing in the country market, portrayed her as pert, bubbly, sweet, energetic. She was, in spite of her two marriages, billed as *Miss* Patsy Cline. Her early coverage reveals something of the developing country promotion strategy and also indicates aspects of the role of women in 1950s country music.

In spite of her reputation within the business as a hard living, rough talking, temperamental hell raiser, Patsy was promoted to the public as a sweet, country girl. Decca's promotion director Shel Silverstein described her in promotional copy as "a god-fearing religious girl who is thankful for all the goodness in her life. There isn't a malicious bone in her body. Patsy is the kind of girl who will go out of her way (no matter how far) to help someone who needs her help. Yes, Patsy Cline is a credit to the music business and a boon to all who love listening to good music" ("In Tune.").

The magazine, *Trail*, had a 1958 feature on Patsy's clothes preferences called "Trail Togs." In gushing prose, the article describes how Patsy's jewelry is "of the sparkly type," but "in excellent taste because she doesn't 'overdress' with it." She is also said to "limit her use of rouge, powder and eye make-up, because she has a very lovely complexion, and looks always as though she's just come back from a morning walk in the cool spring air." Patsy is portrayed as having a taste for simple, quality clothing, even though the pictures accompanying the copy make this an unlikely claim (*Trail*).

One of the most memorable disjunctures between photo and copy is an early 1960s *Country Song Round-up*. The picture of Patsy was taken at the annual Country Music Disc Jockey Association convention in Nashville. A heavily made up, overweight Patsy Cline is sitting on a chair in the middle of a room full of partygoers, singing sleepily into the microphone. The caption reads. "Here's pert Patsy entertaining stars and fans at a Nashville D.J. bash" (*Country Song*).

So-called "girl singers" had a specific role in country music during the 1940s and early 1950s. Package shows assumed they needed one, but only one. She was portrayed as sweet and innocent and protected by safe male companionship. The classic example of this is from the 1940s, when Roy Acuff hired banjo player and comedian Rachel Veach. He got concerned and irate fan mail until he paired her with Pete Kirby as "Cousin Rachel and her great big bashful brother Oswald" (Green 43). This reassured fans that she was being properly looked after on the road.

Patsy Cline was clearly cut from a different cloth. This both angered and frustrated many in the music business, who went to great lengths to protect her reputation. The terms used to describe her—down-to-earth, refreshingly honest, sincere, a real country gal—are very oblique references to her outspokenness. When I first began interviewing people in Nashville I was puzzled by the reserve that crept in when I asked people to describe what she was like. Earthy, open, honest, real—only later, or with evidence that I knew some of the "dirt," would descriptions of her include references to her swearing, drinking, sexuality and even then they would be vague and off the record. It was, and remains, difficult for the country music community to accept a woman performer in the role of honkytonk angel, rather than as her alter-ego, the long-suffering saint at home.

Patsy's voice and performance style were also difficult to characterize in promotional copy. Eventually the idea of her voice being so good that she appealed to country *and* pop audiences became the way to describe her, although early on in her career she was introduced as one of the finest "country-western-blues singers in the world."[8] Certainly things got easier for the writers by the 1960s, when crossovers were far more acceptable and when her membership on the Opry defined her status as a country singer whose songs made it on the pop charts.

Conclusion

Patsy Cline is frequently cited as having "opened doors" for other women in the business. Dottie West, who moved to Nashville in the early 1960s, says:

> In those days record men would tell you that women didn't sell, so on all the package shows there'd be only *one* girl. And I think that was really because they didn't think of us as artists—they just thought they should have a girl on the show. You know, for looks. But after Patsy Cline hit, there were more women making records because record men weren't afraid of them. (Offen 37)

Brenda Lee, Loretta Lynn and others echo this sentiment. The success of Patsy Cline songs helped to convince Music Row and the Opry that women performers could sell records and tickets. Still, they were promoted as "sweet country girls," and sang songs that portrayed them as the wronged woman, not the temptress. Jean Shephard said that her producer "would never let me record a triangle song unless I was on the right side of the fence" (Offen 42).

Patsy is also cited, of course, as one of the major figures in the rise of the Nashville Sound. Her success on the pop charts, while keeping an identity as a country singer, was taken to be an indication that "good" country music could have wide appeal, if it didn't have too strong a country flavor. Other performers, like Marty Robbins and Jim Reeves, did the same. In fact, the lush, orchestrated arrangements of the Nashville Sound came to dominate most country recordings during the period.

Patsy Cline's career, while not necessarily typical, is illustrative of many of the characteristics of the time. She illuminates the tensions between honkytonk angel and country girl, country and pop music, live and recorded performance and rural and uptown styles. Her career spanned a transitional period in country music, and her recording sessions reveal the search for a commercial but a "country" sound. Her identity was bound up in being a country performer, yet her voice was suited to pop songs. Her struggle to maintain a country definition was overt and memorable, demonstrating the definitional power of music as a cultural form. Her career can be used as evidence that country music is a form of symbolic material whose production is always a complex interpretive, negotiational process.

Notes

[1] Don Roy's impressive discography in *Journal of Country Music* 9.2, is the most complete listing available of Patsy's recordings, sessions and albums.

[2] Unless otherwise noted, the following biographical information comes from a combination of a variety of sources. My background research, for both the history of the times and Patsy Cline's biography included reading issues of *Country Song Roundup, Country and Western Jamboree, Folk and Country Songs, Rustic Rhythm, (Country) Music Reporter*, all available in the Country Music Foundation archives. I also surveyed *Billboard* 1954-64. The newspaper file at the CMF contained articles about Patsy; photographs and additional articles were found through personal contacts and the reader's guide. Numerous interviews were conducted, including Patsy Cline's husband, Charlie Dick, producer Owen Bradley, disc jockey Ralph Emergy, manager X. Cosse, promoter Mae Boren Axton, songwriter Harlan Howard, impresario Connie B. Gay, performers Faron Young, Brenda Lee, Kathy Copas Hughes, Ray Walker and Gorden Stoker, columnist Redd O'Donnell, Four Star president Joe Johnson, drugstore owner Ralph Gaunt and bandleader Jim McCoy. Photographs were obtained on sites, from her friends, from publications. Visits were made to the Nashville area in summer of 1979 and 1980.

[3] The information on Connie B. Gay comes from a lengthy interview (20 April 1980), his scrapbooks and articles, including "Country Boy Always Tuned In," by Hank Burchard in the *Washington Post*, 8 February 1971, and "Country Stylist," by McCandlish Phillips in *The New York Times*, 8 September 1957.

[4] Cassette recording given to Jim McCoy.

[5] The arduous task of taping each of Patsy's songs, in order, was accomplished by Don Roy, while employed at the Country Music Foundation Library.

[6] Guitarist Hank Garland had just begun using a device that gave the guitar a bell-like sound, and Howard believes that this new sound contributed to the success of the song he co-wrote.

[7] Owen Bradley said that Johnny Gimble told him that Patsy's version of "Faded Love" was one of Bob Wills' two favorite records.

[8] Arthur Godfrey apparently characterized her this way in introducing her on the show, according to an entry in the *Official WSM Grand Ole Opry History Picture Books* 2.2: 27.

Works Cited

Bageant, Joe. "Patsy Cline: Legends, Ghosts and Goodhearted Gals." *Picking Up the Tempo* 18. Albuquerque, NM: Wowapi Productions, nd.

Bradley, Owen. Interview. June 1979.

Cline, Patsy. Letter to Jim McCoy after 1961 auto a accident.

Country Song Roundup 13.74 (Nov. 1961).

Gantry, Susan Nadler. "A Portrait of Patsy Cline." *Country Music Magazine* Oct. 1979: 64.

Green, Douglas. *Country Roots: The Origins of Country Music* Hawthorne Books, 1976.

Hecht, Donn. "I Remember Patsy Cline." *Country Music Magazine* Oct. 1973: 44.

Howard, Harlan. Interview. June 1979.

"In Tune with Patsy Cline." *Cowboy Songs* 2.59 (Jan. 1959).

McCoy, Jim. Interview. Summer 1980.

Nassour, Ellis. *Patsy Cline: An Intimate Biography.* Tower Books, 1981.

Offen, Carol. "The Big Speakout: L'il Darlin's Know the Score." *Country Music Magazine* July 1974: 37.

Stoker, Gordon. Interview. June 1979.

Trail Magazine 1.2 (March-April 1958): 34.

Walker, Ray. Interview. June 1979.

Elvis, Country Music, and the South

Bill C. Malone

Sometime in 1955 I attended a concert featuring Hank Snow in Austin, Texas. To my chagrin the concert was cut short, and Hank was reduced to giving an abbreviated medley of his songs so that a second show could be scheduled for the accommodation of the large throng clamoring outside to get in. The multitude was not there to see my hero, Hank Snow, nor to hear "old-time" country music. They were there to see the rising new sensation, Elvis Presley. He was just beginning his stint with RCA Victor but had not yet recorded his first smash national hit, "Heartbreak Hotel." Stylistically, he was neither fish nor fowl and, consequently, his managers had not yet determined how to package him. To a rock-ribbed country traditionalist such as myself, it was bad enough to be given only a condensed period of my favorite kind of music. Even more appalling was the tumultuous, and even frenzied, response of the audience to Presley who, in my opinion, was not good and, more significantly, was not country. He came out in his red sports coat (or was it pink?) wearing his pompadour and long sideburns and twisting his lips into that peculiar shy sneer. After one verse and a chorus of "That's All Right, Mama," he shoved his guitar to one side of his body, set his left leg to quivering and began the pelvic thrusts that any stripper would have envied. With each bump and grind, his young women listeners came unglued until, unable to resist any longer, they stormed to the foot of the stage shrieking their pleasure and reacting in a manner allegedly alien to most proper Southern girls. I do not know whether my discomfort arose most acutely from my puritanism or from my musical conservatism. Whatever the source, I felt that Presley was a disrupter and that, as evidenced by the response given to him, the future of country music was dim.

While I still have no greater affection for Elvis' music than I did twenty years ago, time and reflection have made my response more historical than hysterical, and I feel that I now have a more balanced view of his place in the country music continuum. And Elvis *was* country, as much as he was anything, and it is in country music that one must look to find the roots of his style, if not his appeal. Much has been made of Elvis' successful exploitation of the black musical idiom, as if he and Sam Phillips, the director of Sun Records, were the first to stumble upon such an idea. On the contrary, Elvis' fusion of black and white music was merely the most recent phase in a process of interaction that

This essay first appeared in *Elvis: Images and Fancies* (ed. by Jac Thorpe) 123-134. Reprinted with permission of University Press of Mississippi.

51

extend back to the earliest contacts between blacks and whites in the early seventeenth century and has been manifested in American professional entertainment since at least the appearance of the blackface minstrels after 1830.

White country musicians, from Jimmie Rodgers to now, have demonstrated a continuing fascination with black sounds, songs, styles and images. Most people are at least dimly aware of the influence exerted by black styles upon the music of such major performers as Bob Wills, Hank Williams and Charlie Rich, but it may not be quite so well known that the music of a host of other country performers has been tarred with the African brush. Even Louisiana's famous singing governor, Jimmie Davis of "You Are My Sunshine" fame, known for his policy of racial segregation and his soulful singing of gospel songs, got his start in the early 1930s by singing sexy versions of tunes like "Red Night Gown Blues" and "Tom Cat and Pussy Blues." Nevertheless, it is important to stress that these entertainers succeeded because they were able to "mix" or appropriate racial styles, not because they made themselves into replicas of Negro performers (although the Allen Brothers, to their great disgust, were sometimes listed in record brochures alongside "race" performers because they sang blues tunes so convincingly). Similarly, Elvis did not sound like a Negro, despite Sam Phillips' search for such a performer; he sounded like a white boy from the Deep South. That alone was enough to make him unusual in the bland, homogenized atmosphere of American popular music at the end of the 1950s. His exploitation of black material, in any case, has been greatly exaggerated; it was, rather, part of an eclectic and, in fact, largely undisciplined approach to music.

Although country music was once considered the hayseed stepchild of the American popular music industry and perceived solely as a regional genre of limited appeal, it had begun to launch out into the world-at-large long before Elvis made his first test recordings in the Sun studio in 1954. Much of its expansion occurred during World War II when the migrations of defense workers and servicemen promoted musical interchange, but the music's first commercial boom period came after 1946 when the lifting of controls and postwar prosperity generated an unprecedented pursuit of entertainment. With over 650 radio stations carrying live "hillbilly" talent and a proliferation of small record labels promoting all kinds of grassroots musical material (Cajun, gospel, blues), the music began entering homes where it had never before been admitted. While they seldom appeared on the major pop music charts—musical forms were still rigidly segregated until the mid-1950s—singers like Eddy Arnold, Carl Smith, Lefty Frizzell, Hank Snow and Hank Williams gained a name recognition in American popular culture that earlier country entertainers would have envied. And, increasingly, songs of country origin *did* begin to appear on the charts, but almost always by pop singers as in the cases of Patti Page and "Tennessee Waltz," Rosemary Clooney and "Half as Much" and Tony Bennett and "There'll Be No Teardrops Tonight."

The covering of country songs by pop singers is a well-known fact of the early 1950s; the parallel utilization of other forms of music by country singers is insufficiently recognized. Since the 1920s a major preoccupation of country musicians had been with the cluster of musical forms which included boogie, blues and hot dance rhythms. In the late 1940s and early 1950s when Elvis would have been warehousing sounds he would later exploit, Hank Williams, for instance, did songs such as "My Bucket's Got a Hole in It"; Red Foley had smash hits with "Chattanoogie Shoe Shine Boy" and "Tennessee Saturday Night"; and the Delmore Brothers, who had been performing country boogie tunes since the mid-1930s, had great success with songs like "Freight Train Boogie" and "Blues Stay Away From Me." Furthermore, many of the instrumental cliches that would later characterize early rock and roll could be heard distinctly in country music during the immediate postwar years. As an inveterate radio listener Elvis could scarcely have avoided hearing such groups as the Maddox Brothers and Rose (billed as "the most colorful hillbilly band in the land") whose exuberant and jivey songs featured hot electric guitar solos, slapped bass playing and an energetic style of singing similar to and anticipatory of rockabilly music. Nick Tosches, in *Country: The Biggest Music in America*, calls their "Hangover Blues," recorded in 1952, "pure gutter-rock."

Elvis's derivative style, then, was a composite drawn in great measure, but not exclusively, from earlier country music, and one could hear in his performances echoes of country boogie pianist Moon Mullican, the Maddox Brothers, Hank Williams, Red Foley and others whose music he had long absorbed. Nevertheless, it is almost a certainty that his career would never have experienced its rapid ascent had he not unleashed his own charismatic combination of sensuality, high energy and rollicking bad boyishness in tapping a brand-new audience, the youth, which was ready for the music he purveyed and which could not be confined to the traditional country music format.

Elvis began as a member of this audience, sharing its desires and frustrations; he soon became one of its heroes and spokesmen. Up to a point, his biography resembles my own and that of millions of Southern working-class youth. Like many of our generation born on farms or in small hamlets during the Depression, there was, during the war and its immediate aftermath, a move to the city, in Elvis's case, Memphis. This migration brought into focus a confrontation of values which was both generational and social. Many people readily conformed to the city, welcoming its hastened pace as well as its economic enticements. Others never really abandoned the rural scheme of values even though they became permanently domiciled in an urban home and occupation. Elvis rejected neither reality but absorbed them both into his music. Like Jerry Lee Lewis, the wild man of rockabilly music, Elvis was reared in the Pentecostal faith, that wondrous mixture of otherworldly vision and earthly abandon which contributed heavily to the building of modern gospel music and to the molding of an impressive body of musicians ranging from Mahalia Jackson to James Blackwood. No musical instrument was ever taboo in Pentecostal services, and church members felt free to express a joyous emotionalism that was often closed to them in secular life. Elvis did his first public singing in church, and his style certainly bears the marks of this experience, but he has alluded more directly to the influence upon his life of the ministers, that zealous and often flamboyant breed of men and women who intrigued him with their theatrical flair and platform choreography.

The white gospel quartets were also powerful shapers of Elvis' music, and the greatest of them all, the Blackwood Brothers, were Mississippians too who made their headquarters in Memphis when he was still a teenager. The rather affected and throaty vibrato which he used on his slower songs probably came from the quartet singers, and Elvis usually recorded or performed in concert with the Jordanaires or the Stamps Quartet. Elvis never abandoned his affection for gospel music; even at the peak of his professional career, when mainstream pop music was his primary expression and Las Vegas his principal arena of action, he usually sang religious songs during his private moments offstage. Gospel music remained one of the few safe retreats available to him during those lonely days of isolation at the end of his life and a mark of loyalty to the culture of his mother.

Immersed in the traditional culture and music of his parents, yet drawn by the liberating musical trends of his own era, Elvis, like his Southern contemporaries, was torn by conflicting impulses. His eclecticism seems to have been the resolution of this conflict. In addition to the church music he had heard all his life, he listened to any and every kind of music that was available on the radio. Much of his musical experimentation was a trial-and-error search for a successful commercial formula; in his Sun auditions he tried a sampling of everything he knew, from Dean Martin-style pop music to gut-bucket blues.

His first Sun recording included "Blue Moon of Kentucky," a blue-grass song by Bill Monroe, and "That's All Right, Mama," a rhythm-and-blues tune from the repertory of Arthur "Big Boy" Crudup. By successfully wedding the music of the poor whites and poor blacks of the South, Elvis established a new folk consensus that proved commercial enough to alter the course of American popular music as no other singer, from Al Jolson to Frank Sinatra, had ever done. His impact on the larger popular music world has been explored elsewhere; my emphasis will be, instead, on Elvis' effect on the music from which he had first drawn sustenance, the music of his origins, the country music of the South.

Elvis' recording success inspired a similar exploitation of other young singers who could perform his kind of music. Some, like Bob Luman, were directly inspired by Elvis; others, like Carl Perkins and Jerry Lee Lewis, had been waiting in the wings with rocking styles developed independently of Presley. Elvis opened the commercial doors for all of these young singers, many of whom made their recording debuts on the Sun label. Whether they came from the Mississippi Delta or from the Texas Plains, they were generally described as rockabillies because of their alleged fusion of blues and hillbilly music. But again, it would be a gross misinterpretation to view the rockabillies as nothing more than white boys doing black music even if they did "cover" a considerable amount of black songs; more often they just applied their high-energy styles to country music. The term rockabilly means just that: hillbilly music with a rocking beat.

Although it was only for a brief moment, the rockabillies' success marked the most important intrusion made by Southern whites into mainstream pop music. The rockabillies made their Southernness known by their accents and dialects, but they also projected a hedonistic, and even macho, strain that had always been part of Southern working-class culture, the wild, devil-may-care abandon that had helped to fling their earlier counterparts and ancestors onto the battlefields of the Civil War (but more likely today to lure them into barroom fights or into stock car races). If W.J. Cash had lived, he might have recognized them as the simple "men-at-the-center" whom he discussed in *Mind of the South*: men who felt rather than thought and who embodied, without hypocrisy, both hedonistic and puritanical traits (and, as Jerry Lee Lewis has repeatedly demonstrated, the distance from the honky tonk to the revival mourner's bench, and back again, is short indeed). Jack Kirby, in his recent book *Media-Made Dixie*, describes country musicians as conveyors of the myth of "the visceral white Southerner," a character who is "languid, innocent of caprice and wisdom in handling money, moonstruck and often drunk." He would have been more accurate if he had centered his discussion on the rockabillies. The hedonistic strain had always been present in Southern rural culture, but seldom had it been so blatantly displayed in the white man's music. Country singers like Jimmie Rodgers, Charlie Poole and Hank Williams had often conveyed the image in their songs about drinking and rambling, and on occasion someone like Prince Albert Hunt, the Texas fiddler who was shot to death outside a Dallas tavern in 1931 by a jealous husband, could even act out the fantasy. Performing styles, though, have rarely been so uninhibited. A singer like Little Jimmie Dickens might bounce around the stage like a whirling dervish, and a Bill Carlisle could amuse an audience with his jumping antics, but no white country singer prior to Elvis and the other rockabillies had ever fused so closely physical action and sexual suggestion.

To argue that Elvis drew upon cultural and musical sources common to the other rockabillies is not to deny his uniqueness. Roy Orbison projected a "cool" image with his black-leather jacket an dark sunglasses; the Everly Brothers and Buddy Holley exuded the boyish naiveness of a high school sock hop; Carl Perkins came across as a rustic hep cat; Jerry Lee Lewis was definitely macho in his appeal—but Elvis was all of these. And unlike the others, with his appealing combination of vulnerability and aggressiveness, he brought a frank sexuality to both country and pop music. His pouting leer and heavy-lidded bedroom eyes made him fascinating to many people, but his boyish appeal also evoked the motherly instinct in many of his women fans. His physicality, his crucial contribution to country and popular music, was distasteful to many people, especially to the ministers of his own religious denomination (at least in his early nonestablishment days), but he was careful never to offend public tastes as did, say, Jerry Lee Lewis (no hell-raising in public, no marrying his thirteen-year-old cousin, no outrageous interviews).

For two or three years after 1957, "traditional" country music suffered as a result of the rock and roll revolution. Except for bluegrass music, which has always led a rather underground existence, fiddle almost disappeared from country recordings, and the mainstay of the honky tonk genre, the steel guitar, became even more rare. The "rural" sound was discouraged, and everywhere there was a tremendous emphasis on youth, vitality and modernity. Recording companies, booking agents and other music promoters began a rather frantic search for talent that could equal Elvis' appeal among American youth. Under intensive prodding older country singers added rock and roll songs to their repertories or, often with pathetic result, adapted their performing styles to the new phenomenon. Even Bill Monroe, the veteran bluegrass star, speeded up his version of "Blue Moon of Kentucky" after Elvis hit with the song. The most traditional mountain-oriented bluegrass group, the Stanley Brothers, recorded a rhythm-and-blues tune, Hank Ballard's "Finger Popping Time," and hard-core honky tonk singer George Jones recorded at least one rock and roll song, under the name of Thumper Jones. There was also a great profusion of singers who, if not fully rock and roll, at least souped up their styles to appeal to young listeners.

The rock and roll inundation of country music nevertheless proved to be short-lived, and by the end of the 1950s, the mainline country styles were making vigorous comebacks. Led by such entertainers as Merle Haggard, Loretta Lynn and Charley Pride, these styles were experiencing a remarkable resurgence by the end of the 1960s. Rock and roll, however, left what would appear to be permanent marks on country music. High-powered electronics remained permanently wedded to country music, and young guitarists who had begun their careers as rock and roll musicians came back into country bands bringing their instrumental licks with them (one needs only to listen to any Waylon Jennings recording). Rock and roll songs like "Johnny B. Goode" have repeatedly resurfaced in the repertories of country singers. Disc jockeys who had grown up listening to rock and roll, or who had sometimes been rock and roll musicians, often found employment on country radio stations, especially after 1960 when the number of such stations greatly proliferated. As powerful tastemakers, they did much to alter both the style and audience of country music. The country music industry reacted to the rock and roll threat (and to the recognition that there was a vast new audience out there) by creating a form of music that would be inoffensive to listeners who had not grown up in a Southern rural environment or who wanted to forget that they had. The result was a so-called compromise that would supposedly preserve the flavor and ambience of country music while projecting a more urbane image. Chet Atkins and the other architects of this country-pop blending which was designated as the "Nashville Sound" seemed to assume that the "old" country music audience would remain loyal regardless of the changes (they after all had little choice); the "compromise" obviously was designed to attract a new audience.

The rockabillies faded rather quickly from the national consciousness, and rock and roll gave way to a much more aggressive and urban form of musical expression, the rock culture which knows no regional identity or bounds. The rockabillies, however, never disappeared from American music; they, and their successors, remained as a fringe of country music. Some rockabillies such as Conway Twitty became very successful mainstream country singers; others, like Jerry Lee Lewis and Waylon Jennings, effectively combine country and rock music in their repertories. A few, such as Billy Swan, who travels with Kris Kristofferson, adhere closely to the sounds of the 1950s. There is a large body of singers who still dress in costumes reflective of Elvis' post-Sun period, with tight, flared pants (usually white or some bright color) and sequined shirt open to at least the third button, and who strut or swagger around the stage and sing with a great deal of acrobatic vigor: Crash Craddock, Narvel Felts, Joe Stampley, Roy Head, T.G. Sheppard, Ray Griff, Ronnie McDowell, to name only a few. In addition to these successful professional singers, there are innumerable others throughout the land, amateur and professional (including the legion of Elvis imitators who have flourished since his death), who perform for small audiences in clubs or at Saturday night barndances. Their dynamic stage routines, replete with often grotesque displays of leering and bumping-and-grinding, reinforce the faith of an audience who still think that Elvis is king and who enthusiastically welcome any performer who seems reminiscent of him.

In evaluating Elvis' impact on American music, some writers assess him as a conscious rebel who deliberately set out to offend public sensibilities and overthrow both conventional musical tastes and societal standards. Like the motorcycle hellion portrayed by Marlon Brando in *The Wild Ones*, Elvis, in this view, was an indiscriminate rebel against anything that society had to offer. (Questioner: "What are you rebelling against?" Brando: "What've you got?") But those who would interpret Elvis as an anarchistic iconoclast merely project their own consciousness upon Elvis, much in the way that ideologues interpret earlier revolutionaries to fit their own visions. If Elvis was a revolutionary, he was a most unconscious one and he distanced himself from the musical Jacobins, i.e., the protest singers and the acid rock singers, who came later. From the time he decked himself out in flamboyant clothing and ducktail hairstyle as a Memphis teenager, to the rather aimless search for commercial material in the Sun studio which led to his first hit record and on through his fabulous career, Elvis never rejected his origins or his essential Southernness. Nor did he reject that larger world from which his family had long been excluded. Rather than thumb his nose at the middleclass mainstream, he actively sought to enter it, as the children of humble origins have inevitably tried to do. He succeeded in his quest and was imprisoned, tightly sheltered from the adoring public that had given him his success. Some would say that his music was also constricted and that his RCA recordings never achieved the vitality and individuality of those early Sun performances.

Although his musical managers tried to blunt it, Elvis' Southernness remained an essential and defining aspect of the man. He always adhered to his gospel origins, even if some of the musical energy of his Pentecostal background was dissipated. Elvis was almost a parody of Southern courtesy with his deference toward women and older people. By serving unquestioningly in the United States Army and in offering his services to the FBI as an informer against scandalous behavior by rock musicians, he exhibited those stereotypically Southern male responses which also surfaced in his love of guns, high-speed automobiles and karate: the physical, loyal and thoroughly masculine man. He reportedly viewed the Beatles as bad examples for

American youth because of their flaunting deprecation of that which he valued: patriotism and Christian morality. If he ever recognized the English musicians as his cultural offspring, there seems to be little evidence for it. Despite his own indebtedness to black musicians, he never questioned the racial values of his homeland. His fascination with big cars, fine mansions, jewelry and expensive clothes affirmed his endorsement of that capitalistic world that had long been closed to him and his poor white ancestors.

More than twenty years after I first encountered Elvis in that abbreviated Hank Snow concert in Austin, I once again saw Hank in a setting that brought back some of those old memories. In May 1978, I attended the Jimmie Rodgers' Memorial Festival in Meridian and heard Hank Snow, who looked and sounded much as he did twenty years before. He received vigorous applause, but the singers who caused pandemonium in the audience were the rockabillies Ray Griff and T.G. Sheppard. Griff wore a mod leisure suit with musical notes embroidered upon it, and when he went through his sexy dance steps many of the women in the audience squealed the same way the Austin girls had done for Elvis twenty years earlier. Since some of them appeared to be in their forties (and older), they may very well have been the same women reliving the fantasies that King Elvis had aroused in them years before.

Apart from the sense of deja vu which swept over me as I watched the Meridian performances, I was most impressed with the contrasting and seemingly ambivalent strains of country music so strongly displayed there. Despite my earlier fears, country music did not die and its composition today is still flexible and responsive enough to contain both the older (Hank Snow) and the newer (Elvis-derived) entertainers. The tensions I felt at the sensual superimposed upon the traditional make the issues Elvis interjected as alive and controversial today as I felt them to be twenty years ago. That both strains persist indicated that Southern country music has not given up the schizophrenic nature of its identity (the pure vs. the hedonistic), and that it still has not been homogenized into the McDonald's mainstream, but like Elvis himself, bears witness that it is simultaneously both holding onto values and wringing out emotions for all they are worth.

Waltz Across Texas:
Local and Regional Forms and Influences

The dominance of Nashville today in country music masks the very real fact that this music has always had a strong regional componant to it. In the early days of recording, Atlanta was far more important and influential than Nashville and, prior to 1945, Chicago and Cincinnati were both music scenes with a great deal more action than Nashville. In Texas, country music has thrived in cities such as Dallas, Fort Worth, Houston and Austin. California has Bakersfield ("Nashville West") and, of course, Los Angeles—which has produced everything from Hollywood's singing cowboys to the rhinestone-studded dogcollar sound of cowpunk. And then there is New York. And Tulsa. And even the New England state of Maine...

In all of these culturally diverse regions and areas (and others), particular mixes of talent and tradition have combined to create country musics that are similar yet, at the same time, very different.

As Paul Fryer writes in "Local Styles and Country Music;" "Country music is made up of a series of such local area traditions, which have combined to create the generic form of country, but which have risen and fallen in popularity and importance over the years since the beginning of commercial recording in the 1920s."

Fryer traces the rise and fall of various regional styles in his article, connecting this regional popularity with the home states of country singers. "If country music can really be said to be an amalgam of area traditions, then it should be apparent in an examination of the birthplaces of the musicians; if the (new) Western element in country music was Texan (for example), then there must have been a group of musicians from the area coming to popularity at the same time." In addition to this mapping, Fryer attempts to take into account migration patterns (of musicians and audiences) in examining the development of new country genres. Throughout the history of country music, and especially in the post World War II era of modern country, he finds the South to be center for most of the varied stylings, with Texas and Tennessee being the two most influential states.

In "County Music and the 'Southernization' of America" James Cobb looks at the shifts in taste and genre that took place in country music during the key decade of the 1970s. Country songs, once dismissed as the regional music of red necks and the rural poor, were fast becoming fashionable across the country during that decade. As economic prosperity in the "New South" put the lifestyles and values of that part of the country in a more favorable light, country music moved very quickly toward national acceptance as a mainstream style. As Cobb writes; "Obviously, much of the glorification of the South and its music was the result of commercial ballyhoo and popular whim. Behind the mythmaking, however, was the reality that a traumatized post-Civil Rights, Vietnam, Watergate nation had at last acknowledged its regional stepchild." The "Southernization" of America had begun.

This "Southernization" included Texas, as well as Nashville. In the mid-1970s, there arose in Texas a major new regionally based influence on modern country music—a movement that Nicholas Spitzer, writing in 1975, called a "romantic regionalism," centered around the city of Austin. In "Romantic Regionalism and Convergent Culture In Texas," he examines what became an eclectic mix of rednecks, "goat ropers," longhairs, heads—and even gays—who together created and developed this important and improbable regional scene of "progressive country"—a scene which Spitzer describes as a "progressive attitude" toward the many genres (honky tonk, country rock, western swing, etc.) that made up the Austin scene. This enclave of "cosmic cowboys," with Willie Nelson as resident guru, began to lose its luster and fade by the late 1970s and early 1980s, and is today nowhere near as vital as it once was. However, Austin's legacy lingers in modern country music in such forms as the cable television shows "Austin City Limits" and "Texas Connection," country rockers like Steve Earle and, in the late 1980s and early 1990s, a "new wave" of unique country artists from the area, including Lyle Lovett and Nanci Griffith.

In addition to the southern nature of many of its regional styles, modern country music has also been heavily influenced by the music of Mexico, especially in material composed and performed in Texas and other border states. In "Mexican Musical Influence on Country Songs and Styles" I trace these Mexican influences, from Marty Robbins' signature song "El Paso" to Waylon Jennings' version of Los Lobos' "Will The Wolf Survive." Mexican influences in country are, I suggest, far more pervasive than many realize.

Not all country music is created, nor regional styles developed, in the south. California, Chicago and even New York (as examples) are all strong sites in which country is recorded and performed. In addition, there is a strong country audience in Canada, and there are strong regional performers and preferences in areas such as the Maritimes, Toronto and Alberta. This music, though technically not "made in America," is still a strong and legitimate part of the modern country music scene, as its artists look to Nashville in the same way American artists do. On this Canadian-American border, a whole country away from the Texas-Tennessee axis, lies the small New England state of Maine. In "A Tombstone Every Mile," I examine the creation of country music in Maine and its importance, not only in this small—but thriving—regional market, but also in its connections to country music on a national (and international) level in Canada and America.

Playlist

Bob Wills	Best of Bob Wills & his Texas playboys	MCA
Jerry Jeff Walker	Viva Terlingua	MCA
Asleep At The Wheel	Texas Gold	Capitol
Nanci Griffith	One Fair Summer Evening	MCA

Texas Tornados	Texas Tornados	Reprise
Freddy Fender	Tex-Mex	ABC
Dick Curless	Tombstone Every Mile	Tower (Capitol)

Local Styles and Country Music:
An Introductory Essay

Paul Fryer

American popular music, both white and black, has, throughout its history and development, been influenced and to a great extent defined by its place of origin. The cultural geography of city and state has affected both the influences working on the musicians and the attitudes put over in song. A musical tradition for an area is a synthesis of influences; an area where, for example, there is a Mexican local culture will produce a different style to one where the only style is that of the Anglo-American ballad, in terms of instruments used, tunes borrowed and the attitude adopted by the singer, traditionally conservative or exuberantly celebratory.

Country music is made up of a series of such local area traditions,which have combined to create the generic form of country, but which have risen and fallen in popularity and importance over the years since the beginning of commercial recording in the early 1920s. The very term "Country and Western" signifies one such stylistic jump, with the success of a Texas style associated with the simultaneously popular movie cowboy heroes. The Western element involved the adoption of the basic country music style of the southeast by a state further west, in the heartland of the American South, and its development there to fit the needs of an audience and the heritage of a new set of singers. The arrival of this new element in the mid-1930s redefined country music, but also redefined Texas music, which became part of the greater style (Carr 102-37; Malone 145-83).

The determining factor on these changes in local emphasis should, therefore, be the homes of the musicians, the areas where they grew up and from where they assimilated formative influences. If country music can really be said to be an amalgam of area traditions, then it should be apparent in an examination of the birthplaces of the musicians; if the western element in country music was Texan, rather than the result of marketing and changes in repertoire caused by the advent of cowboy films, then there must have been a group of musicians from the area coming to popularity at the same time.

By examining the home states of country musicians, it is possible to see the periods of ascendency experienced by various areas and to align this with the currently popular styles. This can ascertain that assumptions of local influence are indeed true and can be used as an indicator as to the overall

Reprinted with permission from *Popular Music and Society vol.* 8.3&4 (1982): 63-76.

importance of certain states in the commercial development of country music

The source from which details of birthplaces and birthdates were taken was *The Illustrated Encyclopedia of Country Music*, edited and compiled by Fred Dellar and Roy Thompson.[1] The book contains biographical and career details of 465 solo acts and groups influential in the development of country music since the 1920s, nearly all of which are provided with birth histories. These details were examined firstly through the correlation of date of birth of the performer to state of origin, and secondly through the correlation of the year of the performer's first hit to state of origin. In the latter examination, the year was extracted from Joel Whitburn's *Top Country and Western Records* 1940-1971, for artists rising to popularity within these years. For artists coming to prominence in the 1970s, the date of first hit given by Dellar and Thompson was taken; for artists popular before 1949 and the beginning of the *Billboard* chart, the date given for the first significant recording, by Dellar and Thompson was taken. In both examinations, figures were broken down into five year periods, beginning with the decade and with its mid-point (Whitburn).

The encyclopedia has undergone prior sampling, which both causes difficulties and is of benefit to an analysis of the figures it produces. Thompson and Dellar have not based their sample of artists on chart popularity, with all its associated problems of influential performers who either had not hit or who appeared before the birth of the charts and of one-hit wonders likely to distort a sample. Rather, they have selected on two bases, of past importance, popularity and influence in the development of the music, and of present popularity, though that popularity admits of no such lasting contribution to the tradition.

This sampling technique means that past performances have to be more significant than those presently popular to be included and must have made a sizeable name for themselves during their era of popularity. This is counterbalanced by the fact that the country music audience has itself expanded considerably in the years since the Second World War. With the expansion of the media for spreading the style and with the advent of record charts for affirming temporary success for artists, more singers have been able to become popular with a wide cross-section of the national audience and to have that a success historically recorded and affirmed. The imbalance provides a way of accounting for and counteracting the effects of an increased market.

Similarly, the encyclopedia does not accept the definition of country music placed upon the style of the recording industry and its marketing policies and by the record charts. Both of these impose a traditional and conservative definition on the style that is detrimental to the recognition of novel sub-genres, most particularly that of country rock. The boundaries of Dellar and Thompson allow for country rock as an influential new development, one that in turn comes to influence mainstream country music with its attitudes and accompaniments and accept that any differentiation between folk music and country music must admit of some overlap with performers of the like of Doc Watson (Carr 1-29).

The latter-day artists selected suffer from a lack of historical perspective; at the time of the book's completion, it was not possible for the writers to perceive that artists like La Costa and Dennis Weaver were to be of minimal importance to the country market. Artists thus gathering their first hits in the 1970s may carry no guarantee of being as influential or as popular in the long term as artists popular before the beginning of that decade. This, however, would have posed problems in any sample that did not include an artificial definition of popularity, in terms of records sold or of a minimum number of chart hits.

Information on groups was also less detailed than that on solo performers or entrepreneurs. The examination of individual group members' dates and places of birth would have overbalanced the sample in favor of musicians not popular or known as individuals. Too rarely was detailed information given on the place of group formation or of the biographical background of the group leader when that was apparent for groups to be included in the survey, except where group leaders were important figures in the pre-1949 stylings, like A.P. Carter and Dr. Humphrey Bate.

The exclusion of groups from the survey and of entries where only partial or irrelevant information was given, left a survey figure for sole performers, musicians and comedians and for industry figures like producers and entrepreneurs vital to the growth of the country music industry, of 417 entries. A breakdown of this can be found in Figure 1, where the number of entries per state is noted, both as a total and as a percentage of the whole.

From this survey, it becomes apparent that the chief providers of country musicians are the states of Texas, with 16 percent of the total entries and Tennessee, with 11 percent. No one state can be said to be the centre of this demographic spread, but, when these totals are plotted on a map, it becomes noticeable that the main density area is that of the south-east states and of the deep southern states, those states lying east of a line running from Virginia to the north of Texas. Despite the spread of country music to a national audience, the number of country figures provided by the states outside of this area is minimal (Hagarty 177-182; Kahn; Lynn 81-125). On the basis of this, it is apparent that it is reasonable to discuss country music in terms of it being a music local to the south-east. The distribution of entries by state can be seen in Figure 2.

Any local styles impinging on and influencing the development of country music can be seen to be local traditions from within its home area. Even California, with its country-rock traditions in the 1960s and 1970s, provides no significant input into the demographic analysis. These figures can be related to arguments that much of the expanding country market was the result of migration out of the south, and that northern country record buyers were usually displaced southerners (Malone 184-295; Petterson and DiMaggio). Should any northern country traditions have developed by the mid-1970s, they were not, at that stage, strong enough to have produced a successful local tradition. It can also be said that not only was the expanding audience dependent upon migratory southerners, but that musicians working on new genres within country, like country rock, were also likely to be migrants, redefining home traditions in the light of new but temporary surroundings, often on the West

State	Total	Percentage
Texas	67	16
Tennessee	46	11
Kentucky	38	9
Oklahoma	29	7
N. Carolina	21	5
Missouri	20	5
Arkansas	17	4
Virginia	17	4
Alabama	15	4
Georgia	15	4
Louisiana	15	4
Mississippi	14	3
Florida	9	2
Indiana	8	2
W. Virginia	8	2
New York	7	2
Kansas	6	2
S. Carolina	6	2
Wisconsin	6	2
Canada	5	1
Ohio	5	1
Illinois	5	1
Arizona	4	1
California	4	1
Other	20	5
: Australia	3	
: Maine	3	
: Pennsylvania	3	
: Colorado	2	
: Maryland	2	
: Massachusetts	2	
: Michigan	2	
: New Jersey	2	
: Washington D.C.	2	
: England	1	
: Idaho	1	
: Iowa	1	
: Minnesota	1	
: N. Dakota	1	
: Nebraska	1	
: New Mexico	1	
: Oregon	1	
: Washington	1	
Total	417	100%

Fig. 1 Number of entries by state of birth (solo singers, musicians and comedians; producers; entrepreneurs)

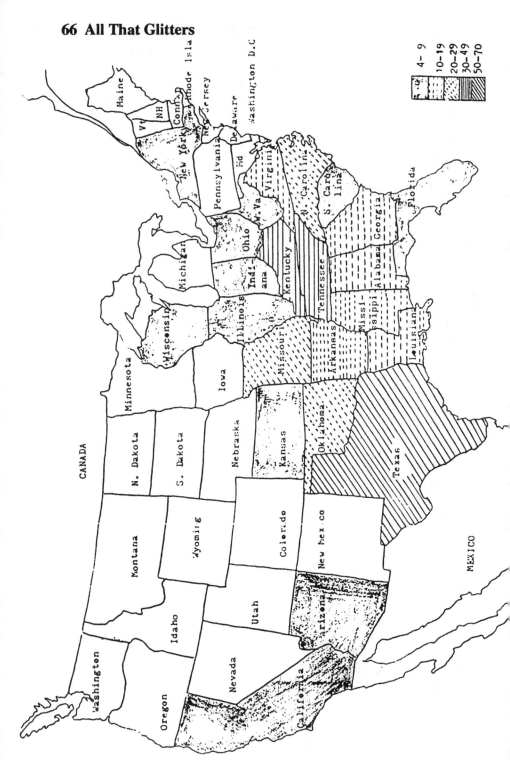

Figure 2. The density of Country people, by state of birth

Coast. Country rock, then, can perhaps be best seen as a southerner's view of rock, rather than a rock musician's view of the south.

Given then that the South can be shown to be the centre of country stylings, it becomes possible to examine the importance of individual states within the South through time, to find periods of popularity and of decline within the music industry. This examination was conducted using two methods, a correlation of state to date of birth and of state to date of first hit. These two facets of the examination can demonstrate two sides of the importance of local traditions, dates of birth providing an insight into the growth of local styles in a local context and dates of first hit proving an insight into when local styles suited market needs and were adapted to suit the general style.

The musical style, its conventions and assumptions, of a performer must be related to the influences upon him, or her, in the formative period of musical learning. Once the rudiments of music have been learnt, other foreign elements can be added, but, in a folk music environment, musical skills are learnt by watching, copying and being taught by local musicians around the learner. It is perhaps not unreasonable to consider this learning and influence period as being between the ages of five and twenty years old. By looking at the dates of performers, it is possible to see whether there were strong local traditions that were later to pass into the marketplace, and, if so, whether these areas produced groups of musicians in limited periods, who were to go on to be successful.

It is impossible to trace any such local styles before the turn of the century. Only seven entries were born in the United States before 1890, and none were born outside of the south-east. The older styles represented by these performers, like Fiddlin' John Carson from Georgia and Uncle Jimmy Thompson from Tennessee, were archaic by the age of recording, recognizably rural folk music at odds with the increasingly-industrializing America, to which country music was in part a reaction (Carr 30-72).

Factors other than developments in the music in the twentieth century influenced the demographic spread of the early years: states in the midwest were still in the process of, or had just succeeded in, obtaining statehood, and the settled society that implied, suitable for the entry of the record industry; and perhaps as important, the only entrepreneurs were born around 1890 and concentrated their recording efforts upon performers who were their contemporaries. Thus Ralph Peer was born in 1892, Art Satherley in 1889 and Fred Rose in 1897.

Taking the two states providing the most entries, Texas and Tennessee, it is possible to see two completely different demographic patterns. When the number of entries is converted into a percentage figure of total entries for that five-year period, then Tennessee provides a steady influx of performers, nearly always between 5 percent and 15 percent of the total, while Texas' provision comes in a series of peaks and troughs, the peaks occurring in the years 1905-1909, 1925-1929, 1935-1939 and 1945-1949,

For the other states, peak periods are occasional but notable. A summary of these major peaks, expressed in terms of a percentage, are noted below (Figure 3):

Years	State	Percentage
1900-1904	Kentucky	31%
1905-1909	Kentucky	21%
1910-1914	Oklahoma	15%
1915-1919	Arkansas	12%
	Kentucky	15%
1925-1929	Virginia	12%
1930-1934	Missouri	12%
	Oklahoma	12%
1935-1939	Kentucky	10%
	Oklahoma	10%
1940-1944	New York	8%

(of a total of 7 entries by the state, 4 were during these years)

Fig. 3 Peak periods for states' provision of entries, by year of birth

It can be noted that Kentucky is a heavy provider of country musicians from 1900-1920, and that the general trend, in terms of peaks, is for the south-eastern states to provide large proportions of the entries through till the 1930s, at which stage Oklahoma becomes significant. The peaks assumed by state in the 1930s may be related back to a previous peak, from 1910 to 1914, just after the conferring of statehood; those born during those years could be expected to be prominent musicians within the community during the Depression years and to be able to achieve media attention. Of these, the most important may be Woody Guthrie, born in 1912 in Okema, whose propagation of Okie culture was coming to influence in the 1930s.[2]

Two other factors are of interest. Firstly, the national adoption of country music after the Second World War led to a decentralization of states of origin, with a greater variety of states providing musicians, and with no regional peaks that could be said to indicate a rise in provincial styles in later years. Secondly, New York has over half of its entries, 57 percent, grouped in the years from 1940 to 1944, those artists born during this period coming to popularity with the New York folk song revival of the 1960s. Only Texas was able to secure high percentages of artists born after 1940, with 21 percent in 1945-1949, following 23 percent in 1935-1939 and 15 percent in 1940-1944.

An examination of the dates of birth recorded by Dellar and Thompson reveals fruitful periods for states in the provision of musicians, those generations likely to succeed musically and to interact with both the local tradition and with other musicians within a specified geographic area. By looking at the years when those local styles became nationally popular, however, it is possible to ascertain periods when these strong localized styles were acceptable to the market. The existence of local traditions and predominances could only become important, in the world of the record industry, when those styles sold records, and, in doing so, became no longer rurally-local folk song styles but commercially profitable trends within the marketplace.

That there is no direct correlation between dates of birth and the year of ascent to popularity is not surprising, for the country music never accepted the necessary relationship between youth and success presupposed in the field of rock music; it is not valid to assume that performers gain success before the age of thirty, and periods of influence of performers born in the same year group can differ by ten years or over. Interest lies, nevertheless, in the relationship between dates of birth and hit record, for that tells of the speed by which strong local traditions were presented to, and accepted by, the market and the industry.

Following through these two states providing over one-quarter of the entries, Texas and Tennessee, a peak-and-trough pattern is found for both states, Tennessee largely abiding by the percentage range created by the dates of birth of performers while Texas assumes the exaggerated peaks of her own dates of birth. Thus, Tennessee has in influence peak for the first hits of musicians in 1925-1929 and in 1950-1954, with that percentage at each period being around the 25 percent mark. Apart from a low trough of 4 percent in 1965-1969, the graph shows a steady pattern of between 8 percent and 16 percent of the total entries for each period.

Texas, though, has a higher general level, with successive peaks in 1930-1934, 1950-1954 and 1970-1974 ensuring that the state did not have a long period of a settled market share. Noticeable rises in popularity for the state's music can be seen every ten or fifteen years, and the total entries' percentage for Texas never drops below 7 percent in 1920-1924. A graph plotting both dates of birth and dates of first hit for these two states can be seen as Figure 4.

As for the years of birth, other states experience occasional but important peaks, when local artists become successful commercially during a limited period. Here, the success of a local style is often dependent upon the breakthrough of one artist, which creates a market for other performers in the same style. It may be that a later artist, within the same period, may go on to become more successful than the market-breaker, but concerted market success is nevertheless related both to the initial breakthrough and to the marketing and recording policies of the record companies, in their attempts to cash in on a new style's market. Ultimately, though, success depends on the market's desire for a music and what it represents, a desire that can be stimulated but never created solely by marketing executives.[3] Figure 5 (below) illustrates occasional peaks achieved by states other than Texas and Tennessee.

Years	State	
Percentage		
1920-1924	Georgia	23%
	Virginia	23%
1930-1934	Kentucky	32%
1935-1939	Oklahoma	13%
1945-1949	Kentucky	15%
1955-1959	Missouri	10%
1960-1964	Oklahoma	15%

Fig. 5 Peak periods of states' provision of entries, by year of first success

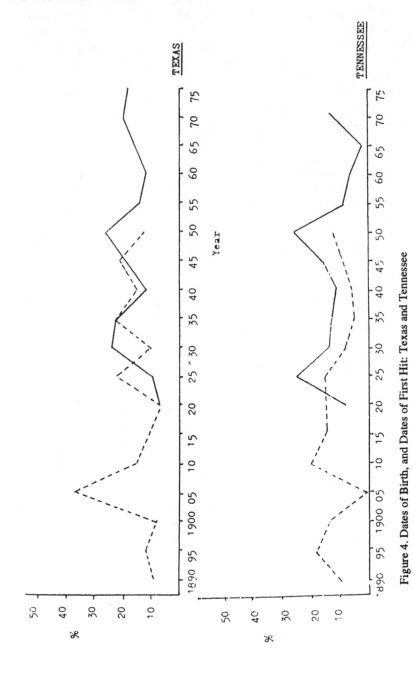

Figure 4. Dates of Birth, and Dates of First Hit: Texas and Tennessee

Peak Periods:

State	Year of Birth	Year of First Hit
Kentucky	1900-1909	1930-1934
	1915-1919	1945-1949
Oklahoma	1910-1914	1935-1939
	1930-1939	1960-1964
Missouri	1930-1934	1955-1959

Fig. 6 Comparison of states' peaks for dates of birth and initial success

Peak periods can be seen to be separated by the length of a generation, twenty-five to thirty years. It is notable that Oklahoma should provide three peak periods that overlap and in doing so demonstrate the importance both of local styles and of the stimulus given to their commercial development by the record industry. The first wave of Oklahoma musicians become successful in the late 1930s, influencing a generation born in that decade with their example, a generation that was itself to become successful in the early 1960s. Oklahoma, as a newly-admitted frontier state, could be expected to have fresher traditions, more self-contained and less influenced by the outside world, which still held a local identity in the 1930s, an identity aided by the mythologising of the "Okie."[4]

The states important in the early years of recording were those of the south-eastern states, where the initial recording sessions were held; while musicians either were located in their own states or were prepared to travel to recording centres in a nearby state, musicians from Texas and Oklahoma were isolated. When these states began to provide a significant number of musicians for the popular market in the early 1930s, they were thus able to bring with them styles that still bore local traits, untainted by a previous contact with the commercial needs of the media.

The styles from Texas, and peaking in the years 1930-1939 and 1950-1959, were, respectively, Western Swing and "honky tonk," (Malone 162-183; Carr 102-137; Stricklin and McCoral; Townsend), both music with a strong regional flavor and an internal stylistic continuity. Performers in both styles were recognizably following a genre. Similarily, Oklahoma developed a tradition of individualistic solo singers whose attitude could be related to frontier belief in the need to preserve integrity.

These styles were to combat styles popular in the south-eastern states that had merged into one another, to create a south-eastern, but rarely a state, type of country music. These music were south-eastern in that they were invariably acoustic and based on stringed instruments, but it would be difficult to identify from within this the music of Georgia, Kentucky and Virginia. Regular contact over a hundred years between local musicians was sufficient to merge styles originally local, a process aided by geographical proximity and an almost simultaneous settlement. Texas and Oklahoma, conversely, had been the frontier of the South for several decades, with the western borders of each state being many miles away from the influence of any states to the east.

It is notable that these south-eastern states were not the main providers of country musicians after the 1930s, yet the centre of the country music industry, Nashville, lies firmly within the area. Record industry interest in the city developed prior to World War II, when south-eastern musicians were still in control and combating what appeared to be the "fad" of cowboy music; its continuation after 1945 was representative of a protection of initial investment, and this protection, by the record industry, took the form of bringing local stylists to Nashville to record. Then, those local styles could be worked in such away that they were diluted, mixed with the ingredients of the south-east's music. Most notable within this attempt by the record industry to centralise and standardize country music was the development of the "Nashville Sound," a pop-oriented version of country music, that imposed the attitudes of the east on the music, folk-styled, of the frontier; the "Nashville Sound" imposed the smooth strings traditionally part of south-eastern music on the rawer frontier styles, these strings being now amplified and utilizing the benefits of sophisticated urban technology Electric guitars and soft-toned fiddles were a post-war version of the east's belief in melody rather than in rhythmic drive and individualistic lyrics, the desire for conformity rather than the stress on integrity and individualism for so long associated with the frontier of the American West with its music

The move of country musicians like Willie Nelson (born Abbot, Texas) and Waylon Jennings (born Littlefield, Texas) away from Nashville, to Austin, in the early 1970s was a direct rejection of Nashville's insistence on making Texas country suit the needs of a south-eastern hierarchy. Western Swing had been tolerated by the record industry as a surprise novelty, while "honky tonk" music had quickly lost its stars, like George Jones, to the Nashville establishment. Austin's self-conscious celebration of the rugged integrity of cowboy culture, though, set up a base for country music that was indirect opposition to Nashville, that initially opposed both its principles of standardization and its corporate direction. It was not surprising, however, that the record industry then reassessed tactics and priorities, and moved into the Austin scene. In doing so, however, in gaining control of the rebels, principles of standardization had to be removed, and the "Nashville Sound," and the concentration of country music in that city fell into necessary decay, in the process vindicating the basis premise, in favor of untampered local music, put forth by the Austin musicians (Spitzer; Reid).

The rise of Austin as a country music centre was perhaps the last flowering of local genres within country music, a conservative attempt to defend the past rather than a development for the future, for the Austin musicians were unable to keep away other media influences. Despite the rise of Freddy Fender and Johnny Rodgriguez as new Texas singers, most Texas singers worked either within or from the rules of country music, dictated by market desires. It was no longer practicable, either for singer or for record company, to present music to a wide audience in the hope that it would sell, as had been the case before 1940. A market had to be assured, so that both musician and company made a profit, and this entailed a recognition of the currently-popular styles. even in the last fling of a separate Texas culture, its musicians had to consider the ingredients necessary for their music to sell, and merely by so doing, brought their music out of the realm of the purely local folk song style, the idea that they held up for themselves.

The spread of country musicians, by date of birth, since the late 1930s, is indicative of the fact that country music is no longer that of a regional market, within which are local styles. The predominance of one state, even for short periods, is no longer possible because of, firstly, the number of states providing musicians, and secondly, the erosion of local stylistic cohesion. The issue and sale of recordings brought the sounds of different regions to all of the United States, and gave local musicians a point of comparison and of emulation. Folk styles could no longer develop in isolation, feeding off local circumstances, and once Nashville was established as an industry-defined centre for country music, all local styles were given a yardstick to which they were to compare themselves. The attitude of the industry in defining Nashville as the home of true country music led local musicians to emulate the sounds emanating from that city, and, in doing so, to destroy the local bias so important in the origins and the commercial rise of country music.

Notes

[1]Fred Dellar and Roy Thompson, eds., *The Illustrated Encyclopedia of Country Music* (London: Salamander Books, 1977). *Melvin Shestack" The Country Music Encyclopedia* London: Omnibus Press, 1977) deals with similar ground, with the inclusion of biographical data, but adopts a more informal tone, giving less detailed information on recording careers and maintaining a sample that stresses mainstream traditions rather than the interdisciplinary offshoots of country rock and folk music.

[2]See *Woody Guthrie, Bound for Glory* (New York: E.P. Dutton, 1943); Joe Klein, *Woody Guthrie: A Life* (London: Faber & Farber, 1981); Richard A. Reuss, "Woody Guthrie & His Folk Tradition," *Journal of American Folklore* 83.329 (1970: 273-303).

[3]The influence of commercial pressures on an originally folk-based music is discussed in Carl I. Belz, "Popular Music and the Folk Tradition," *Journal of American Folklore* 80.316 (1967): 130-142; and Steve Chapple and Reebee Garofalo, *Rock 'N" Roll is Here to Pay: The History and Politics of the Record Industry* (Chicago: Nelson-Hall, 1977).

[4]See Alan Lomax, comp., *Hard Hitting Songs of Hard-Hit People* (New York: Oak Publications, 1967); John Steinbeck, *The Grapes of Wrath* (Harmondsworth: Penguin, 1951: first published, 1939); and John Ford's 1940 film of *The Grapes of Wrath.*

Works Cited

Carr, Patrick, ed. *The Illustrated History of Country Music.* New York: Dolphin Books, 1980.

Dellar, Fred and Roy Thompson, eds. *The Illustrated Encyclopedia of Country Music.*

London: Salamander Books, 1977.

Hagerty, Bernard G. "WNAX: Country Music on a Rural Radio Station, 1827-1935." J.E.M.F. *Quarterly II* (Winter 1975): 177-182.

Kahn, Edward A. "The Carter Family: A Reflection of Changes in Society." Ph.D. Thesis UCLA, 1970.

Lynn, Loretta, with George Vecsey. *Coal Miner's Daughter*. London: Panther Books, 1976.

Malone, Bill C. *Country Music. U.S.A.* Austin: U of Texas P, 1968.

Peterson, Richard A. and Paul DiMaggio. "From Region to Class, the Change Locus of Country Music: A Test of The Massification Hypothesis." *Social Forces 53* (1975).

Reid, Jan. *The Improbable Rise of Redneck Rock.* Austin: Heidelberg Publishers, 1974.

Spitzer, Nicholas R. " 'Bob Wills is Still the King': Romantic Regionalism and Convergent Culture in Central Texas." J.E.M.F. *Quarterly II (1975):* 191-96.

Stricklin, Al and John McCoral. *My Years With Bob Wills*. San Antonio: Naylor Co., 1976.

Townsend, Charles. *San Antonio Rose: The Life of Bob Wills*. Urbana: U of Illinois P, 1976.

Whitburn, Joel, comp. *Top Country and Western Records 1949-1971. Wisconsin: Record Research,* 1972.

Country Music
and the 'Southernization' of America

James C. Cobb

In 1969 Merle Haggard's "Okie from Muskogee" paid tribute to militant "hippie-haters" and generally reconfirmed the traditionalism and authoritarianism long associated with the South and country music. Eight years later Waylon Jenning's "Luckenbach, Texas" described another small town in the South not as a citadel of intolerance but as a "live-and-let-live" haven where jeans-clad residents had rediscovered the "basics of love." Whereas Haggard's "Okie" had enjoyed its greatest appeal among conservative, country music-loving southerners, Jennings' "Luckenbach" was on the lips not only of traditional country fans but of shaggy teenagers and young middle-class adults across the nation. The dramatic expansion of country music's appeal in the 1970s was particularly significant because for most of its existence the music had encountered all the hostility and condescension traditionally reserved for things southern. The nation that embraced country music in the 1970s had been deeply affected by the twin shocks of defeat and disillusionment, traumas previously associated only with the experience and heritage of the southern states. Thus the factors underlying country music's increased respectability in the 1970s also provide important insights into the nation's belated acceptance of the South, a phenomenon which some called the "Americanization of Dixie" but others more accurately identified as the "Southernization of America" (Egerton).

The image of a "benighted" South emerged in mature form in the 1920s. World War I had unleashed a number of forces that spotlighted the region's deficiencies and even worse inspired many of its leaders to defend these shortcomings. The war had tossed southerners, black and white, into a whirlpool of new experiences—travel, interaction with non-southerners—even non-Americans. Concerns over the potential aggressiveness of returning black veterans resulted in intensified repression and occasional anti-black riots. Caught up in militant patriotism southern leaders made their defense of the region's social and political hierarchy synonymous with their devotion to traditional "100 per cent Americanism." Thus the Scopes-Trial, other examples of entrenched religious fundamentalism, and even the resurgence of the Ku

Reprinted with permission from the *Journal of Popular Culture* 16.3 (Winter 1982): 81-91.

Klux Klan were not embarrassing examples of regional backwardness but badges of honor proudly worn. With the rest of the nation hurtling down the road to modernism, relativism and almost certain ruin, the South led an uncompromising defense of the absolute and the familiar (Tindall).

Not surprisingly, its reactionary position as defender of the faith subjected the South to a torrent of derision. Henry L. Mencken, the region's super-detractor and arch-nemesis, led the way, reviling Dixie as the "bunghole of the United States." To Mencken, even Virginia, the best of the southern states, had "no art, no literature, no philosophy, no mind or aspiration of her own." On the other hand, Georgia, the region's most primitive state, was "crass, gross, vulgar and obnoxious." Between these two lay "a vast plain of mediocrity, stupidity, lethargy, almost of dead silence" (Tindall 210; Mencken)

It was significant that country music began to have its first commercial impact as Mencken was deriding the South for its cultural barrenness and particularly for its spirited defense of traditionalism. Essentially the music of low-income, rural whites, early recorded country music was an amalgam of British and American folk and fiddle tunes, hymns and old popular songs that had been preserved within the self-perpetuating, conservative matrix of values and tastes in the region. Recording companies began to realize the market potential for southern rural music after Georgian Fiddlin' John Carson's recording of "The Old Hen Cackled and the Rooster's Going to Crow" sold several thousand copies on the "Okeh" label. Talent scout Ralph Peer had described Carson's singing as "pluperfect awful," but conservative rural customers nonetheless seemed anxious to own recordings of songs that they had been hearing for years at minstrel shows, dances and fiddling contests (Malone, *Southern Music* 62).[1]

Much of the original material performed by Carson and his contemporaries consisted of folk tunes and hymns, but as recording opportunities increased, the need for new material spawned the first generation of country songwriters. Like the nearly recorded folk and gospel music, the first commercial compositions expressed the values and prejudices of the rural south. Fiddlin' John Carson was a regular at Ku Klux Klan rallies and his "Ballad of Little Mary Phagan" helped to exacerbate the anti-semitism that was a major factor in the lynching of Mary's alleged murderer, Leo Frank. Fiddlin' John made light of the evolution controversy in "There Ain't No Bugs on Me" when he asserted "there may be monkey in some of you guys, but there ain't no monkey in me," but his contemporary Vernon Dalhart took a more serious view in "The John T. Scopes Trial," concluding that "the old religion's better after all." In addition to religious fundamentalism and ethnic bigotry, early country music stressed the sadness of life on this earth, particularly the pain of unrequited love and the inevitable sorrow brought on by man's sins. As it became increasingly commercialized, "hillbilly music" (named for a band known as "Al Hopkins and the Hillbillies") proved acceptable neither to educated northerners who maintained a romanticized vision of the sturdy Anglo-Saxon "folk" nor to progressive, upper-class southerners who saw the music undermining their efforts to revive the "culture" and "refinement" which they, and others, believed had been a prominent characteristic of the ante-bellum South (Lund 80-83; Malone, *Southern Music* 28-37).

Although most Americans rejected country music as the primitive mode of expression of the southern "po white," Jimmie Rodgers broadened the music's audience in the 1930s by employing a number of vocal and instrumental innovations. "Singing cowboys" like Gene Autry and Roy Rogers also lent appeal to country music by encouraging the use of "country-western" to describe what had once been "hillbilly" entertainment. Taking a cue from this development, country performers abandoned the garb of the rural poor in favor of the lavishly decorated cowboy outfit (Malone, *Southern Music* 70-87).

Sequined shirts, ten-gallon hats and fancy boots made country performers more glamorous, but World War II gave the music its greatest boost toward respectability. As the war scattered southerners and their music all over the world, Armed Forces Radio broadcasts provided reassuring melodies for homesick southerners and won country music many new fans. Broadcasts from the Grand Ole Opry even introduced the "bellow-wail" singing style of Roy Acuff to the Japanese who passed judgement by occasionally changing their battle cry from "Banzai" to "To Hell with Roy Acuff!" (Malone, *Country Music* 206).

The wartime experience convinced Nashville recording and publishing executives that the market for country music was more extensive than they had dreamed. Eddy Arnold typified a move to make the music more "sophisticated" by exchanging his checkered work shirt for a tuxedo, de-emphasizing his "Tennessee Playboy" nickname and crooning the tender ballads that quickly made him RCA's most popular recording artist. Meanwhile, star-crossed Hank Williams was repeatedly demolishing the barriers between country and popular music as his simple but emotionally appealing songs propelled him to stardom and his instability and alcoholism drove him to an early grave (Malone, *Southern Music* 93; Williams).

Despite the beachheads established by Williams and Arnold, traditional country music was forced underground in the mid-1950s as rebellious youth made their ambiguous statement through rock and roll. Country music had fallen on hard times, but at the end of the 1950s a few performers were able to capitalize on the "urban folk revival," an academically-inspired resurgence of interest in the "true" American folk music. Traditional artists like Maybelle Carter, Bill Monroe and Flatt and Scruggs became feature attractions at campus "hootenanies" and others like Johnny Cash were flexible enough to present themselves as folk singers. The urban folk revival had little time for mainstream country music, however, for the movement was in essence another idealistic attempt to celebrate a genuine, undiluted and therefore, of course, nonexistent culture of "the folk" (Malone, *Southern Music* 140-44).

Most country performers were as unwelcome on college campuses during the 1960s as Fiddlin' John Carson would have been at H.L. Mencken's table during the 1920s. Country music remained very much the music of the southern redneck and thus elicited images of pickups with shotguns stacked in the back of the cabs, shotguns waiting to be used to terrorize or kill civil rights marchers or those who sympathized with them. Amidst the liberal fervor of "The New Frontier" and "The Great Society," the ugly scenes of New Orleans, Oxford, Birmingham and Selma made the South seem every bit as primitive and savage as it had in the 1920s.

For years, observers had searched vainly for a genuine spokesman of the proletariat among country music stars, someone who might demonstrate significant commercial appeal as a "poet of the people." Hank Williams, who seemed to some a likely candidate to become the "hillbilly" Woody Guthrie, had proven to be a simple, uneducated country boy who read comic books and shunned politics and social commentary. Johnny Cash's victory over drugs and empathy for the down-and-outer made him country music's first great hope of the counter-culture in the 1960s. Unfortunately, however, Cash's decision to make commercials for the American Oil Company and, ironically, the fact that his success had made him so respectable cooled the ardor of many of his youthful fans.

Cash's most likely successor as country music's Bob Dylan was Merle Haggard, an ex-convict whose songs of poverty and alienation were welcomed as authentic vignettes of life on the other side of the tracks. Haggard seemed the perfect symbol for a campaign to convince blue collar whites they were being exploited and take them out into the streets to join the student protests of the late 1960s. Like Cash, however, Haggard proved a disappointment. In 1969 a road sign pointing to Muskogee, Oklahoma, and a comment about the smoking preferences of its residents inspired "Okie from Muskogee," a song intended as a lighthearted commentary on the generation gap. Regrettably (except in the commercial sense), both hardhats and liberals insisted on interpreting the song literally and when Haggard, a former Okie himself, recorded "Fightin' Side of Me," a musical version of the "America—Love It or Leave It" bumper sticker, his ties to the New Left were temporarily severed (Hemphill 331). Thus, as the 1970s opened and the bitter polarization of American society exploded in the tragedy at Kent State University, country music was there, apparently defending authoritarianism, repression and excessive use of force.

By the end of the 1960s many Americans outside the South were angry and bewildered by the tumult in their midst. Martin Luther King's attempts to take the Civil rights movement north of the Mason-Dixon line had shown that non-southern whites were far more distressed about racism and discrimination in Dixie than in their own backyards. Alabama Governor George Wallace had found a following among blue collar voters (and not a few secretive white collar contributors) in the industrial North. As attention focused on embarrassing racial problems in northern cities, C. Vann Woodward observed that "self-righteousness withered along the Massachusetts-Michigan axis" (98). When the Nixon administration moved to cultivate the South and coopt Wallace, it accelerated a snowballing tendency to forgive, forget and even applaud the South's peculiarities.

Both the Vietnam and Watergate experiences encouraged a revised and more favorable assessment of the South. The Vietnam conflict gave the nation its first taste of defeat and left it without so much as the satisfaction of having fought for a noble cause. Agonizing post-mortems produced no comforting explanations for the Indochina failure. Southern leaders had shown the staunchest support for the war, even to the point of defending accused mass-murderer William Calley. These same spokesmen, however, generally refused to join in the self-flagellation that became almost a national pastime as the United States backed out of Southeast Asia. The South had been saddled with the humiliation of defeat for over a century. Hence it was not surprising that of all Americans, southerners appeared to cope best with the Vietnam failure (Woodward 98).

The South's response to Watergate and other Nixonian excesses was similarly stoic. Despite the blind, last-ditch defense of Nixon offered by a great many conservative southern political representatives, Americans at large were more keenly aware of the ostensibly objective, level-headed performances of Senators Herman Talmadge, Howard Baker and Sam J. Ervin. The last named's record of opposition to civil rights measures was forgotten as he quoted the Bible and the Constitution with equal aplomb and punched holes in the nervous testimony of once-powerful White House advisers (Kirby 137-38). Despite the fact that many of them had supported Nixon to the last, after his resignation, southern political leaders refused to apologize or express disillusionment. To them, like supporting the Vietnam War, backing an embattled (and sympathetic) President had been a simple act of patriotism and was certainly no cause for remorse.

As the nation lay locked in post-Vietnam, post-Watergate paralysis, expressions of confidence and purposefulness were rare except in the South where the confrontation politics of George Wallace and Lester Maddox had yielded to the moderate progressivism of Reubin Askew and Jimmy Carter. Even as a fledgling presidential aspirant who seemed to have little chance of winning his party's nomination, Carter exuded quiet confidence. His staunch Baptist faith and studied humility, two of the most commendable "southern" traits, blended with his Yankee-like energy and commitment to efficiency to make him an attractive symbol of a reunified nation (Miller).

Carter moved toward the White House to the accompaniment of an unfamiliar but welcome chorus of favorable media treatment of the South. *Saturday Review* hailed "The South As the New America" (Murphy). Even the formerly neo-abolitionist *New York Times* joined in celebrating the South's re-entry into the Union by noting that every southern city sported "transplanted Yankees who have adopted open collars, drawling speech and bourbon mixed with Coca-Cola" while the natives had reciprocated by sipping Scotch and "experimenting with skis" ([Feb. 11] 1). The implication of the media "bliss blitz" was clear to southerner Larry L. King who exulted in the November, 1976 *Esquire*: "We Ain't Trash No More!" (88-90, 152-56).

Admiration for things southern was not completely without precedent in American history. Historically, however, the region's rare moments of approval had come when a mythical antebellum South of magnolias, belles and cavaliers was praised by writers for its rejection of the crass acquisitiveness they saw in contemporary American society. Romantic unions between gentle, refined southern belles and energetic but crude Yankees were a popular theme during the Gilded Age as investors scrambled to stake their claims in an economically underdeveloped South. In a sense, this mythical "southern way of life" provided an attractive alternative to the tyranny of technology, bureaucracy and the profit-motive fostered by the nation's relentless pursuit of "progress" (Hackney).

Although not unprecedented, the rediscovery of the admirable, even adorable South in the 1970s was nonetheless striking because the nation appeared ready to look beyond the belles and beaux, put the Tobacco Road stereotype aside and at last embrace that formerly repulsive rustic, the redneck. Movie performances by Burt Reynolds suggested that at heart working class southern whites were too fun-loving and well-intentioned to get much of a kick out of nightriding and lynching. *Time's* portrayal of the "Good Ole Boy" revived the Jeffersonian ideal of the agrarian-as-salt-of-the-earth: "Behind his devil-may-care lightheartedness "runs a strain of innate wisdom, an instinct about people and an unwavering loyalty that makes him the one friend you would turn to." In a more serious vein, "The Waltons" reminded troubled television viewers that lower-class southern whites had always cherished strong family ties. The several movie versions of "Walking Tall" embellished the exploits of Buford Pusser, an impulsive but courageous southern sheriff with special appeal in a law and order decade ("Those Good..." 17; Kirby 142-46, 151-53). The redneck, who had once been scorned for his crudity and lack of sophistication, now emerged as a hero who had resisted the corrupting influences of mainstream society.

The nation's new appreciation for the South had a strong economic component. Spurred by the population and aerospace boom in Florida, the region's economy "took off" in the late 1960s, registering dramatic improvements in almost every statistical category. The South became the cornerstone of the lower tier of fast-growing, easy-living states known as The Sunbelt. Although poverty remained a serious problem, by the mid-1970s the southward shift of population and investments suggested that the wheel of fortune had at least stopped on the South's number. Like the symbolic, if often superficial, cleansing afforded by the Civil Rights movement and the remarkable equanimity with which the region endured the successive traumas of Vietnam and Watergate, Dixie's new-found affluence greatly enhanced its respectability. Urban-industrial growth posed a serious threat to the South's reputation as an uncluttered land of relaxed, gracious living, but the region's leadership, intoxicated by impressive growth statistics and basking in the warmth of national approval, could see no evil in the Sunbelt boom (Breckenfeld 133; "Surging..." 72-73; *New York Times* (Jan. 9) 42; Frady 11).

As economic prosperity put southern lifestyles and values in a new and more favorable light, country music moved rapidly toward mainstream acceptance. No longer did middle class whites in the South or southern migrants to the North have to switch their radios to "pop" stations at stoplights or refrain from playing Loretta Lynn's newest hit on the jukebox. Country radio stations cropped up all over the dial. In 1961 there had been but 80 "all-country" stations in the nation, but by the mid-1970s there were more than 1,000, the most striking newcomer being New York City's WHN, which adopted a country format and doubled its audience in little more than a year (Lord 51). The boom had proven too big for a single town, and while Nashville remained the capital of country music, Austin and Bakersfield could now rightfully claim "sounds" distinctively their own.

Since its inception, commercial country music had sought a larger audience. Jimmie Rodgers had enhanced his music's appeal to urbanites by blending in blues, ragtime and even Hawaiian touches. Hank Williams' songs had regularly appeared on the pop charts when recorded by artists like Tony Bennett and Frankie Laine while crooners like Eddy Arnold and Jim Reeves had attracted a large number of fans who shunned more traditional performers. In the 1960s master guitarist Chet Atkins presided over the creation of a smoothed-out, jazzed up, electrified "Nashville Sound" and "country pop" singers like Roger Miller and Jimmy Dean demonstrated considerable appeal. It was not until the 1970s, however, that country music would enjoy repeated and widespread success among pop fans. Former Rhodes scholar Kris Kristofferson's bearded appearance and independent behavior set him apart from other country artists and his popularity sent a clear message to fellow performers that, "properly packaged" country music could at last stake a claim on the lucrative youth market (Malone, "A Shower..." 416-19, 433-34).

Kristofferson's success paved the way for a number of veteran country performers to strip off their sequined suits and dive belatedly into the counterculture. Willie Nelson, long recognized in country circles as an excellent songwriter and singer, shattered the conservative image he had projected on the Ernest Tubb television series by sporting a beard and long hair and affecting the garb of a 1960s drop-out. Nelson relocated in Texas in 1972 and became the pivotal figure in "the Austin Sound." Another Texan, Waylon Jennings, who once played with rock star Buddy Holly's Crickets, forsook his "ducktail" haircut for the "dry look" and a beard. Jenning's arrest on a drug charge actually seemed to boost his career, a fact of which he was well aware. With Nelson, Jenning's symbolized the "outlaw" movement in country music, a curious phenomenon seemingly out of phase with prevailing trends toward conservatism and respect for "law and order." In fact, however, the appeal of the outlaw movement may well have been that it offered a brief nostalgia trip into the uninhibited lifestyles and flaunted traditions of the late 1960s without requiring any sort of ideological commitment. Nelson and Jennings seemed to have changed their philosophies relatively little, but their new appearance and demeanor had helped to win the hearts of many of their new-found fans. As the seventies unfolded, other performers with roots in traditional country music adopted the Jennings-Nelson style with significant, although less spectacular, success (Malone, "A Shower" 438-41).

By the end of the 1970s female performers like Anne Murray, Crystal Gale (the sister of Loretta Lynn), Emmylou Harris and Linda Rondstadt enjoyed equally high standings in both the country and pop markets. Even the once "down-home" sound of Dolly Parton had been adapted to a more rock-oriented audience. The 1970s witnessed the emergence of "southern rock," a music more "rock" than "southern" whose performers—like Charlie Daniels and the Marshall Tucker Bank—flaunted their "Deep South" heritages but dressed like cowboys. Meanwhile, the country market became so lucrative that traditional performers found themselves in competition with artists seeking to make a "reverse cross-over" appeal to the country audience. Purists bristled as "outsiders" like Olivia Newton-John and John Denver received the industry's highest awards, but even old-timers like Roy Acuff and Maybelle Carter joined the Nitty Gritty Dirt Band on "Will the Circle Be Unbroken," an impressive album tribute to the roots of country music (Malone, "A Shower..." 429, 434-35, 442; Gailliard 147-70; Malone, *Southern Music* 112).

Much of the expanded popularity of country music was the result of shameless image-making by performers and promoters. Still, there had been some changes in the music as well. The heavy bass beat of a Waylon Jennings tune called to mind much of early rock music, a form that appeared to stagnate in the 1970s. Thus former rock fans could hear in country music the pleasing rhythms they could no longer find in rock. Country music continued to act as a preservative for popular music, keeping alive old rock favorites like "That'll Be the Day" (Linda Rondstadt) or "Save the Last Dance for Me" (Emmylou Harris). The traditionally conservative lyrics now expressed a more explicit sexuality, as in Kris Kristofferson's "Take the Ribbon From Your Hair." More significantly, female performers like Tanya Tucker ("Would You Lay With Me in a Field of Stone?") were expressing, even flaunting, their sexual liberation (Malone, "A Shower" 434).

Despite the changes, country music of the 1970s was still more traditionally "country" and "southern" than anything else. Country songs continued to emphasize the darker side of life, the unavoidable pain and punishment that a weak and sinful humanity forced a loving but stern God to inflict upon it. Country music's prescription for coping with life was a large dose of lowered expectations. With humans able to recognize their sinfulness but unable to control their sinning, life on earth could only be a sad experience and even the brief pleasure of rebellious hell-raising only raised the price of atonement even higher. Like Kenny Rogers' "Lucille," the biggest country hits of the 1970s continued to center around lost love and other deep personal tragedies. In early 1977, 36 of the top 100 country songs dealt with marital infidelity (Lyle 143). Country music in the 1970s, as it had been in the the 1920s, was as blunt a reminder of human imperfections as could be found.

Country music's unattractive description of human nature inferentially damned human society and institutions as well, but the music had produced almost no social commentary. For many Americans such causelessness was a welcome release from the crusading and protesting of the 1960s. Merle Haggard's odes to the "hardhat backlash" were a bit crude for some, but country music produced other less primitive expressions of frustration at the rapidity of the changes taking place in American values and lifestyles. Tammy Wynette's "Don't Liberate Me, Love Me," was a commercially motivated appeal to record buyers who belonged to the "barefoot-in-the-kitchen" school of thought concerning the female's role in society. On the other hand, Loretta Lynn's "Don't Come Home A-Drinking (At Least not with Lovin' on Your Mind) and "Your Squaw's on the Warpath" found an eager audience of women clearly tired of second class citizenship at home and in the world at large but uncertain they wanted total "liberation" (Horstman 318-21).

Many Americans probably shared the ambivalence about "progress" reflected in country songs, but to liberal observers the music was a reminder of the unfinished business of the 1960s, a reminder which grated not only on their eardrums but their psyches as well. The hard-core country music fan had long been the enemy of crusaders for social change. Those who threatened blacks and voted for Wallace also idolized Ernest Tubb. Writing in 1973, *New Yorker* Richard Goldstein admitted that country music represented "a culture against which I have very ancient and tenacious biases." Goldstein was even more candid as he explained further, "I can never encounter a white southerner without feeling a murderousness pass between us" (115).

Although the racist influence of the southern redneck had been undermined by the Civil Rights movement, northern liberals came away from the experience unsatisfied and confused. By the mid-1970s the traditional villains in the American morality play, the long-time opponents of social progress, were not only no longer pariahs, they were actually being venerated on juke boxes throughout the land. Johnny Russell's 1974 recording of "Rednecks, White Socks and Blue Ribbon Beer" was a thorough-going celebration redneckery:

No we don't fit in with that white collar crowd,
We're a little too rowdy and a little too loud
But there's no place that I'd rather be than right here
With my redneck, white socks and Blue Ribbon Beer.

(McDill, Holyfield and Neese)

One resentful writer called Russell's song "a truculent hymn to the twice-turned jockstrap that could someday become America's Horst Wessel," but despite such warnings, the odes to the blue collar white continued, culminating in 1979 in Moe Bandy and Joe Stampley's popular album "Just Good Old Boys" (King, "Red Necks..."; *New York Times [Nov. 18] 31D)*.

A number of country songs of the 1970s went beyond a celebration of the common white folk of the South to pay tribute to region and its deliverance from itself. Treatments like Jesse Winchester's "Mississippi, You're on My Mind," expressed confidence in the future but spent little time apologizing for the past. Tanya Tucker recorded the best known version of Bobby Braddock's "I Believe the South is Gonna Rise Again (And Not the Way We Thought It Would Back Then)," a song that rejoiced at the visions of "sons and daughters of sharecroppers drinking Scotch and making business deals." Braddock's tribute to Dixie emphasized a future of "brotherhood" and dismissed the past with "forget the bad and keep the good."

Country music's failure to apologize for the southern past was mitigated to some extent by a fusion of the southeastern "Deep South" with the "Cowboy

South" of the Southwest. Any knowledgeable listener knew better than to expect an apology from Willie Nelson or Waylon Jennings. Moreover, "redneck chic" blended with "Texas chic" in a manner not unlike the marriage of "country" and "western" music in the 1930s. The frantic, booming Southwest offered a paradoxical but appealing vision of "laid back" cowboys sipping Lone Star Beer and living life one day at a time. Waylon Jennings's "Luckenbach Texas" glorified a wide spot in the road near Austin by depicting it as a place to escape the burdens of "keeping up with the Joneses," and Jennings and Nelson offered their own tribute to good ole boys in "Mamas, Don't Let Your Babies Grow Up to Be Cowboys," whose message might actually be translated: "They could do a whole lot worse."

Obviously much of the glorification of the South and its music was the result of commercial ballyhoo and popular whim. Behind the mythmaking, however, was the reality that a traumatized post-Civil Rights, Vietnam and Watergate nation had at last knowledged its regional stepchild. Was this a positive step, a move toward final sectional reconciliation or was it, as some feared, a "copout"—a demonstration that Americans would rather defend than remedy the deficiencies exposed in the late 1960s and early 1970s? Had the worst elements of the national character been allowed to triumph over the best? Were the values celebrated in country music values of which Americans might truly be proud?

The notion that the "southernization of America" marked a turn for the worse not only ignored the social, political and economic advances in Dixie; it reflected the misconception that crusading liberalism and hunger for social justice had persistently characterized non-southern society. Writing in 1964, Howard Zinn had cautioned critics against dismissing the South as "unAmerican" and argued that southerners were correct in insisting that they were the most "American" of all the citizens of the United States. Zinn depicted the South as the regional embodiment of many basic American traits in their most extreme version. The South's flaws were merely the nation's flaws in concentrated and clearly focused form. Thus, the uncouth, racist, traditionalist South was actually an unflattering mirror image of the nation as a whole (217-18).

Such an assessment was understandably upsetting to a generation of Americans who grew up thinking the South represented the antithesis of everything in which they were supposed to believe. Even in the rare moments when the region had been held up for admiration, it had been depicted as an alternative to American society's obsession with "progress." Still the white-backlash/George Wallace phenomenon, the widespread pessimism bred by Vietnam and Watergate and the resurgent conservatism of the 1970s did a great deal to narrow the chasm between Dixie and nation at large. Ironically, some of the best evidence that Zinn's "mirror image" thesis had gained implicit acceptance in the 1970s was the use of southern themes and settings to indict all of American society. Robert Altman's *Nashville* employed the country music capital as a cinematic setting for his argument that American Society was rotten, not just at the top, as Watergate had shown, but at the grassroots, where the music of the masses was made. In conquering the nation, the country music industry had been ambushed by national values. Moved to philosophizing by several scotches, veteran country singer Faron Young ruefully admitted: "You got that dollar, you got America" (Kirby 156, 158-59). In a similar vein the highly successful television serial "Dallas" confronted viewers with J.R. Ewing, a good old boy every bit as greedy and power-mad as a Jay Gould, Jim Fisk or any contemporary northern robber baron. The South had at last arrived. It was no longer more sinful than society at large, but it had also become just as corrupt and cynical.

As the nation embraced southern music, detractors could not resist pointing out that country songs remained "monotonous, sentimental, obvious, musically inferior, and lyrically sub-standard" (Lyle 140). What did a low brow art form so emphatic in its emphasis on human deficiencies have to offer a nation crippled by a crisis of confidence in its leadership and institutions? Was not a more inspiring music in order? Such questions failed to consider the possibility that country music had the potential to encourage Americans to throw off the crippling disappointments of the late 1960s and 1970s. A music which has seen the South through several decades of deprivation and rejection to ultimate acceptance and emulation may convince Americans at large that by acknowledging their weaknesses they do not necessarily deny their strengths.

Note

[1]For an excellent survey of the evolution of country music, see Bill C. Malone, *Country Music, U.S.A.: A Fifty Year History* (Austin: U of Texas P, 1974).

Works Cited

Braddock, Bobby. Copyright 1973. Tree Publishing Co.

Breckenfield, Gurney. "Business Loves the Sunbelt and Vice Versa." *Fortune* 95 (June1977).

Egerton, John. *The Americanization of Dixie: The Southernization of America.* New York: Harper's Magazine Press, 1974.

Frady, Marshall. "Gone with the Wind." *Newsweek* 53 (28 July 1975).

Gailliard, Frye. *Watermelon Wine: The Spirit of Country Music.* New York: St. Martin's, 1978.

Goldstein, Richard. "My Country Music Problem—And Yours." *Mademoiselle* 77 (June 1973).

Hackney, Sheldon. "The South as a Counterculture." *The American Scholar* 42 (Spring1973): 283-93.

Hemphill, Paul. "Merle Haggard." *Stars of Country Music.* Eds. Bill C. Malone and Judith McCulloch. Urbana: U of Illinois P, 1975.

Horstman, Dorothy A. "Loretta Lynn." *Stars of Country Music.* Eds. Bill C. Malone and

Judith McCulloch. Urbana: U of Ilinois P, 1975.

King, Florence. "Red Necks, White Socks and Blue Ribbon Fear." *Harper's* 249 (July1974).

King, Larry L. "We Ain't Trash No More." *Esquire 126* (Nov. 1976).

Kirby, Jack Temple. Media-Made Dixie: The South in the American Imagination. Baton Rouge: Louisiana State UP, 1978.

"Lord, They've Done It All." Time 6 May 1974.

Lund, Jens. "Fundamentalism, Racism and Political Reaction in Country Music."*The Sounds of Social Change*. Eds. R. Serge Denisoff and Richard A. Peterson. Chicago: Rand McNally, 1972.

Lyle, Katie Letcher. "Southern Country Music: A Brief Eulogy." *The American South: Portrait of a Culture*. Ed. Louis D.Rubin, Jr. Baton Rouge: Louisana State UP, 1980.

Malone, Bill C. *Country Music, U.S.A.: A Fifty Year History*. Austin: U of Texas P, 1974
_____."A Shower of Stars: Country Music Since World War II." *Stars of Country Music*. Eds.Bill C. Malone and Judith McCulloch. Urbana: U of Illinois P, 1975.
_____.*Southern Music, American Music*. Lexington: U of Kentucky P, 1979.

McDill, Bob, Wayland Holyfield and Chuck Neese. Copyright 1974. Jack Music.

Mencken, H.L. "The Sahara of the Bozart." *Prejudices: Second Series*. New York: Knopf, 1920.

Miller, William Lee. *Yankee from Georgia: The Emergence of Jimmy Carter*. New York: Time Books, 1978.

Murphy, Reg. "The South as the New America." *Saturday Review* 4 Sept. 1976: 8-11.

New York Times 11 Feb. 1976: 1.

New York Times 9 Jan. 1977.

New York Times 18 Nov. 1979.

"Surging to Prosperity." *Time* 27 Sept. 1976.

"Those Good Ole Boys." *Time* 27 Sept. 1976.

Tindell, George B. *The Emergence of the New South, 1913-1945*. Baton Rouge: Louisiana State UP, 1967. 184-218.

Williams, Roger M. *Sing a Sad Song: The Life of Hank Williams*. Garden City, NJ: Doubleday, 1970.

Woodward, C. Vann. "The South Tomorrow." *Time* 22 Sept. 1976.

Zinn, Howard. *The Southern Mystique*. New York: Alfred A. Knopf, 1964.

Romantic Regionalism and Convergent Culture in Central Texas

Nicholas R. Spitzer

The romantic uses of folklore on the part of writers, poets and academicians is a familiar theme in American culture. From Walt Whitman to John Lomax and J. Frank Dobie, the interest in folklore collection, collation and representation has vacillated between objective scholarship and the desire to build a literature based on folk roots (Bluestein). In the United States it was and is ironic that as intellectuals and the new middle class began to take up the folk aesthetic from the 1920s on in a variety of ways, from Leadbelly's music to Ben Botkin's *Treasuries*, the folk (black, white and ethnic) have often looked to mainstream acceptance, acculturation and a chance to get on the "folk-urban-suburban continuum." In hillbilly music, for example, the growth of Nashville is associated with a demise in regional styles (Malone).

In the post-Vietnam era, unlike earlier post-war eras and other periods producing nationalistic feelings and art forms, there is less of a sense of national correctness or agreement. As we experience what some have called a search for community (i.e., not on the national level), or more metaphysically, a "turning inward," various cultural traits, often regional and ethnic in nature, are being consciously resurrected and reasserted.

In Central Texas, with Austin as its focal point, I dub this tendency *romantic regionalism*. It coincides most closely with what rural sociologist Howard W. Odum called "literary and aesthetic regionalism" (Odum and Moore). However, in Austin, the expressive culture that comes most readily under this aegis is not "high art" or popular written literature. Rather, it is the folk-based popular art of country and western musical performance that is pre-eminent. This music in various forms has served as an expressive cultural bridge reflecting the convergence of socio-economically diverse elements of the population.

Interest in country and western music has not always been fashionable for the youth and student community, many of whom come from middle-class backgrounds which they often reject. At the same time the lower-class, rural affiliated "cedar choppers," "goat ropers," "kickers," and "rednecks" (I will use these terms interchangeably), have clung ambivalently to their rurality as

Reprinted from the *John Edwards Memorial Foundation Quarterly* 12:4 (Winter 1975), pp. 191-197 by permission of the publisher and the author.

expressed in part by the creation of rural suburbias—where the hard-core country and western club is now found in a shopping center.

Of the consciously cosmopolitan Austin youth, many of whom were recruited from rural Texas by the University, psychedelic rock, urban folk music and rock 'n' roll were the forms most subscribed to in terms of expressive self-identity. This youthful population has, since the early 1970s, been seizing upon the image, style and content of Texas country and western music (with an emphasis on western) and fusing it with rock and pop music. The musical forms—and by association, lifestyles—resulting have been variously called "cosmic cowboy," "red neck hip" and "progressive country." These forms are part of and comment upon the strongly self-referrent regional romantic movement.

It must be emphasized that despite the rise of this hybrid music and cultural romanticism among the student-oriented youth, the rural kickers were not initially drawn into accepting the music or the long-haired-cowboy-hat-wearers who sought out shotgun-racked old pickup trucks, drank beer and smoked marijuana under the code of the "neon (or is it 'neo') cowboy." Ironically, many rural people were and are in no sense occupational cowboys themselves; yet they too have historically used the image in defining their lifestyles. Indeed, Bob Wills' music itself reflects the Western imagery of Hollywood rather than the oral and cultural traditions of real cowboys.

These "real" rednecks have been sparse at large local outdoor festivals such as Willie Nelson's 4th of July picnic. The first of such events in 1973 found a larger percentage of rural people in attendance than in subsequent years, due most likely to the more traditional line of commercial country and western stars on the bill and an unawareness of the transformation of Willie Nelson from Nashville stalwart to bearded renegade. In the following years the event, attracting from thirty to seventy thousand fans, has taken on more and more the ambiance of a rock festival. This includes a high degree of alternately dusty and muddy incommodiousness, more country-rock and hippies, less country music and kickers.

This is not to say that the music preferred by the rednecks is unromantic (and here I'm referring to Nashville country as well as the earlier Texas-Oklahoma honky-tonk stylings of Milton Brown and his Brownies, Bob Wills and the Texas Playboys, The Cowboy Ramblers, and in later years, Ernest Tubb, Johnny Bush and Darrel McCall). Quite the contrary, it is equally nostalgic and self-referrential since for many of them, their nostalgia is rooted in the actual experience of leaving the farm, ranch or rural situation. As such it parallels contemporary youthful rural romanticism. This similarity is crucial. The respect for the past implied on the part of the youth culture and the shared, dare I say, neo-populist ambivalence about urban/suburban America has brought acceptance of country-rock on the part of the rural or newly suburbanized redneck. However, this process has been more gradual than the youth-affiliated regional country and western fan magazines such as *Picking Up the Tempo* would indicate. Further, rural acceptance of pop-oriented music and cultural style is not really new in Texas; it goes back to the rockabilly era of

Buddy Holly and Roy Orbison, and earlier to Jimmie Rodgers—perhaps the first eclectic cosmic cowboy.

Indicative of the latest and farthest degree of cultural interpenetration is the song "Bob Wills is Still the King," recorded live at the now defunct Texas Opry House in Austin (it moved to Houston). The song was the first of its kind to be "number one" on the local country Top-40 station (KVET-AM) as well as the FM progressive country station (KOKE-FM). That is, it defies the categories of hard-core and progressive country. Based on record sales it fulfills both genres. The song is sung by Waylon Jennings, whose initial audience had been the fans of hard-core or "straight" country music. Admittedly, Waylon has always defied labels. He was a member of Buddy Holly's Crickets, and in recent years, by utilizing his image as a rock and rolling Nashville rebel, in apparent cahoots with Willie Nelson, he has augmented his following with the young hip to a large degree.

Lyrically the song toughly espouses the virtues of Texas life in the nostalgic terms of cowboy self-reliance and chivalry. Further, it invokes an animistic fashion, a past regional hero as the basis for present day self-pride. Wills incidently is historically more associated with Fort Worth and Tulsa than Austin; but it is the interpretation of the past on the part of the present cultural configuration that is of interest here, not the attempt at an objective account of history.

The musical style is that of country-rock, not western swing, although it is based on an amalgam of Nashville country, rockabilly and western swing. The rhythm is a slow and almost ponderous rock tempering of conventional upbeat country. If any one instrument carries the old western sound here it is the steel guitar, since this, the fiddle and horn sections (optional), were its mainstays. Here a harmonica is added to the overall modern sound to evoke the popular image of the Chisholm Trail campfire. The aesthetic synthesis is complex, reflecting the varied audience tastes reached. Relating more directly to the performance event at which it was recorded, is Waylon Jennings' vague, but all inclusive use of the phrase "our kind of music" in his spoken introduction to the song to establish rapport with the varied concert goers. The introduction also reveals that the song was written in Texas, "on a place between Dallas and Austin," and is about someone who "did as much for our kind of music as anybody."

In the verses, Jennings remembers the "honky tonks in Texas," "the Rose of San Antone" and "Tommy Duncan and the Texas Playboys." He goes on to make a distinction between Nashville's "Opry" music and that of Texas; "When you cross that old Red River, hoss, it (Nashville's music) don't mean a thing."

To audience cheers, Jennings concludes with the lines:

You just can't live in Texas unless you got a lot of soul. (cheers)
It's the home of Willie Nelson (cheers),
It's the home of western swing.
He'll be the first to tell you; Bob Will is still the king. (cheers)

In relation to the function of popular culture artists and art forms in shaping an expanded sense of community and cultural contiguity, I should point out that Waylon Jennings, based on the lyrics of many of his songs is a symbolic, normative outlaw. Country and western music is rife with them as fantasy characters proving *honorable* ways to break the law. His power as a performer for Austin audiences is further amplified in his rebellion from Nashville. That is, he also iconically represents an outlaw of sorts. A supplementary example of a non-normative outlaw in relation to this "outlaw community" of Austin would be Kinky Friedman, the existential Jewish cowboy. He goes beyond mere Texas/cowboy male chauvinism by performing extremely satirical material like "Get Your Biscuits in the Oven and Your Buns in the Bed." He also violates an Austin taboo by singing "The Ballad of Charles Whitman" as a humorous song. Kinky refuses to be considered part of the "Austin scene" and makes only rare appearances in the town—interestingly he is one of the few Texas-linked performers actually from Austin. In a sense, by being outside it, he helps define the community of new "good ole boys."

Apart from Kinky's aberrations and Waylon Jennings' ability to bridge cultural aesthetics, another element of the romantic movement is the clamoring for authenticity—for something that is real. This is not unlike the "purist" advocates of the urban folk movement in the early 1960s. In the recording of "Bob Wills is Still the King," the loud and continuous audience response is indicative of one behavioral manifestation of this authenticity-oriented attitude. The crowd hoots and hollers on cue in a manner that from participant-observation I would describe as self-conscious. That is, they are themselves performing in the fashion presumed to be truly Texan. If the boisterous, independent Texan is the stereotype from earlier years (Fehrenbach), they have chosen to accept and, in so doing, to invert the negative stereotype to a source of pride and self-referential declaration (for a related phenomenon see Green's discussion of the hillbilly, 1965).

The musical result of a search for authenticity has produced a number of bands that recreate the western style. They perform the old songs like "San Antonio Rose" and "Bubbles in My Beer" as well as their own material with new lyrics that localize and update old themes. The performance style emphasizes a strong band leader reminiscent of Bob Wills, chomping on a cigar, pointing out solos and adding jive commentary. The word text below of "Don't Ask Me Why I'm Going to Texas" is performed by Asleep at the Wheel, a group that sought out the growing Austin community after leaving Berkeley. They have since had success elsewhere and play in various styles besides western swing (big band, Kansas City hot jazz, Fifties Honky-Tonk and Nashville country). This song is not pure western swing itself (if such a thing exists). It draws heavily on the Hank Thompson sound found especially in the steel guitar signature. Musically, the song lyrics contains quotations from "The Eyes of Texas" and "San Antonio Rose." Lyrically, the regional feeling is evident in its use of place names as well as the bringing together of "Bob Wills, Bill Mack (of WBAP, Ft. Worth) and me on radio...." The young singer is able to cross the barriers of time and culture by having his music on the mystical medium of Texas radio:

"From Austin up to Dallas, Amarillo to El Paso,
you can hear Bob Wills, Bill Mack and me, on your radio.

Don't ask me why I'm goin' to Texas, it's just the kind
of place I should be."

Asleep at the Wheel has played with many of the older western swing artists like Bob Wills' fiddler, Jesse Ashlock, and singer/songwriter of the late 1940s, Floyd Tillman. Speaking of the band, Ashlock says: "They played from the heart, for the people. They play more for other musicians." This gives us some clue to the self-consciously romantic nature of the new music. Floyd Tillman adds: "They're like the old bands, but with a difference, they play take off solos. That's more like rock. Still I love 'em or I wouldn't play with 'em. They've moved the music back into the dance hall where it belongs." This last comment is particularly telling because it indicates the context in which most of the convergence in Austin expressive popular culture takes place—the play area of the dance hall or the honky-tonk bar. It is the traditional kicker setting for license. Western swing as dance music has thus been far more effective in bringing the diverse groups together of late than the cosmic cowboy music or urban folk/rock tempered styles. These latter genres do not encourage as much overt participation in dance; and the dancing that accompanies them is more free form. Also, they do not satisfy the aesthetic sensibilities of the rural kicker lyrically or musically.

Most importantly, it is socially easier for the youthful participants of the eclectic romantic regional popular culture to enter the redneck honky-tonk to enjoy the hard-core music and dance old style, than it is for the rural person to attend the outdoor country-rock concert or a massive youth-oriented club like Armadillo World Headquarters.

The new long-haired rednecks seem to be playing out their fantasies of a simple self-reliant life in the face of a modern, complex, often unrewarding society. They do this in a variety of ways, including cultivating old dances and music, eulogizing the poor white trash, dumping the equally faddish liberal-tinged ecology movement and adopting conservative rhetoric.

In terms of costumery, long hair and cowboy clothes have become fairly meaningless as markers of cultural identity in Austin, since kickers often have long hair while some of the new rednecks now have short hair. However, the kicker is still less likely to wear a rhinestone encrusted shirt and more likely to have a John Deere cap than a cowboy hat.

Where the romantic redneck has often left middle-class culture behind, at least superficially, the rural-oriented lower classes now have a wide range of choice in cultural models between middle-class mainstream culture and a new reasserted vision of their own, thanks to the massive youth culture with which they have contact. The depth of value and behavior change on the part of the redneck is difficult to assess and demands extensive survey work. It is readily apparent that the youthful cosmic cowboy utilizes primarily surface cultural traits (short hair, conservative rhetoric, pickup truck, cowboy clothes) to show his new affinities without sacrificing his deeper values (reflected behaviorally in cohabitation of unmarried couples, acceptance of drug use, lack of church affiliation, election of a liberal mayor in a recent election). As one extreme example of shifting redneck values, one can see homosexuals dancing unmolested next to kickers in a formerly hard-core country and western club.

Austin's musical popular culture telescopes time and geography. This makes it a particularly effective means of providing a sense of community because performers of the earlier periods are side by side with the contemporaries. Recently the original Texas Playboys (with some exceptions) were regrouped in Austin with great success at a formerly all redneck dance hall. They were on a double bill with a recreating band called Alvin Crow and the Pleasant Valley Boys. Even the earlier Jimmie Rodgers era is well represented by exalted local old-timers such as Kenneth Threadgill and Bill Neely, both of whom learned the Blue Yodeler's material from records and recreate his style and songs. Jesse Ashlock incidentally has taken to jamming with Neely at his weekly club jobs.

Recreation, tradition, commercialization, improvisation and the resultant hybridization are the dynamic forces interacting to create a regionally significant art form. Or perhaps more accurately, a number of forms all under the label of country music. Not all of these are "progressive country," but what is evident is a progressive attitude towards all of the genres (progressive country, hard-core country, Nashville country, MOR country, western swing, honky-tonk, country-rock, rockabilly, old-time country, cosmic cowboy, redneck rock) on the part of formerly diverse audiences. It is at the musical events (in bars, dancehalls, concert halls and outdoor festivals) that intensive culture contact, convergence and change has taken place. The role of the performer in providing such expressive culture through which new social structure can emerge is essential. Whether western swing performer, hard-core country artist, re-creator, cosmic cowboy, or a synthesis of these types, their performance lies within and gives meaning to a matrix of acculturation and self-conscious romanticism that have long been the paradoxical mainstay of country and western music (Green, "Hillbilly…"). In the suburban and rural areas in and around Austin, Texas, the mythopoetic past is contiguous with the present.

Works Cited

Bluestein, Gene. *The Voice of the Folk*. Amherst: 1972

Fehrenbach, T. R. "The Americanization of Texas." *Texas Monthly* Jan. 1975: 60-62; 88-93.

Green, Archie. "Hillbilly Music Source and Symbol." *Journal of American Folklore* 78.309 (1965): 215-225.

_____."Midnight and Other Cowboys." (Commercial Music Graphics 34) *JEMFQ* 39 (1975): 137-152.

Malone, Bill. *Country Music U.S.A.* Austin: Univ of Texas P 1968.

Odum, Howard W. and Harry Estill Moore. *American Regionalism—A Cultural Historical Approach to National Integration.* New York: 1938.

Spitzer, Nicholas R. "The Prodical Son Returns: Whatever Fits." *Pickin' Up the Tempo: A Country-Western Journal* July: 1, 3-4.

Austin Tabloids and Fan Magazines.

Austin Sun. Various issues.

Buddy . Various issues.

Pickin' Up the Tempo: A Country-Western Journal . various issues.

Interviews with:

Floyd Tillman at Texas Opry House, Austin, Texas, April 1974.

Jesse Ashlock at Split Rail Inn, Austin, Texas, October 1975.

Mexican Musical Influences
on Country Songs and Styles

George H. Lewis

Spanish is a loving tongue
Soft as music, light as spray...

Charles Badger Clark

It is late in the year, 1990, and the weather has turned grey in Nashville.
Bare trees clutch at the afternoon sky and the Cumberland River rolls sluggish
and cold through the city. In Emerald Studios, Virginian Kelly Willis—a
newcomer to Nashville recording—prepares for the next take. Her producer,
Tony Brown, who has made hit records with Steve Earle, Nanci Griffith and
Lyle Lovett, makes a last suggestion to acoustic guitar player Richard Bennett.
Everything is ready. The tape rolls. Bright Spanish notes of a near classic
ranchera song tumble from Bennett's fingers as Willis' dusky voice, evoking
memories of Patsy Cline, joins the Spanish guitar in "The Heart That Love
Forgot," a song written by her drummer, Mas Palermo...

Spring in California, the Golden State that has been plagued with drought
for the past five years. But it has rained in March, and the bright orange poppies
that are symbols of the state paint bold colors on the freeway embankments and,
in the country, wink through the green of quick grass, sprung up after the late
rains. It is a sunny April weekend in 1991, and the California Ag Expo is
opening in Sacramento, at the fairgrounds. People mill around the main stage,
waiting for the music to begin. A man in work jeans and a faded checkered shirt
lifts his seven year old son onto his shoulders for a better view. Three women
with dark hair, flashing eyes and babies talk excitedly, sitting on the grass in a
circle. The Texas Tornados, opening act for the Kentucky Headhunters, take the
stage and immediately launch into a spirited version of "Adios Mexico," Freddy
Fender trading vocals with songwriter Doug Sahm. Later, they will play
Fender's "A Man Can Cry" and the late Santiago Jimenez's "Son de San Luis,"
which will feature his son, Flaco Jimenez, on both vocals and accordian. The
country crowd in Sacramento is on its feet, clapping and calling out requests, as
the Spanish drenched music swirls and flashes, like orange poppies, in the
bright California sun...

Country music, if you listen, is filled with the sounds of Mexico. Although

94

the traditional histories of the music, such as Bill C. Malone's *Country Music, USA* emphasize its Anglo-Appalachian roots, and less traditional accounts, such as Nick Tosches' *Country* point to how much country music owes to the Afro-American tradition, it is also true that the music of Mexico has been of critical importance in the development of this musical tradition

From Cowboy Ballads To Texas Swing
Early Mexican Influences On Country Music

Mexican influences came very early, in the 1800s, with the popularity of the *corrido* in the folk music of the Southwest. The corrido, a long ballad form, can be either upbeat (usually in 2/4 time) or played in a slow, 3/4 waltz time. The corrido narrative is of story form—usually tragic in nature—and documents in surprising detail an incident deemed important by the community (McDowell).

Mexican-US border corridos first are documented as appearing in the 1830s to relay the news of the day—Indian raids, the seccession of Texas and the treatment of Mexicans in the United States (Parades). "El General Cortina," written in 1859, salutes Juan Cortina, who shot a Brownsville, Texas city marshall after the marshall pistol-whipped a Mexican who had been working his ranch. Cortina briefly occupied Brownsville before being forced across the border (Birnbaum & Nathan 24). Probably the most famous of these corridos is "Gregorio Cortez"—which was made into a film in 1981, starring *Miami Vice*'s Edward James Olmos, concerning a young Texas ranch hand who, in 1901, shot a sheriff after falsely being accused of stealing a horse, then eluded several posses of Texas Rangers before finally being captured.

This style heavily influenced early Anglo song writers and singers of the West. The cowboy ballad "Texas Rangers" is of corrido form, as is "The Buffalo Skinners," which was performed by, among others, Woodie Guthrie. Many of Guthries' own songs were heavily influenced by this Mexican musical form, which he was exposed to in his early years while playing with his uncle in Pampa, Texas in the late 1920s. Of his corrido inspired songs, "Deportee (Plane Wreck At Los Gatos)" is perhaps the best known and most widely recorded country example, performed by—among others—Johnny Cash and Dolly Parton.

In the late 1860s, another form of Latin music was becoming popular in the U.S. The *habanera* form (Mexican in origin, though heavily influenced by Cuban music being played in Mexico City) took the country by storm, with the publication of Sebastian Yradier's "La Paloma" in New York in 1877 (Geijerstam). This song, an example of mid-century Mexican drawing room ballads, was known as a *cancion mexicana*—a type of music that evolved into the popular *ranchera* song of the American southwest and which has informed American country music from the hits of Freddy Fender to the vocal style and songwriting of artists such as Linda Ronstadt, Rosie Flores, Tish Hinojosa, Jann Browne, and even, to some extent, Emmylou Harris.

The first country recording made by country artists is commonly held to be Eck Robertson and Henry Gilliland's fiddle version of "Arkansaw Traveler," recorded on June 30, 1922 (Scherman 32). The 1920s also saw several Mexican or Mexican-inspired songs become country flavored hits. The long time favorite, "Rose of the Rio Grande" appeared in 1922, while "Mi Viejo Amor," a cancion mexicana, was especially popular in 1926 (and was also republished in 1940). Manuel Ponce's 1909 composition, "Estrellita" was revived in the 1920s by Frank La Forge, and the pseudo-Mexican "Mexicali Rose"—a corrido-derived tune, was written by Jack Tenney and Helen Stone.

Texas swing, developed in the 1930s, was heavily influenced by Mexican music (Pena). Pianist Knocky Parker once described this style as "a mixture of Mexican mariachi music from the south, with jazz and country strains coming in from the east" (Malone 173). The Mexican song "El Rio Grande" is still a standard for Anglo swing bands, and the Bob Wills standard, "San Antonio Rose" is almost certainly a form of the Mexican "Spanish Two-Step."

Al Dexter, who was to record "Pistol-Packin' Mama" in 1943, used a Mexican guitarist in his first recordings in the mid-1930s. As he told Nick Tosches; "He (Bobby Simon) was a Spaniard from San Antone. He was a very refined Spaniard, though. He played electric steel and take-off guitar..., and he played it Spanish style. That's the one I recorded 'Honky Tonk Blues' with" (Tosches 189). With "Pistol-Packin' Mama," Dexter was trying to get a Bob Wills feel to a song that sold a million copies and was the first country record to top the American pop charts. The Mexican influence in Dexter's band and in Wills' swing style were both evident in this historic country recording.

In the southwest, the 1930s also saw the growing dominance of the accordian in Mexican music, with the artistry and innovation of Narcisco Martinez and Santiago Jimenez. Santiago is the father of Flaco Jimenez, who continues today in the tradition of his father to influence Texas popular music and country styles. (Flaco, in 1990, was at the top of the regional charts of the southwest as a member of the Texas Tornados and has recorded the bouncy accordian accompaniment to Dwight Yoakum and Buck Owen's 1988 country hit—"The Streets of Bakersfield.")

Mexican music even found its way into early bluegrass, in the music of Jim and Jesse McReynolds, whose career took them from their native Virginia into the mid-West in the late 1940s. While there, they absorbed western-styled singing and developed a sound close to that of the Sons of the Pioneers, whose harmonies were inspired by songs from south of the border. When the McReynolds moved into bluegrass in the early 1950s, Jesse continued to amaze audiences with the speed and dexterity of his mandolin playing on songs such as "Are You Missing Me," as well as on Mexican flavored tunes like "Border Ride" and "El Cumbancero" (Malone 345).

The Next Teardrop Falls:
Mexican Influences and Modern Country Music

Mexican music, then, has been important since at least the late 1800s in influencing what was to become known as American country music. In fact, Jimmie Rodgers, the "singing brakeman," who many regard as the most important early figure in defining the country music style, was likely influenced in the creation of his famous "blue yodel" by the hollers and shouts of Mexican border singers (Malone 96; Roberts 97). To the extent this is true, many of the yodeling singers who followed in Rodgers' footsteps—including Hank Williams, Patsy Montana, Hank Snow and Yodelin' Slim Clark, to name a few—have been carrying on a musical tradition with some of its roots in Spanish culture.

The corrido, as a song type, is also well represented in American country music. The most well known of these songs is probably Marty Robbins' "El Paso," in which the singer falls in love with Felina, a Mexican bar girl, then shoots a man he sees flirting with her in the bar. The singer flees but cannot stay away from Felina. When he rides back to see her, he is shot down by the posse, dying in her arms on the steps of the cantina in which she works and he fell in love. In addition to the musical form, "El Paso" also features Spanish guitar work, mariachi horns and the long, drawn out syllables of the singer ("West Texas wi-i-i-i-nd")—a distinctive vocal trademark of this type of song (Lewis 235).

Corridos also are very specific in the details of the (usually) tragic incidents they relate. This is most certainly true of Woody Guthrie's "Pretty Boy Floyd" and of his "Deportee (Plane Wreck At Los Gatos)." These songs (especially "Deportee") have been recorded many times by country artists, including Dolly Parton, Willie Nelson, Johnny Cash and Waylon Jennings.

This form is still being used by contemporary country song writers. Townes Van Zandt wrote the enigmatic "Poncho and Lefty" as a corrido. In this haunting song—recorded by Emmylou Harris, and Willie Nelson and Merle Haggard—Lefty betrays his buddy Poncho to the federales in Mexico, where they are involved in an illegal enterprise (probably the drug trade). Poncho is seemingly killed and, because of his bargain with the law, Lefty is allowed to escape across the border to the north, where he finishes his guilt-ridden days in the frigid "hell" of Ohio.

Drug trafficing and the running of contraband has been a recent favorite of Mexican corrido writers and singers, including Los Broncos de Reynosa's "La Banda del Carro Rojo (The Gang in the Red Car)" in which a gang is carrying 100 kilos of cocaine to Chicago and gets involved in a bloody gun fight with the Texas Rangers in San Antonio (Birnbaum & Nathan 25). Another common feature of the corrido, found in "Poncho and Lefty," is the use of two voices in a distinctive duet style—which Willie Nelson and Merle Haggard used in their hit version of the song.

An aspect of Mexican music that was absorbed early on by American country music was that of vocal harmonies. As Hugh Cherry says in his liner notes to the Sons of the Pioneers album *South of the Border*, "from the very beginning (the early 1950s), the Sons of the Pioneers sound was influenced by the vocal harmonies of Mexico." This is as evident on their classics, such as "Cool, Cool Water," and "Room Full Of Roses," as it is transparent on their versions of songs like "Mexicali Rose," "Spanish Eyes" and "Maria Elena."

Mariachi horns show up on country records with surprising frequency, clearly calling attention to the fact that songs like Marty Robbins' "El Paso," or Willie Nelson & Ray Charles' "Seven Spanish Angels" is *supposed* to be about Mexico. The use of mariachi brass in this way is, technically, a borrowing from Mexican music. However, because of the overwhelming popularity of Herb Alpert's Tijuana Brass in the 1960s, the sound had become, by the 1970s, somewhat of a cliché in American pop music and was used to give a Mexican "feel" to many recordings that, otherwise, have little to do with Mexican musical styles—such as Captain Hooks' 1977 "Making Love and Music."

On the other hand, mariachi horns, bolero rhythms and even marimbas have been used in country music to great effect, as in the Amazing Rhythm Aces' "Third Rate Romance, Low Rent Rendezvous," Mel Tillis' "I Believe In You" and in the works of Hoyt Axton and Ian Tyson. Axton's 1974 "When Morning Comes" sets a mariachi-type melody with a bolero feeling solidly in a country song context, while his later "Evangelina" and "Viva Pancho Villa" included Mexican topical material along with musical borrowings from this tradition.

Ian Tyson has consistently written and recorded material with a strong Mexican mariachi/bolero feel to it—first as half of the folk/country duo Ian and Sylvia and, more recently, as a solo artist. His "Play One More" features mariachi horns in a typically country story about drinking in a smoky barroom, while the bolero tinged "Someday Soon," has also been recorded by Tanya Tucker and Crystal Gale. Tyson has also written and recorded "Rio Grande," a western song/story with a strong Mexican flavor and "Gallo de Cielo," a corrido in which a young Mexican steals a rooster, crosses the border in the United States and tries to make enough money on cockfights to buy back his family's land, "stolen" from them by Pancho Villa. As is the case in most corridos, tragedy rules. After winning a large sum, his rooster fights an evil black one (Zorro), who kills it. Penniless, he is alone in San Francisco at the end of the song. He has buried the picture of his wife that he had carried with him, with the body of his rooster. He has not regained the family's honor. The land will never again be theirs. And he will never see his loved one again.

Although the huge majority of popular country artists have been Anglo, there have been two talented Chicano artists who, in the 1970s, brought a large dose of Mexican musical sensibility into country music—Johnny Rodriguez and Freddy Fender. Johnny Rodriguez was the youngest of nine children, born in 1952 in a four room shanty in Sabinal, Texas—a town ninety miles from the Mexican border. He has said of his musical roots that: "I was always around music when I was growing up and I decided to sing country because that is what I am. My older brother...was a rodeo man and he'd sing a lot of country songs, often in Spanish. That's where I came up with the idea of doing some of my songs in English and half in Spanish" (Stambler & Landon 624). Nominated as Country Vocalist of the Year by the Country Music Association in 1973, Rodriguez made hits of songs such as "You Always Come Back To Hurting Me" (in the tradition of the cancion mexicana), "North of the Border," and the Spanish "Eres Tu."

Freddy Fender (born Baldemar G. Huerta in 1937) was older than

Rodriguez and has been in the music business (and regionally popular) since the late 1950s. After coming home from military service in 1952, Fender played local dances and cantinas in Texas, making a name for himself in the Mexican-American community. Looking for major success, in 1959 he cut the Tex-Mex rockabilly song "Wasted Days and Wasted Nights," which broke out of regional popularity and onto the national charts. However, Fender was busted for marijuana possession in 1960 and spent three years in prison. It took until 1974, then, for him to connect with producer Huey Meaux in Houston. They cut "Until the Next Teardrop Falls," with its English and Spanish lyrics. This became Fender's first gold record. In 1975, Fender sang onstage at the *Grand Ole Opry* during the CMA awards, and in 1976 he was nominated for a Grammy for Best Country Vocal Performance (Stambler & Landon 236). He remained strong on the country charts throughout the 1970s and on into the early 1980s.

In addition to these two Chicano country stars, several Anglo greats were born in areas where they were exposed early on to Mexican music and musical styles. Bob Wills, who invented Texas swing from a mix of Mexican mariachi, jazz and country, wrote the Mexican-derived "San Antonio Rose," "Spanish Fandango" and "Mexicali Rose," and is by far the best known and most influential of these individuals. Indeed the central importance of his swing style in nearly all Texas country music that has come since—and the diffusion of swing into many other areas of country music (from the recordings of Waylon Jennings to those of Tanya Tucker and Asleep At The Wheel)—cannot be discounted.

Wills was not the only country artist who was influenced in his early life by Mexican music. Jim Reeves, born in Panola, Texas, had a song he cut on a local label break out nationally for his first top ten country hit, "Mexican Joe." Linda Ronstadt, born in Tuscon, Arizona, has said that Mexican music was the basis for her own country/rock style; "The kind of music I listened to as a child was Mexican music—rancheras, like Lola Beltran. So country it is, but it just doesn't happen to be this country" (Roberts 196). Guy Clark, growing up in Beaumont, Texas, learned guitar as a boy and initially played Mexican songs, rather than country or folk. This early absorption of Mexican music shows in songs of his like "Desperados Waiting For A Train" and "Coat From The Cold," recorded both by himself and Jerry Jeff Walker. Clark's songs have also been recorded by Earl Scruggs, Jim Ed Brown and David Alan Coe, spreading this Mexican influence into many corners of the country world. Buck Owens grew up listening to the "beautiful melodies and harmonies of Mexican people," as he has recently said. "I think specifically my music is very influenced by Mexican music, the way the singing is harmonized, the way the melodies work."

Finally, Doug Sahm, who brought his Texas border sound to the pop charts in the late 1960s, returned to Texas in 1971. In Texas he recorded and released an album entitled *The Return of Doug Saldana*, which he explained in the album's liner notes: "Saldana is a name my friends on the West Side of San Antonio gave me many years ago. Being a white boy, but sharing deep things with my Chicano brothers, they decided to call me that."

On the album Sahm recorded Freddy Fender's "Wasted Days and Wasted Nights" and, throughout the 1970s and 1980s, has continued to record similar border material from Texas. His albums have featured many Mexican musicians, such as saxophonist Rocky Morales and accordian player Flaco Jimenez (as well as pianist Mac Rebennack, saxist Fathead Newman and guitarist David Bromberg). In 1990, Sahm has formed a "Texas supergroup" called The Texas Tornados, comprised of Augie Meyer (from the original Quintet), Freddy Fender, Flaco Jimenez and himself. The group has broken beyond their regional popularity and are hitting the national charts in rock *and* country with songs like "(Hey Baby) Que Paso?," "Adios Mexico," "Laredo Rose" and Flaco's tribute to his father, Santiago Jimenez's own "Son de San Luis," which won a Grammy in 1991.

Conclusion: The Wolf Will Survive

It should be clear from this overview that Mexican influences are very strong in American country and western music, ranging all the way from standard trademarks such as the yodel, through song forms, themes, rhythms and instrumentation. As invisible as it perhaps has been to many, Mexican music from south of the border has always been drifting through this American pop form—commenting on it, modifying it, helping to define it—while, at the same time, even suggesting directions in which it might go....

It was late in the evening, but summer heat still hung in the still night air. They came trooping into the small shadowy club dressed all in black. At least the two men were. The kid, though he was probably old enough to drink, had on an old green plaid shirt and brown wrinkled corduroys. The two women wore dark coats, even in the late summer heat, wrapped round them as though the unfamiliar smoky atmosphere of the club was as threatening to them as the cold winter that was to come. They stared around nervously, as one of the men shuffled sideways between the loose chairs until he came to an empty table. He smiled, and there were spaces where his teeth were missing. Waving his arm like a thin spindly spoke of a windmill, he nervously ushered the others to the table, pointing to where each should sit, fussing about until the cocktail waitress came over for their order. It was beer, though the bourbon he had been drinking outside hung around his head like a cloud.

The lights dim and the singer steps on stage to a roar of whoops, hollers and rebel yells. Waylon Jennings smiles quickly, a flash of teeth in the grey of his beard. He turns his back to the audience as he completes the final tuning on his black and white leather covered guitar. Although he is wearing blue jeans, otherwise Jennings is dressed all in black, like the two men who have come to hear him. He turns back, looks out over the audience. "This 'un was written by some Spanish boys down in L.A.," he says. "It's called 'Will The Wolf Survive?', and you know—I think he will." Waylon grins and fingers the lead notes as the band fills in behind him. The crowd stomps and slaps the beat, carrying the tempo of this Mexican-American country song, rushing it forward into the hot breath of the August night.

Works Cited

Birnbaum, Larry & Debbie Nathan. "Crossover Music."*Village Voice* 33.28(1988): 22-26.

Geijerstam, Claus at. *Popular Music in Mexico*. Alburquerque: U of New Mexico P, 1976.

Lewis, George H. "Interpersonal Relations and Sex-Role Conflict In Modern American Country Music." *International Review of the Aesthetics and Sociology of Music* 20.2 (1989: 229-238.

Malone, Bill C. *Country Music, USA*. Austin: U of Texas P, 1968.

McDowell, John. "The Corrido of Greater Mexico as Discourse, Music, and Event." *Social Process and Cultural Image As Texas Folklore*. Eds. Richard Bauman and Roger Abrahams. Austin: U of Texas P: 44-75, 1981.

Parades, Amerigo. *With His Pistol In His Hand*. Austin: U of Texas P, 1958.

Pena, Manuel. *The Texas-Mexican Conjunto: History of A Working Class Music*. Austin: U of Texas P, 1985.

Roberts, John Storm. *The Latin Tinge*. New York: Oxford, 1979.

Scherman, Tony. "Cuttin' Tracks." *Asymptote* Summer *1991*.

Tosches, Nick. *Country*. New York: Scribner's Sons, 1985.

A Tombstone Every Mile:
Country Music In Maine[1]

George H. Lewis

When it's winter up in Maine, better check it over twice,
That Haynesville Road is just a ribbon of ice...
If they buried all the truckers lost in them woods
There'd be a tombstone every mile...count'em off...
There'd be a tombstone every mile.

Dick Curless/Dan Fulkerson, 1965

Dick Curless, born in the northern Maine community of Fort Fairfield, began his recorded career in country music in 1950 with a song entitled "The Coast of Maine." Influenced and assisted in the early years of his career by Maine country stars Hal Lone Pine and Yodelin' Slim Clarke, Curless moved from regional popularity to national stardom with songs such as "Room Full of Roses," "Tater Raisin' Man" and the above quoted "Tombstone Every Mile"...a song which recounts the saga of hauling potatoes from Aroostook County in the north of Maine down to Boston, a trip that took truckers through the infamous Haynesville woods...100 miles of twisting, icy road with no stops, no towns along the way. Such songs reflected Curless' roots, sunk deep in the rocky soil of this New England state and far from the Tennesse-Texas axis that most people identify as the locus of American country music (Fryer; Malone, *Southern*).

Maine might not be the first place one would think of with respect to country music, but, in fact, the state has a long and distinguished history of contributions to the genre. Paul Metivier, for example, (writing as Paul Roberts) penned "There's A Star Spangled Banner Waving Somewhere" while living in Skowhegan, Maine in the early 1940s. This song became one of the most popular country songs of its time, much in the same way that Lee Greenwood's "God Bless The USA" became a giant country-pop song in the late 1980s and early, Desert-Storm-influenced, 1990s.

Robert's song was recorded by well over 50 artists in the 1940s and was the first country tune to be sung on the Lucky Strike Hit Parade. Elton Britt, now in the Country Music Hall of Fame, sold well over a million copies of his popular version of the song. Roberts, who lived for a good deal of his life on Swans Island, off the coast of Maine, has had well over a hundred songs of his published in Nashville and has, himself, been recognized as a songwriter by Nashville's Hall of Fame.

Portland Maine Is Just The Same As Sunny Tennessee

If country music were not important in Maine, it is hard to understand why performers like Jimmie Rodgers (who wrote the line quoted above) and Mickey Newbury (who "bought a ticket to Skowhegan, Maine" in his "The Future's Not What It Used To Be") would have included references to the Pine Tree state in their songs, as they (and others) have done. Of course, one way of looking at it is these country artists could think of no place *further* off and away from civilization than Maine to use as a reference point. Still and all, there has always been a strong audience for country music in the state. Grandpa Jones, in his autobiography, remembers travelling to Maine, from Boston, in the summer of 1935 to play "Waterville, Portland, Bath, Rockland, Fort Fairfield, Houlton, Bangor and some smaller places" (Jones and Wolfe 55).

At that time Sunday shows were not allowed in Maine, due to old Yankee "blue laws." Jones found that he had been booked into a small Maine town on a Sunday. He and the band pulled in, expecting the worst.

...but when we got to the theater, the manager met us smiling and ready to go. "Don't worry," he beamed. "I've already paid the fine in advance!" Sure enough, we had a full house, and everything went fine...for about 15 minutes. Then a huge storm hit and knocked out the lights all over town, including the theater. We didn't know what to do, but those Down Easters weren't about to give up after having coming this far with our illegal show. About 25 of them lit out of the theater, and in a few minutes they had brought in their flashlights and even a couple of floodlights...That's the way we found the people up there, and it amuses me to hear people today talk about how New Englanders are only now beginning to hear some country music. (Jones and Wolfe 55)

As Grandpa Jones noted, New Englanders...in this case, Mainers...have been hearing country music for at least as long as people in any part of the United States, a fact that would come as no surprise to folklorist Simon J. Bronner. Bronner, writing in 1976, challenged what he called the "myth of Southern origin" of country music (Bronner, "Woodhull's"). Instead, he felt there is a "continuously evolving and *traditional* music known as country music, which has developed independently outside of the American South, incorporating local folk traditions" (Bronner, "Country Music Culture" 71). Bronner has investigated country music in New York State, finding...as he predicted...a strong history of country music and artists who were influenced by local and regional traditions mixing with the evolving, more nationally popular, forms of country music (Bronner, "The Country Music Traditions").

Following Bronner's lead, similar analyses have been done in other areas of the American North (Roberts) and the Canadian Maritimes (Rosenberg, "Ethnicity"). In all these cases, the criteria that country historian Bill C. Malone developed earlier (*Country*) to map regional country music in the South, have been successfully applied in these northern areas as well. According to Malone, in order for country music to evolve and thrive in a region, the following three pre-conditions must be present:

1. A committment to and preservation of traditional cultural values, summarized as a basic conservatism.
2. A rural agricultural population, comprised of White, Protestant Anglo-Saxon inhabitants.
3. A basic isolation due to geographic factors, deficiencies in education, poverty and a lack of communication. (Malone, *Country* 54-65)

To anyone remotely aware of conditions in the state of Maine, it is clear that this state, too, meets Malone's criteria. Bordered on two sides by Canada and one by the Atlantic Ocean, Maine has always been a distinct cultural region. Stoic Yankee characters, downeast humor and Maine accents have long been a part of this regional identity. Yankees have always been known to be protective of their cultural values and...although not as publically extreme as neighboring New Hampshire...have a long tradition of basic conservatism, which evidences itself in a personal lifestyle of thrift, a concern and respect for the environment and a certain stubbornness in clinging to traditional ideas and ways of living and thinking.

Although the Maine population has historically been a rural one, it is somewhat contrary to Malone's second pre-condition, in that it is not made up exclusively of White, Anglo-Saxon Protestants (though the *image* of Maine Yankees as such is a strong one in this country [Lewis, "The Maine"]). There are many sizeable ethnic and cultural groups in the state that are not of traditional Yankee WASP extraction. Easily the largest of these...nearly 150,000 strong in a state with a population of just over 1,000,000, (according to the latest US Census figures) are the Franco-Americans, whose presence in the St. John's River Valley in the north of the state and in old mill towns like Sanford, Biddeford and Lewiston—where they moved from Quebec for work in the late nineteenth century...is strongly felt in the country music of the state.

Historically isolated by its geographic position, Maine's population remained relatively stable during the nineteenth century (with the exception of the Francophile in-migration). Previously, the largest number of Mainers had settled in the area from 1750 to 1800, arriving from England or from settlements in Southern New England. Communities across the state were scattered and separate. As folklorist Edward Ives has pointed out, Maine's culture can be said to have developed along its own lines through this combination of isolation and stability ("Maine Folklore...")...conditions Malone listed as important in the development of a regionally based country music.

Maine also has a history of economic problems, reflected in its relatively high level of rural poverty. At any given moment, even today, the poverty rate is about 15 percent, according to Joyce Benson, senior planner in the Main State Planning Office. For rural areas, this is closer to 21 percent (Lewis, "The Maine"). But thousands of others in the state are so close to the line that a cutback in work hours or a family illness sends them below, bringing the actual figure for the state to more like one out of every five persons. As characterized by regional writer Sanford Phippen: "This Maine is hard on people. It is a life of poverty, solitude, struggle, lowered aspirations, living on the edge" (Phippen 309).

Thus, with the exception of the Franco-American influence in Maine (and fewer over-all educational deficiencies than in many areas of the South), Maine fits Malone's pre-conditions for the development of country music probably *better* than many of the regional areas of the South from which the model was constructed (such as Tulsa and its surrounds, for example, where Bob Wills developed the basics of "Texas swing").

Lay Like A Bulldog: Fiddles, Chanties, Dances and Lumbercamps
Maine's country tradition stems from a series of regional sources that make it unique from that developed in the Southern United States. On the coast from the mid-1700s on, shipbuilding and sailing created a folk tradition of sea tunes and chanties...a tradition that linked Maine, musically and trade-wise, with the coastal areas of the Canadian Maritimes. This tradition is carried on today in country and country-folk music in Maine, from Dick Curliss' "The Coast of Maine," to the work of singers and writers like Gordon Bok and Schooner Fare, whose "Portland Town" and "Salt Water Farm" have been popular with local audiences since they were first written and recorded in the early 1980s (Lewis "Regional").

Inland, especially in the late 1800s, the lumbercamps were where the music was made...ballads created by musicians such as Joe Scott, who would take a knapsack full of his sheet music and go from one camp to another, selling copies for a dime apiece (Ives *The Woodsman*). Singing these ballads was a popular pastime on camps. Indeed, Edward Ives remembers one man telling him that, even though the labor was so bone-killing hard he had left that line of work, the man had returned to the woods, because he "missed the singing" (Ives, "Maine Woods" 23).

Many of these lumbercamp ballads were called "Come All Ye's," as they began with those words. Helen Hamlin, writing in 1948, remembered the community gatherings of the first part of this century in northern Maine as places where these songs were sung and played. "No social gathering anywhere from St. Francis up to Churchill Lake on the Allagash River was complete," she wrote, "without Tom Gardner to dance and fiddle, and sing some of the songs of the old logging days like 'Bogan Brook Line' and 'The Jam On Garry's Rock' " (Hamlin 125).

The fiddling involved in these tunes stemmed from two major traditions...the Celtic tradition of the British Isles and that of the French Acadians, who had relocated from Canada to the St. John's River Valley and worked alongside the English-Americans in the northern Maine woods. This mix of fiddling traditions created a unique style that can be heard in the music of many Maine country bands today, especially those with roots in the Franco-American rural communities of the Allagash and the urban Lewiston/Auburn area (McKeen).

Fiddling was also central to dance...a form in which most early country music in the area was enjoyed. While early country dancers in Maine were familiar with polkas, waltzes and even the foxtrot, the contradance was the most popular form (Hubley). The contradance gets its name from the two opposed lines of dancers who use a variety of steps...swing, promenade, allemende, dos-a-dos...steps that date back hundreds of years on European tradition to ancient English line dances, many of which were taken up by the French in the 1600s and called "contre danse."

In colonial times, in Maine, there were two major types of dance...the English style, which retained the dance lines, and the French, in whose hands the contre danse had evolved into the the more formal quadrille, a dance that had four sets of couples dancing from a square formation. English sentiments in Maine during the Revolution buttressed a strong adherence to the opposed-line contradanse, while anti-English sentiments (likely mixed with pro-French feelings) meant an embrace of the quadrille form, which has evolved into today's formal "square dance," with its emphasis on coordination, practice and complicated steps (Hubley). In contrast, the Maine contradance, even today, is characterized by people joining in and learning on the spot...and by the fact that, contrary to the square dance form...eventually everybody will get to dance with everybody else.

The English derived contradance style and its fiddle music have been influenced by French Americans (and Canadians), who have been dancing and playing it for over 200 years. Dominant strains in the music are both Celtic and French Acadian, with an accordian or two most likely joining the mix of fiddlers and (today) a piano or even a banjo (Dodson).

Of all the country fiddlers who emerged in Maine from this tradition, Mellie Dunham was, in terms of country music, the most important. Born in Norway, Maine in 1853, he made his living working on the family farm and by making snowshoes. He gained some degree of fame in 1909, when Commodore Robert Peary used Dunham-made snowshoes in his trek to the North Pole. However, Dunham's fiddling at a local Norway club for contradances was to be the thing that propelled him, late in life, into the national spotlight musically. Acting on a dare from a friend when he was 72 years old, Dunham entered a fiddle contest held at the Lewiston Armory in 1925 where, beating out both Anglo and Franco fiddlers, he was declared the Champion Fiddler of Maine (Whitman).

A Boston newspaperman, who was originally from Norway as well, heard of Dunham's triumph. He also knew that Henry Ford, concerned about maintaining the "purity" of traditional American music in the face of the many foreign musical styles coming in the great turn-of-the-century wave of immigration, had evidenced an interest in old time dances and fiddlers. Ford had especially negative feelings about jazz, which he felt demoralized America. He thought if he could encourage and promote old time fiddling and dancing, he could "help America take a step...toward a saner and sweeter idea of life" (New York Times 1952:2). Ford also had a summer home on Mt. Desert Island, off the coast of Maine. So when the Boston newsman sent him a clipping chronicling Dunham's triumph, Ford took notice.

Dunham, as had other fiddlers before him, received an invitation from Ford to come to Dearborn, Michigan and play for him. Dunham came and played, charming the industrialist with his music. (What Ford would have done, had he known of the French Acadian influence present in Dunham's fiddling, is interesting to speculate upon.)

Dunham's personal style was such that he generated a huge amount of publicity both before and during his visit to Henry Ford. He was described by the press as a "sawed-off Mark Twain," and he began to receive offers (which he accepted) to play in New York and Boston on the vaudeville circuit. He was especially successful in Boston, where he played the Keith House to capacity crowds and had his first engagement extended from one week to three. Dunham's stage act was the simulation of a barn dance, with the stage decorated to supposedly resemble the interior of a weathered, New England barn. Dancers, many imported from Maine, appeared on stage to contradance to Dunham's fiddle music (Wells).

At about this time, in 1926, Tennessee's Uncle Jimmy Thompson, who had been a featured performer on WSM in Nashville in a show that was to evolve into the Grand Ole Opry, won a fiddling contest in Texas and was named America's Champion barn dance fiddler. A Boston paper, having interviewed Mellie Dunham about this, reported:

The Maine fiddler takes exception to the crowning of Thompson as America's champion...following a contest that lasted eight days in Dallas. "He may have defeated 86 opponents in the Dallas contest", declared Dunham today, "but they were all southerners and they don't know as much about barn dance fiddling in that section as they do down in Maine. I'm ready to meet any and all of them, but I'd rather like to meet Uncle Jimmy Thompson, who claims the title." (Wolfe 57)

Thompson's reply to Dunham, when it came, became one of the most famous in American popular entertainment: "If Mellie Dunham will come down..." he said, "I'll lay with him like a bulldog" (Wolfe 56).

Dunham and Thompson never met, yet their reputations were both made. And, of the two, Dunham was clearly the most well known nationally. As Paul Wells, Director of Middle Tennessee State's Center for Popular Music, wrote; "This small fiddler, without even trying, had thrust upon the nation an awareness of traditional fiddling. Although he is little remembered today, he was, for a time, one of the most influential figures in American music" (Wells 115).

Hard, Hard Travelin' Men: The Rise Of Regional Stars in Maine

The antagonism that revealed itself in the Dunham-Thompson exchange in 1926 continued to be present as the regional styles and commercial country musics of the two areas evolved through the 1930s and on into the 1950s. As Al Hawkes, the owner of Maine's first country recording company and, himself, an accomplished country musician, said: "It was hard to get the southern stations to play records from Maine. They'd maybe play them in the studio, but they wouldn't put them on the air" (Hawkes). In this he was echoed by Betty Cody, one of Maine's top country stars of the era, who toured with Hank Snow, Chet Atkins, Minnie Pearl, Kitty Wells and others. Cody said bluntly: "It didn't set in too good, if a Northerner had a hit" (Cody).

But it was radio, not records, that was the route to success in country music in the 1930s and 1940s, especially in economically depressed Maine. The big stars from Chicago's National Barndance, Nashville's Grand Ole Opry and the Louisiana Hayride beamed from powerful transmitters in the mid-West could be heard, sporadically, in Maine...depending on weather and broadcast conditions. Also, and ultimately of greater importance in Maine, was WWVA's Jamboree, broadcast live from Wheeling, West Virginia. This station (and program) became *the* most listened to extra-regional country music source in Maine. As Al Hawkes recalls, usually "in the daytime, you couldn't get it at all, and at nighttime, well, it skipped. Faded in and out." If the weather conditions were just right, though, WWVA came in loud and clear at night, and many country listeners kept their radios tuned, even if it was skipping or all they could hear was static, knowing that "it's going to come back in, so leave it there" (Hawkes).

To perform on WWVA became a goal of many of Maine's country stars of the 1930s-1950s. It was the mark of making it to the top...a mark many attained, including Betty Cody, Hal Lone Pine and Gene Hooper, all of whom became regulars on the Jamboree. WWVA, increasingly in competition with southern stations like Nashville's WSM, welcomed this chance to sign up Maine country singers (and others from the north and mid-west) who, because they were not "good old boys and gals" from the south (and also because the southern audiences these radio stations reached were not familiar with these artists) very seldom contracted to put them on the air.

But, with few exceptions, the country stars who sang on these "big time" stations did not tour into the New England area, nor up to Maine. (Earlier in this paper a 1935 tour Grandpa Jones made in Maine was mentioned. But Jones was originally from Boston, so he had a "built-in" New England following to draw on.) For the most part, country fans in Maine had to put their faith in the crackling, static-filled airways in order to pick up bits and pieces of these singers and their songs. As a result, local stars who toured from community to community and performed on strong local radio stations had a loyal following. From the 1930s into the late 1950s, these were the real country stars in Maine...regional artists in direct touch with their fans.

The first of these major regional artists was Hal Lone Pine (Harold J. Breau), born near Old Town, Maine in 1916. He is credited as the first, in Maine, not only to have his own radio show but also the first to put together a package show and take it on the road to big city concert halls and grange halls not only in Maine, but also in the Canadian Maritime Provinces. Lone Pine broadcast from both CFBC in St. John, New Brunswick and WABI in Bangor, Maine, where his weekly program was eventually picked up by the ABC radio network and broadcast coast-to-coast.

Betty Cody, who sang with Lone Pine and became his wife, remembers that "he had charisma...he'd speak right to the audience...and he had beautiful costumes. Beautiful. He was one of the first to get tailormade suits. All embroidered, rhinestones, all that. He had all of those... (Cody).

Betty Cody (Rita Cote) was herself a star of this era. She was born in Sherbrooke, Canada in 1921, the sixth of eleven children. Her family moved to Lewiston/Auburn Maine when she was nine months old. When she was 14, Cody won a WCOU radio contest singing "I Want To Be A Cowboy's Sweetheart." By the age of 15, she was singing (and yodelling) regularly on live programs on that station. With Hal Lone Pine, Cody toured successfully in Maine and the Maritimes. Then, in the early 1950s, she signed a recording contract with RCA. At about the same time she and Lone Pine became regulars on WWVA's Jamboree. Betty credits part of her success to the fact of her Franco-American heritage (Cody). She sounded a bit different than other, southern, country stars.

Indian? Spanish? It was a guessing game for her audience, and it kept public attention on her, enabling her to record more than twenty successful songs for RCA, including "Tom Tom Yodel" and "Please Throw That Glass Away."

The way the Lone Pine Show (and others like it) worked was the group would pick a local radio station, audition and get a daily half hour program...usually in the early morning, when they felt the largest part of the country audience would be listening. Then the group would moniter their fan mail. If enough came in (it usually did...to the tune of 200 to 300 letters a week), they would begin scheduling concerts at all the local grange halls in a 150 mile radius of the radio station. The idea was to stay on a particular station long enough to play each hall in the listening area twice, on average...which might take a few months, or as long as a year. Then, when the group had become familiar to that local audience and everyone had seen their "big hats and fancy boots," the show would move on.

Many times this way of performing meant a concert and a dance each night, six nights a week, at some local grange hall. When the dance was finished, usually well after midnight, it was time to drive back to the hotel, catch a little sleep, and be up in time for the next morning's live (and early) radio show. As Cody says: "All we did was travel and rehearse and eat and sleep. That was our life... In the winter, it got so cold... there'd be a little pot-bellied stove in the middle of the grange hall, but you get away from it, you'd freeze...We'd take the tickets, then go backstage to change and the uniforms were frozen. Just frozen...But we enjoyed it" (Cody).

This local broadcasting, performing and promoting was terribly taxing, if it was done correctly. Another important country personality of the time, who became very successful on the radio and later on television, was Ken Mackenzie. Mackenzie first came to Maine to work with Buck Nation and the Cowboy Caravan in 1938. (By this time, the "singing cowboy" films were all the rage in Maine and country groups were dressing in fringes, big hats and boots and calling themselves and their groups "cowboys," even though the furthest west they may have been was to Westbrook, Maine, where Al Hawke's

Event Records was located.)

In early January, 1939, Mackenzie began a 7 a.m. show on WGAN in Portland, a station that had just commenced broadcasting four months previously. Also in 1939, Mackenzie organized what was billed as the first country-variety show in Maine. He remembers "appearing with the show over 80 consecutive nights in a row, one night off, and then 14 more. This was besides doing the daily radio shows on WGAN" (Maine Hall of Fame). Mackenzie kept this sort of pace up until 1954, when WGAN moved into television broadcasting. At that time he launched a highly successful country television show, while later developing a regular country disc jockey program for KGAN radio as well.

This formula of touring, variety shows and appearances on local radio stations made major stars of several Maine artists, including...of those not already mentioned...Yodelin' Slim Clark (an inductee in the National Yodeler's Hall of Fame); Curly O'Brian (a singer on WWVA and a staple for many years on Bangor television and cable television in the Maritimes); and Dick Curless (who appeared on the The Grand Ole Opry and was a regular member of WWVA's Jamboree and the Buck Owens All American Music Show).

As Neil Rosenberg has pointed out, country music is many times the end result of a process which occurs when the music of a group...usually having regional, class and/or ethnic identities...achieves access to commercial media (Rosenberg, "Big Fish..." 152). When this happened in Maine, not only did these performers put the state on the country music map, they helped define a *style* of country singing, playing and song writing that is regionally distinct from any other in America...a style that, while partially echoing the pop sound of the big time southern market, also carries its unique blend of Anglo/French (and Canadian) musics and styles, as well as a penchant for songs that reflect a love and appreciation of the north woods and coastal waters of the region, from Charlie Gilliam's "Casco Bay," to Rusty Wellington's "The Allagash" and, more recently, Betty Decoteau's "Winter In Oxford Hills." In this way, Maine country artists of the era were, to use Rosenberg's terms, both "mirrors and instruments" of local/regional and nationally popular tastes (Rosenberg, "Big Fish..." 161).

Pine Tree Country: Two Tiers Of Maine Music

As with many regional country musics, the advent of national television created major changes. No longer were the regional stars the only ones an audience could "see." And with visual recognition from television, national distribution of recordings and a national "networking" of stars came an equally national based touring network. By the 1960s, national country stars could make money touring in markets like Maine, and venues such as Lewiston, Bangor, Augusta and Portland became common stops on national tours.

Also in Maine, live local radio shows gave way to the national playlists of commercial country radio. Headliners at local fairs were, increasingly, nationally known performers from out of the region. It seemed as if the regional country music of the state had been driven out and passed by for the commercial sights and sounds of Nashville Central.

And yet, even though the strength of the regional market has been sapped since the mid-1960s, it is by no means appropriate to pronounce regional country music dead in Maine. What has happened is the constant promotional hype of the commercial star network has, because of its glitter and electric shine, obscured the fact that country music in Maine has become, today, a two-tiered phenomenon.

On the top because of its dollars and influence, is the national commercial star network, which controls most television and radio playlists and which sells the most CD's and country music tapes. Indeed, there is a strong country music scene of this sort in Maine, with over 20 radio stations classified as full time country in this limited market. When Rockland-based WMCM moved from a classical to a country format in 1990, the radio station hosted a picnic with three country bands that was very well attended. Jack Armstrong, disc jockey for the station (who had previously been working at stations in Louisville and Lynchburg) noted: "Country and western has become mainstream. It's very popular in coastal Maine and throughout the state. And country listeners are active consumers. They frequent convenience stores, yes," he said. "But they also buy BMW's" (Boyd 3). As Ken Minott, Program Director for WCME noted: "Most stations seem too attached to the Top 40 format to take a chance on a Maine artist, which is a shame" (12).

And yet, hidden under all this commercial glitter is a second network of regional performers and stars...people playing and singing much as the past generations of Maine country artists did. People such as Elmer Larson and Jeanie Carter of Country Fever; The Okey Doke Band, with Charlie Brown and Miss Marilyn; Norm and Betty Decoteau; Theresa Cormier; and Jeff McKeen and The Old Grey Goose Band. Although it is far less likely that any of these performers will move on to the national level, as did several performers of the previous generation, they enjoy a strong and steady popularity in the state, playing regularly at clubs, picnics, parties and other social gatherings. (And some of them have had a song break out nationally...Theresa Cormier's 1990 recording of "Hello Mama" and Malinda Liberty's 1987 "Working Days," which reached #3 on *Cashbox's* Country Chart, are but two examples.)

These performers also have strong local networks of support. In Maine there is the Maine Country Music Association, The Down East Country Music Association and the Maine branch of the New England Country Music Historical Society. Each of these organizations has a monthly publication devoted to country music artists and their work. In addition, the Maine Country Music Association has put together a Hall Of Fame and gives annual awards for the top local performers in the state. They also perform an important "networking" function for performers in the pages of their *Maine Country People*, which includes items as diverse as birthdays, hospitalizations, benefit concerts, artists looking for work and recipies for carrot cake.

Many local artists record their own music...sometimes in album form but increasingly on "cassingles" like Al Wing's "Ice Around Your Cold Heart" (which was written by Maine songwriter Sylvia Munsey). This song was recorded by Jerry Dunning at his studio on Orr's Island, then (to show a Maine-Nashville industry connection), it was sent to Dayle Grisham, who plays steel guitar for Randy Travis and who worked on several Maine artists' records when he was stationed at the Brunswick Naval Air Station several years ago. Grisham added some touches and created the final mix for the song (Adams, "In the Spotlight" 9).

These cassingles and albums are sold to fans at live shows throughout Maine and are also used in attempts to get on the air on local radio stations. Although these artists are generally not successful in getting their material played on shows featuring a national playlist, most stations reserve some time and/or slots for local artists. But as Ken Minott, Program Director for WCME in Newcastle says of Maine country radio: "Some stations do play Maine artists but they are few and far between and when they are played, they don't provide any information on who it is or where they are from." WCME and some other Maine stations have tried to counter this inattention with shows devoted entirely to local talent. Minott's "Home Cooked Country," on the air every Saturday from 7 to 8 p.m., uses "a format of a full program of Maine country music, information and interviews, verses, occasionally putting a song or two into the daily rotation...We provide the artists, the writers and especially the fans a definite time when they know they can hear good Maine country music" (Minott 12).

Maine artists continue to tour and play instate and, to some extent, in other areas of New England, the Canadian Maritimes and beyond. Harold Crosby, for example...born in Houlton, Maine, in northern Aroostook County...tours as far south as the Carolinas and has had hit songs, such as "Old Slewfoot," on the charts in places as far away as Holland, England and Austria (Adams, "In the Spotlight" 10).

And contemporary Maine artists are not unknown at the national level. Theresa Cormier and Malinda Liberty's recent nationally ranked recordings have already been mentioned. In addition, in both 1990 and 1991, Norm Decoteau was named National "Male Entertainer of the Year" in the Country Music Associations of America annual competitions in San Dimas, California. In the same competitions, Al Hawkes was named "National Instrumentalist of the Year" in 1990 and Moe Greenleaf was "Male Vocalist" in 1991 (Adams, "Norm Decouteau..." 7).

In New York City, in November of 1990, the Maine French Fiddlers played Carnegie Hall in a show billed as "French Fiddling Meets Its Celtic Kin: Irish, Scottish and Country Music." The *New York Times* reviewer noted, in a very favorable review, that "in one song, each fiddler played separately, revealing the variations behind their unaminity and, for a finale, 11 year old Daniel Guillemette joined the group, proudly fiddling along side his grandfather, Ben Guillemette of Sanford. When Daniel was asked why he took up the fiddle, the boy's answer was quick: 'Because my grandfather does it' " (Pareles).

Also in 1990, Allan McHale's recording, "Old Country Radio Songs," was one of only four country CD's included in *CD Review*'s "Elite Greatest CD's

Ever," as selected by the editors of that publication (the others being Emmylou Harris' "Ballad of Sally Rose," The Dirt Band's "Will The Circle Be Unbroken" and K.T. Oslin's "This Woman"). As McHale said of his national honor; "growing up in Bangor, Maine, country music was my whole life" (McHale 5).

So, although there is in the 1990s, no set of artists of long lasting national stature, as there was in the previous generation, there is not only a strong regional "scene" of country music in Maine, but several Maine artists who continue to be noticed on the national level.

Conclusion: I'm Gonna Live Life My Way

Country music has always been a popular musical form in Maine, from the early contradance fiddlers and lumbercamp ballad singers to today's professional musicians. As in other areas of the United States, a strong regional style—in Maine developed from the state's unique mix of Anglo and French/Acadian traditions—merged with the evolving national country music sound of Nashville to become the musical platform from which several Maine artists have sprung to national attention. Many of these did so in the 1940s and 1950s, lending a decidedly Downeast flavor to country music of the time.

Though there are no contemporary major name country artists on the national scene from Maine, the regional picture in the 1990s is strong, as it always has been. Local artists are supported by fans throughout the state, who buy their CD's and cassingles, come to their live shows and dance to their music at honkytonks and bottle clubs throughout the state. Indeed, it is at this level of club performance where Maine's country blood runs richest; places like Reggie Greenlaw's "Musitorium" in Stonington—a converted five car garage where the mike on the bandstand is in a ship's wheel surrounded by fish nets and two large lobsters; or Millinocket's Bottle Club—a dark, no-windowed hall with rough, chainsawed log benches; or Le Passe-Temps in Lewiston...a cinder block joint with peeling blue paint in the old French part of town; or a weathered hen coop in Machias—where Gene Hooper learned his first country chords from Lyman Beal, who came upriver from Jonesport to buy clams. This is the heritage of country music in Maine—driving the icy roads of the great north woods, trying to make it home safely to friends and family, determined not to become one of those marked forever by a tombstone every mile.

Notes

[1] I would like to especially thank the following persons and organizations who have generously given of their time, information and advice. They have all helped me immensely in my study of country music in Maine: Marie Adams and the Maine Country Music Association; The Maine Country Music Hall of Fame; Jeff McKeen; Anne Dodson; The Northeast Archives of Folklore and Oral History; and Neil V. Rosenberg. Thank you one and all.

Works Cited

Adams, Marie. "In The Spotlight." *Maine Country People*. July: 10.

_____. "Norm Decouteau Wins." *Maine Country People* June 1991: 7.

Boyd, Stephany. "Cowboys and Classical Clash for Cash." *Preview: Maine's Guide To The Good Life* Sept. 1990: 3.

Bronner, Simon J. "Country Music Culture In Central New York State." *JEMF Quarterly* 13 (1977): 171-182.

_____. "The Country Music Traditions In Western New York State." *Journal of Country Music* 7 (1978): 29-59.

_____. "Woodhull's Old Tyme Masters." *JEMF Quarterly* 12 (1976): 54-63.

Cody, Betty. "Interview" on "Pioneers of Maine Country Music." Maine Public Broadcasting Program Tap. Orono, Maine: Northeast Archives of Folklore and Oral History, 1990.

Dodson, Anne. "Interview" by the author, Oct. 11, 1990.

"Ford Party Dances To Dunham's Music." *New York Times* 12 Dec. 1925: 2. Fryer, Paul.

_____. "Local Styles and Country Music." *Popular Music and Society* 8.3&4 (1982): 63- 76.

Hamlin, Helen. *Pine, Potatoes and People*. New York: W.W. Norton, 1948.

Hawkes, Al. "Interview" on "Pioneers of Maine Country Music." ME Public Broadcasting Program Tape. Orono, Maine: Northeast Archives of Folklore and Oral History, 1990.

Hubley, Doug. "It's A Country Dance." *Maine Sunday Telegram* 26 June 1988: 26-27.

Ives, Edward. "Maine Folklore and the Folklore of Maine." *Maine Historical Quarterly* 23.3 (1984): 111-132..

_____. "Maine Woods Ballads." *SALT* 39 (1990): 21-25.

_____. *Joe Scott: The Woodsman-Songmaker*. Urbana: U of Illinois P, 1978.

Jones, Grandpa and Charles Wolfe. *Everybody's Grandpa*. Knoxville: U of Tennessee P, 1984.

Lewis, George H. "The Maine That Never Was: Myth and the Invention of Meaning In Regional Culture." Paper presented at the Pacific Sociological Association Annual Meeting, Irvine, 1991.

_____. "Regional Music in the American State of Maine." *International Review of the Aesthetics and Sociology of Music* 21.2 (1990): 207-218.

Maine Country Music Hall of Fame. "Ken Mackenzie Biography," 1978.

Malone, Bill C. *Country Music, USA*. Austin: U of Texas P, 1968.

_____. *Southern Music, American Music*. Lexington: U of Kentucky P, 1979.

McHale, Allan. "Old Country Radio Songs." *Maine Country People* Jan. 1991: 5.

McKeen, Jeff. Interview by the author, Oct. 3, 1990.

Minott, Ken. "Home Cooked Country." *Maine Country People*. March 1991: 12.

Pareles, John. "Eleven Year Old Plays Carnegie Hall." *New York Times* 8 Nov. 1990.

Phippin, Sanford. "The People of Winter." *The Best Maine Stories*. Augusta, ME: Lance Tapley, 1986. 309-314.

Rosenberg, Neil B. "Big Fish, Small Pond: Country Musicians and Their Markets." *Media Sense*. Eds. P. Narvaez and M. Laba. Bowling Green, OH: Popular Press, 1985. 149-166.

_____. Ethnicity and Class: Black Country Musicians In The Maritimes." *Journal of Canadian Studies* 23 (1988): 138-156.

Roberts, Roderic J. "An Introduction to the Study of Northern Country Music," *Journal of Country Music* 7 (1978): 22-28.

Wells, Paul. "Mellie Dunham: Maine's Champion Fiddler." *JEMF Quarterly* 12 (1976): 112-118.

Whitman, Vic. "Fiddler For Henry Ford." *Down East* 14 (1968): 59-61.

Wolfe, Charles. *The Grand Ole Opry: The Early Years, 1925-1935.* London: Old Time Music, 1975.

There'll Always Be A
Honky-Tonk Somewhere:
Country Culture

The first reference to honky-tonks, according to writer Nick Tosches, was in the Saturday, February 24, 1894 edition of the *Daily Ardmorite*, the newspaper of Ardmore, Oklahoma, which reported that "honk-a-tonk last night was well attended by ball-heads, bachelors and leading citizens." Although the meaning of "ball-head" may well be lost in history, the term "honky-tonk" has become well known in music, perhaps appearing in country for the first time in Al Dexter's "Honky-Tonk Blues," in 1936. Dexter himself owned and operated a honky tonk called The Round-Up Club in Turnertown, Texas. He described these places as "beer joints up and down the road where the girls jump in cars and so on."

As such, these establishments of dim lights, thick smoke and loud, loud music have always been a major influence in country culture—an influence more local, rough-shod and immediate than the countrypolitan glitter and bright lights of the big time performers and polished recordings of Nashville's music industry. In the honky tonk, by contrast, one drank beer, danced, laughed and cried. The world outside could (and probably would) go to hell, but in here, country people were not quite sober, safe and warm.

In "Honky-Tonking," Joli Jensen examines these places as social institutions which "offer a special area for studying social and symbolic interaction." In the taverns and the bars, songs are sung to an audience who finds their themes of loss and dislocation to be personally meaningful. However, as Jensen notes, this specific form of culture production and consumption has come to have an increasingly marginal relationship to the industry that first produced the music—the live music and country culture of the honky-tonk is "distinct from the mainstream of country music." As she writes, "it is *selected* for its appropriateness by an interaction between the band and the audience...it is *altered* to become unique and to foster comraderie...it is *shared* in a way that creates feelings of openness and kinship...and it is *incorporated* in conversation to understand everyday experience." As Jensen concludes, "the honky-tonk is a setting that authenticates music by making it personal and connecting it directly to social experience."

Aaron Fox, in "Split Subjectivity in Country Music and Honky-Tonk Discourse" examines this connection, viewing it as a "complex, apparently contradictory intertwining of intense, devastating affect with easy-going, playful sociability." This intertwining creates what Fox calls the "split subject," a concept he develops in an ethnographic study of a blue collar country music

116

bar in which, as he says, "the lived 'texts' of real working class lives are inextricably intertwined with the artistic texts of country music, and vice-versa."

Not all participants in the honky-tonk are necessarily members of the local culture. In contrast to the tavern studied by Jensen, where the band was local, in many cases musicians travelling the regional or local honky-tonk circuit may play in one town for no more than a week or two, then move on. In these cases, the musicians never do develop any real ties to the local country culture. Instead, they—the very ones who create the music around which culture develops—are likely to be the ones most alienated from it, a situation analyzed by Karl Neuenfeldt in "Alienation and Single Musicians on the Honky-Tonk Circuit" his study of single country musicians in British Columbia.

Playlist

This Playlist consists of a set of instructions. Visit any place advertised in your local paper with a name like "The Ranch House," that promises LIVE country music; or venture into any bar with a jukebox playing country music loud enough to hear from the doorway and a parking lot at least half full of pickup trucks and old Cadillacs. Wherever you go, relax, smile, order a longneck and listen.

Honky-Tonking:
Mass Mediated Culture Made Personal

Joli Jensen

The cabarets and honky-tonks,
Their flashing signs invite
A broken heart to lose itself
In the glow of city lights...

"City Lights"
Bill Anderson

Overview

Honky-tonk music developed in the 1930s in live performance by local musicians in roadhouses and taverns. It developed out of an intimate connection between the performer and the audience; songs were written by, and sung for, people who shared an experience of rapid social change. The singer/songwriter performed songs about lost love, broken dreams, loneliness and nightlife to a bar full of people who knew what he was talking about; all were experiencing the dislocation of the rural dweller in an urban environment.

Honky-tonks trained a generation of musicians who wrote and performed much of the country music that was recorded and broadcast during the 1930s and 1940s. The broadcasting and recording industries acted mostly as a conduit during this period, transmitting songs (developed in honky-tonks) to a more distant audience. This changed during the 1950s, however, as the broadcasting and recording industries became increasingly complex and interdependent.

Technological, social and economic forces acted together to transform the popular music industry in the 1950s and thus to transform country music production. It became "big business"; songs were produced and marketed to appeal to a maximum audience. The honky-tonk genre, whose characteristics developed in a specific context for a specific audience, diminished in importance in the country music industry during this period.

Yet the period involved continued urbanization and industrialization of the South and continued migration of rural southerners to northern cities. The tensions engendered by those changes, tensions expresses in honkytonk music, still affected segments of the population. The hodgepodge of country music on radio and records in the 1950s and early 1960s, however, offered little symbolic material that directly addressed those particular concerns.

While the nature of produced country music changed in the 1950s, honkytonks still thrived in urban areas. In these taverns, songs continued to be sung to an audience who found their themes of loss and dislocation to be personally

118

meaningful. However, this specific form of culture production and consumption came to have an increasingly marginal relationship to the industries that created and disseminated the music. The music performed live in taverns today continues to be distinct from the mainstream of country music.

Origin

Country music historian Bill C. Malone locates the origin of honky-tonk music in Texas taverns and roadhouses. The Texas oilboom of the 1930s created a number of frontier-like areas on the outskirts of town where tax rates were low, police supervision lax and where "farmers, laborers, truckdrivers and displaced rural dwellers gathered to relax and drink beer or to work off their frustration (or add to them) by an occasional round of merriment or 'hell-raising' " (162).

Country music changed in the context of the honky-tonk. Lyrics became franker and more realistic, to address the problems of the "wild side of life." Themes of temptation, adultery, alcoholism, loneliness and loss became prominent, reflecting the experiences of the patrons and performers who found solace in taverns.

Instrumentation changed too, in order to be heard above the din of laughter, the clink of glasses, the shuffle of feet and the buzz of conversation. The beat got louder, using string bass and later drums. By the end of the 1930s these, along with the plunk and wail of electric and hawaiian steel guitar, were established as fixtures in a honkytonk band.

The music derived from a variety of influences in the southwest and was a mingling of jazz, hillbilly and blues traditions. As folk music scholar D.K. Wilgus describes the genre, it emphasized a variety of blues vocals with supporting instrumentation, a "syncopated backing of lyrics expressing the problems of sexual and marital relationships in which the neon sign of the tavern is seldom absent" (169).

Setting

Honky-tonk songs are performed in a special context, the communal atmosphere of beer, smoke and sound in a neighborhood tavern. Taverns are social institutions, and taverns with live music offer a special arena for social and symbolic interaction. The relationship between the songs and the setting is heightened by the singing of songs about the setting ("Honky-tonk Blues," "Bright Lights and Country Music") as well as by the comraderie generated by small dance floors, regular patrons and free-flowing alcohol.

There is a surprising dearth of systematic studies about taverns and their role in community life. One such study, done by Macrory in 1950 (636), labels neighborhood tavern as the most numerous and functionally varied of all tavern types. Macrory conducted extensive interviews and observations to determine why taverns are popular and concluded his sociological analysis by noting that taverns provide certain satisfactions that are difficult to come by in an urban culture.

Men yearn for a sense of belonging; for recognition, for response and security, but urbanism as a way of life if not conducive to meeting these social-psychological needs. While many make satisfactory adjustments through their homes, through satisfying marital and family experiences, or relationships with other institutions, others are not so fortunate. Many of these people turn to the tavern as the most convenient medium for meeting those needs. (636)

Audience

The pattern of communal relationships Macrory describes as alternative to tavern patronage was reconfigured by southern industrialization and urbanization and by immigration to northern cities. The period 1940-1960 has been labeled as "the great migration" from the Southern Appalachian region; high industrial productivity in northern cities brought a tide of rural southern white laborers to urban industrial centers like Chicago, Cincinnatti, Cleveland, Dayton, Baltimore and Detroit (Brown and Hillery).

Kinship networks were involved in the migration process (Choldin), with family members helping more recent migrants find jobs, homes and social contacts. Still the adjustment of southern white migrants to northern urban norms was neither simple nor complete. Honky-tonks had an important role in the lives of southern white migrants in urban areas.

A case study of a colony of white southerners in Chicago, done by Lewis M. Killian from 1947 to 1949, reveals that migrants were "in, but not of, the Near West Side community" ("The Adjustment..." 67). They existed as a quasi-minority, considered by non-southern whites to be a distinct, cohesive group called "hillbillies."

Killian defines the tavern as an important gathering place, as well as a form of voluntary segregation, for the displaced southerner. A contemporary article in *Harper's* (1958) describing the "hillbilly invasion" of Chicago, states that the "chief social diversion is to gather with friends in the one social institution that they have originated up North—the hillbilly tavern" (Votaw 65). The article then quotes a Chicago Sunday Tribune expose: "Skid row dives, opium parlors, and assorted dens of iniquity collectively are as safe as Sunday school picnics compared with joints taken over by fightin' feudin' southern hillbillies and their shootin' cousins."

Killian gives a somewhat less xenophobic description of the bars:

Quiet except for the jukebox during the day, after dark these taverns were filled with the whine of electric guitars and the nasal tones of country singers. There was no floor show—the patrons were the show. Drinking cheap beer, dancing, talking with kindred spirits from the South, occasionally fighting among themselves or with Yankees who invaded their turf, the migrants found escape from the impersonality of urban living in a true ethnic tavern. (*White Southerners* 110)

To review, honkytonk is a genre of music that developed in a social institution that addressed the needs of rural dwellers exposed to urban pressures. The music was originally formed in oilboom Texas in the 1930s; as southern migration to the north continued and expanded in the 1940s, the urban honky-tonk and its music offered solace to the dislocated rural dweller. For them, songs about broken dreams and love gone wrong, about the temptations of neon lights and hard liquor, had experiential meaning. This audience would frequent taverns, buy records and listen to radio stations that offered them that array of themes and images in which to share.

The Industry

During this time honky-tonk material dominated country music radio and record fare. The musicians, songwriters and performers who gravitated to Nashville as it became a recording center had learned and honed their craft in honky-tonks. Thus the Nashville country music industry acted mostly as a conduit for the sounds and lyrics created in the intimate performer-audience relationship of the tavern, and the connection between live and recorded performance was extremely close.

This situation was altered in the transformation of the popular music industry after World War II. The 1950s were a period of upheaval in the whole industry. Postwar prosperity and the baby boom resulted in a dramatic increase in the size and wealth of the youth market. A hit in the teen market could make millions, and the teenage taste for a new form of music, rock 'n' roll, affected all other forms of popular music.

Radio was moving to an all-recorded music format in response to television's adoption of its other programming. Market research began to be used to garner advertisers, so that radio programming became increasingly tailored to fit specific tastes and habits. This led to format radio, increasingly dependent on top hits in various music categories, because format programming was found to be both predictable and profitable.

At the same time, the recording industry was expanding, diversifying and becoming more closely linked to radio airplay. Independent companies sprang up in the 1950s, due largely to the lucrative teen hit market and also to the formation of BMI (Broadcast Music, Inc.), which challenged ASCAP's (American Society of Composter, Authors and Publishers) licensing control over new material. Also, new and more sophisticated recording techniques were being developed, new distribution channels were formed and new and aggressive promotion techniques were becoming popular.

These forces interacted in the transformation of the country music industry. In short, it became "big business"; and as sales were increasingly tied to airplay on format radio, musical content was altered so that songs would have crossover potential and thus maximum sales.

Two processes became important in this more complex and radio dependent recording industry: preselection and filtration. Hirsch's analysis of the popular music industry notes that in it, as in all culture industries, more items are available and produced than ever reach the consumer and that there is no way to accurately predict which items, once in the consumer domain, will have appeal. To cope with this plethora and uncertainty, the industry develops a system that preselects material via a filtration process. The process is designed to minimize risk and maximize profits.

In Hirsch's analysis, popular music has a creative sector that is made up of selected artists and recording company agents. They generate the raw material that will then be selected for release by record company policy makers. Once released, a record must receive radio airplay; airplay is determined to a large extent by regional distribution and promotion. Given format radio, the record must demonstrate strong appeal before it receives frequent airplay; there is a problematic interactive relationship between record sales and radio airplay.

The business consideration operating at every level of the structure is "will this record sell?" Beginning in the 1950s, sales for the country music industry are generated by songs that appeal to a range of country music fans and that can also "crossover" into the popular Top 40 charts.

In summary, the burgeoning country music industry of the 1950s changed from being a conduit to being a filter; it developed a process of preselection heavily weighted toward wider appeal and weighted against the situation-specific sounds and symbols of honky-tonk music.

The 1950s Sound

The result, in the 1950s, was a bewildering melange of styles. Popular tunes were "countrified" with steel guitar and rural twang, country tunes were "sweetened" with violins and harmony backup vocals. Rock 'n' roll licks were added to ballads, blues tunes were growled and yodeled. As a top producer said of the period, "We'd try anything to find a hit sound" (Bradley).

Lyrics, too, reflected the upheaval—they would be sprinkled with jive talk, or be cloyingly Tin Pan Alley, or obviously created for effect. Fans call the 1950s the period where country music got commercial, people in the business will blame rock and roll, saying that it "almost killed country music."

The honky-tonk genre diminished in prominence, but did not totally disappear, during this period. Hank Williams songs were recorded by other performers and Nashville-based singers like Webb Pierce, Lefty Frizzell, Hank Thompson, Hank Snow, Ray Price and George Jones recorded many songs that were well-suited to performance in smoke filled bars. They did not always make it to the top of the charts, but they were available on records and on the radio and found a smaller but loyal audience.

They also found their way into the repertoires of live honky-tonk bands. The genre continued to be performed and have meaning in honky-tonks, where people drank beer and danced to songs like *Night Life*, *Detroit City* and *Faded Love*.

Contemporary Honkytonking

Although the country music industry has expanded greatly since the mid-1960s, its essential character has not altered significantly. It is a commercial industry that produces material called "country," material designed to become a country hit and/or crossover into other markets. Its artists and songwriters are professionals whose careers depend on their generations of material that will have wide audience appeal.

It is this industry that provides new material for local bands that play live country music in taverns. The cultural material generated in Nashville is validated in complex ways by its performance in a honky-tonk. What follows is a description of some of this complexity based on participant observation in a central Illinois tavern. This honkytonk owned and operated by the leader of a band, Sunny Norman; he and his Drifting Playboys play there five nights a week (Jensen).

On most evenings the band members start to come in around 9 p.m., just after the pool table has been covered and the row of flourescent lights has been turned off. Around 9:30, Sunny pulls the plug on the jukebox, orders a round of drinks for the band over his shoulder as he walks, stomach jutting, up to the bandstand—bottle in one hand and cigar in the other, a smile and a wave to the people he knows sitting at the surrounding tables.

The stage is barely large enough to hold the amplifiers, microphones, instruments and band. It is a plywood platform covered with shag carpet, bounded by an iron fence that was covered, for Christmas, with a silver tinsel. The tinsel is still there in March, as are the decorations around the top of the walls left from the Christmas before. The fence is waist high, the platform raises the band about a foot and a half off the dance floor, which is in front of the band. The stage is lit by soft red and white lights so that the band looks healthier, happier, larger than the people sitting at the bar. Those who dance will be washed by the same light as the band.

Sunny and Scotty tune up, Scotty strumming a chord on his steel guitar, while Sunny leans over him, matching it with a flurry of notes, his eyes closed, carefully. Then Sunny stands straight, looks around, nods and with fast sharp lead guitar the band is playing their quicktime intro tune; as they play Bobby steps up to the microphone to say in a cheerful showman's voice "We'd like to thank you all for coming out to our house tonight, we're Sunny Norman and the Drifting Playboys and we'll be up here playing country music for you until one o'clock in the morning. If you've got songs you'd like to hear, come up and tell us about it, and we'll try to do them for you" and then he steps back smiling while the music ends and people hunch over their drinks and smile back.

Specific songs are selected by a direct interaction between the band and the crowd. The band wants to please the crowd; they must keep people drinking, dancing and coming back the next night. This means that they will play the songs that the audience wants to hear at the moment—there is a direct connection between the tavern setting, the audience mood and the content generated.

Sunny may talk some about a request they are going to do—who wrote it, who sang it, what he thinks of it ("Starts out sad, ends up plumb pitiful"), whether they can do it ("We used to know it, we'll see what we can come up with was we go along").

The band will include uptempo tunes to accommodate dancers as well as listeners. Unattached women are more likely to dance a fast song with a stranger; if that dance goes well she may be willing to dance to the slow songs that appeal to the more established couples. The mix of songs also helps keep the mood of the place from becoming overly melancholy—an unmitigated stream of songs about love gone wrong, dreams gone awry and being lonely with only the bottle as your friend can become oppressive. So every so often the band plays an uptempo tune that celebrates the joys of drink, dance and driving the big rig home to see your baby, which adds an element of rowdy comraderie to the basic honkytonk theme of poignant perserverance.

Older songs make up the bulk of the material; there is little pressure on the band to play a preponderance of recent hits. The audience will select from contemporary playlists those songs that they want to hear in the tavern setting and the band will play mostly the ones that they like. Often these are recent hit songs that deal with traditional honky-tonk themes (e.g. "I Cheated Me Right Out of You") in the traditional manner. Still, "classics" are the rule in the honky-tonk. People want to hear the songs they've heard a hundred times before; they are familiar, well-loved and still have personal meaning.

The audience does not want, or expect, the song to sound "just like the record." One characteristic of a honky-tonk band is that they alter a record's arrangement. The musicians take pride in their ability to phrase, harmonize and play in their own style. The goal is not to sound like the record, but to "sound good," a personal evaluation of what good country music is all about. The characteristic becomes evident when a performer broadly imitates a certain vocal style, or plays a lick exactly like the original—it is parody shared with each other and with a usually knowing crowd.

The alteration of lyrics is another important part of the performer-audience interaction. Words are changed to become suggestive or obscene ("four hungry children and a crop in the field" becomes for Bobby and Sunny, "four ugly children and a crotch that won't heal"), or frankly sexual ("darling, let's go all the way...").

Songs are also altered to include the names of patrons present or absent and may commorate special occasions, such as Sunny's special "happy anniversary, my darling, thanks for all the misery."

This alteration of lyrics keeps the artist-audience interaction unexpected and lively. Usually this treatment is reserved for recent country rock hits, or ballads that Sunny or Bobby feel are "too commercial." The sad, sweet standards are usually sung straight; the band rarely ridicules the emotions expressed in "good" songs.

Another feature of the music, as it exists in the tavern, is that it promotes and legitimates a special type of shared interaction. Many bars have dim lights, smoke and alcohol, but honkytonks have a unique atmosphere, due in large part to the presence and nature of the music.

Honky-tonk music lets you clap, stomp, dance, sway, sing along, sigh or cry into your beer. The volume precludes extensive conversation, instead you smile, nod, lean close to your neighbor in order to communicate.

The depth of identification with the music is reflected in the content of conversations held in the tavern. Lyrics are frequently incorporated word for word when someone talks about their life, their hopes, their philosophy. This incorporation of lyrics can be conscious or unconscious, but indicates that lyrical content is being used to understand and explain lived experience.

In summary, the consumption of honky-tonk music is affected by the setting in special ways. First, it is *selected* for its appropriateness by an interaction between the band and the audience, based on the contingencies of their relationship. Second, it is *altered* to become unique, and to foster comraderie and conviviality. Third, it is *shared* in a way that creates feelings of openness and kinship among audience members, and finally, it is *incorporated* in conversation to understand everyday experience.

The music itself expresses deep feelings; it deals directly and frankly with pain and loss. By being in the tavern and responding to the songs, the patrons express their sharing in those emotions; they tacitly admit that loneliness and emptiness are common experiences. This sharing of highly emotive images, in an atmosphere of alcohol, soft lights, smoke and conversation, allows an aura of warmth and closeness to develop. This atmosphere defines the honkytonk experience.

What Holds True

What follows is a series of paragraphs, meanings that are made in the honky-tonk. They are cumulative, moving from separate human emotions and activities to a sense of what the world is like. Being in the tavern, with its soft lights, cheer, music and people known, seems to weave the meanings together in a way that is enveloping and sustaining. It seems to wash them in an aura that makes them simple, shared and true.

Love

Love cannot be trusted. Hearts are broken, tears fall. Lovers marry others. Husbands and wives cheat.

Yet love can be found, in affairs, in marriage, by being good and kind, by being gentle, by waiting and hoping and forgiving.

You always carry the torch. Unrequited love is inescapable, noble and hurts deeply. It is to be borne in silence and strength. The loved one is worthy, but through your flawed ways or their confusion, they are forever lost to you. You can do no more than cherish their memory.

Work

Work is hard, unending, underpaid, emasculating. It is done for strangers. It drives you to drink. It is the only way to pay the rent and feed your children. It drains you of your soul.

It is to be done because you must do it. It is not to be chosen or changed. Only gamblers, hustlers and con men make it big, and in doing so they lose home and family.

You may long for a rich and easy life but if you find it, you will not find happiness.

Drink

Drink is anesthesia and danger. It brings temporary solace but it breaks up your home and takes food from your children's mouths. It can soften the edges of a harsh world, but in the end the bottle lets you down and it hurts even more. You cannot drink things off your mind.

Women

Women are tarnished angels. They can bring light and beauty into your life, but they are tainted and so give pain. They are to be protected from temptation, because they can succumb to wealth and flashy dress. Some good women will stick by you, though you falter, others will not and will hurt you by turning to bright lights and bourbon.

Girls are unaware of their sexual power. They can, but should not be seduced. They are looking for a kind of love you cannot give. You can only long for them. They will tempt you, but no good can come of it.

Men

Men are struggling to maintain their self-respect. They do the best they can but are misunderstood and mistreated. They want to find a woman who will be good, kind and true.

They can overcome the temptations of sex, drink and easy money, but it is a hard fight. Sometimes they just want a night on the town, to drink and pretend they are single. They want to find someone who will listen to them and understand.

Chivalry

Some people are too naive and trusting and it is your duty to protect them from the evil others will do them. In the end, the only people who count are the ones who mean well and do the best that they can. You help these people out and leave the rest alone.

Home

Home is far away. It is safe, simple and pure. Life here is city life, dangerous, complicated, poisoned. You can long to return but you can't go home again. All you can do is find people who come from where you come from. They will do right by you.

Time

Memories never die, old loves never fade, broken hearts never mend. You learn to live with pain. It is to be borne, through eternity or until you die.

Loneliness

You are alone and it hurts. Your true love has died or left you. Your wife or husband no longer cares. Your children have grown up. You are far from home, searching for something you cannot find. You try to find solace in drink and smokefilled bars, but they cannot replace the love you have lost.

Dreams

Dreams shatter. Ideals crumble. What you seek you cannot find. Nothing turns out the way you planned.

You can become bitter, or remain true to your vision and hope to find someone who will make your dreams live by sharing them with you.

Us and Them

There is us and there is them. We are hardworking, honest, far from home, patriotic, vulnerable. They are slick, dishonest, untrustworthy, powerful, cruel. They are threatening. They own the factories, they have more education, they think they are better than us, they do not respect other people or what makes this country great. They use big words. They hold all the cards. They will stab you in the back.

But we are better than they are, because we work hard, care for our families, stick together and keep faith with each other. We made this country. We hold the key to what makes happiness, because we know it is home and family and doing right by each other. We have good friends who go way back with us. If we do the best we can it will all work out all right. They can never take that away from us.

Out There and In Here

There is out there and in here. Out there it's the same thing day in and day out and nobody cares if you live or die. Out there it is cheap and shallow, everybody is looking out for number one. You have to be on your toes all the time.

In here the lights are soft and low. You have friends who touch you and call you by name. The bartender knows your drink and you know almost everyone here. You can listen to the music you like, maybe hold somebody close while you dance, see people you haven't talked with for a while, have a few drinks and feel good about yourself. In here you matter to other people, in here it is soft, safe and kind.

Conclusion

Folk art has been classified as unsophisticated, localized culture, an art that deals with the concrete world and arises from a close relationship between performer and audience (Real 7). It relies on tradition and is shared in face-to-face communal interaction. Honky-tonk music, when it developed in live performance in taverns in the 1930s, had these characteristics.

In the 1940s, as performed by honky-tonk trained musicians in live radio broadcasts and on records, country music maintained the qualities developed in live performance. The country music industry transmitted the music to a diffuse audience with little selectivity or conscious design.

As the recording and broadcasting industries became more complex and interdependent and as Nashville became a haven for professional musicians dependent on a large and more vaguely defined audience, the nature of mainstream country music changed. The industry came to select and filter the music, creating material designed to appeal to a mass audience. As country music became big business, it came to display many of the characteristics of mass art; it was created *for* people rather than *by* people.

Honky-tonk music, as a genre, was eclipsed by this process. While there was still an audience who found its symbolic content to be meaningful, that audience did not connect well with industry structure. The genre is strongly tied to the tavern setting; songs like "Oh Bottle Take Effect" lose power when heard on the car radio or on the stereo at home. The audience for honky-tonk songs did not buy records, or form a radio audience, in large enough numbers to influence industry production.

It is tempting to idealize pre-1950s honky-tonk music as being somehow authentic and thus to denigrate later Nashville fare as inauthentic "mass culture." In fact, the "new traditionalism" of the late 1980s can be seen as an attempt to once again reconfigure country music's "authenticity" by creating, in today's Nashville, songs that have a 1950s honky-tonk sound.

Authenticity is a vexed issue, and I hope that this discussion of honkeytonk music suggests the inadequacy of evaluative schemas that anoint some forms of culture as worthy and others as unworthy, based on an unspecified mistrust of institutional, profit-oriented production. What I suggest here, in conclusion, is a more complex account of authenticity, based on connection to lived experience.

In the mass culture debate, a debate that still figures (often unacknowledged) in discussions of media in society, culture is deemed to be less authentic, the more it is "commercial" or "mass." Authentic culture is deemed to be culture that is "folk" or "popular," communally created and performed. This kind of idealized authentic culture is contrasted with mass or commercial culture, made in an impersonal way, solely for profit.

This contrast becomes a way to critique contemporary life, contemporary cultural forms and contemporary taste. Once, the story goes, things were communal and personal and genuine; now, they are commercial and impersonal and spurious. What the honky-tonk experience demonstrates and this analysis attempts to illustrate, is that meaning is created in situations, it is constructed in interaction—it is in reception, not conditions of production, that meanings are made.

What this means is that a cultural form's "authenticity" is best defined in relation to its deployment in actual people's everyday lives. Understanding what a cultural form "means" requires an understanding of what a cultural form means to specific groups of people in specific contexts. Evaluation of its "worthiness" should be based not on origins, or textual characteristics, but on how it "lives" in everyday experience. Evaluation of worth is thus sociological and ultimately moral, not aesthetic or ideological, and therefore it is much more difficult to sustain.

My initial claim is that a song's origins in commercial institutional processes does not automatically define it as false or inauthentic or (even) ideologically suspect. Just because a big, elaborated, industrial system supports the production of a cultural form does not mean it is inherently tainted. In other words, in spite of the mistrust of the mass mediation process, commercially produced material is not by its nature corrupt. Tautologically but still significantly, the meaning of cultural material is in its use, its context of consumption, in what it means to those who find it meaningful.

In the honky-tonk setting, performers and patrons define certain songs as "good," based in overlapping and related beliefs about country music, about the honky-tonk setting and about the lyrics and the sounds of the songs. Sunny Norman, who owns the context of performance; and thus has unusual latitude in song selection, still must negotiate between what the music industry has made available, what the audience requests, what "works" in the setting (to maximize pleasure and drink consumption and thus returning paying patrons) and what he himself values as "good" or "real" country music.

To the honky-tonk customer, the song is "good" when the lyrics speak directly and seemingly honestly about particular aspects of life and when the instrumentation is "right" (in other words, has a honky-tonk sound). Such a song can be (and almost always is) created for profit, via a formula. It can even be written totally cynically, by someone utterly outside of the tavern experience and promoted and distributed by people who think it is hillbilly garbage. Yet it can still be made "good" or "meaningful" or "authentic" in its reception—the honkytonk is a setting that authenticates music by making it personal and connecting it directly to social experience.

My argument here is that connection to lived experience, in the honky-tonk setting, validates the values and beliefs expressed in a particular genre of country music. This argument can easily be extended to other kinds of media fare, kinds that are similarly denigrated as "commercial" and mistrusted as "inauthentic."

Cultural and social critics rarely acknowledge or respect the relationship between fans and the media forms they enjoy. From Adorno's critique of radio music to the chronic complaints about television's vast wasteland, critics presume that cultural forms carry their origins like a virus, ready to infect their recipient with either the debilitating disease of commercialization, or (with luck) the bracing anodyne of authenticity.

What I hope this analysis of the meanings made in honky-tonks suggests is that country music, like other cultural genre, can be best understood as a form of experience, rather than as an industrially created text or product. The honkytonk setting is a particular form of experience in which meanings are constituted and celebrated, using commercially created and disseminated cultural material. Performers and customers select, alter, share and incorporate cultural meanings in complex and personal ways. This process of validation through experience is surely not limited to country music and it deserves our recognition, attention and respect.

Works Cited

Bradley, Owen. Interview. July 1979.

Brown, James S. and George A. Hillery, Jr. "The Great Migration, "1940-1960. *The Southern Appalachian Region, A Survey* Thomas R. Ford., ed. U of Kentucky P, 1967.

Choldin, Harvey M. "Kinship Networks in the Migration Process." *International Migration Review* 7 (Summer 1973).

Hirsch, Paul M. *The Structure of the Popular Music Industry* Ann Arbor, MI: Institute for Social Research.

Jensen, Joli K. "The Rose Bowl: A Cultural Analysis of a Country Music bar." Unpublished manuscript.

Killian, Lewis M. "The Adjustment of Southern White Migrants to Northern Urban Norms." *Social Forces* 32.1 (Oct. 1953).

_____. *White Southerners*. New York: Random House, 1970.

Macrory, Boyd E. "The Tavern and the Community." *Quarterly Journal of Studies on Alcohol* 13 (1952).

Malone, Bill C. *Country Music U.S.A.* Austin: U of Texas P, 1968.

Real, Michael. *Mass Mediated Culture*. Prentice-Hall, 1977.

Votaw, Albert N. "The Hillbillies Invade Chicago." *Harper's* 216. 1293 (Feb. 1958).

Wilgus, D.K. "Country-Western Music and the Urban, Hillbilly." *Journal of American Folklore* 83 (April 1970).

Split Subjectivity in Country Music and Honky-Tonk Discourse

Aaron A. Fox

Tim: If anybody told me that they were gonna stop country music tomorrow, I'd possibly commit suicide (laughs)...I really would. If there was not gonna be any other music on the radio, shit, I'd probably leave this world tomorrow. You can relate to this shit, at least I can anyway (...) Like if you're gettin' over a heartbreak or somethin' like that, it might tear you up, just listenin' to the songs...
AF: But that's the point, isn't it?
Tim: Yeah, but I mean, a lot of people don't want to get tore up. And that's a lot of the bitch about country music. God do you want to cry in your beer? No! (...) Hell, the cryin' in the beer part is not part of it.[1]

Introduction

"The bitch about country music"—at least for its working-class, beer-drinking, honky-tonkin' constituency and arguably for those of us who study it in order to practice cultural criticism—is country's complex, apparently contradictory intertwining of intense, devastating effect with easy-going, playful sociability. As Tim implies, country music is intimately associated with getting "tore up" and "cryin' in your beer." On the other hand, Tim also claims that "the cryin' in your beer is not part of it." Which of these is the "true" face of country music? They *both* are, and that's the bitch about country music.

At one extreme, the discursive subject—both the subject of the country song narrative and a "real" person like Tim who "relates" to such narratives—is immersed in the experience of loss, pain, misery and heartbreak. Such feelings are represented as anti-social, dangerous, obsessive and crazy in country music texts and by working-class country music fans. They mark a disengagement with ordinary modes of sociability and a descent into self-immolation (cf. Stewart, this volume). At the other extreme, the discursive subject in country music culture achieves a reflexive distance from these same feelings. This subject watches—and narrates—its obsessive, fixated *doppelgänger* with amusement, as if it were a reflection in a distorting mirror. By means of this talkative, sociable gaze, the dangerous and anti-social figure "cryin in his (or her) beer" is recovered and re-socialized. A potentially disruptive (or as Tim remarks, even "suicidal") moment is brought within the interpretive boundaries of "ordinary" social life, and a withdrawal from sociability is converted into something good to talk about.

This essay explores this sort of double or "split" subjectivity and argues

131

that the trope of the "split subject"—at once immersed and distanced, silent and talkative, inarticulate and artful—is central to the poetics of country music and to "ordinary" discourse in the cultural context of the rural, working-class beer joint. The "split subject," in other words, articulately speaks its inarticulate silence in both the country song and in "real life." Finally, I argue that the trope of the split subject contains an important lesson for a cultural criticism which studies country music as socially located artistic expression, because it enables us to understand the "bitch about country music" for those of us who study the genre.

The Poetic Function:
Country as Socially Situated Artful Discourse

This paper is informed by a particular theoretical orientation toward the relationship between "art forms" such as country music and "real life," such as that encountered in the country music honkytonk bar. In recent years, drawing in particular on the work of Roman Jakobson, scholars in a range of disciplines have articulated a "cultural poetics" approach to the study of the relations between artistic discourse and the "ordinary" life which such artistic expression represents and from which it emerges. Jakobson defined the "poetic function" as the tendency for the artful use of language to focus on its own formal and conceptual structure and thereby to reveal the conventionality of the "ordinary" referential meanings used in everyday, non-artistic genres of discourse which are constructed from the same linguistic raw materials (Jakobson). A "cultural poetics" approach further emphasizes that such "ordinary" meanings normally have a "natural," non-reflexive character which conceals the conceptual assumptions and the desires and interests which undergird everyday social life (cf. Bauman & Briggs for an overview).

In other words, artful or poetic expression reflexively examines the ideological structure of the "ordinary" events and discourses it takes as both its raw materials and as objects of scrutiny. This "poetic" mode of attending to the "ordinary" is precariously situated. On the one hand, it functions as a potential *critique* of the "ordinary," a stripping away of the ideological veneer of naturalness and a probing of the concealed structure of motives and interests revealed thereby. On the other hand, artful discourse also heightens and intensifies otherwise unremarkable situations and genres of discourse, providing a pleasurable reassertion and reinforcement of ideological *a prioris* and fundamentally implicating the poetic function in the reproduction of ideology. Artful discourse, then, is at once a challenge *to* and a celebration *of a particular social order.* More precisely, artful discourse is understood to involve a *dialectical movement* between challenge and recovery, or between ideological critique and culture reinforcement.

Country music, as a mode of artful discourse intimately linked to complexities and contradictions in the language, experience and culture of American working-class whites, exemplifies this dialectical oscillation at many levels. As I have argued at length elsewhere, the play of critique and affirmation which is the essence of the "poetic function" is evident in the relation between the discursive tasks of song-writing and song performance, in the relation between "ordinary" working-class language and its representation in country song texts, in the cycles of resistance and commodification which weave through the history of the genre and in the set of tropes, figures, metanarratives and themes which are ubiquitous in and unique to country music (cf. Fox). In ways both subtle and apparent, country polemically engages in both the critique and the affirmation of the "ordinary" social and psychological experiences and ideological discourses of its constituency.

The country music trope of the "split subject" can be understood as a particular manifestation of this double, dialectical thrust of the "poetic function," albeit one which functions at the most intimate and microcosmic level of "ordinary" social experience, namely, the construction of the "self" as a discursive position, that is, a place from which one speaks. For country, as for other discourses, an understanding of characteristic subject positions is crucial for understanding the larger dialectical movements of the discourse and ultimately for understanding the relationship of country music, as an art form, to its ideological and cultural contexts.

For example, a characterization of the particular mode of subject-construction in country music and in the cultural practices associated with country music must underlie any attempt to specify, as I have attempted to do elsewhere, the ways in which country both criticizes and affirms unequal class relations in late capitalist society (Fox). Put briefly, culturally appropriate readings of *what* is being said must be informed by a sense of *who* is speaking and *how* such a subject expects to be interpreted—or, often, productively misinterpreted—in particular contexts.

Furthermore, any discussion of the relationship between an artistic genre and the forms of social consciousness which it articulates and shapes must be predicated upon an understanding of the modes of subjectivity characteristic of the artistic genre and of the discourses which surround the production, consumption and interpretation of that genre. Although questions of consciousness and ideology are not the subject of this paper, any treatment of such issues entails claims about subjectivity. In what sense is the speaking subject of the country *song* a representation of "real" speaking subjects? And how does this representation in turn influence the modes of subjectivity of "real" individuals?

These last questions raise one further theoretical issue which I shall address before turning to a discussion of the split subject of country music and honky-tonk discourse. In order to deal with such questions, it is necessary to engage in an *ethnographic* mode of inquiry, one which examines the insertion of artistic texts and performances in concrete contexts of discursive production, consumption and interpretation; and which examines the interrelations between the multiple levels of textualization and contextualization which surround every artistic discourse. My examples here, then, are drawn both from the realm of country songs and from fieldwork in a rural, working-class honky-tonk bar in central Texas (cf. f.n. 1).

Split Subjects: "there's a fool in the mirror..."

The "split subject" of the sad country song represents a "real" subject position in honky-tonk discourse. On any given night, in any given honky-tonk, a visitor is bound to notice at least one person who appears to be withdrawn from the joking, banter, and easy-going, bawdy, good-time solidarity which characterizes the "ordinary" social life of a rural beer-joint. Although this figure may be a long-time patron, well known to all present, and although he or she may be sitting at the middle of the bar, surrounded by talk on all sides, the figure will seem darkly silent and ominously introspective. And although conversation goes on as usual around the bar, everyone is highly aware of this figure, who has the power to draw down all the talk around him/her into an attentive silence when s/he finally does speak, if only to order another beer or to mutter a cryptic *non-sequitur*, or when s/he gets up to feed the jukebox a few more quarters.

This figure—the "fool" of so many country song lyrics, who sits "gettin' tore up" or "cryin' in his/her beer" while all around him/her life goes on—occupies a marked discursive position in the honky-tonk. I say "discursive," because even though the figure may be "silent," s/he is at the center of the storm of "ordinary" talk swirling around him/her. Nobody is unaware of the "fool" and of the challenge—even the danger—that s/he represents to "ordinary" honky-tonk sociability, least of all the "fool" him- or herself.

Periodically, attempts will be made to draw the figure back into the ordinary sociability of the bar. The figure at the margin of the conversation will suddenly be made the focus of "unwelcome" attention as someone shouts "ain't that right?" to the figure, seeking corroboration of some controversial or polemical point. Often the reply is a growled *non sequitur*, usually in the form of a pithy aphorism (e.g., "If the world was logical, men would ride side-saddle") which disrupts everything, challenging the others to come up with a quick pun or a new topic of conversation of some kind or equally absurd reply.

If this attempt at recovery fails, the silence of the "fool" descends uncomfortably over the entire group until someone restarts the conversation; sociability is shattered. On the other hand, when this drawing out of the "fool" succeeds—when the "fool's" comment is skillfully re-integrated into the barroom conversation—it results in the most memorable and creative kind of honky-tonk talk: an accelerating stream of puns, *double entendres* and intensifications which results in a magical peroration of hilarity and artful verbal brilliance.

This "real" discursive figure of the silent "fool," sitting alone drinking and "gettin' tore up" is, of course, a *texted* position in honky-tonk discourse, no less than in the country songs which represent this figure. The "fool" is a role played by certain people at certain times—a dramatic production of a familiar narrative, the assumption of a particular, culturally salient subject position. In "reality," the individuals who play this part are rarely inarticulate or at a loss for words—indeed, when they *do* enter barroom banter, it becomes apparent that they are among the most skillful talkers in the place. This is precisely what makes their silence such a potent anti-social force. These articulate individuals are deeply immersed in and fascinated by the inadequacy of words to express their "tore up" situation, a fact to which their silence testifies. Thus, when they *do* talk about their texted silence, they enact a critical distance from their "silent" selves.

One such figure at Ann's Other Place (cf. f.n. 1) is Maria, a Hispanic woman in her mid-30s. Maria often sat silently at the bar for hours on end, nursing her beer, smoking and intermittently singing along with the jukebox for a line or two. Talking to Maria over the course of many nights, I discovered that she was immersed in—indeed, obsessed with—memories of her happy marriage which had ended several years before in a bitter divorce and left her in poverty with an adolescent son to raise. Our talk centered on the lyrics to sad country songs and on phrases from those songs which she would repeat over and over as touchstones for reflection, as if to say that she lacked her own words with which to explain herself. When she talked to me, it was as if she was watching *herself* "going through the motions" of coming out to beer joints to be alone in a crowd. She often expressed amusement and fascination with the effect certain songs had on her.

Maria's objectifying, amused distance from her own pained silence closely parallels the construction of the "fool" in country songs such as Becky Hobb's "Jones on the Jukebox," in which the narrative subject watches herself as a "fool in the mirror, looking back across the bar," sitting alone with her memories in a crowded bar. Like Maria, who spoke in the words of country songs, the protagonist of Hobb's song marks the inadequacy of her own words by speaking intertextually, in phrases drawn from a series of George Jones songs. The progression of the subject from observer to observed is marked by a perspectival shift from deictic description ("There's a fool in the mirror...") to self-reflection marked by the pronominal shift to the first person: "*I've* got Jones on the jukebox, and you on *my* mind." The silent, devastated self has become a character in a song—or rather a series of George Jones songs—watched from a distance by the amused, talkative self of the narrating voice.

The explicitly "split subject" image of the "fool in the mirror" is also used in Lefty Frizzell's classic song "I Never Go Around Mirrors," in which the perspectival shift of the subject from observer to observed is foregrounded. The song begins with an elaborate third-person description of a drunken, dishevelled, unshaven, crying "fool," ("one who never combs his hair or shaves his face") but the singer then suddenly pulls off a disorienting identification of the foolish figure being described with the speaking subject of the song, by singing the first-person title line of the song. It becomes apparent that the slobbering, pathetic fool is the "I" of the narrative. The pronouns describe the split subject by means of a grammatically dubious image: "I can't stand to see me/without you by my side." Here, again, the subject is split into two parts, one inarticulate and "tore up" and another who speaks of his or her own inarticulateness in the richly poetic language of a country song.

Of course, in the country song narrative, the articulate, observing side of the split subject always predominates. The narrative subject has been returned to the realm of the social through the use of artful speech, and the "tore up" figure of the fool is held at a distance, only asserting itself in a clogged, sobbing vocal inflection or in a dramatic, dangerous pause, as in the bar of silence immediately preceding the title line in "I Never Go Around Mirrors," when the listener begins to wonder who this "fool" really is. The intensity of that pause is the equivalent of the pointed *non sequitur* spoken by the silent "fool." Everything social hangs in the balance: how will the dangerous moment be integrated into the flow of poetic discourse?

In a country song, the recovery of articulate speech after the moment of discursive free-fall is virtually guaranteed, although it is the mark of a great singer like Lefty Frizzell that he can convince the listener to suspend knowledge of this "guarantee" long enough to engender a delirious, vertiginous sensation prior to the recovery of sense even after repeated hearings. In honky-tonk discourse, however, there are no such guarantees. Sociability is on the line every time the split subject threatens to come completely apart.

This risk is especially pointed when the "tore up" figure *has* been tentatively "drawn out" of his or her silence and brought into the conversation. In the tense, electric moments that follow, we encounter another highly texted version of the split subject, rather like an inversion of the figure of the "fool" who sits silently immersed in his or her own world, muttering *non sequiturs* and singing lines to country songs. The figure of the "drawn out" fool is another figure familiar from the country song narrative: the self which presents a laughing, joking, "good time" public face which *hides* the "tore up" and inarticulate self.

Like the country singer, this figure often achieves great heights of artful verbal brilliance, but these heights are understood by co-participants to conceal depths of affect which could swallow up the entire company with the slightest provocation. The challenge, of course, is to push the split subject as far as possible without pushing him or her over the edge. In the following example, Randy and Rich have "drawn out" the articulate side of Pat, a woman who had spent most of the afternoon "crying in her beer" because her longtime boyfriend had left her the previous night. Pat has just responded with a brilliant display of bravado and raunchy humour, insisting that the breakup was "his [her boyfriend's] loss," but the strain of this show of unconcern is showing, and Randy and Rick are flirting with disaster:

Randy: Well, now you're braggin! Hah! I love ME! Hey Yeah... HIS LOSS! God damn!

Pat: Would you rather see me like this or would you rather see me sittin up here cryin?

Rick: I'd console you.

Randy: Boy, I'd like to have your ego.

Pat: What'd you say?

Randy: I'd like to have your ego! His loss!

Pat: I could be sittin up here cryin...

Randy: His loss!...

Pat: I could be sittin over here cryin cuz I'm broken hearted.

Rick: (sings very softly); "I've got this cryin'..." (silence descends on the entire bar) (spoken) You got the right attitude, always go through life thinkin' what someone else is missin out on. Someone tears me down, I go, Ppppt, get lost. (long pause, uncomfortable silence)...Then I go home and cry! (Everybody laughs)

Here, Randy reveals the split subjectivity which Pat occupies by challenging her bravado repeatedly, until Pat finally admits that she could be crying "because I'm broken hearted." Rick seizes this moment to risk destroying the sociable atmosphere entirely, by softly singing a line from a sad country song which he has heard in Pat's repeated use of the verb "cryin'." In the silence that follows, he pushes even harder making a show of sympathy for Pat's bravado which explicitly diagnoses her condition, as privately "tore down" (a variant of being "tore up") and only publicly indifferent. At this moment, the silence around the bar grows palpably uncomfortable, and Pat is at a loss for words—the inarticulate side of the split subject comes welling up—when Rick suddenly saves the day with a brilliant punchline delivered with perfect timing, engendering raucous laughter and allowing the conversation to continue. (Pat then returned to her "good time" public subjectivity, levelling a stream of raunchy insults at Rick for the next five minutes.)

Pat occupies a split subject position which is ubiquitous in country music. She presents an aggressively articulate face to the others which conceals an unspeakable, shattered private world. This is the brash but shattered subject of songs like Dwight Yoakam's "Guitars, Cadillacs," Mickey Gilley's "A Headache Tomorrow (Or A Heartache Tonight)," or Moe Bandy's "Someone That I Can Forget" and thousands of other honky-tonk songs in which the subject buries his or her desperate misery in a show of outward sociability and good time partying.

Maria and Pat enact two moments in the life of the split subject, whose public "self" oscillates between the two positions of articulate self-reflexivity and inarticulate, even silent abjection. These moments are figured in various combinations in countless country music narratives, and these narratives are the soundtrack and the script for the "real" lives they represent and which in turn enact and re-textualize the songs. These texted oscillations which afflict both "narrated" and "real" subjectivities are fundamentally implicated in the dialectic of the establishment, disruption and recovery of "ordinary" social life around the honky-tonk bar. The lived "texts" or real working-class lives are inextricably intertwined with the artistic texts of country music and vice-versa. And that's "the bitch about country music" for those who live within its lure.

It's also "the bitch about country music" for cultural critics who study country music as a socially situated expressive cultural practice, and this is my final point. Although, as I said above, this paper has not dealt with larger issues of ideology and social consciousness, I contend that the issues raised here must be dealt with in any treatment of country music which *does* attempt to address the connections between the texts and performances of the genre and the lives of those who make and listen to this music.

As I have tried to demonstrate, country music and "ordinary" life are intertwined in complex, mutually determining ways. Country music is the highly articulate, overtly arrogant, unabashedly polemical, public face of its working-class "subject," but the trope of the "split subject"—the pervasive speaking voice of the country narrative—also suggests that this working-class "subject" is split, secretly "tore up" and immersed in vivid memories and inarticulate silence and in a sense of loss so powerful that it threatens to shatter the ever more fragile facade of community and sociability in post-Desert Storm American society. In order to grasp the dialectical, historical character of this "threat"—which may have progressive possibilities—we must grasp the allegorical salience of the split subject. For cultural critics, this task is our own version of "the bitch about country music."

Acknowledgements: My immense debt to my teacher, Kathleen Stewart, will be obvious to those who read her paper in this volume. I am also grateful to Steven Feld, Ted Gordon, Greg Urban, Mari Keefe, fellow students at The University of Texas at Austin, and to all of my consultants and friends at Ann's Other Place, Lockhart, Texas, and in other beer joints where I have been welcomed.

Note

[1]Quoted speech and descriptions of honky-tonk culture in this paper are drawn from a four-month period of intensive fieldwork in a small, rural honky-tonk bar near Lockhart, Texas, called "Ann's Other Place." Reported dialogue is transcribed from tape recordings. Participants in tape-recorded discourse were aware of the tape-recorder, which was always in plain sight on the bar during my recording sessions. Most of the participants in quoted dialogue have also read at least an initial write-up of my fieldwork, and I have worked through objections I have encountered with those who have raised them. At my own discretion, however, I choose to respect my consultants' privacy by using pseudonyms for patrons of Ann's. I gratefully acknowledge their hospitality and assistance. In quoted dialogue, triple-dots [...] indicate a long pause. My editorial elisions are indicated by triple dots in parentheses[(...)].

Works Cited

Bauman, Richard and Charles L. Briggs. "Poetics and and Social Life." *Annual Review of Anthropology* 19 (1990): 59-88.

Fox, Aaron. "The Jukebox of History: Narratives of Loss and Desire in the Discourse of Country Music." Forthcoming in *Popular Music* 11.1.

Jakobson, Roman. "Closing Statement: Linguistics and Poetics." *Style in Language*. Ed T.A. Sebeok. Cambridge: Harvard UP. 350-77.

Songs Quoted

"Jones on the Jukebox" by Mack Vickery, Becky Hobbs, & Don Goodman. Copyright

Alienation and Single Musicians on the Honky-Tonk Circuit

Karl Neuenfeldt

For many country musicians playing the bar, tavern and honky-tonk circuit as single musicians, a good deal of "road work"—many times lasting for months on end—is unavoidable. A recurrent complaint about the occupation is the rigor and necessity of travel. Willie Nelson's popular country song, "On The Road Again," paints a romanticized version of musicians as a band of gypsies rolling down the highway, seeing things they'll never see again, excited about going places they've never been before. This may happen occasionally, but often road work is tedious, redundant, lonely and, ultimately, alienating. Nelson's musical myth represents the road as the ultimate freedom from the world of 9-to-5: only occasionally does this myth lend itself to reality.

The question of alienation is very important in any examination of the work of being a single country musician. In the course of doing research and in private conversations with singles and personal experiences over the years, I have often encountered attitudes of extreme alienation. Although there exist different approaches to alienation (i.e. Durkheim), the causes of alienation among singles can profitably be examined from the perspective of classical Marxist thought because of its applicability to work situations. A single is only worth what someone is willing to pay for their musical labor, so talent becomes a commodity. They also work within a service industry where work tasks are fragmented and where workplace protocol and territoriality precludes their involvement in the larger economic activities of the venue. Singles very rarely are the owners of the venue at which they perform, although they may and usually do own their 'tools'.

Marxist analysis also suggests that human beings are quite literally made for work. In the case of some workers, like singles, the producer and that which is produced are one and the same thing. To separate the singer from the song is difficult. Therefore when there is a disjuncture between the goals of the producer/product (the single and his act) and the consumer (the audience and management) as to the value and intent of what is produced (the performance), alienation can result.

Alienation is the disconnection and separation that results when workers

This is an edited version of a paper entitled: "How Many Baths Can you Take In One Day?: Killing Time On The Road," that was presented at the American Anthropological Association Convention, Phoenix, 1988

140

are unable to maintain a stable connection to their social world because of "unnatural, alien work arrangements" (Erikson 2). Alienation can assume various forms; such as, the loss of contact with the product workers produce; the lack of involvement in the work process itself so that work is no longer creative; the cessation of a sense of community because workers are in direct competition with each other; and the onset of a sense of ennui when work becomes merely a means to make a living. This all-too-brief summary of Marxist thought about alienation reiterates opinions expressed by informants about what they felt were negative aspects of the occupation. Single musicians felt that when their acts were ignored they lost interest in the music they performed; they began to lose musical creativity; they became disconnected from any sense of musical or social community because of competition for work and attention. Music ended up as merely a "job," no longer directly concerned with esthetic considerations

Data

The data for this study was gathered from ten extended career histories (Langness; Crapanzano) of solo musical subcontractors, hereafter referred to as 'singles' in the Vancouver region of British Columbia, Canada.[1] The informants perform in taverns, restaurants and lounges throughout western Canada. These observations are also informed by 20 years of personal experience as a musician, writer and performer.

All of the informants include some country music in their repertoires. Country music itself is a major radio and television format in Canada. Playlists closely resemble those of American stations albeit with the addition of legislated requirements to include 33 percent "Canadian content." Many singles emphasize the country content of their act through their instrumentation, clothing styles and repertoire. One informant is so wrapped up in his country image that he recounted that patrons do not recognize him without his cowboy hat. He has been asked if wears his hat and boots to bed. Country audiences are recognized by singles, and agents, as loyal and supportive of acts as long as they are not "played down to." Although the gigs themselves are not always high paying or in upper scale venues, country singles appreciate that country gigs are often more consistent and dependable than Top 40 gigs.

Aspects of Alienation

There are three aspects of alienation connected to 'road work' that informants felt were primary in retarding occupational and personal satisfaction in their careers: first, the lack of a sense of community; second, the difficulty of establishing and sustaining personal relationships; and third, a pervasive sense of anonymity. These elements of alienation need to either be surmounted or resolved if a single is to continue to ply his or her trade successfully.

Lack Of A Sense Of Community

They say the road will cost you your wife. Now, I never believed that until my marriage broke up and yeah, it does cost you a lot of personal [and community] relationships. It costs a lot because you don't get to see the people you love as much as you should and God knows, they're not going to last forever and neither are you. There's a lot of precious time that gets lost by being on the road. (Duke)

A perceived lack of community can be a direct outgrowth of a single spending extensive periods of time travelling. Road work, by its very nature, entails the suspension of close ties not only with intimate partners but also with kith and kin.

There are two aspects of community present in this investigation: that of a larger musical community of singles; and that of the single as a part of a larger social aggregate. Whether or not there exists a musical community of singles is debatable. (Community here is used to refer not to a geographic locus, but rather a "community of interest" where individuals "share a set of norms which in turn define roles for them" [Merriam and Mack 211].) Singles possess a sense of community different from that of other popular musicians such as country or rock band members because singles do not operate as part of a collectivity, but rather as soloists. Also, a distinct musical community of singles does not exist, partly because they consistently compete directly with each other for employment. Co-operation within an occupation is difficult when the work force is solitary, fragmented, dispersed and/or independent by inclination. Thus, the sense of musical community for singles is fundamentally different from that of group musicians; singles often lack the mutual support, or the "us and them" attitude found in touring bands or entertainment troupes (Becker; Peterson).

In their study of the emerging jazz community, Merriam and Mack identified three elements of alienation and self-segregation in the social, psychological, and physical world of jazz performers. They suggested that the underlying causes of the jazz musicians' attitudes of rejection were: the rejection of jazz itself and the jazz musicians by the general public; their isolation from the general public by the nature of the occupation; and the inherent occupational dilemma that places being a creative artist and a commercial artist in contradictory roles, at opposite ends of a continuum, leaving the musician in the middle to effect a compromise (Merriam and Mack 213).

These criteria also apply to the working world of singles, with a few qualifications and may contribute to a sense of alienation. First, the music singles perform is not necessarily rejected by the general public; rather audiences are often indifferent due to the environment in which singles present their music. Second, the single is in many cases isolated, spatially and temporally, by the nature of the occupation, especially if the single must resort to road work to insure fuller employment. Third, whether one performs conventive or inventive music is usually decided quite rapidly when a single enters the occupation since most venues and agents demand conventive music. A single may be able to present a limited amount of inventive material, but the overwhelming emphasis is on being inventively conventive.

Rather than being classified as a full blown community, singles could more accurately be described as members of an occupational category because they remain atomized individuals who may or may not share an occupational ideology and may or may not exhibit expected behaviors. Singles are often precluded from extensive interaction with other singles because typically they work in isolation from one another and are often in direct competition for limited available employment. Singles may think of themselves as musicians, but most often lack a clear cut identification of themselves as singles and consequently, any extensive sense of specific musical community. When financial demands require that a musician perform, working as a single often ends up as a 'court of last resort' because of the ease with which singles can come and go from the occupation.

One of the informants, Leo, expressed a yearning for a sense of community, perhaps because he grew up in an isolated British Columbia coastal village where a sense of community was instilled early on. When Leo left performing and took a 'day-job' he noted there were two immediate changes in circumstance: first, he had a steady income which was positive in terms of his self-image; and second, he felt a return to a sense of community:

[It was good] just to feel part of the community again. [One] aspect of being a musician that is quite hard to take is the loneliness of it and the sense that you really are an 'odd duck' because I tend to think work is a very social thing. For most people who work 9-5, the social aspect of the job means a lot more than they would care to admit. I've always been a sort of social animal, and that *didn't* happen nearly so much when I worked as a musician.

Personal Relationships

[Introduction Moe uses when performing] 'Good evening ladies and gentlemen', I'm Moe and I am a 'born again' bachelor. I don't intend to get married anymore, but just about every three years I'm going to find a woman I hate, and buy her a house. (Moe)

You can maintain [a relationship] if she is willing to go through the extra work involved in staying at home and keeping the home fires burning while you're out conquering the world. Not many women are willing to do that in this day and age and I can't say I blame them. I mean, why should they? Would I be willing to do that? Would I be willing to bury my life? (Leo)

I meet a lot of guys out there [as an agent and musician], they sing their hearts out and when they get their cheques, they send off and support payments. They're paying for kids they had from a woman they lost while doing the job. (Moe)

These remarks illuminate an area of the informants' personal lives that has a critical influence on how well they adapt to occupational demands, the difficulty of establishing and sustaining personal relationships when intimacy is all too often limited to phone calls, usually collect. Many singles find themselves accumulating sizeable phone bills trying to keep in touch with someone, back somewhere, but they are not always successful in keeping contact with significant others in their lives.

Informants' statements, often a blend of poignancy and cynicism, emphasizes several problematic concerns about personal relationships: coping with loneliness and the issue of sexual fidelity; and, the effect of a negative self-image on relationships.

Moe, having been both a single and an agent, had a blanket assessment of singles, the occupation and relationships: "It ruins personal relationships you have 'cause you're on the road all the time." Moe doubts relationships can remain monogamous, or committed: "Let's face it, if you're six weeks on the road, you can't expect her to be there when you get back, and if she is, she's lying."

Jon was ambivalent about going on the road on an extended tour. He enjoyed the travel and adventure but admitted that loneliness and the lack of prolonged intimacy often dogged him. He said it was hard to remain faithful, "You can't really have a steady girlfriend if you go on the road, I mean, how do you remain faithful after 7 or 8 weeks. You know there's always someone who takes an interest in you, or you in them." When asked if the recent AIDS issue had affected his sexual activity on the road, he remarked, "Well, you have to be a little more selective, but it doesn't seem to matter now because disease can be with very classy people as well as all the way down to skid row." However, he would prefer a monogamous relationship: "I'd rather have a steady girlfriend [because] you're not going to get a disease as long as you're both faithful. Maybe if the woman was special enough I could maintain being faithful after 2 or 3 months of being on-the-road." Like Moe, he is dubious his partner could remain faithful during his long absences, even if he did: "I can't expect a woman to be faithful to me if I am gone for two or three months. Or even want to maintain a relationship unless they really liked their freedom."

Leo also found maintaining intimate relationships while he was working as a single to be difficult. He said that with the stability of his present relationship and the AIDS scare he does not meet a lot of women. In the past he did establish liaisons, some lasting and some proverbial 'one night stands'. He feels some musicians stay on-the-road because: "you do meet people sometimes. The musician is seen as having a skill or talent, but that can be a negative thing because the women you meet aren't necessarily the ones you *want* to meet. They are often lonely people running away from something, and you're the person they can sort of dump on and jump on."

The myth of singles engaging in an endless stream of one night affairs was laughable to Benny, "Since I've been on the road [three years] I had one, one night stand and that was that!" Brief romantic encounters are not what Benny prefers. He recognizes that that might be an incentive for some singles, but not him. He did try to maintain a relationship with a woman while performing out of town but she was a 'workaholic' and he was mostly gone. When he came back into town she had her life organized around him not being there so he felt left out. Benny finds relationships "very hard." Even if he had a woman back home he admits she would have cause to be leery of his fidelity because "when you're around women all the time, temptation is right there."

Aside from the effects of loneliness on relationships, another concern of some singles was how a negative self-image could have a deleterious effect on their personal lives. For both Eric and Leo, a negative self-image was a problem while working as singles.

Eric recalled that keeping a relationship going while performing in bars put a lot of strain on his primary relationship because: "I was so unhappy. I felt under a lot of pressure all the time because I was not financially secure. And there was a lot of pressure to be danceable and give the people what they wanted, even though it really wasn't what I wanted to give them." Being a single did have a major positive influence on his life since Eric met his wife at a gig where she was a manager. He realized that to give the relationship the opportunity to remain strong and viable he had to quit playing in places that put a strain on him, his self-image and his primary relationship.

Leo also felt strongly that being a struggling musician made him harder to live with and made it harder to keep a relationship afloat. None of his relationships survived when he was doing music full time. When asked why he thought that had happened he replied: "I think it was hard for me to carry on a serious personal relationship when my mate is making two to three times as much money as I am and I am working just as hard, or harder. You feel sort of stupid in a way, because, whether we like it or not, our self worth is determined to some extent by the amount of money we make." Leo thinks that particular view of success is, in itself, too simplistic because he objectively knows he does not need much money to be happy, but he does require recognition that what he is doing is recognized as being accomplished in his field of endeavor. Being a financially marginal musician, who felt he was working hard but was as of yet unrecognized, was very hard on Leo and whatever relationships he established. He knows that leaving full-time music and branching out into other fields contributed to the stable relationship he now enjoys.

Personal relationships are not totally tied to occupational considerations but they do color a single's perception of themselves and therefore their work. Many singles sing and write love songs, living them is another matter entirely.

Anonymity

Generally, I think all musicians feel that when you're up there, and the lights are shining, and you're doing it, you're God. And when you're walking around in the day, you're just a bum. (Mac)

A final aspect of alienation that singles experience is anonymity both at and away from the workplace. For many singles, two paradoxes they deal with constantly contribute considerably to a feeling of anonymity: 1) being the sonic centre of attention while performing and yet at times being completely ignored while performing and 2) being the social centre of attention while on-stage and socially invisible when off-stage. To work in an innately social occupation yet not necessarily feel a part of the socializing is a confusing contradiction that can necessitate a difficult separation of ego from art.

These conflicts are most in evidence when singles work on-the-road where they may not have a social support group to help them cope with an unsupportive work environment. Singles also often find themselves with large blocks of free time. The usual performance is four to five hours. If a single sleeps 8 hours there still remains 12 hours which the single must fill with meaningful activity.

Continual movement from place to place, gig to gig, makes superficial social encounters the norm, often times precluding the development of more intimate relationships and friendships. If a single is made to feel, or allows himself to feel, an outsider often enough, eventually he will define himself thus. He must adopt strategies to cope with the social and occupational reality that a solo musician in a strange place is going to be perceived as a stranger. If he does not implement survival strategies, the self-fulfilling prophesy of musician as perennial outsider can leave him a victim, a "burned out" casualty of life on-the-road.

Benny noted that he had had some good times on-the-road, but had to force himself to be outgoing and active rather than remain anonymous and inactive. A major solace for him when on-the-road is songwriting because "it's a great emotional time to write because you're feeling this loneliness, and you have to have emotions to write a song." Benny gets incentive and song ideas from the people he meets. He finds songwriting beneficial because "it keeps you interested, for a little while. You get kinda bored shopping." Benny tries to fight anonymity by socializing, writing and rehearsing, but still finds that sometimes it is a losing battle. He cannot always overcome the tedium of the road, "you try to keep yourself busy and when you've got nothing to do, that can be very, very tiring sometimes."

Jon also recounted experiencing the pangs of anonymity while on-the-road. He summed up how he feels overall about road work with this bleak assessment: "You can only sit in the hotel so long, or go down to the coffee shop for so long, or walk in the rain so long before you're totally drenched and depressed." "Killing time" when the weather is good is no problem for Jon, since he engages in an array of outdoor activities. Winter time is the most difficult for him because British Columbia's climate can be cold and rainy. When he finds himself inside a lot he either hangs around the mall or his room. However, he said, "You can only watch so much TV and only practice so much a day because when you're performing four hours a night your throat gets worn out." His main recourses are to get out into nature and force himself to interact with people. He enjoys the out of doors: "Being out in nature is like being with my God, my maker. When I get out and walk for a whole day, just consuming the fresh air and the scenery, it rejuvenates me and really helps me keep going." Interacting with people is also important, "there's always nice people on the road. If you have an open mind, open heart, and are susceptible to talking to strangers and being the first one to take that bold step and say 'Hello', you can combat that lonely feeling somewhat. But that lonely feeling is usually the need to be close to someone."

Moe succinctly stated how he felt about being anonymous while performing as a road musician, "You're a hero at night, you're a real star and everybody wants to take you back to their house for a party and they want you to bring your guitar. But when you're not on the stage you're a nobody, you're a bum." He recalled a three week gig he had done in a small logging town on Vancouver Island that seemed to go on forever. He felt there was nothing to do there and he did not know anyone. What made it worse was that his accommodation was even poorer than the business the bar was doing. He had to be 'on-call', but "there were no customers in the bar, which made it really depressing. I had no TV in the room and it was the kind of place where the bed had three legs on it. Whenever a customer came into the bar the manager'd take a pool cue and bang on the ceiling and I'd have to come down and sing."

When asked how he had eventually filled his days he replied, "I took a lot of baths or I'd just wander around and look in the shop windows. And when I got really depressed I'd go and buy a shirt or something or go across the street to the pet store window and watch the gerbils go at it. [Being on the road] is horrible. I mean, how many baths can you take in a day?" Three weeks of being a stranger in a strange land had had a decidedly deleterious effect on Moe. His recollections may appear to present a surreal scenario, but similar situations are experienced by many singles.

Summary

If a single musician cannot cope with the three aspects of alienation addressed here, they may quit the occupation entirely. If they do not quit they may scale back their performances to part time and try to reintegrate themselves into the larger social community, or, they may retreat further into themselves until they end up "burnouts." If the hours of a single's day remain unstructured or are perceived by others as bereft of purposeful activity, then the single truly is "killing time," in an often desperate attempt to try and impose some sort of regime and by projection, meaningfulness, on his solitary existence. When a single ends up just "killing time," too often his creative spark also dies in the process.

A single's place within a larger social community is problematic because their life and work styles are structured along fundamentally different lines than those of the bulk of the population. Singles work while most others pursue recreation, they sleep while others work, and they move through time and space cut off from consistent interactions with family and friends. Informants remarked they often find it difficult to feel a part of a social community when they are on the social periphery of both the venues at which they work and the places to which they travel. A sense of anonymity, being a perpetual "stranger in a strange land," perhaps goes hand in hand with a sense of a lack of community; the former existing on a personal level, the latter on a societal level.

All the informants felt the establishment and maintenance of intimate personal relationships were exacerbated by the culture, organization and structure of the occupation. Most had been married or in serious relationships that had evaporated somewhere along the way in the midst of their career aspirations. Many had children who did not live with them, but who they supported.

Even given the problematic aspects of 'road work', however, informants held out hope that it was possible to affect a compromise between the emotional needs of their hearts, the creative call of their muses, the financial demands of their pocketbooks and the means that they believed might help them realize their musical dreams, becoming a country music star.

Note

¹The data does not claim to be "statistically representative" but rather "logically representative" since it does allow for "logical inference" as emphasis was placed on the "theoretically necessary linkages, among the features of...[the] case stud[ies]" (Mitchell 206-207).

All informant names appearing in this text are psuedonyms.

Works Cited

Becker, Howard. "Some Contingencies of the Professional Dance Musician's Career." *Human Organization* 12 (1953).

Crapanzano, Vincent. "Life Histories in Review." *American Anthropologist* 7 (1984): 953-959.

Erikson, Kai. "On Work and Alienation." (Presidential Address to the American Sociology Association in 1985) *American Sociological Review* 51 (1986): 1-6.

Langness, Louis L. *The Life History In Anthropological Studies*. New York: Holt, 1965.

Merriam, Alan and Raymond Mack. "The Jazz Community." *Social Forces* 38.3 (March 1960).

Mitchell, J. Clyde. "Case and Situational Analysis." *The Sociological Review* 31 (1983): 187-211.

Peterson, Richard. "Artistic Creativity and Alienation: The Jazz Musician vs. His Audience." *Arts in Society* 3 (1965): 244-248.

Nashville Skyline:
The Business Of Country Music

In 1946, in Nashville, the newly formed Acuff-Rose publishing company signed Hank Williams to a song writing contract. In so doing, the company followed in the footsteps of Ralph Peer, the legendary Okeh/RCA record executive who, in the 1920s, realized that popular recordings of folk tunes and standards sung in twangy voices by "hillbillies" were not likely to be terribly commercially successful.

Peer began searching out those singers who also could (and did) write their own material and signed them to contracts. Instead of purchasing their songs outright—which was the way things were done at the time—Peer asked for a share of the royalties that would be realized on each song. This new system emphasized the development of on-going relationships with particular singers and songwriters in the country field, thus creating the underpinnings of an industry dependent on the creation and marketing of new musical material that only *sounded* as if it was traditional in nature.

This developing country music industry, at first located in various cities such as Chicago, New York and Cincinnati, began to center in Nashville after World War II and has altered the skyline and image of that city ever since. The industry has also created a strong and on-going debate (touched upon in Jensen's article in the previous section of this book) concerning the authenticity of the music thus produced. Is country music a modern form of folk tradition, or, by dressing itself up in rhinestones, electric guitars and audit sheets, has it become only another crass, commercial urban noise?

Folklorist Neil Rosenberg, in his essay, discusses this question with respect to modern country music—is it popular, or is it folk? His conclusion: "Yes, at various times it was, is, and can be either or both." Rosenberg identifies a major schism in country music, yet shows just how difficult it is to categorize a particular song as traditional or folk. As he shows, the same song, under different performance and recording conditions, can easily be seen as reinforcing folk traditions of the people or as forcing bar musicians, in their playing of it, to be "grinding out products they often care little about."

The creation of modern country music is a complex process and clearly not an idealized situation of a single artist sitting down and creating a song all by herself. In "The Commercial Art World of Country Music" I use sociologist Howard Becker's concept of "art worlds" to view the process of country music creation. This perspective draws attention to the complexity and interdependence involved in the industry, from the area of song writing to the creation and marketing of singer and group images—the social production, in a complex decision-making matrix, of country music.

149

150 All That Glitters

In what Charles Jaret calls a "vinal crap game," is there any way of predicting the success of a country song with any real degree of accuracy? Jaret, in "Characteristics of Successful and Unsuccessful Country Music Songs," addresses this question with a statistical analysis of hit country songs in which he looks at the lyrical and musical traits of the songs, as well as the fame and gender of those who sing them, to see if any particular patterns emerge.

In contrast to Jaret's statistical survey of the pop charts, John Planer focuses on a single song, Conway Twitty's "Tight Fittin' Jeans"—a song that reached the number one spot on the country charts in September of 1981. Plane dissects this song lyrically, musically and with respect to styles and conventions to illuminate the complexities involved in creating a "simple" country tune.

Playlist

The Lilly Brothers	Early Recordings	Rebel
Chet Atkins	Picks The Best	RCA
K.D. Lang	Shadowland	MCA
David Briggs, Norbert Putnam, et al	Area Code 615	Polydor
Dirt Band	Will The Circle Be Unbroken?	United Artists
Waylon, Willie, Tompall and Jessi	Wanted: The Outlaws	RCA
Conway Twitty	Classic Conway	MCA

Country Music—
Popular or Folk?*

Neil V. Rosenberg

Is country music popular or folk? My short answer to this question is: "Yes, at various times it was, is, and can be either or both." My explanation follows, but first a few words about definitions.

The term "country music" came into general use in the 1960s, a few years after the Country Music Association (CMA), a trade association, was established. Folklorist Bill Ivey, Director of the CMA's Country Music Foundation, has pointed out that in 1968 the first edition of Bill C. Malone's *Country Music U.S.A.*:

established 'country music' as the term describing an entire musical tradition (as opposed to, for example, 'country and western'), and...clearly placed bluegrass, western swing and cowboy music as subsets within that large tradition—relationships that were by no means accepted in the late 1960s. (91)

So the term "country music" was created by this branch of the popular music industry during the 1950s and accepted within a decade by consumers and scholars alike.

The distinction between popular and folk is a modern one; prior to and during much of the nineteenth century scholars used the two words almost as synonyms. William Thoms' 1846 coinage of "folklore" was an act of linguistic politics which replaced the Latin root words "popular antiquities" with the Germanic root words "folk lore." Professor Child called the ballads he canonized "popular," but throughout the twentieth century they have been considered the epitome of "folk" (Bell). In recent years some British scholars of what I would call folksong have returned to using "popular," again for reasons of language politics.[1] Today for working purposes let us start with the distinction between popular and folk as set forth by Narvaez and Laba:

...popular culture refers...to cultural events which are transmitted by technological media and communicated in mass societal contexts...folklore performance is artistic performance which is transmitted and communicated by the sensory media of living, small group encounters. (Narvaez and Laba 1)

*An earlier version of this paper was read at "From Folk To Pop And Back Again," a conference and project sponsored by *Salt* magazine on the interaction of folk culture and popular culture, June 20, 1989, in Portland, Maine.

This distinction focuses upon event and performance rather than upon product, mentifact or artifact—a focus reflecting the recent interests and priorities of folklorists. An earlier and still essential folkloristic perspective is one which focuses upon the contents of performances as discrete cultural items: songs, tunes, stories and so on. It was from this perspective that folklorists pioneered the serious study of what was then called hillbilly and is now called country music. In the 1930s and 1940s brief reviews and discographical comments by Halpert, Lomax and Seeger identified folk songs and tunes on hillbilly records (Halpert; Lomax; Seeger). In 1951 Wilgus argued in the *Journal of American Folklore* that hillbilly records were the modern day equivalent of broadsides, the cheap popular print media which folklorists have long recognized as playing a pivotal role in the transmission of folksong. Subsequent research by Wilgus and other folklorists in collaboration with hillbilly record collectors like John Edwards paved the way for the establishment in 1962 of the John Edwards Memorial Foundation (JEMF) under the auspices of the folklore program at UCLA and led to a hillbilly music panel at the 1962 American Folklore Society meetings from which came the 1965 "Hillbilly Issue" of the *Journal of American Folklore* (Green 68-80; Greenway 231-5; Wilgus, "Hillbilly Issue" 195-288; Wilgus, "A Note" 320). By 1968, the year in which the American Folklore Society published Malone's canonic history *Country Music U.S.A.*, Wilgus could write with confidence in an American folklore textbook that: "A knowledge and understanding of hillbilly music is an essential part of the equipment of the American folklorist" (Wilgus, "The Hillbilly" 271).

By the 1970s American folklorists had successfully established a beachhead for country music as an acceptable topic for academic research, based on the argument that as a working-class expression based on folk tradition, it was a legitimate component of national culture. Since then, there has been a tendency to accept the connection without question—many studies of and commentaries about country music allude to it as a kind of folk music. Often this is nothing more than a way of affirming its legitimacy as a cultural topic. But folklorists have questioned this facile connection for a number of reasons. Let us look first at the question of the producers.

In a recent review of Malone's second edition of *Country Music U.S.A.*, Bill Ivey argues that Malone has uncritically accepted folklorists' interpretations of country music as a popular-culture extension of a community-based oral tradition. He suggests that evidence from the biographies of country performers emphasizes their individuality and shows that they actually are attempting to distance themselves from their communities and families. "Their work," said Ivey, "may do nothing more than reveal the depth of their need to stand before an adoring multitude" (92).

In *The Anthropology of Music*, Alan Merriam made a case for viewing such distancing as inherent in the social role of the musician. He called the question of social status "among the most complex and fascinating aspects of the behavior of musicians" and presented cross cultural evidence for "low status and high importance, coupled with deviant behavior allowed by the society and capitalized upon by the musician" (Merriam 133, 137). This issue was central to the debate among Anglo-American folksong scholars during the 1970s about whether or not folksong composers must be "deviant" in order to create.[2] If Merriam is right about deviance, then both folksingers and country singers may be socially distanced from their community in certain ways and still have a close connection with it.

Another way of examining Ivey's point is to ask if folksingers and country music performers are cut from the same social fabric, or do they represent fundamentally different cultural impulses? Anne and Norm Cohen were confronting this question when they observed that while at the dawn of country music in the 1920s folksong collectors and record company agents combing the southern mountains frequently worked in the same communities, sometimes even recording the same performers, they ultimately documented different repertoires. The Cohens concluded that these differences were explained by two types of folk performance tradition, a domestic (or private) one to which folklorists were drawn and an assembly (or public) one which provided the record companies and radio stations with their hillbillies (Cohen). Behind these distinctions, subsequently confirmed by other research, lie two assumptions: first, that a continuum exists between the two traditions and second, that both reflect close, though different connections between traditional musical performers and their communities. This is one way of explaining why not all folksingers become professionals and why some do.

As the Cohens' example shows, a consideration of divergent repertoires can easily lead to a discussion of divergent performance traditions, traditions, personalities and the like. But what about the repertoires themselves? Scholars who analyzed the earliest country music repertoires found that many of the hillbilly musicians performed songs and tunes which folklorists could identify as folksongs. It appeared that later, as the profession became commercialized, the competitive demand for new material diminished this folk component.

This model of old folksong product being replaced by new popsong product in country music is an oversimplification. First of all, the boundaries between the two forms are never clear. As far back as we have good data about popular song, we can find evidence that some of this music finds its way into folk tradition. Often it is altered in the process. This still happens today in country music. We also can find in the history of popular song that old songs are offered to consumers as new ones, and that new songs are sometimes offered as old. This too still goes on in country music. In fact the history of every song is unique. Moreover, when people make genuinely new songs, whether for personal or commercial reasons, they not only draw from their own imagination but also utilize both contemporary and older ideas from other songs. This mixing of seemingly divergent streams happens because the rhetorical goals of the producers frequently overlap: they write in similar ways about the same kinds of things.

Folklorists' decisions about identifying certain performances as folksongs depend upon their definitions. The performance definition articulated at the beginning of this paper clarifies a distinction that appears to underlie all of the divergences and confluences I have discussed so far: that when people perform or compose music for a living they must produce more and do so within a marketplace of some kind. Usually they do not radically alter their social perspectives when they become professionals. Folk culture knowledge persists alongside the mass society context and technological media tools of their trade and can be an important part of their professional life, as the following example shows.

This is a recording made on September 23, 1957, in what might seem an unlikely spot—Westbrook, Maine, on the outskirts of Portland in the studio of Event Records, a small company owned by a local businessman, Allerton "Al" Hawkes. On it is heard a four man band, the Lilly Brothers. It features Everett Lilly singing "John Henry" and accompanying himself on the mandolin. The other band members also play instruments: Mitchell B. Lilly, guitar; Don Stover, banjo; and Bob Libby, bass. At two points in the recording an unidentified individual—probably Al Hawkes—uses some kind of percussion instrument to recreate the sound of John Henry's hammer striking the spike.[3]

"John Henry"
As recorded by the Lilly Brothers and Don Stover for Event Records in 1957. Issued on Event E-4272 (Westbrook, ME, 1959); reissued on County 729 (Floyd, VA, 1971); and on Rebel CD-1688 (Roanoke, VA, 1991). (sound effects: Hammer: x x x)

1 (mandolin break)

2 John Henry he was a little bitty boy
   No bigger than the palm of your hand
   His mammy looked down at John Henry and said
   Johnny gonna be a steel driving man, lord lord,
   Johnny gonna be a steel driving man.

3 (banjo break)

4 John Henry he said to his captain
   Captain, you're going into town
   Bring me back a nine-pound hammer
   For I want to see that railroad down, lord lord,
   I want to see that railroad down.

5 (mandolin break)

6 John Henry said to his shaker
   Shaker you better pray
   For if I miss that little piece of steel
   (x x x)
   Tomorrow'll be your dying day, lord lord,

Tomorrow'll be your dying day.

7 (banjo break)

8 John Henry went up on the mountain
He looked down on the other side
The mountain was so tall, John Henry was so small
He laid down that hammer and he cried, lord lord,
He laid down that hammer and he cried.

9 (mandolin break)

10 John Henry he had a pretty little woman
Her name was Polly Ann
John Henry took sick and had to go to bed
Polly drove steel like a man, lord lord,
Polly drove steel like a man.

What is folk and what is pop about this recording? First of all there is no doubt that the song itself came to the three principle band members directly from oral tradition. This is a song about their home, for the Lilly Brothers and Don Stover are natives of Raleigh County, West Virginia—the heart of the coal fields, next to Summers County, site of the Big Bend Tunnel where the legendary steel driving man is said to have fought his battle with the steam drill. This is one of the best known folksongs of the American South, so well known that most people who sing it have heard versions which differ from theirs.[4] In 1962 Carter Stanley, a musician of about the same age as Everett Lilly from Dickenson County, Virginia, one county away across the border form Raleigh, told an audience at a folk music nightclub in Hollywood:

This next song, if there was a, in my opinion, a folk song, this is one of 'em. It's a story about a colored boy from the state of West Virginia. Been lots of stories told about it, in many different ways, and I've always liked 'em all. By that I mean there's been many versions of this song done. All about John Henry. We'd like to tell you the story in our way of John Henry that died in the Big Bend Tunnel near Beckley, West Virginia. (*Copper*)

Beckley is the seat of Raleigh County. Carter Stanley and his brother Ralph performed at least two distinctly different versions of "John Henry." Bill Monroe, another musician in the same cultural orbit as Lilly and Stanley, told a rowdy crowd at his festival in Bean Blossom, Indiana, in June, 1978:

John Henry? You don't like that? Boy you ought to like that, that's one of the old timers that we all heard when we was kids, John Henry the Steel Driving Man.

Monroe does the song differently every time he sings it, knowing more verses to it than he ever uses in a single performance.

This is testimony for the primacy of folk tradition in the Lillys' and Stover's knowledge of the song. At the same time we can be certain that early in life they heard it performed by professionals on radio and record, and probably saw it in songbooks too. This is typical of the pop-folk connection in country music: folksongs appear in popular culture contexts which serve to reinforce and spread such songs in folk tradition.

What about this recording? If it functioned to bolster "John Henry" in tradition, what was the intention of the performers on September 23, 1957? Was this music being made as pop or folk? Luckily there are ethnographic documents concerning the Lilly Brothers and Don Stover which can help us examine the connections between sound and intention in this performance (Charters; Fleischhauer; McDonald; Tribe). In voice production, melodic ornamentation and choice of text, singer Everett Lilly was attempting to be true to his own cultural ideals. These are dominated by a combination of a sense of personal style with a sense of appropriateness based on the singing of his elders and peers and on the early radio performers who became his models. He was not singing in a way that was consciously calculated to reach a wider market by making changes that would appeal to listeners far removed from his own culture.

As we move from the voice to the instruments we move from folk towards pop in some ways. The guitar and mandolin of the two Lilly Brothers reflects their synthesis of a widely popular southern hillbilly sound of the 1930s and 1940s, the brother duet. It was a new sound then; today it persists in rural southern folk music traditions and is resurgent in contemporary country music.

The banjo of Don Stover is another move in the direction of pop; Stover grew up playing an old traditional brush style of banjo and began picking in the three-finger style heard on the record only when he was in his early twenties and heard Earl Scruggs playing with Bill Monroe on the Grand Ole Opry and on Columbia Records. Today this style is more or less accepted as a traditional mode in West Virginia. But in 1947 Stover chose this as a new way of playing old tunes and new tunes on a traditional instrument (although he still maintains his skill in the older style). Ten years later his banjo breaks on this recording were innovative, yet reflected his training in traditional music. He chose to use an older traditional open D tuning—one often associated with "John Henry" in both banjo and guitar performances—but the way in which he actually picked the melody was unique. Of all the aspects of this recording, this is the one most copied by other musicians.

The bass player provides an underpinning to the recording just as he would have in live performances; Libby played sometimes with the band, but not regularly, and it is probably safe to say that the bass was present to make the music more solid and to flesh out the sound—rather than because the bass had some traditional connection with the song. Finally, what about the sound effects, made to denote the hammer's sound? These are unique to the recording and represent an attempt to aurally dramatize the music and the text on the record for a mass audience. Only on this recording was that sound heard in a performance of "John Henry" by the Lilly Brothers.

So much for what happened on September 23, 1957. But what about the broader cultural context of the record and the musicians? Are they pop or folk musicians? All began as folk musicians, performing in small group contexts. By the late 1940s the Lilly Brothers were performing on radio and making records in West Virginia. They were full-time professional musicians. From 1950 to 1952 Everett Lilly worked as a member of the Flatt and Scruggs band, then moving from regional to national popularity in country music. To use my own descriptive terminology, the Lillys were journeymen professionals on the regional level; Everett had served an apprenticeship on the national level (Rosenberg).

In 1952, at the urging of fiddler Tex Logan, who was moving from West Virginia to Boston to begin work on a Ph.D. at MIT, the Lillys moved to Boston, taking childhood friend Stover with them. From then until 1970 they worked more or less steadily at "Hillbilly Ranch," a working class bar in downtown Boston. It was a hard and often unrewarding job, but a steady one, and one which is the norm for many journeyman country musicians. They played as much of the down home old-time and bluegrass music they liked as they could, but over the years had to develop a repertoire which catered to the serious drinkers who wanted to hear the country hits of the day, music they found necessary for their living but esthetically much less appealing.[5]

By 1970 they had become nationally known as a bluegrass band. This happened largely because of their recordings. How did people outside of West Virginia and Boston come to know of the Lilly Brothers? First of all, Everett's name was placed on the labels of the Flatt and Scruggs Columbia records on which he sang with Lester Flatt. Next came their Event records. A 1956 recording session in Westbrook produced the first Event single. In a nationally circulated monthly pulp, *Country Song Roundup*, it was advertised as "bluegrass style music" by Jimmie Skinner's mail order record shop in Cincinnati. Following that Don Stover spent a season working with Grand Ole Opry star and bluegrass patriarch Bill Monroe, a move which enhanced his credentials and made his name known to fans who saw him on tour with Monroe. He had just rejoined the band when they recorded "John Henry." Event did not, however, release the single until February, 1959, probably because soon after it was made Everett left the band for another stint with Flatt and Scruggs, who were now also on the Grand Ole Opry and becoming more popular than Monroe. In the meantime Don Stover, B. Lilly and Tex Logan had been included on Mountain Music Bluegrass Style (FA 2318, 1959), an album produced by Mike Seeger for Folkways Records of New York. This album presented bluegrass as a kind of contemporary folk music and was not released until after the Event single of "John Henry." In the summer of 1959 this single and the Folkways album were both being marketed nationally by Jimmie Skinner.

Everett Lilly was never comfortable calling his music bluegrass, but by the early 1960s their band was regularly tagged with that label, and while playing country music at Hillbilly Ranch remained their regular job, they were ideally placed to take advantage of the folk revival interest in bluegrass. From

Cambridge and other New England hot spots of middle-class interest in folk music came enthusiasts who took banjo lessons with Stover, booked the band at hootnannies and festivals and bought Lilly Brothers albums on the Folkways and Prestige-Folklore labels.

To folk music enthusiasts in New England the Lilly Brothers and Don Stover were authentic folk. In view of the fact of their long professional careers some folklorists might contest this conclusion and characterize them as pop musicians. Using the performance definitions mentioned earlier we can see that they have had their feet in both camps all along. But I think that the picture is not complete without considering its symbolic and metaphorical dimensions. If performers like Dolly Parton, Bob Wills, Stompin' Tom Connors, Dick Curless and the Lilly Brothers are clearly unique individuals in the world of pop music, they are also potent wielders of the symbols of folk culture. They, and country music in general, hew to a populist rhetoric, a self-conscious tying of their image to their own personally declared roots. Moreover they participate in a continuing dialectic which is central to country music. This is the modernist versus traditionalist debate—the dialogue between uptown and downhome. This can also be seen as a battle between the bourgeois music industry that uses country music to sell ads on the radio, wanting it to be as slick as possible in order to be commercially successful, and the working class fans who claim country music for their own and think of it as tough, realistic and true.

When Everett Lilly sang "John Henry" at that studio over in Westbrook, he was sending a letter from home. It described familiar personalities and events in a personalized but familiar vernacular way. It was a successful attempt to make a living in a mass culture market utilizing a personal symbol of folk culture. Though it might mean more to the southerners who grew up with the song, it was heard and embraced by sympathetic listeners from New England to Japan who found their own meanings in it.

This accessibility of "John Henry" to outsiders can be explained in terms of its metaphorical meaning. It is a song about the personal hazards of industrial work—about death, alienation and the personal sacrifices of a loved one. Born to work, John is at first eager to "see that railroad down" even if it is costly to those working with him, as the second occurence of the sound effect warns us: if he misses with his hammer, it's death for his helper. Eventually though, John cries when he recognizes the magnitude of his task. Forced to sickbed, his job is maintained by a companion's extraordinary effort when his woman "drives steel like a man." As urban working class bar musicians, the Lilly Brothers and Don Stover became musical machines, forced for years to grind out products they often cared little about. In this sense the song "John Henry" can be seen also as a letter *to* home about life in Boston. In 1970 one of Everett Lilly's sons was killed in an auto accident in Boston. Grief-stricken at this sacrifice of a loved one to the urban way of life, Everett Lilly "laid down his hammer" and returned home. He moved with his family back to Clear Springs, West Virginia. The Lilly Brothers and Don Stover have reunited occasionally since then, but this marked the end of their professional careers together. When they recorded "John Henry" it was folk and it was pop. It told of their past and it foretold their future.

Notes

[1]The contemporary English position is articulated by Michael Pickering and Tony Green, in "Towards a Cartography of the Vernacular Milieu," the introductory essay to the collection of essays they edited in *Everyday Culture: Popular Song and the Vernacular Milieu* (Milton Keynes: Open UP, 1987) 1-38.

[2]In Henry Glassie, Edward D. Ives and John F. Szwed, *Folksongs and Their Makers* (Bowling Green, OH: Bowling Green State U Popular P, 1970) both Glassie and Szwed advance this argument. Ives dissented in his *Lawrence Doyle, The Farmer-Poet of Prince Edward Island* (Orono: U of Maine P, 1971) 243-53, observations which Glassie later accepted in his *Passing the Time in Ballymenone* (Philadelphia: U of Pennsylvania P, 1982) 799.

[3]Event E-4272, a 7" 45 rpm disc, lists "John Henry" as "(arr. Everette [sic] Lilly)" and published by Darleen Music, BMI. It also identifies Lilly as the vocalist and Don Stover as playing the "5-String Banjo." On the other side is a Carter Family song, "Bring Back My Blue Eyed Boy to Me" listed as performed by "Mitchell Lilly and Trio."

[4]A good survey of the scholarship and a listing of the many commercial recordings made of "John Henry" is given by Norm Cohen in *Long Steel Rail* (Urbana: U of Illinois P, 1981) 61-89. See also Brett Williams, *John Henry, A Bio-Bibliography* (Westport, CN: Greenwood, 1983.

[5]Michael J. Melford. "Working the Hillbilly Ranch" *Autoharp* (published by the Campus Folksong Club at the University of Illinois in Urbana) 27 (18 Dec. 1965): 1-3, conveys some of the ambiance of this seedy watering hole.

Works Cited

Bell, Michael J. " 'No Borders to the Ballad Maker's Art': Francis James Child and the Politics of the People." *Western Folklore* 47 (1988): 285-307.

Charters, Sam. "The Lilly Brothers of Hillbilly Ranch." *Sing Out!* 15 (July 1965): 19-22.

Cohen, Anne and Norm. "Folk and Hillbilly Music: Further Thoughts on Their Relation." *JEMF Quarterly* 13 (1977): 49-57

Copper Creek CCSS-V3N2. *Stanley Series Issue 10*. Roanoke, 1989. This is an LP album publication of a tape made at the Ash Grove in Hollywood, August 29, 1962.

Fleischhauer, Carl. "The Public Named Bluegrass Music." *Old Time Music* 21 (Summer1976): 4-7.

Green, Archie. "The Death of Mother Jones." *Labor History* 1 (1960): 68-80.

Greenway, John. "Jimmie Rodgers—a Folksong Catalyst." *Journal of American Folklore* 70 (1957): 231-5.

Halpert, Herbert. "Some Recorded American Folk Song." *American Music Lover* 2 (Nov. 1936): 196-200.

Ivey, Bill. Review of Bill C. Malone's *Country Music, U.S.A.*. 2nd ed. *Journal of Country Music* 11.1 (1986).

Lomax, Alan. "List of American Folk Songs on Commercial Records." *Report of the Committee of the Conference on Inter-American Relations in the Field of Music.* William Berrien, Chairman. Washington: Department of State, 1940. 126-46.

McDonald, James J. "Principle Influences on the Music of the Lilly Brothers of Clear Creek, West Virginia." *Journal of American Folklore* 86 (1973): 331-44.

Merriam, Alan P. *The Anthropology of Music.* Evanston: Northwestern UP, 1964.

Narvaez, Peter and Martin Laba. "Introduction: The Folklore-Popular Culture Continuum." *Media Sense.* Eds. Narvaez and Laba. Bowling Green, OH: Bowling Green State U Popular P, 1987.

Rosenberg, Neil V. "Big Fish, Small Pond: Country Musicians and Their Markets." *Media Sense.* Eds. Narvaez and Laba. Bowling Green, OH: Bowling Green State U Popular P, 1987. 149-66.

Seeger, Charles. "Reviews." *Journal of American Folklore* 61 (1948): 215-18.

Tribe, Ivan M. "Pros Long Before Boston: The Entire Career of the Lilly Brothers." *Bluegrass Unlimited* 17.12 (June 1974): 16-26.

Wilgus, D.K., ed. "Hillbilly Issue." *Journal of American Folklore* 78 (1965): 19 288.

_____. "The Hillybilly Movement." in *Our Living Traditions.* Ed. Tristram Potter Coffin. New York: Basic Books, 1968. (The book grew out of a series of Voice of America Broadcasts.)

_____. "A Note on 'Songs from Rappahannock County'." *Journal of American Folklore* 64 (1951).

The Commercial Art World
of Country Music

George H. Lewis

God bless the boys
Who make the noise
On 16th Avenue...

Lacy J. Dalton

The creation of popular music is a complex process and one that deserves a good deal of analysis. The old illusion that music is created in an artist's head, in a relative isolation from the world around him or her, is just that—an illusion. This sense of illusion is especially strong with respect to the creation of country music. As Bill Ivey, director of the Country Music Foundation, has remarked: "Critical writing about country music...has nearly always treated country music as a free-floating art form, subject only to the ebb and flow of musical style and cross-influence...as if business were something outside the music, rather than the music's reason for being" (Ivey 407).

The creation of music, especially popular music such as country, is a multi-stage social and organizational process involving many types of skills and persons and ultimately is judged by the economic criterion of financial results. It is, to paraphrase Howard Becker who has considered the creation of many types of culture in his seminal work *Art Worlds* (1982), a commercial art world in which the creation of music is not a lone artistic endeavor, but instead a joint product of all the people who cooperate to bring this work into existence, with the bottom line being the hope that this product will make money. Although, as Ivey notes, the country music business employs many who are deeply committed to artistic integrity, particular musical styles and even particular artists, the business itself is incapable of such loyalty. When Chet Atkins was asked to define the Nashville Sound, he put his right hand in his pants pocket and gently jingled the change. "That," Atkins said, "is the Nashville Sound" (Ivey 407).

Culture—in this case, the creation of country music—is more a process of manufacture, of social production, of sales, royalties and balance sheets, than it is the result of romantic, unfettered inspiration from the muse. My concern in this essay is with this social production of country music within its "art world."

The ideas and argument of this paper were first presented in a slightly different form by the author in the Keynote Address of the Western Regional Honors Conference, Portland State University, Portland, Oregon, April 1984.

161

I want to look at a segment of what C. Wright Mills has called the "cultural apparatus—all the organizations and milieux in which artistic...work goes on, and the means by which such work is made available to critics, publics and masses" (Mills 406). An art world consists of all people whose activities are necessary to the production of the characteristic works which that world defines as art or, in this case, country music. As Becker explains it:

> Members of art worlds coordinate the activities by which work is produced by referring to a body of conventional understandings embodied in common practice and in frequently used artifacts. The same people often cooperate repeatedly, in similar ways to produce similar works, so that we can think of an art world as an established network of cooperative links among participants. (Becker 34-35)

Take, for example, a live musical performance by Reba McIntyre or Garth Brooks. Although the audience usually reacts to it as such, the performance is not solely the creation of the artist who happens to be performing. It is created by many cooperating individuals, established in a network within a specific art world, of whom the performer is one, albeit fairly important, element.

The musical instruments that the band uses have had to be invented, manufactured, afforded and purchased. Rehearsals have had to have been held so everyone can learn to play the instruments and, more importantly, to play together. Back-up musicians must be recruited locally and rehearsed.

A sound system, with engineers to supervise the mixing from the various microphones and sound pickups, must be created and set up at the concert site. Lighting and costumes must be decided upon, made available and coordinated. Materials and musicians must be transported to the site and the stage must be set up.

Ads must have been placed, publicity arranged, legal contracts and documents scanned, agreed to and signed. Tickets must be sold and an audience that is capable of understanding and responding to the performance must be recruited—and must show up. Gate receipts must be added up and divided.

And that's really just the most obvious and immediate cast of characters in this one small segment of one musical art world. In this essay, I have chosen to focus on what I consider to be three major areas of critical concern in the production of country music, though there are other important facets of this process that I shall have time only to mention in passing.

First, I shall examine the process of the creation of the original cultural artifact, or, the translation of the initial idea in a creator's mind into a rough, tangible, cultural form. Second, I shall look at the coordination of tasks that are necessary to the production of culture and conventions that arise in art worlds as a result of repetitions of tasks necessary for cultural creation. Finally, I shall focus on the culture industries themselves—complex organizations that are uniquely characterized by a high degree of uncertainty as to what, out of all that they choose to work with, they should process into cultural product and, when they have made their choices, of how and to whom this product should be disseminated.

Song Writing: The Creation of Culture

As Mayakovsky, the Russian poet said, "those who wait for the 'heavenly soul of poetry' to descend on them are not likely to produce much culture" (57). This is true, in spades, when one considers the musical world of songwriting. As one of the Nashville songwriters interviewed said

> You should be able to sit down and write some kind of song after selecting a subject without the benefit of lighting, thunder, and bells. Occasionally, the lightening does strike and you have an idea dropped on you from nowhere that is complete and seems to write itself. But you shouldn't wait for this to happen. And if you concentrate on the work that you're doing, you don't have time to worry about that mood you're in.

From the perspective of professionals in the business of writing country songs, it is hard work—a process that has more to do with discipline and routine than it does inspiration. One of the best of these songwriters described his songwriting technique as follows:

> What I do is get up every morning, if I'm in a writing process, and take a yellow legal pad, think, jot down titles, little lyrics, thoughts, etc. To turn my mind on I listen to music—not country because I'd come out sounding like somebody else...I doodle and if I get something I like, I'll pick up the guitar and I'll sing it. I write in batches, 6 or 8 songs at a time. And depending on the mood I'm in, I'll pick the song I want to work on at that time. Sometimes I'll be working on one and I'll get an idea so I have to stop and work on that idea for a while. When I write, I write a lot at a time. (Gant 77-78)

Another writer claims to work himself into almost a trance-like state. He stays in one room and writes for about three days at a time. If he is not naturally inspired, which is often, he builds himself up to such a state deliberately by forcing himself to sit down and write. "I write 10 or 12 songs the first day, decreasing day by day until I have to quit because I'm exhausted. The first song is usually lousy, but they get better and better until after about the fifth or sixth song, I'm writing hits" (Lewis 40).

The creation of songs in the country field has become highly routinized, to a great extent because of the kind of division of labor that exists in this musical art world. Singer-songwriters like Rodney Crowell, Nanci Griffith or Loretta Lynn in her early years are the exception to the rule. Usually, songwriters are writing for somebody else and, if they are successful songwriters, they work for a publishing firm, like Acuff-Rose, that coordinates their efforts and tries to link recording artists with their "stable" of songs.

Generally, the songs accepted by a publisher are those which fit his image of a successful artist or type of artist and thus are the easiest to pitch. Typical judgements take forms like: "That's a perfect Ricky Van Sheldon song," or "This will be the new 'Islands in the Stream' for Kenny Rogers," or "I can hear Kathy Mattea or almost any of the new girl singers doing that," or "It may be fine as a personal statement, but it's not commercial; it starts off like Waylon

Jennings and ends up too intellectual."

Songs that the producer feels have only a good line or two, or in which they like the general idea or approach, may be accepted if they believe the songwriter is able and willing to take suggestions on rewriting the song to make it a more commercial product. Fred Rose, a writer-publisher who helped Hank Williams and many others, was known in Nashville as the "song doctor," for his work in this area (Ryan and Peterson 15).

Song doctoring is common in the industry and even artists who come to a session with their own material are likely to have it altered according to the whims of the producer before the session is over. Exceptions to this are artists and writers with a strong track record of hits, who have a financial argument to back up their creative ideas.

Much of the effort of publishing firms is devoted to what is called "pitching" songs to recording artists or those persons who choose the songs for the recording artists. When a firm hears, through the grapevine or via an industry tipsheet, that an artist is recording soon, the first step is to find out what sorts of songs are needed.

These requests, from the artist, might be for a "new woman's song," a "positive ballad," or "an up-tempo drinking song." If the publishing company has any songs that might fit, or might be altered to fit, demonstration tapes are played to the artist. If the songs are not available, the publisher may well ask one of his contracted songwriters to get something out in a hurry.

Songwriters will, many times, write songs aimed at certain artists, then try to pitch them successfully. Steve Goodman, for example, took "The City of New Orleans" first to Johnny Cash's *House of Cash*, but he rejected it, claiming later that he had been too busy to review any songs coming from individual songwriters at the time. The song, finally recorded by Arlo Guthrie, went on to become a huge hit in both the country and pop fields.

Sometimes songwriters can convince artists that they have the perfect song for them. Then, unless the artist is riding a string of hits and thus has power in the industry, what usually happens is the artist is left attempting to convince the producer of his or her session that the song is "right" and should be recorded. For instance, early in her career before she had much artistic clout, Patsy Cline would often attempt to convince her producer Owen Bradley to let her record certain songs. Songwriter Harlan Howard recalls:

I'd sit up in Owen Bradley's office and see her just about to cry fighting over material…Maybe the song wasn't all that great, but she was your friend, she was a good friend to have, and she'd go in and try her best. But Owen Bradley's sitting there, and he's the guy responsible for the production, he's looking for hits, and the more time you waste on mediocrity, the less chance you've got." (Jensen, "Patsy's…" 43-44)

Coordination of Tasks and Art World Conventions

A focus on the coordination of tasks and art world conventions is central to an understanding of the production of culture. To create the systems of meaning, an elaborate division of labor has evolved within most art worlds.

This means it is most important, in order to ensure smooth cooperation among specialists, that there be conventional ways of doing things, that actions can be anticipated and that the meaning of these actions can be fully understood.

This concern with convention is nowhere better illustrated than in the world of country music. For many years, the most powerful talent spotlight in the field was WSM's Grand Ol' Opry program, broadcast from the Ryman Auditorium, a large converted church located in downtown Nashville, Tennessee. This radio show, broadcast live, developed the conventions necessary to operate smoothly. And there were real challenges here. How to shuffle acts on and off stage quickly, do live commercials in between and not get tangled up in the jungle of cords and electrical equipment that covered the stage.

Early performers, with perhaps just an acoustic guitar or two, a banjo and a string bass, were fairly mobile. They could set up, play and scramble off stage during the Brown Mule Tobacco commercial and still leave time enough for the next group to set up. This ordered chaos of the early Opry is reflected well in Paul Hemphill's recollections of his first visit as a young boy:

> Lord, Lord. For the better part of the night I sat there mesmerized, undeterred by the stultifying heat and blinded by rhinestones as one by one my radio heroes meandered front-and-center, larger than life. Here came Roy Acuff yo-yoing and balancing a fiddle on his nose and singing "Great Speckled Bird," Little Jimmie Dickens shouting 'Sleepin' at the Foot of the Bed' while standing on an apple crate, big old raw-boned Martha Carson whapping out a gospel boogie called "Satisfied" on a guitar bigger than Dickens, Carl Smith (little Junebug Carter's husband, everybody knew that) with a powder-blue western-cut suit and pompadour hair crooning "'Am I the One?" And Ernest Tubb and Webb Pierce and Faron Young and Hank Snow, who had my father singing along when he did "Movin' On," all of them moving in and out of the spotlights as the huge canvas backdrops were raised and lowered every fifteen minutes to denote that segment's sponsor (Martha White Flour, Goo Goo Candy Bars)...(Hemphill 354)

With such a performance, it was better to have experienced musicians who worked relatively smoothly together and with the technicians who had to get the program on the air, than it was to work with those who had never done the Opry before. So the pattern became one of a large group of "regulars" and only a few invited guests—a predictable show that developed and sustained conventions of song length, singing style and choice of instruments, as well as smooth coordination in the backstage aspects of the show's presentation.

Drums, for example, were not allowed on the Opry stage for many years. Nor were electrified instruments. Part of this was due, of course, to the conservative nature of this art world, and thepredictability its producers and audiences dictated. But part of it also was due to the nature of coordinating and producing the show. In the social and physical environment of the Ryman and in the context of a live show, drums and electric instruments were just too disruptive of a worked out, semi-smooth routine.

Since the Opry's move to the huge slick sound stage at Opryland, things appear to go more smoothly. They have to, as shows from the new stage are televised, most often on the TNN cable network. And yet, though not as visible, the degree of coordination necessary to create the visually exciting show necessary for television is, if anything even higher than it was in the Ryman.

Similar coordinative routines have existed in the recording of country music along "Music Row" (16th Avenue) in Nashville. Although it has loosened up in the 1980s, in general the tradition in town has been not to have artists use their road bands for studio recording. Again, smooth coordination and the development of a certain predictable sound by the producer of the session plays an important part in this sort of decision. There is no hassle of rehearsing untested musicians. When a performer comes to town, he or she can be scheduled at a certain hour at the studio, walk in, and the regulars will be ready.

Although it's a bigger and less coordinated effort today, in the late 1960s there were only 25 or so musicians (out of a union of well over 300) who regularly worked all the sessions in Nashville (Denisoff 121). No wonder the music produced was so predictable and sounded so much the same.

These musicians, working together in this way, developed over time their own musical notation system. An artist or song writer, ready to record a song, would play or sing it and the session men would take notes on chord progressions. These notes, scribbled on bits of white paper, were the musical charts for the session.

The chart might, for example, read: 1 1—4 4—1. If the musicians decide to do the song in the key of C, then 1 refers to C. Two 1s means stay in C for two bars, then change to F (C, D, E. F). And so on. This example, 1 1—4 4—1, would come out as C C F F C in five bars of music.

Now, if the producer decided to do the song in the key of B Flat, then there is no lengthy transposition to be done. Just call 1 B Flat, then 4 would be E Flat. That's all the musician needed to know.

Not only is this convention—developed by a small group of musicians—important in that it facilitates coordination and speeds up Nashville recording sessions, it also serves the purpose of further locking other musicians, who do not understand the meaning behind the system or who are not experienced in using it, out of contention for jobs. This ensures regular employment for the inner group, many of whom can make $70,000 to $80,000 a year.

The Fate of Art in Culture Industries

The third, and final, aspect of the production of culture I want to look at more closely is the organizational setting in which this activity takes place, especially when the culture produced is popular and business involved is big. Paul Hirsch has labeled such organizations "culture industries," and they are different from most other formal organizations that exist to manufacture products. Characterized by *uncertainty* rather than predictability, with respect to what cultural products they should create and promote, culture industries exhibit a constant tension between, on the one hand, the bureaucratic need for rationality and control and, on the other, the need for novelty and innovation in product.

At what is known as the input boundary of the cultural industry, there stand selectors and screeners who try to make manageable an endless stream of cultural material—demonstration tapes, screenplays, songs—that compete for their attention. At the industry's output boundaries, those in charge of distribution seek to rationally sift through the created product, deciding how and to what extent it should be promoted in order to achieve maximum sales. In between, the product, in various stages of its production, is shepherded from one specialist to another on its way to completion (Lewis 35).

In no area—and especially at the input and output boundaries—is there any real certainty as to what products are going to do the best commercially in the market. Under such conditions of uncertainty, and with a need to make the most efficient, rational choices, power accrues in the hands of those who can most effectively convince others that what they are creating is what deserves the most support from the system as it moves through. "The point," as one country music producer put it, "is to make money, not art" (Ryan and Peterson 25).

In the world of country music, there is no dearth of material from which to choose at the input boundary. Outside of the hundreds of novice songwriters and performers that try to make it into the system each year, there is also the regular "stable" of artists and songwriters, all creating output from which the decision makers at this boundary have to choose.

In just considering the professionals, for example, Dennis Lecorriere lead singer for a group called Dr. Hook, claimed that over 2,000 songs were screened to find the 10 that fit the image and mood for their 1981 album (Peterson and Ryan 24). And even then, the album was not highly promoted by the record company—nor did Dr. Hook realize high hit sales from it.

The artists or songs most likely to be considered by the input decision makers are those that either adhere to a tried and true theme or pattern, or those who can be developed in line with such patterns. Producers who have a track record of hits are counted on to repeat themselves. Often times, they do so by following whatever pattern first broke for them, rather than by trying for something new.

Chet Atkins, for example, in looking back over his career as producer for RCA, pointed out that, in a session, "I started in telling everybody else what to do. I've always been that way, because most of the time I knew four chords and the other guys knew three" (Ivey 431). "I usually had about thirty-five to forty artists that I recorded myself. Of course, we'd make an album back then in one day—just go in a make twelve sides, four songs on a session" (Atkins 429).

The Nashville producer, as Chet Flippo has noted, is truly king. "He chose the songs, the pickers, the arrangements, the album cover, the strings and vocal backing used to 'sweeten' the whole package. The singer was almost an afterthought...The companies were selling records, not individual careers" (Flippo 456). As Rich Blackburn, head of CBS Records in Nashville, noted with respect to Ricky Scaggs: "When I signed him, he wanted to produce himself. I said, 'You can't.' And he said, 'Why not?' 'Because you're not qualified. You tell me you played in Emmylou Harris's band—big deal. So that makes you a producer? No" (Blackburn 16-17). In the case of Scaggs, Blackburn finally relented, but only because he checked with Rodney Crowell and Brian Ahern, Emmylou's producer and found both men vouched for Scaggs' ability in the studio. And then, Blackburn was taking a chance—this was a very big exception to the general rule.

Artists, many times, will be moulded into an image in order to get a contract and the promotional backing of a company. Or, in some cases, the company will fist develop the image, then go looking for the artist.

This latter was the case with Ricky Scaggs. Rich Blackburn recalls that with Scaggs, "we needed that sound on the roster, and we knew exactly what we were looking for. We had done enough research to know there was a strong feedback from consumer groups who had discovered country music through artists like Kenny Rogers, Dolly Parton, Willie Nelson—as these fans got into it, they wanted to know more about a traditional sound—with energy. So we knew *specifically* what we were looking for with Scaggs" (Blackburn 17).

The image the record company wants may, and often does, have little to do with how the artist sees him/herself—or even with the directions in which he or she wishes to go creatively. With the early success of Ricky Scaggs on Columbia, RCA wished to market a similar sound and signed the late Keith Whitley, who had played traditional music with Scaggs in Ralph Stanley's band. Whitley's traditionally oriented first album was, in the words of Joe Galente, head of RCA, a "commercial disaster." And so RCA decided to change Whitley's image and sound to a softer, more pop country sound. As Galente said: "We made the change on Keith Whitley...it's really altering your direction so you can become more commercially successful" (Galante 25).

Perhaps the most famous image created by contemporary country music is that of the "outlaw" associated with the careers of Willie Nelson and Waylon Jennings. The story that is perpetuated by the industry is that these two, showing great artistic integrity, held out against the closed Nashville establishment and finally, uncompromised, got their "sound" out to the public. The public, of course, loved it—and the reaffirmation of the romantic vision of the lonely, suffering, outsider as creator that it suggested. This is, of course, country music's version of the romantic vision of the artist as creator, discussed earlier.

For the industry, the good news is that this promotion tied into a deeply held cultural belief, worked. Willie and Waylon became superstars.

And the bad news is, as you might suspect, that's not how it happened.

Outlaws have been a theme in country music for many years. Both Johnny Cash and Marty Robbins, in the early 1960s, posed for albums in black gunfighter attire. The ploy then was to cash in on the popularity of westerns in both film and television viewing in America.

In about 1970, Lee Clayton wrote a song called "Ladies Love Outlaws," because, as he says, "country music from its inception has always been outlaw music...When I wrote the song, I wrote it tongue in cheek, then I saw it all get out of hand" (Thomas 18).

Waylon Jennings recorded the tune in 1972 and an album, with the song as its title cut, was released late that year. The song helped to revive this older concept in Nashville's consciousness. At about the same time, a disc jockey in Ashboro, North Carolina, telephoned Hazel Smith, who worked as a columnist in Nashville and in publicity for the Glaser Brothers. The disc jockey was doing a show featuring the music of Tompall Glaser and Waylon Jennings, among others, and was looking for a name for the show. Smith suggested he call it *Outlaw Music*, which he did. Eventually, the station took this on as a slogan of the sort of music they were broadcasting. They became very successful and regionally popular—a fact not unnoticed by the big Nashville recording companies (Denisoff 194).

Meanwhile, Waylon Jennings' new manager, Neil Reshen, while searching around for a concept to make the singer, under his management, more marketable than he had been, hit on emphasizing this same theme. Reshen had seen Waylon, who up until then performed clean shaven and with hair neatly combed and cut, ragged and with a beard he grew during a bout with hepatitis. The image of Waylon as outlaw began forming in Reshen's mind:

"I was totally instrumental in it," he said. "We laughed a lot because after we got the whole publicity thing done and that whole campaign—we shipped the promotion booklets—Waylon called me up and told me he shaved his beard and mustache off. But fortunately, he grew it back...Willie Nelson also grew his beard and we've been very successful with the image...There were literally hundreds of people who then added on to it. But Waylon and Willie got all the attention." (Denisoff 191-193)

The attention spread to the RCA production staff. Producer Jerry Bradley put together an album of previously recorded songs which he described to Chet Flippo. "I'm putting Willie and Waylon and Tompall (Glaser) together as the Outlaws, because that's the way they are regarded here in town. This is a package, a total package that I'm looking to break outside the country market" (Flippo 458).

The album, *Wanted! The Outlaws*, was released on January 12, 1976 with a large promotional effort by RCA. It not only raced up the country charts, but crossed over to the pop charts as well and was certified as gold by April. By December, it had sold over one million copies and was country music's *first ever* platinum album. Subsequent albums by Jennings and Nelson also went gold, selling over 500,000 copies apiece.

And yet, for all the publicity and fame, the image began to wear, on Jennings especially. He felt constricted by it. It began to dictate what he could record, what the public expected. Finally he wrote a song chiding the promotion campaign that made him a star. He called it "Don't You Think This Outlaw Thing's Done Got Out Of Hand?" and it referred to the image as a self-fulfilling prophesy, which it had become.

Manipulation of artist and product does not stop with image creation. Decisions are made, too, on whether particular songs will ever be released, and if so, their placement on an album—or if a certain one will be released as the next single and shipped to the country DJs. As Joe Galante has said with respect to The Judds and their targeted appeal to both the traditional fan and the younger pop audience: "It's the choice of singles. We try not to stray too far from either end of the mainstream. And certainly when they do their album they go both ways. They do something that tends to be more traditional, more country, and something that tends to be more rock" (Galante 24).

Marketing of the song also must be discussed, timing of release date, publicity, whether to do a video, how much to spend on the total promotional package. A strategy for getting critics to notice the song favorably, and those who make up radio playlists to listen to it, must be formulated and put into action. Finally, the record must be physically manufactured, art work for the sleeve created, pricing decided and shipping and distribution accomplished.

During these several stages of the decision-making process through which a song passes, it is referred to in the industry as "product." What is more, there are specific words used to depict the stage at which a cultural product is at: a song is called a copyright, a property, a demo, a tape, a dub, a transcription, a cut, a master, a side, a release, an A side, a pick, a selection, and finally, a hit or a dud (Ryan and Peterson 25). This nomenclature helps underscore the extent to which a piece of creative work is viewed by the industry as product, something to be manufactured in order to make a profit.

The important thing, in order to successfully get a piece of work through the system and distributed with enough promotional money attached to give it a chance in the market, is to develop a product image that is geared to most likely be accepted by the decision makers at the next link in the chain. And the easiest way to do this is to develop an image that is much like that of materials that have most recently passed successfully through the chain. In this way, increment by increment, piece by piece, country music is reshaped to look, sound and feel like what came before it.

This conservative shaping of the product has gotten the industry into trouble more than once, as listeners—turned off by the repetitious nature of the sound, stopped buying the product. This occurred in the late 1970s, for example, when the "Nashville Sound" had gained an aesthetic stranglehold on the music. This establishment sound, the creation of Chet Atkins, Owen Bradley and others who had been cranking out many hits with it, was finally effectively challenged by the Outlaw image and sound of Waylon, Willie and the boys. But, as Chet Flippo points out, this new image and sound did not have a real impact on the Nashville industry until their records began selling better than those of the establishment artists. As he says: "until their efforts translated into money—which is after all, what the system really understands and appreciates—they were laboring in the wilderness, as it were" (Flippo 468).

The Outlaw sound, in its turn, was co-opted and commercialized by the *Urban Cowboy* fad and became as predictable and formulaic as the Nashville sound was before it. Spurred on by falling record sales in the late 1980s, the country music industry has been searching for another sound upon which they can rely. But in this period of uncertainty, and largely because of it, a wider range of music is being marketed—the folk sensibilities of Nanci Griffith, the country rock of Steve Earl, the electric hillbilly blues of the Kentucky

Headhunters, the traditional purism of Ricky Scaggs and the feminist protest music of Rosanne Cash, to name but a few of the popular artists of the late 1980s and early 1990s. As Jimmy Bowen of MCA Records has remarked: "that's the only way to survive down here for the next ten years. Who knows tomorrow what the audience is gonna want" (Bowen 21).

Conclusion

In conclusion, I would like to re-emphasize a point made early on. Culture, no matter what its form, is created or produced by people working together. The process of cultural production is social in nature. It takes place within what Becker has labeled "art worlds," and is, overwhelmingly, oriented toward a market. The artist must get his or her message out to the people and it must be in such a form that the people receiving it can understand and appreciate it. As the Spanish critic Adolfo Vasquez has pointed out: "The artist is subject to the tastes, preferences, ideas and aesthetic notions of those who influence the market. Inasmuch as he produces works of art destined for a market that absorbs them, the artist cannot fail to heed the exigencies of this market—they often affect the content as well as the form of a work of art" (Vasquez 84).

With respect to the country music industry in Nashville, market forces to affect, considerably, the form and content of country music. As Bill Ivey has pointed out, "the players in each segment of this system invent each day their sense of public taste and then act on that invention, choosing those songs, artists and records to be blessed with the endorsement of the business. For a publisher, record executive or radio programmer to be radically and continuously out of step with popular taste produces observable failure—and, eventually, turnover" (Ivey 409).

What I have attempted to sketch in this essay, very briefly, is the social nature of artistic constraints and cultural production in the commercial art world of country music. In the presentation, I have focused on three major areas of critical concern in the production of culture; 1) the creation of the original artifact—in this case, songwriting; 2) the coordination of tasks and the emergence of art world conventions; and 3) the fate of art as it moves through culture industries characterized by high degrees of uncertainty at their input and output boundaries. Each of these areas is, of course, far more complex than I have had time to illustrate here. And there are other areas—such as the distribution of product—that are also important and which I have, here, done little more than mention in passing.

But what I hope I have done is give a hint of the complexity of the issue. In truth, the creation of culture is a many faceted process that can be understood only within the context of the social environment within which it is created and consumed. As Janet Wolff has pointed out in *The Social Production of Art*: "All action, including creative or innovative action, arises in the complex conjunction of numerous structural determinants and conditions. Any concept of `creativity' which denies this is metaphysical and cannot be sustained" (Wolff 9). But she goes on to emphasize what I would also underscore, in closing. "The corollary of this line of argument is not that (artists) are simply programmed robots, or that we need not take account of their biographical, existential or motivational aspects...Practical activity and creativity are in a mutual relation of interdependence with social culture" (Wolff 9).

After all, as Ivey points out in Nashville, the industry and the country music artists actually possess considerable control over what is created and what succeeds in the marketplace. As he says, popular taste is generous and many songs and records fall within its broad limits (Ivey 409). The power of those who are creating the music is, then, in selecting and promoting appropriate alternatives within this pool of acceptable work.

Or, as Lacy J. Dalton sings: "God bless the boys who make the noise on 16th Avenue."

Works Cited

Atkins, Chet. "How Chet Atkins Did It." *Country: The Music and the Musicians*. Ed. P. Kingsbury. New York: Abbeville P, 428-29.

Becker, Howard. *Art Worlds*. Berkeley: U of California P, 1982.

Blackburn, Rick. Interview. *Journal of Country Music* 10.2 (1985): 15-18.

Bowen, Jimmy. Interview. *Journal of Country Music* 10.2 (1985): 15, 19-21.

Denisoff, R. Serge. *Waylon: A Biography*. Knoxville: U of Tennessee P, 1983.

Flippo, Chet. "Waylon, Tompall, and the Outlaw Revolution." *Country: The Music and the Musicians*. Ed. P. Kingsbury. New York: Abbeville, 1988. 452-475.

Galante, Joe. Interview. *Journal of Country Music*. 10.2 (1985): 15, 22-26.

Gant, Alice. "The Musicians In Nashville." *Journal of Country Music* 3:2 (1974): 24-44.

Hauser, Arnold. *The Sociology of Art*. Chicago: U of Chicago P, 1982.

Hemphill, Paul. "A Fan's View of Country Music." *Country: The Music and the Musicians*. New York: Abbeville, 1988. 342-372.

Hirsch, Paul. "Processing Fads and Fashions: An Organization Set Analysis of Cultural Industry Systems." *American Journal of Sociology* 77 (1972): 639-659.

Ivey, Bill. "Business Practices That Shaped Country Music." *Country: The Music and the Musicians*. Ed. P. Kingsbury. New York: Abbeville, 1988. 406-451.

Jensen, Joli. "Patsy Cline's Recording Career: The Search For A Sound." *Journal of Country Music* 9.2 (1982): 34-46

Lewis, George H. "Country Music Lyrics." *Journal of Communication* 26.4 (1976): 37-40.

_____."Uncertain Truths: The Promotion of Popular Culture," *Journal of Popular Culture* 20.3 (1986): 31-44.

Mayakovsky, Vladimir. *How Are Verses Made?* London: Jonathan Cape, 1970. (Originally published in Russian, 1923).

Mills, C. Wright. "The Cultural Apparatus." *Power, Politics and People*. Ed. L. L. Horotwitz. New York: Oxford, 1963.

Moulin, Raymonde. "La Genese de la Rarete Artistique." *Revue d'ethnologie Francaise* 8 (1978): 241-258.

Pellas, Geraldine. *Art, Artists and Society: Origins of a Modern Dilemma*. Englewood Cliffs, NJ: Prentice-Hall, 1963.

Peterson, Richard and J. Ryan. "Success, Failure, and Anomie in Art and Craft Work."

Research in the Sociology of Work. Beverly Hills: Sage, 1983.

Ryan, John and R. Peterson. "The Product Image: The Fate of Creativity in Country Music Songwriting." *Individuals in Mass Media Organizations.* Eds. J. Ettema and D. C. Whitney. Beverly Hills: Sage, 11-32.

Shils, Edward. "Mass Society and Its Culture." *Culture For the Millions?* Ed. N. Jacobs. New York: Van Nostrand, 1961. 1-27.

Thomas, Gail. "Lee Clayton." *Country Music* 5 (1978): 17-19.

Williams, Raymond. *The Long Revolution.* Harmondsworth: Penguin, 1965.

Wolff, Janet. *The Social Production of Art.* New York: St. Martins, 1973

Vasquez, Adolfo. *Art and Society.* London: Merlin, 1973. (Originally published in Spanish).

Characteristics of Successful and
Unsuccessful Country Music Songs

Charles Jaret

The popular music business has been characterized as a "vinyl crap game" in which major record labels, in search of the elusive hit, indiscriminately flood the market with product (Denisoff). This scattershot approach to record release might have been feasible during prosperous times but can hardly be justified today when the industry shares the economic woes of the country in general. Music business executives have become increasingly cautious about releasing new material unless popular success is virtually assured. But how, in fact, can a hit record be predicted? Can specific lyrical or musical traits be identified as pecular to hit songs as opposed to less successful ones? How significant is the fame (and gender) of the performer? This paper attempts to deal with these questions with regard to country music songs.

For several reasons, the study of country music is now an especially important area of inquiry. Country music has become popular with an increasingly large audience during the last few years. The crossover success of such performers as Dolly Parton and Willie Nelson, who have had major hits on the popular as well as the country music charts is one manifestation; another is the popularity of such films as "Coal Miner's Daughter" and "Urban Cowboy." Country discos are now chic. Several major Top 40 radio stations have recently changed to a country music format. Neil Rockoff, general manager to KHJ-AM in Los Angeles, thus explained the change at his station: "What country music seems to do is reflect and mirror life. It is a return to what is familiar and warm in difficult times. Country, with its honesty, roots, warmth and familiar way it touches people is the way to go" (Harrison). A key notion here is the idea of familiarity. Country music is often considered to set forth certain clearly delineated themes, characters, settings and values in a traditional vocal and instrumental style. Thus, it may be argued that successful country songs merely follow a formula that has proven popular with fans in the past. Rockoff suggested that familiar aspects may be especially comforting during hard times. Country music is acknowledged to the economic foundation that has helped major record companies survive during business recessions. The hardcore country music audience is noted for its loyalty; country albums and singles are steady sellers. A problem arises, however, in selecting which product will be likely to sell the most albums and singles because the companies have limited

Reprinted with permission from *Popular Music and Society* 8.2 (1982): 113-124.

promotional advertising revenues to spend.

Impressing country music radio station program directors has become harder as these stations are adopting tighter Top-40-like formats to appeal to broader audiences. Stations are unlikely to broadcast songs that are not certain hits. Len Anthony, assistant operations manager and disc jockey at WPLO in Atlanta, uses reports from trade magazines and tip sheets, calls to local record stores, telephone requests, advice from fellow DJ's, and "gut reaction" to pick songs to add to the playlist at his station, which he characterizes as "mass appeal with country overtones." Anthony believes that a country song should tell a story but that professional arrangements are important as well. During his interview, he played a single with which he was impressed, "Sweet Red Wine and Painted Women," which features a traditional theme along with lush pop arrangements (Anthony).

As mentioned by Anthony, one major avenue that stations use in selecting hits is the tip sheet such as *Rudman's Friday Morning Quarterback*. It is questionable, however, whether these tipsters apply scientific techniques in selecting potential hits. Rudman's publication is filled with advertisement from record labels (Simon). The importance of promotion and advertising to the hit-making process is unquestionable.

Still, it is generally accepted that a "stiff," a record that does not "have it in the grooves," cannot be promoted to hit status. Some market research has identified what aspects of popular music appeal to listeners and buyers. One study found that the artist is the most important factor in record success. Melody and lyrics are more important than arrangement and production, while record label and packaging are of virtually no importance to the consumer ("Label and Packaging"). Our study takes a different approach in assessing the degree to which a country song's commercial success and popularity is related to its lyrical and musical characteristics and qualities and discovering which of those qualities and characteristics are most important in determining the song's success.

Methodology

Our methodology may be divided into three major steps, as follows: a) selecting and obtaining an adequate sample of country songs to study, b) identification and formulation of the relevant variables for the analysis: adequate measures of the dependent variables (song popularity and success) and the independent variables (the relevant lyrical and musical qualities in the song), c) application of multivariate statistical techniques to examine the relationship between the song's musical and lyrical content and its commercial popularity and success.

Our Sample. In the summer of 1978 we drew and tape recorded a random sample of 235 country music songs that were played on a variety of different types of country music stations in Georgia. Details of this sampling are given in a 1979 article in *Popular Music and Society* (Thaxton & Jaret). Our initial expectation, that it would be best to separately analyze the records made by male and female singers, was confirmed by preliminary analysis. This report is based on samples of 108 songs by men and 48 songs by women singers. (Instrumental recordings, "oldies," or songs more than two years old and songs by male-female duos were excluded.) Each of these songs was subjected to a detailed content analysis in which we noted and coded the most important features, qualities and characteristics.

Identification of Variables. The object of study here, or the dependent variable, was the song's commercial success and popularity. We wanted to know how strongly song success and popularity is dependent upon a variety of musical and lyrical characteristics (independent variables) and, more specifically, which of them are most important. As an operationalization of song success and popularity we chose two indicators: one is the highest position that the song rose to on *Billboard*'s listing of Top Country Singles and the second is the number of weeks that the song remained in the top 100 on the *Billboard* list. Both of these indicators of popularity are compiled and published in an annual volume entitled *Top Country Singles & LPs* by Joel Whitburn, and it was by referring to these volumes that we obtained our data on the dependent variable.

The task of formulating the independent variables was less straightforward. We had to identify the characteristics or qualities (lyrical and musical) that might affect audience response to and popularity of a country music song and then somehow measure these qualities. Some of the characteristics that came to mind were fairly simple, like the song's tempo and seemed more complex. For the identification and measurement of the more complex country music themes and images, we made use of the statistical technique of factor analysis and construction of factor scales. Our factor analysis resulted in the identification of a number of factors that could be interpreted and recognized as common themes and dimensions found frequently in country music, many of which, such as rambling, honky-tonking and sad love, have been described in more qualitative studies. Technical details and statistical results of the factor analysis are available on request from the authors. Table 1 gives a brief description of each of the independent variables used in this analysis. Those numbered 5 through 16 are the ones developed through use of factor analysis.

Another obvious variable that affects the success of a song is the singer. A record released by a well-known superstar in all probability will be more successful than a song by a relatively unknown singer, regardless of other independent variables. To take this into account, we included a variable that measured the stature or ranking of each singer on a scale of 1 to 5 (1 = superstar, 2 = big star, 3 = average or typical performer, 4 = lesser renowned singer, 5 = unknown). The authors independently judged and rated each singer on this scale and were able to do so with a high degree of reliability ($r = .87$). Any difference in ratings were reconciled through discussion and reference to the Whitburn volumes. Use of this variable in the multivariate analysis gets at an intriguing question: Is the fame of the singer more important than the lyrical and musical content in determining the popularity of the song?

Table 1

Listing and Description of Independent Variables
(Potential Determinants of Song Success)

1. Tempo
On this variable, songs were classified into the categories of slow, moderate and fast.

2. Mood
On this variable, songs wereclassified into the simple categories of sad, serious and happy.

3. Instrumental Performance
On this variable, songs were classified as nontraditional, mixed and traditional as follows: nontraditional rock/electric, brass, orchestrated strings
mixed traditional: instruments plus either rock or orchestrated strings
traditional: acoustic guitar and/or fiddle, banjo mandolin, piano, harmonica, steel guitar

4. Interpersonal Conflict
On this variable, songs are classified as to their lyrics' emphasis on personal conflicts, misunderstandings or incompatibilities.

5. Sexual theme
On this variable, songs are scaled according to the extent that the lyrics mention or describe making love, kissing, flirting, picking up someone and cheating.

6. Rambling theme
On this variable, songs are scaled according to the extent that the lyrics mention or describe being corrupted, working, having a good time, driving and travelling.

7. Sad Love theme
On this variable, songs are scaled according to the extent that the lyrics mention crying and breaking up.

8. Violence theme
On this variable, songs are scaled according to the extent that the lyrics mention fighting and dying.

9. Honky-tonking theme
On this variable, songs are scaled according to the extent that the lyrics mention drinking, flirting or picking up someone in a bar and having a good time.

10. Music theme
On this variable, songs are scaled according to the extent that the lyrics mention performing music, travelling and dancing.

11. Make-up/Break-up Theme
On this variable, songs are scaled according to the extent that the lyrics mention forgiving and making up, breaking up and arguing.

12. Traditional Country Images theme
On this variable, songs are scaled according to the extent that the lyrics mention stock characters*, typical settings** or home.

13. Men-Women Basic Nature theme
On this variable, songs are scaled according to the extent that the lyrics provide a message about what men or women are really like, or a moral concerning men or women's nature.

14. Irony theme
On this variable, songs are scaled according to the extent that the lyrics contain some form of irony i.e., twist endings, wordings that literally have the opposite meaning from what is actually meant or are deliberately understating the idea, or meaning that is clear to the audience but not grasped by the character in the song).

15. Work theme
On this variable, songs are scaled according to the extent that the lyrics mention an occupation orother work related images.

16. Religion-Morality theme
On this variable, songs are scaled according to the extent that the lyrics make religious references and provide the listener with a moral.

17. Singer's rating
On this variable, the singer's fame or status as a big star was measured on a scale ranging from 1 (a superstar) to 5 (a virtual unknown.)

* Stock characters included here are the "angelic" wife, bartender, city slicker, country girl, cowboy, Devil, factory worker, farmer, grandma, grandpa, hillbilly, honky-tonk queen, Jesus, Mama, musician, "no-good" husband, Papa, prisoner, rambler, truck driver, vagabond, waitress.
** Typical settings included here are bar, bedroom, cabin, factory, farm, highway, mine, motel, prison, small town, truck cab

Multivariate Statistical Analysis. Having obtained a sample of country music songs and formulated the variables for study, we then applied statistical techniques that describe the relationships between these variables. We were interested in knowing the amount of a song's total variation in success and popularity that could be explained or accounted for by the indicators of musical and lyrical qualities and characteristics (Table 1), as well as the direction of the relationships between these indicators, which of these qualities is most important, and whether they are more, or less, or of equal importance than the rating or fame of the singer. In more simple terms, some questions we asked were whether slow songs are more or less successful than songs of moderate or fast tempo, whether songs that contain much sexual imagery are more or less successful than songs having little sexual imagery and whether, overall, tempo is more or less important than the sexual theme in determining song success.

We used two statistical techniques that are designed to answer these sorts of questions: multiple regression and discriminant analysis. We used stepwise multiple regression to compare the relative explanatory power of our independent variables and to access their importance taken all together. Discriminant analysis provides complementary results, as it enables the researcher to define two or more groups (such as top 10 songs, songs that variables best explain and predict which group the songs will fall in. Due to space limitations, we will only present results based on our regression analysis, though these were supported and in no way contradicted by the discriminant analysis

Findings
Success of Songs by Male Singers.
After analyzing the musical and lyrical characteristics and qualities of country music songs by male performers, our conclusion is that the success of a song is not strongly related to the musical and lyrical qualities considered here. Our list of independent variables, or any subset of them, could not explain much of the variation in the dependent variables, nor does knowledge of what a song is like in terms of these variables allow one to very accurately predict how many weeks the song will be on the hit list or how high on the charts it will rise. Table 2 presents the quantitative results of our regression analysis. Next to each variable is the zero order correlation coefficient (the upper number) and the beta weight (lower number) for both indicators of song success.

Given these statistical results, we must be cautious in making any further generalizations about the relationship between specific lyrical and musical characteristics and song success. With this qualification, we feel that it is defensible to suggest, on the basis of our results, that the only song characteristics that seem to affect the popularity and success of songs by male artists are the sexual theme, the honky-tonking theme and the tempo. Our finding is that, in general, songs that contain sexual references and innuendo, provide the honky-tonk setting, imagery and action and are slow in tempo achieve a somewhat higher degree of success than songs that do not have these characteristics. Of slightly less importance are the presence of an ironic note in the song's lyrics or story line, the presence of the music theme and the absence of the traditional country images (except for that of the honky-tonk). As for the other independent variables we studied, the relationship between them and song success is so weak that we cannot make any statement about them, even in qualified terms.

Table 2
Song Success and Song Characteristics:
Male Singers
The top numbers are simple (zero-order) correlations between the
independent variables and our measures of song success. The number below it
is the standardized regression coefficient (beta weight) for the variables that had
a non-negligible impact on song succession in our best regression model.
Asterisks (**) indicate the most important variables

Independent Variable	Weeks on Hit List	Highest Point on Chart
1. Tempo**	-.19	-.16
	-.26	-..22
2. Mood	-.05	.00
3. Instrumental	.00	.03
Performance		
4. Interpersonal Conflict	.12	.09
5. Sexual Theme**	.23	.25
	.19	.21
6. Rambling Theme	.05	.04
7. Sad Love Theme	.05	.02
8. Violence Theme	-.04	-.02
9. Honky-tonking Theme**	.24	.25
	.20	.20
10. Music Theme	.04	.02
	.19	.16
11. Make up, Break-up	.03	.01
Theme		
12. Traditional Country	.01	.03
Images Theme	-.17	-.14
13. Men-Women Basic	.16	.16
Nature Theme	.12	.11
14. Irony Theme	.18	.18
	.17	.15
15. Work Theme	.07	.06
16. Religion-Morality Theme	-.03	-.07
17. Singer's Rating**	.37	.35
	.31	.33
R^2 (without singer's rating)	.14	.12

Compared to the musical and lyrical characteristics of a song, the rating or
status of the performer is a much more powerful determinant of the success that
a record will have. Our regression analysis indicates that, all things being equal,

for male performers the ranking or popularity of the singer is about twice as strong a determinant of a record's success as the individual factors mentioned above. When we include the rating or popularity of the male singer along with the song characteristics in a regression model, we are able to explain about 25 percent of the variation in both indicators of song success.

Success of Songs by Female Singers^frl. For women performers we were better able to specify the musical and lyrical song characteristics that are related to commercial success. Here, without even including the rating of the performer, our best regression model was able to account for just over a quarter of the variation in our dependent variables. Table 3 presents the results for women singers in the same format as Table 2. Given these results, we can be more confident in our statements about women artists then men, though we are still cautious in our conclusions. Our results provide us with a thumbnail sketch of the successful country music song by a woman performer, which in some interesting ways is different from that of men.

Table 3
Song Success and Song Characteristics:
Female Singers
The top numbers are simple (zero-order) correlations between the independent variables and our measures of song success. The number below it is the standardized regression coefficient (beta weight) for the variables that had a non-negligible impact on song success in our best regression model. Asterisks (**) indicate the most important variables.

Independent Variable	Weeks on Hit List	Highest Point on Chart
1. Tempo**	-.11	-.06
	-.31	-.31
2. Mood	.11	.15
3. Instrumental	-.24	-.29
Performance**	-.34	-.26
4. Interpersonal Conflict	-.08	-.15
	-.12	-.22
5. Sexual Theme*	.14	.26
	.15	.13
6. Rambling Theme**	.31	.29
	.63	.41
7. Sad Love Theme**	.18	.13
	.30	.26
8. Violence Theme	.00	.00
9. Honky-tonking Theme**	.12	.17
	-.33	-.19
10. Music Theme	-.11	-.10
	-.24	-.22
11. Make up, Break-up Theme	.06	.03

12.Traditional Country Images Them	-.06	-.04
13. Men-Women Basic Nature Theme*	.18	.22
	.14	.21
14. Irony Theme	.20	.22
	.13	.06
15. Work Theme	.18	.17
	-.14	-.05
16. Religion-Morality Theme	.04	.04
17. Singer's Rating**	.42	.44
	.28	.33
R^2(without singer's rating	.26	.27

By a rather large margin, the single most important element in successful women singers' records is the rambling theme. There are four other factors that are of moderate importance: the type of instrumental performance and backup, the tempo, the sad love theme and the honky-tonking theme. Other characteristics that were found to make a small but significant impact on song success are the music theme, the sexual theme and the men-women basic nature theme. The other characteristics seem to have no meaningful relationship to song success.

Let's examine these findings a little more closely. We were surprised to see the rambling theme appearing as so strong a determinant of women's songs popularity. On closer examination, we found that in most cases the woman is *not*^frl the "rambler" in the song: Rather, she is singing about the rambling ways of an important male in her life and the resulting problems or sadness that he has caused her. It is not unknown, though, for a female singer to use the rambling theme in a more active way, as did Emmylou Harris with "Two More Bottles of Wine," a song written by and probably intended for a male artist.

Among the other moderately important patterns, we found that the instrumental performance and accompaniment was related to song success in the following way. In terms of weeks on the chart and the highest point reached on the chart, it is better for women singers to have a *less* traditional country music instrumentation and arrangement. Orchestrated strings and country-rock accompaniments are more successful than acoustic guitar and/or piano, banjo, fiddle, steel guitar and harmonica. Another finding was that the honky-tonking theme was related to song success in the opposite direction than it was for male performers. For women, lyrics with much honky-tonking action and imagery seem to reduce the level of popularity of the song, while lyrics that omitted or dealt with this theme peripherally were more successful. Tempo, however, was related to success in the same way as it was for males: the slower tunes were more popular than the fast-paced songs. Also a significant factor in women artists' song success was the presence of the sad love or heartbreak theme: songs that mentioned characters crying or breaking up were more successful than songs in which this theme was weak or absent. Finally, among the weaker influences of song success we found that the presence of the music theme was linked with lower levels of commercial success and the presence of the sexual theme was related to greater song popularity, as was the presence of the men-women basic nature theme.

We also analyzed these data with the rating of the performer taken into account, as we did with the males. Our results, however, were different, and our main conclusion is that the star-ranking of the singer is not as important a factor in the song's success among women singers as it is among the men. Our evidence for this is the fact that the singer rating variable was not the strongest influence on our dependent variables when it was added to the regression model. Instead, for weeks on the hit list, it was fourth in importance (behind the rambling theme, honky-tonking and instrumental performance) and, for highest point on the chart, it was second in importance (behind the rambling theme). In practice this means that the singer's renown does influence how well the song is received; however, for women artists this is not the most important factor. There are some musical and lyrical characteristics that are of greater importance. Quite a few of the successful songs by women, in our sample, were performed by young singers or newcomers who were not well known in country music and who have since gone on to become much more popular. The implications of this finding and the contrasting pattern to that of male singers will now be discussed.

Discussion and Conclusion

There are two issues emerging from our research findings that we would like to address. The first pertains to our discovery that for country artists, especially males, the aspects of musical and lyrical style that we captured in our measurements were not sufficient to explain the level of success that a song achieves. Even when we took the fame and status of the singer into account, we could not fully account for a record's reception by the listening public. What additional factors might be important?

Our discussions and interviews with knowledgeable, experienced people active in commercial music suggest a few answers. Every country record that is released does not get a chance to be heard and judged by the radio audience: many records never reach a radio turntable. There are simply too many, and most radio stations are committed to some system of frequent playing of a relatively small number of "hits." This results in keen competition among records for a limited amount of exposure and air time, a situation that record companies have responded to by using various promotional means, such as advertisement in music magazines, publicity flyers, personal appearances and distribution of positive reviews. Thus, the amount or strength with which a record company promotes a record is an important determinant of its success that our analysis has not taken into account.

Another factor, in addition to musical and lyrical content, the singer and level of promotion, that influences a song's success is a random element. As mentioned earlier, program directors utilize every method from sophisticated marketing research to "gut reaction" in determining what songs to play. Random occurrences may sometimes give records that would otherwise be ignored a chance to be heard and possibly a chance to become popular.

Finally, we admit that our measurement of some musical characteristics of songs was not extremely precise. We roughly categorized tempo and rather simplistically treated musical instrumentation and accompaniment. If we were more detailed and sophisticated in measuring these and other musical qualities we might find a greater association between musical content and song popularity. Research by McMullen suggests that this is so, as he has identified specific pitch levels, degrees of musical redundance and rhythmic structures that are generally preferred by listeners and found that these do not appear to vary much among musical styles. Lomax has also developed a more elaborate system for analyzing popular song structure and incorporation of these approaches with our work would be an interesting avenue for further research.

The second matter to be discussed is our finding that the singer's rating or fame seems to be a relatively less important influence on the success of a record among women performers than men. This has the following two-edge implication: Women who do not have an established reputation or big name in country music have a better chance of having a successful record than do male singers who are also unknown, but famous women artists have less assurance than famous male performers that their records will be highly successful.

While we cannot be sure of the reason for this pattern, we do suggest the following as a hypothesis or partial explanation. What we have described seems similar to the career pattern so common among Hollywood actors and actresses and is grounded in American sex roles and norms. Hollywood is known for its starlet syndrome, in which young, sexy, beautiful women are constantly being discovered and being given roles in movies that become successful. Some young actresses rise to star status. Then, as they begin to age, these actresses, with a few notable exceptions, find themselves in fewer movies, in less choice roles and in less successful films, being passed over for a new crop of starlets. For actors, however, the career pattern usually starts off and develops more slowly; once fame has been achieved, however, it lasts longer, with actors often continuing to make successful films when they are middle-aged or older.

We suggest that the same factors, American sex roles and preferences and male control of the industry, also operate in the country music business, though perhaps in a weaker or more subtle way. The career patterns of male and female country music performers appear to show the same tendencies, whereby young, talented, good-looking female performers are brought into the limelight, win the hearts of many fans and make successful records. With some prominent exceptions, however, "mature" female country artists begin to find a drop in record sales or popularity as younger women singers appear on the scene. Among men singers, though, we find a slower climb to success but a longer-lasting career, as big name male performers seem to develop a more loyal set of fans who continue to buy their records.

All our data are consistent with this interpretation and substantiate our general impression of country music career patterns. Proof of validity would require a separate research project addressed to it specifically. In this paper we have tried to apply some rather sophisticated quantitative methods to an area that usually is approached with qualitative research methods. We hope that our approach can be followed up and improved on, and we would be delighted if this work stimulates ideas or raises issues that result in more sensitive and sophisticated analyses, both quantitative and qualitative, of popular music.

Works Cited

Anthony, L. Personal interview. 19 September 1980 "Label andpackaging not important, survey reveals." *Billboard 16* Sept. 1978: 46.

Denisoff, R. S. *Solid Gold.* New Brunswick, NJ: Transaction, 1975.

Harrison, E. "Country music mushrooms on radio and TV." *Billboard* 13 Sept. 1980: 1, 26, 50.

Lomax, A. *Folk Song Style and Culture.* Washington: American Assn. for the Advancement of Science, 1968.

McMullen, P. T. "The influence of complexity in pitch sequences on preference responses of college-age subjects." *Journal of Music Therapy* 11 (1974): 226-233.

McMullen, P. T. and M. J. Arnold. "Preference and interest asfunctions of distributional redundancy in rhythmic sequences." *Journal of Research in Music Education* 24 (1976): 22-31.

Simon, J. "Kal Rudman picks the hits." *Rolling Stone* 19 Oct. 1978: 42.

Thaxton, L. and C. Jaret. "Country music and its city cousin: A comparative analysis of urban and rural country music." *Popular Music and Society* 6 (1979): 307-315.

Whitburn, J. *Joel Whitburn's Top Country Singles & LPs.* Menomonee Falls, WI: Record Research, 1978

Function in the Country Song
"Tight Fittin' Jeans"

John H. Planer

The essence of country music, at its best, lies in its lyric integrity and that hasn't changed. It still deals with the real experiences of life—love and work, temptation and failure. And that's what appeals to people.

Ed Benson, Country Music Association

...the common man would rather be entertained than edified.

Robert E. Park

The country song "Tight Fittin' Jeans," composed by Mike Huffman, was popularized through a recording by Conway Twitty which was issued on three MCA records[1] The song ranked first on the country music popularity charts for the week of 26 September 1981 (Downing and Berger). The lyrics relate an encounter between a cowboy and a wealthy, upper-class, married woman wearing tight jeans.

> A cowboy once had a millionaire's dream,
> And Lord, I loved that lady wearing tight fittin' jeans.

In examining "Tight Fittin' Jeans," we must be careful not to generalize about all popular music or all country music any more than we can generalize from a single example about all serious music, literature or art. In addition we must identify the exact object of our investigation of function, for the popular, commercial recording represents the efforts and judgments of many different individuals. Mike Huffman wrote the music and lyrics; Prater Music Inc. (ASCAP) copyrighted them. Bergen White then arranged Huffman's music for strings (violin, acoustic guitar, steel or Hawaiian guitar, bass), women's chorus and percussion (a drum set).[2] Then Conway Twitty[3] and specific individuals performed that arrangement. Finally, an individual or collective decision then occurred to release a single (or perhaps a composite) performance, with specific tempos, phrasing and improvisation. Audio engineers then manipulated electronically the dynamic levels of the different instruments to achieve a specific balance. Therefore when we study the song which became popular, we

Reprinted with permission from *Popular Music and Society* 14.3 (Fall 1990): 27-50. Edited version.

study a recording which combines Huffman's lyrics and music with White's arrangement in one particular rendition by specific individuals. The public, however, associates "Tight Fittin' Jeans" with Conway Twitty, not with the composer, arranger, producer, publisher, record company or supporting musicians; and when the song is mentioned, listeners recall his specific recording.

Popularity depends not only upon the intrinsic merits of the music and lyrics as well as their realization in performance, but also upon its publicity, particularly its exposure on radio stations which play popular and country music, and the persona of the soloist (Rogers 17-21). An excellent song, with the potential to become widely popular, must be promoted effectively if it is to sell well. Fan magazines, country music newsletters and books and concert tours further promote a song *once an audience is familiar with it* from repeated listening, usually over the radio.

Kasha and Hirschhorn describe the successful country song as follows:

...the basic secret of writing a good country lyric is to make it sound as though it sprang spontaneously from the tongue of the speaker. Any trace of overelaborateness will mark it phony. As country words must sound like rhymed dialogue, tunes must come across as a musical equivalent of ordinary speech. It's as if the melody were only an extension of conversation, one more way of talking. (134)[4]

Their description does indeed match the characteristics of most country music.

Once we recognize and articulate the limits which a mass market imposes, once we clarify the intent, then we can move within those limits to criticize popular art not as serious but rather as *Popular* art.

Popular Intent in "Tight Fittin' Jeans"

It is difficult to find in "Tight Fittin' Jeans" either insight into reality or a significant cause. While the lyrics relate the details of a plausible incident, we can draw little significance from it, other than "a good time was had by all" or "a cowboy's life ain't all that bad!" The song promotes no cause; it advocates neither chastity, prohibition, nor Christian fundamentalism. The popular intent of its composer, arranger, performers and producers is obvious: to entertain the mass audience which enjoys country music and thereby to provide a livelihood for its creators, performers, producers, distributors and investors. The very fact that the song *did* rise to the top position on the country music charts, that it was issued on three different records and that the music was published and widely-distributed attest to the successful achievement of its creators' objectives.

Although we can identify a group of characteristics which may explain the popularity of "Tight Fittin' Jeans," we cannot isolate one or two specific characteristics which, by themselves, would account for its success. We cannot do so because popularity involves not only a recording but also the individual and collective psychological responses of its listeners. Market research can identify the characteristics of listeners of country music in general and of

Conway Twitty in particular, but devising a procedure to elicit profound information from the subconscious feelings of listeners with little knowledge of musical terminology lies far beyond the scope of this study of criticism and the training of its author.

We can, however, group the characteristics of "Tight Fittin' Jeans" which collectively help account for its popularity under the following headings: 1) contemporary appeal to a particular social class; 2) conformity to rigid stylistic limits which restrict originality; 3) a style which is clear, unambiguous, regular, repetitive and non-cerebral; 4) pervasive sexuality; 5) predominance of emotional fantasy over intellectual realism; and 6) avoidance of painful realities.

1) Contemporary appeal to a particular social class. Country music generally appeals almost exclusively to white listeners between 25 and 49; they are likely to have completed only grade school and few have completed a college degree. Most hold low-prestige jobs: unskilled and service workers or skilled and semi-skilled blue collar workers; few professionals, managers and executives listen to country music. In 1975, incomes of country western fans ranged generally between $5,000 and $15,000 per year. The music does not appeal exclusively to rural audiences, however, for concerts of country music in large cities are well attended. The appeal of country music extends well beyond the southern and southwestern United States; it has become a music which appeals more to a class than to a geographic area (Peterson and DiMaggio).[5]

The text of "Tight Fittin' Jeans" does not identify a particular time or geographic region; nevertheless, the references to a "good ole boy," "pardner," "cowboy" and "cowgirl" all suggest a southern or southwestern context. The appeal, however, is contemporary: an unescorted, upper-class woman wearing faded denim clothes enters a lower-class tavern seeking union with a hard-ridin' cowboy. The musical arrangement is typical of country music of the 1980s. Although the singer is "stuck" in his world, the text, nevertheless, flatters a lower-middle-class life-style, for the wealthy experience it. And in their relationship he quickly dominates her.

2) Conformity to rigid stylistic limits which restrict originality. The music and lyrics of "Tight Fittin' Jeans" fit perfectly within the boundaries which Kasha and Hirschhorn have identified. Huffman produced a new, copy-righted, attractive song without the significant innovation which could alienate a mass audience. He uses only four chords: tonic, subdominant, dominant (seventh) and the dominant of the dominant. When the arrangement modulates up a half step for the second half of the song, from A to B-flat major, again only those four chords sound. The rhythms are also not exceptional: the duple meter is evident aurally, and the tempo is sprightly. The "Scotch snap" rhythm ♪ ♩· ♪ ♩. alternates with ♩· ♪ ♩· ♪ .

Bergen White's arrangement is well-crafted, but again, not sufficiently innovative to detract from the lyrics or to attract the casual listener's attention. Its excellence lies in its unobtrusive enhancement of Huffman's music. a) The instruments and women's chorus add interesting tone colors. b) The upper strings bridge the ends of phrases and those which follow. c) The addition of the female chorus in the second verse helps maintain interest and underscores important words and phrases. The contrast of male-soloist with female-chorus also reflects the sexual subject of the song. d) The counterpoints which the melodic instruments and chorus add provide a more interesting texture and flesh out the harmonies. e) The modulation midway helps provide tonal variety which is necessary when two short sections are repeated several times. f) The instruments and chorus emphasize the two contrasting, dotted rhythms which together form the "figure" or "riff" of the song (Kasha and Hirschhorn 99-100). The bass emphasizes the first rhythm; Conway Twitty, the chorus and the other strings emphasize the Scotch snap. Thus the opposition of the two rhythms provides variety. Although few non-professional listeners of popular music would notice the arrangement, much less try to distinguish between Huffman's song and White's arrangement, that arrangement enhances the song significantly.

3) A style which is clear, unambiguous, regular, repetitive and non-cerebral. The text of "Tight Fittin' Jeans" utilizes simple, direct vocabulary and syntax, mixing direct discourse with narration. All but four words are monosyllabic or bi-syllabic. The "hook" or "key lyric or melodic line (Mason 276-77) is the title, "Tight Fittin' Jeans," which ends each strophe. The verses of each of the six quatrains generally contain seven accents and are approximately iambic heptameter. The rhyme scheme is aabb ccbb ddbb. In addition to the chronological unfolding of the narrative, the lyrics also employ effective contrasts: female and male, cowgirl and cowboy, queen and peasant, tiger and man, champagne and beer, crystal candle lights and a bar, wealth and poverty, pearls and denim jeans, opportunity and being "stuck." Such polarities (male-female, me-him/her, us-them) pervade country music (Buckley; King).

The text itself is explicit. The first stanza is narration; the dialogue and offers commence in the second; the third is the woman's explanation; the fourth represents her transformation; the fifth is sexual and the sixth is separation and retrospection. Although the climax occurs, appropriately, near the end, the sixth stanza nevertheless is no anti-climactic let-down. As the sexual heat cools, the broken cowboy compares his economic and social status with that if his tiger: the millionaire's dream could choose to go slumming, but he was stuck.

The length of the text is typical of most country songs. "Tight Fittin' Jeans" contains 267 words instead of the normal 120-160 words, a figure which excludes repeated verses or a chorus (Mason 278).[6] Conway Twitty's performance lasts only two minutes and forty-eight seconds; two-and-a-half to three minutes is typical in the broadcasting and country music industry (Rogers 17).

The music reflects the clarity and simplicity of the text. The dynamics are constant—no gradations occur. Balance therefore is effected by an engineer who mixes the various tracks rather than by interplay among the musicians themselves. The harmonies are thoroughly familiar and functional; no unusual dissonances or modal influences invigorate them. The music of the six stanzas comprise an AAB AAB pattern, the medieval "bar form." Within each section considerable repetition occurs. For example, the melodies of the four lines in the A section can be described as ABAB'; the melodies of the B section then correspond to CDAB'. These internal repetitions produce a highly-unified melody which musically-unsophisticated listeners can readily recall.

The rhythm is similarly constant. The pulse is steady; no pauses or fermatas break its march. While syncopations and Scotch snaps provide relief, the effect of the accentuation and balanced four-measure phrases is rhythmic regularity. Huffman, however, introduces some relief by adding an extra measure between the second and third lines of each stanza and by beginning some lines without an anacrusis.

The harmonies and tonality are also traditional. With the exception of a secondary dominant-seventh chord, all chords are major triads. Cadences define the tonality clearly, and the melody consists almost exclusively of chord tones and passing tones.[7]

4) Pervasive sexuality. The sexuality of "Tight Fittin' Jeans" lies primarily in the lyrics, though the performance by a male vocalist and female chorus reflects the heterosexual encounter related in the text. The sexuality is explicit from the first stanza; Huffman effectively sets his hook when the cowboy sees right through the lady's jeans. And the woman not only knows that he sees through her pants—she aggressively affirms her availability by admitting that a tiger inhabits her jeans. The fifth stanza contains the most numerous sexual references to the liaison. The woman remains a lady, but the cowboy has been broken; he held a gorgeous woman the night he "knew" the lady. But as orgasm approaches, pseudo-modesty prevails: the cowboy refuses to state explicitly what occurred, though his hints leave absolutely no doubts, the reference to "knowing" a woman, though archaic, is perfectly unambiguous to those familiar with the King James translation of the Bible; thus the concluding reference to loving the lady refers to sexual passion.

References to sexuality are common in lyrics of country songs.[8] And to varying degrees performers of country and popular music make the musical eroticism visual as well. Some performers reinforce the associations of their lyrics by dressing the part and/or by their physical motions on stage. Men wearing open shirts and tight pants may rock and roll appropriately. Women wearing spandex pants or body suits may gyrate; they may separate and lift their breasts, displaying lesser or greater areas of flesh; their facial expressions may suggest the ecstasy of orgasm.

Conway Twitty's repertoire contains numerous, directly sexual references. The songs he records often emphasize "adult themes" (Mason 16), and his following is largely female (Mason 119).[9] Bill C. Malone explains:

An intense bond of loyalty exists between Twitty and his fans, many of whom are middle-aged women whose devotion to him began when he was a gyrating rock-and-roller. The sexuality of his lyrics is much more overt than that found in most other singers' material, and such songs as "You've Never Been This Far Before, "Slow Hand," "I'd Love to Lay You Down" and "Tight Fittin' Jeans" have aroused controversy while also being major commercial hits for him. Twitty's performances, however, are physically restrained and contain none of the sensual body movements witnessed in the acts of many of the modern rockabillies. (382)

But "Tight Fittin' Jeans" appeals not only to Twitty's fans—its appeal was much wider since it rose to the top of the country listings.

5) Predominance of emotional fantasy over intellectual realism. The lyrics of "Tight Fittin' Jeans" reveal little cerebration, save for the narrator's reflection upon socio-economic status in the last stanza. Both partners are willing for a fling; there is little personal or emotional involvement between them; the words "adultery" and "cheatin' " do not occur, and only the reference to "married money" suggests infidelity. The narrator exclaims twice, "Lord," but the reference is not serious: God, present in the background of many country songs, does not enter the bar to condemn or condone the liaison.[10]

What makes "Tight Fittin' Jeans" so effective is its appeal to both male and female fantasies.[11] For men, the idea of being picked up by a wealthy, beautiful, hot woman eager for sex flatters the masculine ego, probably because it rarely occurs for most men. Although the cowboy initiates the dialogue, he promptly asserts dominance not by offering to buy her champagne but rather by stating that he will buy her a beer. Her response indicates her willingness to converse and contains an offer of her own: a dance in exchange for her story. Huffman wisely avoids mentioning whether the man was married or not, thereby appealing both to bachelors and husbands.

For women, the fantasy is attracting and arousing a good-looking male and then enjoying him. In general, women purchase far more country records than men (Mason 278). For Twitty's fans, however, Conway Twitty becomes the cowboy, and some women fantasize about being his "pardner" as they listen to the song.[12] The genius of Huffman's lyrics thus is their sexual appeal to both men and women: the references are sufficiently obvious, but the pseudo-reticent phrasing at the climactic moment would appeal to women, while the directness would satisfy men. Not only does Huffman appeal to sexual fantasy, he also repeatedly refers to dreaming and fantasy in the lyrics. While the context indicates that the dreams and fantasies are those of the lady and the cowboy, their fantasies are also those of the listeners.

Despite the adult subject and participants, the lyrics refer frequently to them as boy and girl, rather than man and woman: a cowboy meets a lady who wants to be a "good ole boy's girl," and later that night she is transformed into a cowgirl. While Huffman does refer to her as both a woman and a lady, those nouns refer more to her wealth and upper-class status than to the personality which emerges in the honky-tonk. Indeed adults do occasionally refer to themselves as boys and girls in colloquial speech,[13] but given the nature of the sexual liaison and the importance of erotic fantasy, the reference to two adults reverting to designations of children is intriguing.

Perhaps these references reflect a strong desire to revert to the "good old days" of childhood in order to escape the monotony and responsibilities of adulthood.[14] The woman realizes her adolescent fantasy by donning the tight jeans and picking up a cowboy, to their mutual delight.

6) Avoidance of painful realities. Huffman underscores the fantasy of

"Tight Fittin' Jeans" by citing no unpleasant or realistic details before, during, or after the one-night affair. No fears of venereal disease, discovery, or conception inhibit them. The cowboy performs well, though he admits that by dawn the cowgirl has broken his plow; he suffers problems from neither premature ejaculation nor impotence. Neither participant has a hangover or nausea, despite the beer that they went through. (While Huffman mentions the beer the couple drank, he does not allude to the concomitant excretion.) No unpleasant after-effects occur: the lady's husband does not come to the bar with a shotgun; her children do not discover her infidelity; the preacher does not denounce her infidelity from his pulpit the next Sunday; neither party contracts herpes or syphilis; neither abortion nor divorce transform that dream into a nightmare. The passion is present without any responsibility, and that indeed is an alluring fantasy.

Conclusion

It is inappropriate to criticize the lyrics of "Tight Fittin' Jeans" as dishonest or unrealistic. Huffman, Twitty and most listeners know well that maturity involves responsibilities and that our actions have unpleasant as well as pleasant consequences. Their intent, however, is not to depict reality or to provide intellectual insight for people who want entertainment. Once we acknowledge the popular intent, serious critics must then move within the parameters of popular intent to evaluate "Tight Fittin' Jeans" by the most appropriate standard of popular entertainment: commercial success. Its success lies not in innovation, subtlety of poetic image and nuance, or formal integration. Its popular success is measured by its ratings, sales and the income it produced; these attest to the composer's, arranger's, performers' and promoters' capacity to anticipate correctly the preferences of the country music market. The critic who sneers at "Tight Fittin' Jeans" demeans not the music but himself, for he utilizes inappropriate standards of criticism.

And "Tight Fittin' Jeans" *is* effective. Its simple directness fits the requirements of effective popular art, and its ranking as first on the country music charts attests not only to the song's appeal but also to its newness, its characteristics which attract attention above its competition and which attest to its originality within the limits of the formula. "Tight Fittin' Jeans" seeks neither to change the formula nor to attract attention to innovation; its appeal to both male and female fantasies is brilliant; it maintains interest in the narrative, and the music neither bores nor attracts undue attention to itself; the style of the lyrics is clear and colloquial. In short, the song conforms closely to a formula which has repeatedly proven popular. And that success reveals the attractiveness of the formula itself. The songwriters, performers and producers in Nashville know well their audiences and the restrictions within which they must operate, the limits of innovation and the patterns which please their listeners[15]

"Tight Fittin' Jeans" is excellent popular art, not only because of its demonstrated commercial success, but also because of its high craftsmanship, musicianship and technical standards within the restrictions of country music.

The "hook" is effective, and the idea that our cowboy sees *through* the tight denim jeans is titillating. The text builds toward the sexual climax. The arrangement enhances the song effectively without obtruding, melding one phrase with another, providing a modulation and counterpoints to avoid monotony and underscoring key phrases with the women's chorus. Although we cannot determine with precision exactly how "Tight Fittin' Jeans" would have fared with a different arrangement, Bergen White's arrangement is musically effective, typical and well-crafted. Finally the song is ideally suited for Conway Twitty since it appeals to both male and female sexual fantasies. The song "works" not because of the vagaries of popular taste but rather because it satisfies those tastes perfectly; consumer satisfaction attests to the knowledge, skill and craft of the song's creators and promoters.

Notes

[1]Prater Music Incorporated (ASCAP) of Naperville, Illinois holds the copyright (1980); the sheet music was printed by Columbia Pictures Publications of Hialeah, Florida (2757 TSMX). The recording by MCA recordings was issued as a 45 rpm single and then was included on two different 33 rpm albums: *Classic Conway* MCA- and *Mr. T* MCA-37246. I am grateful to Jean Prater Bolin of Prater Music and Ronnie Pugh of the Country Music Foundation for their assistance in gathering information on this song

[2]The citation for the arrangement appears on the record labels and the album jackets.

[3]Stage name for Harold Jenkins. For biographical information see Bill C. Malone, *Country Music U.S.A.*, revised and enlarged edition (Austin: U of Texas P, 1985) 381-82; Irwin Stambler and Grelun Landon, *The Encyclopedia of Folk, Country & Western Music*, second edition (New York: St. Martin's, 1983) 756-58; Melvin Shestack, *The Country Music Encyclopedia* (New York: Thomas Crowell, 1974) 282-87. On the recording *Classic Conway* are the songs "I Can't Believe She Gives It All to Me," "We Had it All," "Your Love Had Taken Me That High" and "Red Neckin' Love Makin' Night." On the disk *Mr. T.* are "Cheatin' Fire," "I Made You a Woman," "Slow Lovemakin'" and "Love Salvation."

[4]Kasha and Hirschhorn, 134.

[5]See also Paul DiMaggio, Richard Peterson, and Jack Esco, Jr., "Country Music: Ballad of the Silent Majority" in *The Sounds of Social Change: Studies in Popular Culture,* ed. by R. Serge Denisoff and Richard A. Peterson (Chicago: Rand McNally & Company, 1972), 47-50.

[6]Kasha and Hirschhorn observe that popular songs *in general* have between 50 and 80 words.

[7]In performance Conway Twitty changes the appoggiatura notated in the printed music in the second measure into a chord tone: above an A major, tonic triad, the notated music is a a f e; Twitty sings this as a a a e.

[8]For examples see Nich Tosches, *Country: Living Legends and Dying Metaphors in America's Biggest Music*, revised edition (New York: Charles Scribner's Sons, 1985) 120-56 and elsewhere in abundance. See also Kasha and Hirschhorn, 113-18.

194 All That Glitters

"Sometimes sex is blatantly handled...This kind of straightforward approach works excitingly well with a pulsating beat. The aim of a rhythmic sex record isn't to instruct or analyze or enlighten—it's the musical equivalent of a stag movie, and must turn on the dancers (or lovers) listening to it, or it has failed to accomplish its objective," 117.

⁹"Conway is the essence of the male country persona. Alone among country men singers, he seems to have found a direct pipeline into the hearts of women country fans."

¹⁰It is intriguing that fundamentalist Protestants often condemn the sexuality, drugs and hedonism in the lyrics of rock music and overlook similar sins in much country music. Perhaps the distinction is that Protestant fundamentalism appeals to the same people who enjoy country music; thus fundamentalists would be unlikely to condemn the very music many co-religionists enjoy. Since rock music generally attracts young non-believers, such condemnation is easier. Yet another explanation may be that rock lyrics suggest no guilt; in country music people sin, but they know it is sin, and weakness rather than choice excuses it.

Country music also presents an ambivalent attitude toward drinking. It is acceptable both as a test of manhood and as a means of escaping problems Yet drinking also facilitates sin and irresponsibility, which produces suffering. H. Paul Chalfant and Robert E. Beckley, "Beguiling and Betraying; the Image of Alcohol Use in Country Music," *Journal of Studies on Alcohol*, 38.7 (1977): 1428-33. Neal R. Peirce and Jerry Hagstrom observe that country music is "rooted in rural conservatism ("You've got to have smelled mule manure before you can sing hillbilly," said Hank Williams, a revered country star), blatantly patriotic, distrustful of wealthy city folks and intellectuals, fundamentalist but loving sweet Jesus and tolerant (as one observer put it) of "homegrown vices like boozing and philandering when accompanied by a footnote that they don't come free." Peirce and Hagstrom, *The Book of America: Inside Fifty States Today*, revised and updated edition (New York: Warner Books, 1984) 379.

¹¹"True, entertainers depend on the fantasies their audiences build around them, and you have a responsibility to deal gently with those who take their fantasies to heart." Kenny Rogers and Len Epand, Making It with Music: Kenny Roger's Guide to the Music Business (New York: Harper and Row, 1978) 191.

¹²Malone observes that Twitty's family life stands in marked contrast to the sexual life he sings about (382).

¹³One explanation is that many people conceive of themselves in a manner similar to the way they did in their youth; hence we refer to a "night with the boys" or an "afternoon with the girls."

¹⁴Recent literature in psychology refers to such desires as the Peter Pan Syndrome (for men) and the Cinderella Syndrome for women. Dan Kiley, *The Peter Pan Syndrome: Men Who Have Never Grown Up* (Dodd, 1983); and Colette Dowling, *Cinderella Complex: Women's Hidden Fear of Independence* (Summit, 1981).

¹⁵In short, more people prefer accessible, succinct pop songs to twelve minutes of instrumental noodling, abstract guitar soloing, or impenetrable lyrics and rambling melodies. And that fact makes the songs commercial: they sell.

Commercial. A decade ago, that word was as dirty as capitalist pig. Today it has regained its respect in pop music. No longer a euphemism for bubble gum, it broadly describes those songs that invite mass appreciation. Anyone who has tried writing good, salable pop songs knows it takes a highly talented and experienced songwriter to create two or three minutes of sensational perfection that can be enjoyed—and bought—by millions." Rogers and Epand 85-86.

Works Cited

Buckley, John. "Country Music and American Values." *Popular Music and Society* 6.4 (1979).

Kasha and Joel Hirschorn. *If They Ask You, You Can Write a Song*. New York: Simon and Schuster, 1979).

King, Florence. "Red Necks, White Socks and Blue Ribbon Fear." *Harper's* 249.1490 (July 1974): 30-34.

Malone, Bill C. *Country Music, U.S.A.* Revised and enlarged edition. Austin: U of Texas: P, 1985.

Mason, Michael. *The Country Music Book*. New York: Charles Scribner's Sons, 1985).

Peterson, Richard A. and Paul DiMaggio. "From Region to Class, the Changing Locus of Country Music: A Test of the Massification Hypothesis." *Social Forces* 53.3 (March 1975): 497-504.

Rogers, Jimmie N. *The Country Music Message: All About Lovin' and Lyin'*. Englewood Cliffs, NJ: Prentice-Hall, 1983.

Reasons For Rhymers:
Sensibility, Emotion and Country Values

Country music has always hewn close to the values of its people, reflecting in its lyrics and in the "high lonesome sounds" of its music the core of suffering and care that binds this audience together. Hank Williams wrote (and sang) a lot of people's lives and so have George Jones, Willie Nelson and Roseanne Cash, to name just a few significant artists of the genre. Such a connection, when established between artist and audience, may help explain the relative longevity of country music careers—a musico-emotional bonding that can last for many years.

Using an analysis of country songs that have appeared on *Billboard's* country charts, John Buckley examines the relationship between country music, as expressed in its lyrics and its audience, suggesting that the music offers "a symbolic world with which audience members can identify." This world, according to Buckley's analysis, has in it eight major themes that get repeated over and over in country songs. He also identifies five perspectives *on* these themes, any one of which is likely to be taken, depending upon the particular song being analyzed. In sum, Buckley concludes that, although the fictive world of country music is not the same as the real world of its audience, it is a stable and predictive one—a world country listeners can "easily understand and with which they can identify."

In "Tension, Conflict and Contradictions in Country Music" I move on, from identification of the "core values" articulated in country music songs, to a consideration of these values in their musical context. I note that there are, in many cases, inconsistencies, conflicts and, in some cases, contradictions among them. In fact the tensions, conflicts and contradictions in the values expressed in country music seem at times more intense than their degree of similarity and inter-connectedness. As I conclude, such conflicts and contradictions reflect both the social upheavals the country audience has been subject to in post World War II America and the internal contradictions and oppositions contained in the cultural values themselves, which I suggest viewing, not as centers of agreement, but as axes of potential cultural variation along which these tensions, conflicts and contradictions—many times triggered by social change—play themselves out.

But, in the end, at the heart of country music are its sad songs—those that, as Katie Stewart points out, make up its origin story, wrapped in a tear-jerking poetics of intensification. These songs, beginning at "that unmappable point where a person's sensibilities are overwhelmed" with pain, find the singer suspended in a dream of "floating extremes" in which the narrative movement "rises into wish fulfillment or sinks into anxiety and nightmare." These songs, the "sad, slobberin' tearjerkers," as George Jones calls them, work their magic on the country audience by "repeatedly twanging the strings of a knowing, broken heart."

Sentimental extremity, as Michael Dunne calls it in "Romantic Narcissism in 'Outlaw' Country Music" has always been present in American cowboy music. In his article, Dunne examines the songs of the country "outlaw" movement that peaked in the mid-1970s. These songs, which on the surface are designed to be read as modern day "cowboy" songs, are less like the "externally grounded lyrics of anonymous trail hands" and more, Dunne claims, like the self-referential verse written in the 19th century by English romantic poets such as Shelly and Keats. To Dunne, there is a strong strain of self-pity and romantic narcissism running through songs like "My Heroes Have Always Been Cowboys" and the poses and images of country stars like Waylon Jennings, Willie Nelson and Jerry Jeff Walker—a strain that echoes these earlier romantic poets. "Like their English predecessors," he writes, "each of the outlaws chose the unconventional path of the artist and then lyrically lamented the culture's unsupportive response."

Playlist

Rodney Crowell	Diamonds and Dirt	Columbia
Loretta Lynn	Don't Come Home A'Drinkin'	Decca
Dwight Yoakum	Just Lookin' For A Hit	Reprise
George Jones	I Am What I Am	Epic
Ricky Van Shelton	RVSIII	Columbia
Waylon Jennings &		
Willie Nelson	Waylon and Willie	RCA

Country Music and American Values

John Buckley

In recent years, country music has become an increasingly popular form of entertainment. Its audience has been steadily expanding for the last decade and a half. In 1961, only 81 out of 4,400 radio stations in the United States broadcast country music full-time. In 1974, the number had grown to 1,020 out of 6,900 with another 1,450 programming three or four hours of country music a day. Altogether it is estimated that about half of the radio stations in the nation play some country music ("Why Country" 59; Stein 4). There is a country music station in every major market in the United States (Toy 41; Hemphill 180-84). Record sales are also increasing. In 1973, slightly more than half of the single records purchased in this nation were country music (Lewis 37).

Despite this popularity, much of the public thinks of country music as an artistic and intellectual wasteland. The music has been criticized for being both too vacuous and too reactionary. It is, moreover, often seen as a persuasive medium for the transmission of rural conservatism. Both *The Nation* (Dickson; King) and *The Saturday Review* (Rockwell 32) have, in recent years, described country music as reinforcing the values of its listeners, while a *Harper's* article concluded that, "It is not too farfetched to say the violence of the 1973-74 truckers' strike was fired, in part, by the Nashville sound" (King 34).

It is the purpose of this paper to examine the relationship between country music, as expressed in its lyrics, and the values of its audience. It is suggested that country music does not reinforce or alter attitudes. Instead, it offers a symbolic world with which audience members may identify.

Since there is no exact agreement as to what is "country music" ("Crossovers" 75), only songs are studied which appeared on the *Billboard* "country" charts after January 1, 1973. Some songs recorded prior to 1973 and some songs recorded after 1973 but which did not appear on the *Billboard* survey are included when particularly illustrative. *Billboard* surveys are drawn from record sales and radio play and as such, provide a general index of the public's conception of "country" (Carey 723). Consequently some songs of performers such as Kris Kristofferson and Linda Rondstadt are treated as country music while others are not.

It is worth noting that, although banjos and fiddles are still an important part of the "Nashville sound," not all of country music is the stereotyped steel guitars and whining vocal. A number of country recordings have "crossed-over"

Reprinted with permission from *Popular Music and Society* 6.4 (1978): 293-301.

to the pop charts, becoming hits in two different markets simultaneously (Cook; "Country"). Both country and pop audiences are usually unaware of this process and selectively perceive such songs to fit their preconceived notion as to what is "country." Different groups may listen to the same song for different reasons; country fans enjoy the qualities they identify with "country," and pop fans hear the elements they believe characteristic of "pop." John Denver and Olivia Newton-John, for example, have received major awards in both country and pop music in recent years.

Attention is confined to the lyrics for three reasons. First, country music lyrics are meant to be heard. In general, the melody is the more important factor in the selection of material in rock music (Peterson and Berger, "Entrepreneuship" 99), while lyrics are the more important consideration in country music (Lewis 38). The instrumental is subordinate to the vocal.

Second, the lyrics are unambiguous. Unlike some other musical forms, there are no allegories and no double-meanings. Both performer and audience clearly understand the meaning of a song.

Third, the lyrics are often an attempt at identification. The landscape, people and situations encountered in country music, unlike much of popular music (Hayakawa 399), are intended to be realistic reproductions of life. That relatively few listeners have experienced some of the situations described in the music (i.e. going to prison, committing murder) is less important than that the music attempts to elicit universally shared emotions. Loneliness, trust, suffering, insecurity, human weakness and personal dignity are all constant, integral parts of the country idiom.[1]

In order to examine the relationship between country music and audience values, this paper will 1) sketch the characteristic themes of country music. 2) outline the perspectives toward personal and social relations displayed in the music, and 3) describe the country music audience and its relationship to the music.

Country Music Themes

Eight basic themes characterize country music. Sometimes songs contain only a single theme, but, more often, they are crowded with several. The pattern, however, is for one to dominate, while the others assume a subordinate role. Consequently, the central theme of a song determines its classification.

1) Satisfying and fulfilling love relations. Like popular music (Peterson and Berger, "Three Eras" 228; Carey, "Courtship" 721), the majority of country songs deal with love. In a content analysis of country songs from selected years, 1960-70, DiMaggio, Peterson and Escoe found that 75% of the songs deal with love in its various forms (41). A minority of these songs treats satisfying and fulfilling male-female relationships.

Such relations are almost always depicted as within the frame-work of marriage. While both sexes are forever "slipin' around" and "hav'n one night stands," there are no hymns celebrating the joys of cohabitation. Songs treat relationships between men and women, not boys and girls. Except for an occasional song reminiscing about an old high-school sweetheart, adolescent courtship is wholly ignored. Songs tell of the relations, good and bad, of adults. Consequently, marriage is a pivotal consideration.

Sex is an integral, but not a dominant, part of satisfactory relationships. The chorus of Charlie Rich's "Behind Closed Doors" suggests the sexual dimension of the relationship while the stanzas describe the public dimension. The same attitude is expressed more concisely by Ronnie Milsap when he sings, "I'm not just her lover; I'm her friend."

2) Unsatisfactory love relationships. Easily the single most prominent theme in country music is unsatisfactory love relations (DiMaggio, Peterson and Escoe 41). An earlier study of popular music found expressions of romantic discord to be common (Horton 576). In country music, however, the audience not only knows that the singer is unhappy but is candidly told why. If satisfactory male-female relations are equated with good marriage, then unsatisfactory relations are most often associated with a marriage that is going, or has gone, wrong. One or both partners are unfaithful, weak, or inattentive which leads to divorce, regrets and, in some cases, repentance.

Sex is a more volatile factor in unsatisfactory relations. It is frequently emblematic of other interpersonal difficulties. Titles such as "Barrooms to Bedrooms," "I'd Rather Be Picked Up Here Than Be Put Down at Home" and "Out of My Head and Back Into My Bed" are representative of the emphasis. Male-female relations, in sum, do not go awry because of lack of money or meddling-in-laws but because of loneliness, jealousy, and human weakness.

3) Home and Family. Family relations, while not given anything like the attention devoted to male-female relations, are seen as equally complex. When set in an identifiable locale, these songs are most likely to tell of a farm family and rural life. Typical is David Allen Coe's "Family Reunion," the narrative of a mountain family gathering to play fiddle tunes. Like many other songs in which the family is sympathetically portrayed, Coe is recalling an earlier time.

Home, however, is also the setting for unhappiness. Life is hard for both parents and children, and the problems encountered are not easily solved. "Rocky Mountain Music," for example, tells of a father's death, the mother's subsequent illness and bad temper and a little brother whose mental illness causes him to be "taken away." Like the male-female relationship, the family and home present the individual with a range of experience, some rewarding and some debilitating.

4) Country. It is no accident that family life is more likely to be better in the country; there is a positive agrarian image in country music. "Country" may be a recognizable physical location, but it is more than this; it is a state of mind, a way of life. "Country is," as Tom T. Hall sings, "workin' for a livin', thinkin' your own thoughts, lovin' your town," but, above all, "country is all in your mind."

5) Work. Country music does not feature traditional work songs so much as it does songs about work. "The Workin' Man Blues" and "One Piece At a Time" describe dull, repetitive physical labor "with the crew" or "at the factory." There are no songs about school for, as Charlie Daniels notes, "A rich man goes to college / and a poor man goes to work." Work in country music is

almost exclusively a male purview. Women are mothers, wives, lovers, barmaids and truck-stop waitresses. Housework, to be sure, is drudgery, but, with rare exceptions, is discussed only when justifying a love affair.

6) Individual worth. Country music is rooted in a belief in the worth of an individual. People live lives of quiet dignity, their strength and character not always appreciated by others. They meet and come to terms with, but do not always conquer, blindness, death, poverty, alcoholism and being orphaned. "MacArthur's Hand," for example, tells the story of an old man being sentenced for vagrancy. Once decorated for heroism by the General himself, the proud veteran is now destitute. The old man summarizes his case for the judge, "I was fit to fight your wars, / Am I not fit to walk your streets?" The quality of the man's life is not measured by his conventional accomplishments but by the content of his character.

7) Rugged individualism. Not only is the individual important, but he, for it usually is a man, controls his own destiny. As Charlie Daniels boasts, "I ain't ask'n nobody for noth'n if I can't get it on my own." Travel, violence, prison and drink constitute the world of the rugged individualist. The jobs of these men are more expressions of their personality than sources of income. The cowboy has given way to the trucker as mythic hero, symbolizing self-reliance and personal independence. The danger, the uniqueness of the life and the sense of camaraderie are evident in songs such as "White Knight" and "Big Mama." The trucker is answerable only to himself.

Barroom fights, time in jail, wild parties and getting drunk are seldom glorified as ends in themselves but, instead, as rites of the rugged individualist. They are actions emblematic of a life style.

There are, however, occasional doubts as to whether the life style really brings happiness. Titles such as "Here I am Drunk Again" and lyrics such as "Today I'll face the big fight / But I really had a ball last night" express an ambiguous love-hate relationship for the wild life, albeit a minority one.

8) Patriotism. Perhaps no aspect of country music has received more attention than its patriotic theme. The aggressive militancy of the Vietnam era, when approximately 10% of country music dealt with social or political issues (DiMaggio, Peterson and Escoe 44), will be discussed later, but, suffice it to say here that contemporary songs are overwhelmingly non-polemical. Indeed, social and political issues have almost entirely disappeared as song topics. Of the eight themes, the patriotic currently receives the least emphasis.

Of course, country performers are not alone in singing about true love, the wild side of life, or love of country. Not all the themes in country music, to be sure, are unique to the idiom. What is unique is the symbolic world that is sketched by these themes. It is peopled almost exclusively by adults in the prime of life. Affairs of significance center around the male. The rural life, which has been recently embraced by other genres, has been a favorite image of country writers for over fifty years. Adolescence is infrequently recalled. College, like business and the professions, is all but non-existent, and work is dull, physical and unrewarding. Marriage, whether good or bad, is at the center of romantic relations. In this world, people, above all, retain their individuality, whether struggling for control over their own destiny or preserving through inner dignity.

First, although it uses some of the same themes as other genres, only country music features all eight themes described here. These themes form a symbolic world that is endemic to country music. Some aspects of the landscape are found in other musical idioms, but nowhere else are social relationships exactly so constituted.

Second, these themes do not change over time. Writers may fashion new and different ways to present the themes, but the themes themselves remain essentially unchanged year after year. Whether the setting is the railroads, mines, or Harlan County in the 1930s, or highways, factories and urban bars in the 1970s, the message is the same.

Third, the presence or absence of certain instruments, generally, does not make music country. To be sure, many country songs may be identified by the stylized steel guitars and fiddles. Traditional instruments and instrumentation, however, are not the reliable trademark that they once were. Guitars, fiddles and banjos have been appropriated by other genres. Some country performers, in turn, added electricity to their instruments and engineering to their voices. At the same time, an increasing amount of recording is done with orchestral accompaniment.

Fourth, the appeal of country music, like other musical idioms, is not always confined to its own listeners. Successful songs may "cross-over," achieving popularity in more than one genre, by attracting a country as well as a non-country audience. Glenn Campbell and Ann Murray are as much country entertainers as pop celebrities. Some "progressive country " and "country rock" performers, such as Charlie Daniels and Jimmy Buffet, have both a rock and a traditional country following, with each group drawing something different from the music.

Country Music Perspectives

These eight themes unambiguously express daily problems and primal emotions. In addition, song lyrics provide perspectives on the social and personal relations represented in the themes. Perspective is provided when the audience is informed of the singer's attitude toward the primary theme in a song. For example, what is the performer's attitude toward being a trucker? Basically, five perspectives appear to characterize country music. Although many can be, and are, taken toward all eight themes, certain perspectives are more closely associated with particular themes.

1) Expressive. The performer's purpose in a number of songs is merely to express or describe his/her feelings. An exuberance for life and a need to communicate one's satisfaction undergird the expressive impulse which occurs most frequently in the extremes of rugged individualism and the satisfactory love relationship. Songs like "Dear Woman" and "I've Got a Winner in You" so obviously disparate from "The Red-neck National Anthem," spring, nonetheless, from a shared desire to glorify life choices.

The need to communicate feelings is also manifest in narrative songs.

These three-minute morality plays are most often employed in describing unsatisfactory love relationships or instructing the audience on the importance of individual worth. George Jones and Tammy Wynette's "Golden Rings" follows the prescribed formula, the first verse describing a couple's purchase of a wedding ring in a pawnshop, the second their marriage "later on that afternoon" and culminating in the break-up of the marriage in the third verse. The expressive perspective is common, but not preeminent, in country music.

2) Utopia. Many of the people who are not happy with their current situation imagine affairs as being, or having been, better at some other time and/or place. If life is somehow insufficient, it was better in some other place or at some other time. "Paradise," for example, looks back on an agrarian utopia. "A backwoods old town" in western Kentucky is nostalgically recalled as the setting of childhood memories. Its idyllic landscape, however, is a thing of the past since "Mr. Peabody's coal train has hauled it away." While most songs are not so explicit, performers, nonetheless, express an acute awareness that there are conditions which are more desirable than the one in which they currently find themselves. Past and present utopias can be found in most characteristic themes.

Other themes are sometimes also approached from a utopian perspective as, for example, lost love in "The Most Beautiful Girl in the World" and trucking on "Convoy." The latter song is a saga of a cross-country truck convoy that evades the law and violates the speed limit. Utopias are real or fictive, occurring in the present and the past, but it is singular that there are almost no future utopias in country music. Emmylou Harris's "One of These Days," a general reaffirmation that things will be better in the future, is a rare exception.

3) Escape and fantasy. Perhaps the most prevalent attitude expressed in country music is escape and fantasy. Sometimes the flight is physical, but, more often, it is psychological. It characterizes unsatisfactory male-female relations, rugged individualism and work. Assignation is often portrayed as flight from an unsympathetic spouse. Titles such as "Help Me Make It Through the Night," "She's Helping Me Get Over You" and "From Woman to Woman" are suggestive of the attitude. Work is confronted with psychological fantasy as well as physical escape. In "Daydreams About Night Things," Ronnie Milsap, for example, sings, "While my hands make a livin' / My mind's home lovin' you." Fifteen years in the factory have cost Johnny Paycheck his "woman" and given him nothing in return. He fantasizes that he will hit his foreman and walk out, after telling the boss to "take this job and shove it." Much of rugged individualism is also escape and fantasy. The destination is less important than the trip in songs like "Ridin' My Thumb to Mexico," while the bar, with its attendant drinking and fighting, appears as a refuge from daily problems (Tribe 44).

4) Forbearance. Forbearance, the determination to persevere, is often an indication of individual worth as well as being a perspective that is frequently adopted in family relations. People in these songs do not conjure visions or try to escape into fantasy but confront their problems directly. Like the veteran in "MacArthur's Hand," they continue to strive, although the tide of events may

run against them. When laid-off "down at the factory" before Christmas, Merle Haggard recalls how he had "wanted Christmas to be right for daddy's girl" but now hopes only to "make it through December." He does not recall better days or get drunk, but instead, makes plans for the family's future.*

5) Polarization. Although the polarized perspective is almost entirely absent from contemporary country music, the attitude deserves attention since it played such a prominent role in the songs of the 1960s. Polarization is, of course, a rhetorical strategy as well as a perspective, but the concern here is with its function as perspective, with what it suggests about people's attitudes and world view.

Country music has long defended the values of its audience, and its defense has been most aggressive when those values were most seriously challenged. Comparing the advantages of farm and city life is an old theme in country music, but the social upheaval of the 1960s, with songs like "I Wouldn't Live in New York City If You Gave Me the Whole Darn Town," introduced a shrillness seldom heard before. New issues, like the changing role of women, were cast in extremist alternatives. Tammy Wynette, for example, sang the polemical "Love Me, Don't Liberate Me" as well as the more traditional "Stand By Your Man."

But it was the Vietnam War and domestic dissent that elicited the strongest reaction from country artists. From December 1965 through August 1966, "there were always at least four Vietnam songs on the *Billboard* country charts" (Lund 211-23). Most defended the justness of the War and the wisdom of American involvement. The lyrics of these songs, frequently set to martial music, often conveyed a "love it or leave it" tone. By December 1969 and the release of "Oakie from Muskogee," comment was channeled into attacking dissenters, defending traditional American values and generally ignoring the propriety of American involvement (Lund 224). If some country music frequently presented a polarized perspective during the 1960s, it was reflecting political and social attitudes of the day (Lund 224).

The Country Audience

To say, as some critics have, that country music is "Southern white, working-class music" (qtd. in Reagan 67) is only partially true. Its following has grown in recent years until, today, it is more national than regional. This is only one characteristic that emerges from a rough profile that it is now possible to draw of the country music audience. It is clear that the average country music fan is increasingly likely to live in the North. Moreover, research indicates that he/she will not be a transplanted Southerner but a native Northerner (Peterson and DiMaggio). This trend enabled radio station WHN in New York City to increase its audience 50% within eight months to 1.2 million after adopting an all-country format (Stein 4; "Why Country" 48). The shift is also reflected in record sales. Approximately 10% of Loretta Lynn's records are sold in the

*The release of "If We Make it Till December" coincided with the Arab Oil embargo and a Detroit auto strike in the fall of 1973. Although coincidence, the timing may have influenced audience perception of the lyrics.

New York metropolitan area (Stein 4). Furthermore, "there is no regional difference between the South and the rest of the nation in the distribution of country music listeners by age, occupation, years of schooling and family income" (Peterson and DiMaggio 402).

Evidence suggests that the country music audience clusters between the ages of 25 and 49 (Peterson and Davis 307). Country music also has the greatest appeal for the less well educated. As years of education increase, the probability that one will be a country music fan decreases so that high school and especially grade school graduates are significantly over represented in the country audience (Peterson and Davis 308).

If country music is no longer a primarily Southern idiom, it remains predominantly working class. It is the rare executive or professional who is a country music fan. More common, but still disproportionately small, are the numbers of fans among the ranks of managers, clerical and sales workers (DiMaggio Peterson and Escoe 49-50). Peterson and Davis in their 1974 study of "The Contemporary American Radio Audience" point out that "fully 45.5 percent of country music listeners are craftsmen, skilled or semi-skilled workers." They also report that unskilled workers (farm and manual laborers, cooks, porters, bartenders, service workers, etc.) are over represented in the ranks of country fans. The country audience, therefore, is concentrated in the "middle income category," earning a family income of between $5,000 and $15,000 in 1975 (310). Few of the very poor or the very wealthy are attracted to country music.

Part of the attraction of country music for this audience would appear to be in the lyrics. Its themes and perspectives reflect common experiences. It is music of identification, written for and about working class adults. Like the people portrayed in the songs, country fans also get married, raise a family, hold a job, take pride in their country as well as confront marital and family problems, illness and death.

Marriage and family are probably fulcrums of everyday experience. Their real work holds out as much opportunity for personal enrichment as do the fictional jobs of Ronnie Milsap and Johnny Cash (McCarthy, Peterson and Yancey 59). It is not surprising, therefore, that negative perspectives outnumber positive in country music and that any type of future utopia is almost nonexistent.

The growth of country music in recent years, however, has attracted increasing numbers of Northerners, urbanites and even some college students (McCandlish 1), groups less likely to identify with some traditional country themes. Nonetheless, the music is able to express the values of both its old and new constituencies. That it is able to do this is attributable to the audiences' perception.

Popular culture materials, such as music, may serve different purposes for the same, or different, audiences (Reisman 409). It would appear that country music, by communicating values of newly acquired significance, is mirroring an important portion of Northern urban opinion. As the Program Director for New York City's WHN explains, "There is a back-to-the soil feeling among urbanites now-a-days. People are ecology conscious. They long for simple days when music reflected love and loneliness and death and going to jail, the stuff country music is all about (qtd. in Krebs 62).

Recent converts in Northern cities, then, are attracted by the ability of the music to articulate their problems. They can identify not only with the common themes of marriage, home and family and individual worth, but they can also appreciate the importance of self-reliance, forbearance, the agrarian life style and the general emphasis on the quality of life. In this, they are not appreciably different form their counterparts in the South where "apparently, a larger number of working and lower-class urban whites dream of some day resigning from their jobs and moving to the country to earn a living on a small farm."

In sum, the lyrics of country songs reflect the values of its audience. The fictive world created by country music is not the same as the real world of audience members, but it is one they can easily understand and with which they can identify.

Notes

[1]Legal regulations and community standards of good taste prevent the overt expression of certain audience values. Most notable is the underground market for racist records. Jens Lund, "Country Music Goes to War: Song for the Red-Blooded American, "*Popular Music and Society* 1 (1972): 221-223, John D. McCarthy, Richard A. Peterson and William L. Yancey, "Singing Along with the Silent Majority," *Side Saddle on the Golden Calf*, ed. George H. Lewis (Salt Lake City: Goodyear, 1972) 59.

Works Cited

Carey, James T. "The Changing Courtship Patterns of Popular Songs." *American Journal of Sociology 64 (1957: 723.*

Cook, Bruce. "Nashville's Counter-culture." *Saturday Review* 3 (4 Oct. 1975): 48-49.

"Country Goes Pop." *Horizon* 20 (Nov. 1977): 52-57.

"Cross-overs to Country Music Rouse Nashville." *New York Times* 4 Dec. 1974.

Dickson, Paul. "Singing to Silent America." *The Nation* 23 Feb. 1970: 211-213.

DiMaggio, Paul, Richard A. Peterson and Jack R. Escoe, Jr. "Country Music: Ballad of the Silent Majority." *Social Change.*

Hayakawa, S. I. "Popular Songs vs. the Facts of Life." *Mass Culture: The Popular Arts in America.* Eds. Bernard Rosenberg and David Manning White. Glencoe, IL:Free, 1957.

Hemphill, Paul. *The Nashville Sound.* New York: Simon and Schuster, 1958.

Horton, Donald J. "The Dialogue of Courtship in Popular Song." *American Journal off Sociology* 62 (1957).

King, Florence. "Rednecks, White Socks, and Blue-Ribbon Fear." *Harper's* July 1974: 30-34.

Krebs, Allen. "WHN Joins Camp of Country Music." *New York Times* 26 Feb. 1973.

Lewis, George H. "Country Music Lyrics." *Journal of Communication* 26 (1976).

Lund, Jens. "Country Music Goes to War: Song for the Red-Blooded American. *"Popular Music and Society* 1 (1972): 221-23.

McCandlish, Phillips. "Leaders in Country Music See Chance to Win City." *New York Times* 16 April 1973.

McCarthy, John D., Richard A. Peterson and William L. Yancey. "Singing Along with the Silent Majority." *Side-Saddle on the Golden Calf*. Ed. George H. Lewis. Salt Lake City: Goodyear, 1972.

Peterson, Richard A. and David G. Berger. "Entrepreneurship in Organization: Evidence from the Popular Music Industry." *Administrative Science Quarterly* 16 (1971).

_____. "Three Eras in the Manufacture of Popular Music Lyrics." *The Sounds of Social Change: Studies in Popular Culture*. Eds. R. Serge Denisoff and Richard A. Peterson. Chicago: Rand-McNally, 1972. 288-289.

Peterson, Richard A. and Russell B. Davis, Jr. "The Contemporary American Radio Audience." *Popular Music and Society* 3.4 (1974).

Peterson, Richard A. and Paul DiMaggio. "From Region to Class, The Changing Locus of Country Music: A Test of the Massification of Hypothesis." *Social Forces* 53 (1975).

Reagan, Mike. "The Pious Rhetoric of Country Music." *Music Journal* 27 (1969).

Reisman, David. "Listening to Popular Music." *Mass Culture*.

Rockwell, John. "Blues and other Noises, in the Night." *Saturday Review* 3 (4 Sept. 1976). Street Journal 24 Dec. 1973.

Toy, Steve. "C & W Road Widening $300-Mil Nationwide: Biz As Appeal Soars." *Variety* 12 June 1974.

Tribe, Ivan M. "The Hillbilly vs. the City: Urban Images in Country Music." *John Edwards Memorial Fund Quarterly* 10.2 (1974).

"Why Country Music is Suddenly Big Business." *U.S. News* 29 July 1974.

Tension, Conflict and Contradiction in Country Music1

George H. Lewis

He's a walking contradiction,
Partly truth and partly fiction...

"The Pilgrim"
Kris Kristofferson

John Hartford, the country music singer and songwriter, has called country songs three minute word-movies and that is, to a great extent, exactly what they are. Deriving from a long line of tradition that casts back into the shade and shadows of turn of the century Appalachia, successful country songs reflect, usually from an intimate sort of perspective, the everyday trials, troubles, hopes, fears and dreams of their audience. The messages of these short word-movies are clear and simply put. Many times one needs only to hear the song title to know what the movie is about. Who could mistake the messages in songs entitled; "Pick Me Up On Your Way Down," "Dim Lights, Thick Smoke and Loud, Loud Music," "I'm The Only Hell My Mamma Ever Raised," or "Thank God and Greyhound You Are Gone?"

As country music historian Bill C. Malone has pointed out, this form of music has remained vital to its audience across nearly a century of complex and rapid social change because it "mirrors the social mores of a broad stratum of people, thus both reflecting and shaping their values...In thousands of homes, churches, cafes, taverns, auditoriums, dance halls, and radio stations, the music...gives evidence of being the chief cultural staple of a large group of people who can neither understand nor accept any other form...Country music...is a manner of viewing or reflecting life. To many people, it has been a way of life itself" (Malone 359-61).

This way of life has, increasingly since the 1950s and the close of the Korean War, been subject to the tensions and strains of a nation undergoing tremendous social and technological change. And yet, when country songs are analyzed over time, their lyrical content seems surprisingly steady, revolving in general around the topics of home and family, patriotism, work, love, liquor and the passing of the good old days.[2] Indeed, as DiMaggio, Peterson and Escoe

Reprinted with permission from *Journal of Popular Culture* 24.4 (Spring 1991): 103-117.

note in their analysis of core country music listeners, they are, in general, "urban living, white adults with rural roots who are established in home, family, and job, and yet who are content with none of these" (41). The author asserts that *tensions* raised as a result of economic problems, social change, migration from rural to urban settings and the shifting lifestyles of these persons help to keep their attention focused on these central life topics—the topics most often addressed in country songs. As the lyrics of one such song wryly comment; "I may fall again, but I'll never get up this slow" (Sons and Todd 122).

Although, as referenced above, there has been attention paid to mapping the "core values" of the country music audience by social scientists—especially over the past twenty years—nearly all of this research has been focused on the task of isolating common sets of values and concerns as they appear in the music, topically listing these values and concerns and attempting to establish linkages, sometimes inferential, sometimes based on questionnaire data, sometimes based on song popularity and preference, from these songs to the core values and concerns of their audience. This is an important first step in cultural analysis, and it has uncovered a set of topics of concern that has changed very slightly over the time of analysis, although there have been some shifts in emphasis and even in how the topics have been approached, over time.

For example, in love relationships, the treatment of divorce seems to have become more central over the past decade, as well as reflecting new bitterness and anger on the part of the male, as can be seen in Jerry Reed's "She Got the Goldmine and I Got the Shaft," or George Strait's "All My Ex's Live In Texas." These sorts of emotions connected to the breakup of a love affair, or marriage, have taken on a stronger emphasis lately, doing so not by directing more anger toward the woman directly, but by focusing this anger on the legal institutions of the society, against whom the country boy is powerless to defend himself and with whom his ex-spouse has made an exceedingly dirty deal.

Yet, as suggested by this example, if one looks further and more closely at these core values that are expressed in country music, one is immediately struck with the inconsistencies, conflicts and, in some cases, contradictions among them. In the case of divorce, to continue the example, at the same time blame is diverted from the woman to the greedy and powerful state in terms of the economic consequences of divorce, it is laid at her door in an interpersonal, psychological sense, as expressed bluntly in the line; "I gave her a ring, she gave me the finger" (Sons and Todd).

Other conflicts and contradictions in contemporary country lyrics include concerns for individual expression and freedom being voiced, but also (and many times in the same song) yearnings for the security and dependence of a stable family life. There are expressions of social conservatism, yet also an economic position that can be, in many ways, interpreted as liberal. There are strong expressions of patriotism as an unquestioning acceptance of the political order and, at the same time, a respect for personal autonomy and freedom. There is the importance of work and the rejection of it as alienating, dull and demeaning. And there is the glorification of illicit sex, yet the yearning for a stable, loving marriage (Lewis 9-10).

In fact, the tensions, conflicts and contradictions in the values expressed in country music seem almost more intense than do their degree of similarity and interconnectedness. Viewed in this way, country songs are many times, in Kristofferson's apt phrase, "walking contradictions" and certainly "problems" for any social analyst who seeks to find in them harmonious and consistent value patterning.

Tensions, Conflicts and Contradictions

So far I have grouped the terms tension, conflict and contradiction together, in suggesting the disharmonious nature of the lyrical content of much of country music. But these are strange bedfellows and it now seems time to distinguish among them, for each concept refers to distinct and different types of disharmony.

By *tensions*, I mean problems arising from competing social expectations that derive from various facets of a social position one holds. For example, it is expected in most country audiences that a wife tend to the needs of her children and also be a social support for her husband. This can lead to tension and frustration, as Loretta Lynn points out in "One's On The Way," a word-movie in which a pregnant wife, trying desperately to cope with overwhelming housework and sick and screaming kids, gets a call from her husband, who announces from the local bar that he is bringing his drinking buddies right over for dinner. Her response? Repressed anger, directed at women media stars, like Jackie O, who can jet around the world without cares or responsibilities while she, with resignation, deals with the tensions of real life.

By *conflict*, I mean problems arising from the clash of perspectives' of differentially socialized individuals, whether this difference is a result of differences in gender, social class, age, region, or other major demographic differences. Such conflicts involve different views of the world and what is appropriate, or involve conflicts between mutually incompatible expectations and values, whether these are in the area of male-female sex roles, conflicts between the young and the elderly, between rural and urban expectations, or conflict between social classes, such as that reflected in Merle Travis' 1947 classic "Sixteen Tons," with its refrain of "I owe my soul to the company store," or the more recent hit, "9 To 5," by Dolly Parton, in which both class and gender conflict are reflected in lines like: "They let you dream just to watch them shatter; You're just a step on the boss man's ladder..."

Finally, by *contradiction*, I refer to inconsistencies *within* a value pattern—inconsistencies that can reach the extreme of opposition, in that, if logic is to prevail, one cannot hold simultaneously to both values or behave appropriately according to expectations derived from these values, taken together. For example, Porter Wagoner, in "The Pain Of Loving You," sings of loving and hating a woman at the same time: "The two have bound me heart and soul, so strong that I can't let you go." A second example of value contradiction, this time in the political realm, is the notion that unquestioning acceptance of the external authority and activities of agents of the state is a form of patriotism that *supports* the concept of individual freedom, a contradiction found in many "red, white and blue" country songs of patriotism, such as "Proud To Be An American," or Merle Haggard's "Fighting Side Of Me."

As with most good works of art, whether they be labeled folk, popular or elite, country music is most successful when it probes these central tensions, conflicts and cultural contradictions of its audience. These, the "duellin' values," referred to in the title of this paper, give the song its sharpness of purpose, its interpretive power, its cultural cutting edge. Such pieces, in whatever genre one is analyzing, seem to engage their audience more thoroughly, to be talked and thought about more, than do pieces that more statically reflect cultural harmony. In country music, as elsewhere, the "silly love songs" are played and forgotten, while the quiet but constant tension and masked bitterness that tears through to the surface at the close of a song such as Willie Nelson's "Funny How Time Slips Away," will be recalled and rerecorded for years.[3]

Point and Counterpoint

As Kai T. Erikson pointed out in his study of Appalachian culture and the destruction of community caused by the 1972 Buffalo Creek flood, "the identifying motifs of a culture are not just the core values to which people pay homage, but also the lines of point and counterpoint along which they diverge (81). In examining individual responses to this sudden and disastrous flood, Erikson noted seemingly conflicting shifts in value based responses on the part of flood survivors, as well as contradictory patterns paralleling, but in a more dramatic fashion, what has been described thus far in this paper. He points out that "when a person is caught between two competing strains in his cultural surround...both halves of the dilemma remain as active potentials in his consciousness, ready to assert themselves if conditions change. Thus, every human culture can be visualized, if only in part, as a kind of theater in which certain contrary tendencies are played out (82). When these "contrary tendencies," be they in the milder forms of value tensions or more dramatic forms of conflicts or contradictions, become primary, Erikson suggests that it is "only reasonable to suspect that the potential had been there all along—hidden away in the folds of the culture," and represents a slide along what he terms "lines of point and counterpoint," or axes of cultural variation (82).

This concept of axes of cultural variation which stretch between points of "contrary tendency" is similar to the concept of polar oppositions, which Swindler has used to analyze changes in the mythology of love in American culture. As she describes the polar opposites, she sees them as symbolic "tensions which have given the myth its richness, its seeming power to reconcile divergent needs and opposing parts of the self" (131). This concept of cultural opposition, whether seen as tensions between pairs of polar opposites or as axes of cultural variation along which individuals and groups may move, is a useful way of viewing the tensions, conflicts and contradictions that exist in country music.

Following from an analysis of the common core values that appear in country music and the cultural concerns reflected in these values, I have abstracted what seem to be three very general axes of cultural variation along which the tensions, conflicts and contradictions in the music can be charted. These are; 1) connections between the individual and society; 2) social relations of freedom or restraint; and 3) orientations toward the past (usually defined as rural) as opposed to the present (usually defined as urban). These axes are, admittedly, highly abstract and general; however, together they form a conceptual structure within which one can move to more specifically identified tensions, conflicts and contradictions, as will be done later in this paper.

At this point, it is instructive to illuminate, by example, the three general axes of cultural variation that have been proposed.

Although there are many areas in which connections between the individual and society are problematic in country music, one major area is in one's relation to the state. What are the appropriate patriotic attachments and responsibilities of an individual in this culture? Concerns in this area are pointed up by Waylon Jennings' song "America," in which the singer first lauds the country and its political leadership in traditional patriotic ways, then contradictorily points out the unfair way Native Americans have been treated and suggests, in the spirit of patriotism, that reparation is due and should be supported by us all.

Another major area of problematic individual—society connections is of a social nature and is exemplified by a range of alienated reactions, ranging from the anger of David Alan Coe's "Take This Job and Shove It" to the quiet desperation of drinking songs like Merle Haggard's "Misery and Gin," or Kristofferson's "Sunday Morning Coming Down," in which, hung over and alone in the city, the singer "stumbles down the steps to greet the day."

The second cultural axis, revolving around the social relations of freedom and restraint, is also addressed by Kristofferson in his "Me And Bobby McGee," where he defines freedom as "nothin' left to lose." The subtext here is, paradoxically, that true freedom can only be defined by social restraint—that the social ties of interpersonal intimacy, if they are genuine, are the very restraints that can make one free. On the other hand, after having longed for and finally attained the social restraints of marriage and a family, Rodney Crowell sings on "Diamonds And Dirt," only "when I'm free again, I'll be somewhere bein' me again."

The mystery involved in this contradiction is probed in K.T. Oslin's "Hold Me," in which both husband and wife are running away from social

With no warning to each other one day as they leave for work in the morning, they each drive separately away, "determined I was never comin' back." Yet, for reasons they do not understand, they each turn their car around and head back to the social restraints of their lives, asking only of each other that evening in quiet mutual confessions to "hold me."

Finally, orientations towards the rural past as opposed to the urban present usually involves romantic nostalgia for simple, rural settings filled with the imagined warmth of primary, gemeinschaft relations and are seen in songs such as Bobby Bare's "Detroit City," in which the singer whose urban present is a nightmare of alienating assembly line work in an automotive plant alternated with desperate nightly escapes into alcohol and bar life, falls asleep and dreams of "those cotton fields and home...I dreamed about my mother, dear old papa, sisters and brothers, and I dreamed about a love who's been waiting there so long...I want to go home."

Yet the contradictions are there, in this set of oppositions as well, as pointed out in Dolly Parton's "In The Good Old Days, When Times Were Bad" and John D. Loudermilk's bitter "Tobacco Road," in which the singer tells of being "born in a dump," where "Mamma died and daddy got drunk," leaving him on his own to "die or grow." Even then, to the singer, Tobacco Road is home, "the only life I ever knowed. I despise you 'cause you're filthy, but I loves you 'cause you're home."

Keeping the three general axes of cultural variation in mind, I would now like to discuss two representative settings and situations in which tensions, conflicts and contradictions are highly in evidence, although these two are certainly not the only two areas of such disharmony in country music. The first area of discussion has to do with situations of relatively dramatic social change, both in the society at large and with respect to the country music audience, as subculture, within that society. The second has to do with the problems involved in interpersonal relationships, especially the interpersonal relationships of love and attraction.

Social Change and the Country Music Subculture

Country music has always had a strong strain of traditionalism and conservatism running through it. This is nowhere more evident than in its reaction to the major changes wrought in the past century by the forces of urbanization, industrialization and the secularization of society. Nowhere does this general concern with the macro effects of social change come through better than in Roy Acuff's "Wreck On The Highway," recorded in 1946, just as the forces of modernization developed during World War II were beginning their massive reshaping of the American cultural landscape. Interestingly, the song was written ten years before by the Reverend Dorsey Dixon, as a direct reaction to technological change. As his son recalls: "My father wrote this song when the '36 Fords came out with a V-8 engine and began to kill people all over the nation. The wreck took place at the Triangle Filling Station in Rockingham, North Carolina. Dad went down and seen the wreck, seen the whiskey, blood and glass on the floor of the car (Horstman 99-100). When Roy Acuff recorded it ten years later, he changed the song slightly, and the specific and horrifying image of the crash became a metaphor for America—rushing blindly down a rain-soaked highway, jacked up on whiskey and relying on the secular values of technology, not the sacred ones of religion, to guide the country through the night. As the song ends: "I heard the groans of the dying, but I didn't hear nobody pray."

Social change in this century has prompted massive migrations among members of the country audience as well, from the 1930's Oklahoma-Arkansas-Texas exodus to California, fueled by automation, dust storms and the depression; to the movements in the late 1930s and 1940s from the poor rural south to the more northern urban centers, factories and assembly lines of Baltimore, Detroit, Cincinnati and Chicago[4] These migrations not only spread country music and its audience across the country and into the major urban centers, it also created a sort of culture shock for the displaced rural Southerner trying to cope with a radically new environment—one in which culture conflict and potential value contradiction awaited in every new social encounter and at every unfamiliar streetcorner (Killian).

These new experiences soon became a part of country music. Danny Dill, who wrote "Detroit City," a song discussed earlier in this paper, recalls seeing these southern people while he was playing in little clubs in Detroit. "They did go north. I sat there and talked to these people. They were from Alabama, West Tennessee, Kentucky, and they'd go to Detroit and work in the car factories. And to keep from being so lonely they'd go sit in a bar and drink. And when they did get home, they'd get there with no money" (Horstman 9-10).

Southern servicemen, coming home from World War II and the Korean War, spread country music further, exposing non-Southerners to it in the military barracks and, after the wars, settling down outside the rural south, usually in urban areas of the north and west (Killian; Lund). And so the conflicts and contradictions continued—and continued to be reflected in country songs. In the "Streets of Baltimore," written by Tompall Glazer and Harlan Howard in the early 1960s, a man sells his small Tennessee farm to take his woman to Baltimore, "where she longed to be." But while she is taken in by the bright lights of the city, he works at a long, dull factory job and is tired to the bone when he gets home. Finally, realizing she loves the bright lights "more than me," he leaves alone, broke and broken, for home, while his baby, another kind of victim of the urban trap, continues on her own to "walk the streets of Baltimore."

This musical reaction to what are seen as the problems of the impersonality and strangeness of urban life as contrasted with the past rural simplicity of home continues into the late 1980s to be a theme in country music, even though the rural-urban transformation of the country is nearly complete. In "South of Cincinnati," Dwight Yoakam contrasts the southern woman, writing to her love in the north from "where the dogwood trees grow, south of the Mason-Dixon line, in the home you left long ago," to her departed lover, lying drunk in a "cold grey apartment in Chicago," with a cigarette drowning beside him in a glass of gin. In "I Sang Dixie," Yoakam recounts the story of a southern drunk, down on his luck, dying alone in cold, unfeeling Los Angeles, a city he also paints harshly in "Guitars, Cadillacs, Etc." in which the singer is carved by the sharp knives of urban culture into a new man—soulless, but better able to survive the modern urban environment because of this. As he sings, there "ain't no glamour in this tinseled land of lost and wasted lives." Observing that "painful scars are all that's left of me," the singer does thank his urban girl "for teaching me brand new ways to be cruel."

Finally, in looking at social change and the country music subculture, one must note the diffusion of this music, in a standardized, mass culture form, to an audience far larger than the original subculture.[5] Although detailed examination of this phenomenon is beyond the scope of this paper, it is important to note its impact on the traditional audience and its music. This explosion of popularity of country music, building in the early 1970s and peaking in the early 1980s in America, coincided with the conservative, even reactionary climate of the country. This new popularity of the music, reaching far beyond its original audience, was as much lamented by them as it was lauded by the country recording industry, which made fortunes with slicked down, easy listening "urban cowboy" music. As William Ivey, Director of the Country Music Hall of Fame put it in 1984: "The gloomiest prophecies were coming true. Country music was about to disappear. After having evolved to a point where it was virtually identical to pop music, and after pop artists were successfully imitating country style and generating country hits, it seemed that the artistic tradition, begun in the 1920s, was about to end in a flurry of crossover hits and pop impersonations" (Ivey 15).

This diffusion of pop country music to a culturally alien audience was reacted to on record with songs such as "I Was Country When Country Wasn't Cool," which invoked images of listening to authentic country music artists, such as George Jones, in an earlier period and having members of the larger culture, who now were soaking up the songs of "pop country," look down their noses at the original stuff, or Tammy Wynette's sarcastic word-movie about the urban cowboy who "came into my life on a bucking bull machine."

With the exception of some songs such as these, which pointed out the value conflicts between the traditional audience and its now much larger pop public, most of the successful urban cowboy music of the late 1970s and 1980s stayed in the safe area of songs about romantic relationships or the pleasures of drinking, with an occasional Kenny Rogers "story song" or pious patriotic hymn thrown in for good measure. Buried in this larger pop mix, the traditional themes and songs survived, carried on by singers and writers such as George Jones, Merle Haggard, Loretta Lynn, Conway Twitty and even Willie Nelson.

As country music sales dropped off in the mid-1980s and the larger middle-of-the-road audience turned elsewhere for its entertainment, there began a revival of traditional forms and themes in country music. As RCA vice president Jerry Bradley said in 1984: "It's all going back to fiddles and pedal steel guitars, back to the basics of the music" (Ivey 17). This neo-traditional music of the late 1980s looks to the themes of the past, the common core of concern that has always existed in country music and attempts to update these concerns, conflicts and contradictions, making them fresh and relevant for the contemporary country audience. New stars include singers and writers like Dwight Yoakam, Ricky Skaggs (who, among other things, is bringing sacred concerns back into the secular music) and Nanci Griffith, who is writing new songs in the tradition of looking to the rural past. Griffith, though, in the late 1980s, questions the reality of such a position, although she does not deny the emotional lure it offers. As she bemusedly sings in "You Can't Go Home Again": "This 'ol town never did really care that much for me...I don't know why I always come here in my dreams."

Interpersonal Relationships
In turning attention to the micro level of interpersonal relationships and

how tensions, conflicts and contradictions in these relationships are mirrored in country songs, one should, perhaps, first note the central place in the male country audience of the "buddy" phenomenon. Male bonding in this culture, whether for the purpose of leisure activities such as hunting or fishing, or for bar hopping, chasing women and brawling, is a standard, nearly cliched, aspect of interpersonal association. This buddy phenomenon is mirrored in the popularity of male country singers, such as Waylon Jennings and Willie Nelson, banding together in pairs to record whole albums of duets.

And yet, if one examines the lyric content of the country songs that relate to this idealized phenomenon, one is more likely to find jealously, conflict and even betrayal, than one is to find a reflection of harmonious relations.

This is highly in evidence on "Pancho and Lefty," one of the most lyrically ambiguous, yet best, of the buddy songs. Written by Townes Van Zandt, the song became a hit with the hard core country audience in Willie Nelson and Merle Haggard's "buddy" style duet. In the song, which has been interpreted to be about topics as diverse as drug smuggling, homosexuality and the Mexican Revolution (Thompson), one thing is very clear—Lefty, the American member of the outlaw male pair, betrays his Mexican buddy Pancho to the federals. Pancho is apparently killed, and, because of his bargain with the law, Lefty is allowed to escape across the border to the north, where he finishes his guilt ridden days in the frigid northern "hell" of Ohio.

In another, near reversal of this theme, Eddie Raven's "Joe Knows How To Live," Joe quietly slips away from his boring, deadend urban job in the north, deserting his buddy who is trapped in the urban factory system. Joe drives, this time south, across the border to Mexico, where the singer jealously, but enviously, envisions him lying on the beach, drinking tequila and having an affair with a beautiful woman.

Songs such as these suggest the buddy phenomenon is one as likely characterized by competition, conflict and even betrayal, as it is by mutual support and respect and that emotions such as jealousy and guilt are as likely to be involved in it as are emotions of admiration, care and concern. This, of course, points to a major contradiction in the male culture these songs reflect. Men are supposed to be tough and competitive and are likely to see other men as rivals for jobs, women's affections and even social approval (Weitz; Rubin). With such a cultural overlay, it is tough to establish any sort of primary support system of mutual caring and emotional help.

It can be done, though, and in some buddy songs this bond is portrayed more as the idealistic one of strong mutual support. Yet this support is usually cast against a social backdrop of tensions and conflicting responsibilities, as it is in Billy Joe Shafer's "Willie The Wandering Gypsy And Me," a hit for Waylon Jennings. In this song, the singer is married and his wife is "tight with an overdue baby," but his buddy Gypsy keeps "yellin', Willie, let's go." Gypsy wants the two of them to follow the rodeo, recalling the days when the west was wild and male-bonded buddies, without the social obligations of family, could ride free, partaking of women's favors where and when they wished and not being tied down by the social order that has now stuffed their heads "full of figures and angles." Willie, on the other hand, is caught between the expectations and responsibilities of family and those of the free roaming buddy system. "Rolled from the same makings" as Gypsy, how can he leave his wife at this point in anything but his memories and dreams?

This conflict, revolving around the axis of freedom and restraint, is a central problem built into the expected male role of this culture and one that is mirrored in many country songs. Men are supposed to be free and independent in their relationships, moving about the social landscape with little to tie them down. Yet, at the same time, they are supposed to be entering into the restraining social bonds of marriage and family. Cowboy songs, railroad songs and trucker songs—of which there are many—celebrate life on the road, but usually include a yearning for the settled life as a subtext, as in Red Foley's "Freight Train Blues," in which the singer admits he's "tried a hundred times to stop and settle down," but he can't make it work, or in Leon Payne's "Lost Highway," in which the advice is given not to go on the road, like a "rolling stone, all alone and lost... You'll curse the day you started rollin' down that lost highway."

On the other hand, when a man is entangled in the yearned for set of family social relationships, he usually, in song, hopes for the chance to "break these chains" and be free, as does Willie Nelson in "On The Road Again" and Rodney Crowell, in "When I'm Free Again," in which the singer feels that only at that point will he be able to "be me" again.

The contradiction contained in the female role in this culture, in its most simple form, is between acting like the "honky tonk angel" or like "momma." The woman is, before marriage, supposed to be free and sexual enough to attract a man but, at the same time, be socially responsible enough that she, like mamma before her, can be considered a legitimate candidate for marriage. After the marriage, this duality is expected to continue. The woman is to take care of the house, cook the meals, raise the children and, at the same time, be sexy enough to keep her man true, at home and off the road. Leona Williams, for example, sings of "sewing all day long...so tonight you'll see a country girl with hot pants on."

The consequences of a wrong move in this pattern of contradiction are aptly spelled out in country songs. Honky tonk angels are sexual buddies and pals, like the "Queen of the Silver Dollar," but they will never become wives, or if they do, they will never be true, as the lure of the honky tonk is too great. They, inevitably, will break the heart of any man fool enough to marry them as they cast him aside and return to the wild side of life where they belong.

And, if they don't break your heart, falling in love with them can kill you, as the singer in Marty Robbins' "El Paso" learns. He falls in love with Felina, a Mexican bar girl, then shoots a man who he sees flirting with her in the bar. He flees, but cannot stay away from Felina. When he rides back to see her, he is shot down by the posse, dying in her arms on the steps of the cantina in which she works and he fell in love. This theme is replayed in Mickey Newbury's "San Francisco Mabel Joy," in which the socially innocent singer, a young "Waycross, Georgia boy," falls in love with a prostitute in San Francisco and suffers the same fate—shot down, he crawls to the door of the whorehouse. But, ironically, Mabel Joy is not there. She has left to seek him out and the boy dies, alone but hopefully content in the knowledge that Mabel Joy, at least, did love him in return.

Men also define the consequences of a woman not acting sexy *enough* to attract attention. In Don Williams' "Maggie's Dream," the woman, who has worked as a waitress in a truck stop cafe since she was seventeen, is now close to fifty and still unmarried. Maggie is always up at 4 a.m. and by 5 she is behind the counter of the diner, her life a drudgery of "thirty years of coffee cups and sore feet." The truckers who eat at Cafe Carolina, "take her to places far away with their stories," then leave her with their dirty dishes. And yet, her only dream, since seventeen, has been to "find a husband and be a wife."

As the social changes of the 1970s ushered into country music more songs sung and written by women (Ivey 14-16), and as the country audience absorbed the social impact of the earlier begun and originally middle class women's rights movement, country songs concerning traditional male-female role relationships were increasingly overlayed with comment, reaction and critique. From the women's perspective, as K.T. Oslin sings in "80s Ladies," "We've been educated, we got liberated, and that's complicated matters with men." And in Dolly Parton's "To Daddy," made a hit by Emmylou Harris, the mother, after being ignored and treated like a house servant for years, quietly leaves home. The note she writes explains that, now that the kids are grown, she's "gone in search of the love I need so badly." As the singer concludes; "she never meant to come back home...if she did, she never did say so to Daddy."

The male reaction in country music to such traditional sex role busting sentiments is, perhaps, predictable. The woman is portrayed as taking over the "freedom" portion of the male role, but—and this is critical—*not* being subject to the pulls of the "restraint" pole of the axis, which she is accused of abandoning in her search for liberation. Thus, in contrast to the man, who is constantly torn in both directions—which makes him appear both tragic and noble, even as it offers him an excuse for excess in the area of freedom—the new female is seen as one-dimensional in intent, turning her back on the social responsibilities defined by proper social restraint, and thus, blameable. In contrast, the male, in trying to play out his traditional role against this new femininity, finds himself all alone in attempting to uphold the ties of social responsibility and, ultimately, failing to do so well. In this way, the man emerges as a suffering figure, to be both pitied and respected, while the new woman is seen as a one-dimensional bitch.

This reversal is perhaps most evident in Dan Seals' "All That Glitters," which is even played out in the man's arena—the rodeo. The woman here is a rodeo queen, who grabs the limelight and abandons her husband and small baby to become a full time star in this man's world of all mens worlds. The husband, with very little money, bravely follows the rodeo around in his old pickup truck and small trailer, so his little daughter can at least see her mother perform from time to time. But the rodeo queen has abandoned them both, failing to remember her own little daughter's birthdays with even a simple telephone call or card. As the husband, himself an old rodeo hand, wryly recalls about both his wife and the stage upon which she preens; "all that glitters is not gold."

Conclusion

This paper has examined the place of country music as a reflector and articulator of the values and concerns of its audience, suggesting that a view of these values and concerns as, many times, tension-filled, conflicting and contradictory, is more realistic than to assume them to be harmonious and logically interconnected. This is not a quiet web of culture being sung about, nor one that reflects uniformity of thought and action. Instead, it more resembles a battlefield of cultural conflict and contradiction.

Such conflicts and contradictions reflect both the social upheavals the country audience has been subject to in America and the internal contradictions and oppositions contained in the cultural values themselves, best viewed not as centers of agreement, but as axes of potential cultural variation, along which these tensions, conflicts and contradictions, many times triggered by social change, play themselves out.

Although there are other obvious areas in which such conflicts and contradictions can be seen, such as the treatment of social class in country music or the conflict between self-assertion and fatalism, the two focused on in this paper—that of the impact of urbanization and modernization on the country music audience, and of the conflicts, contradictions and changes in interpersonal relations of attraction and appropriate sex role behavior, have long been central thematic areas in country music and thus, following from the assumptions on which this paper is based, of central concern to the members of its audience.

Notes

[1]A version of this paper was first presented at the 1988 Annual Meeting of the American Anthropological Association, Phoenix, Arizona.

[2]Content analyses of country music values span nearly a quarter of a century now and include, chronologically: Archie Green, "Hillbilly Music: Source and Symbol," *Journal of American Folklore* 78 (1965) 224-228; Paul Ackerman, "The Poetry and Imagery of Cowboy Songs," *Billboard: The World of Country Music* 78.44 (1966) 14-16, 20; Paul DiMaggio, Richard A. Peterson and Jack Esco, "Country Music: Ballad of the Silent Majority," *The Sound of Social Change*, eds. R. A. Peterson and R. S. Denisoff (Chicago: Rand McNally, 1972) 38-55; Dorothy Horstman, *Sing Your Heart Out, Country Boy* (New York: Dutton, 1975); John Buckley, "Country Music and American Values," *Popular Music and Society* 6.4 (1979) 293-301; George H. Lewis, "Mapping The Fault Lines: The Core Values Trap In Country Music," *Popular Music and Society* 11.4 (1985) 7-16.

[3]In 1975, Willie Nelson called "Funny How Time Slips Away," his most financially successful song to date. Written in 1961, it "has been recorded maybe 80 or 90 times so far—right now, on the average, someone records it once a month." Quoted in Horstman, 169.

[4]See Malone; Richard A. Peterson and Paul DiMaggio, "From Region To Class: The Changing Locus of Country Music" *Social Forces* 53.3 (1975) 497-506; and Robert Coles, *The South Goes North* (Boston: Little, Brown) for more detailed information on

these patterns of migration and their effects on country music.

⁵See Joli Jenson, "Genre and Recalcitrance: Country Music's Move Uptown," *Tracking* 1.1 (1988) 30-41, for the industry background that preceded this pop music explosion.

Works Cited

DiMaggio, Paul, Richard A. Peterson and Jack Esco. "Country Music: Ballad of the Silent Majority." *The Sound of Social Change*. Eds. R. A. Peterson and R. S. Denisoff. Chicago: Rand McNally, 1972.

Erikson, Kai T. *Everything In Its Path*. New York: Simon and Schuster, 1976.

Horstman, Dorothy. *Sing Your Heart Out, Country Boy*. New York: Dutton, 1975.

Ivey, William. "Country Music Goes Back to Basics." The Encyclopedia of Folk, Country and Western Music. Eds. I. Stambler and G. Landon. New York: St. Martins, 1984.

Killian, Louis. *White Southerners*. New York: Random House, 1970.

Lewis, George H. "Mapping the Fault Lines: The Core Values Trap in Country Music." *Popular Music and Society* 11.4 (1985).

Lund, Jens. "Bluegrass in a Detroit Bar." Unpublished paper presented at the 1973 American Folklore Society Annual Meeting.

Malone, Bill C. *Country Music, U.S.A.* Austin: U of Texas P, 1968.

Rubin, Lillian B. *Worlds of Pain: Life in the Working Class Family*. New York: Basic Books, 1976.

Sons, Larry and Doug Todd. "The Worst You Ever Gave Me." *Cosmopolitan* Dec. 1987.

Swindler, Ann. "Love and Adulthood in American Culture." *Themes of Work and Love in Adulthood*. Eds. Neil Smelser and Erik Erikson. Cambridge: Harvard UP, 1979.

Thompson, Stephen. "Come Here My Dusky Darlin': Interracial Love Affairs in Country Music." Unpublished paper presented at the 1988 American Anthropological Association Meeting.

Weitz, Shirley. *Sex Roles*. New York: Oxford, 1977.

Engendering Narratives of Lament in Country Music

Katie Stewart

Country music is accused of being a degradation of an "earlier" and more "authentic" "folk" music. According to this particular origin myth, the commercial fashioning of southern rural music to appeal to the broadest possible audience reduced historically specific and narratively detailed ballads to basic, generalized theme songs of lost love and human downfall played to trite, whiny excess.[1] This is a story of the destruction of an old local culture by a new popular culture that manipulates and degrades consciousness into a newly naive and excessively sentimental form. But this is a critique written from a place firmly outside the "lure" of the genre and so ignorant both of the actually quite mixed blood ancestry of its supposed primitivist "original" and of country's continuing cultural conventions—that is, the interpretive practices that work on its participants but lie dead at the feet of those who keep their distance. The naive schlock that this critique *sees* is the naive shlock that it *produces* in its own polemical poetics of sophisticated distance—a poetic traced as a movement to rise above a something base (whether that is figured as (mere) emotion, or as circumstance or ignorance).

But country music has its *own* origin story which has been written into its most excessive (and most conventionalized) sad songs—what George Jones calls "them sad, slobbin tear jerkers." And while these songs do indeed propose a countervailing poetic of a *downward* movement into the gutter, the prison, the grave or the bottle, they are just that—a proposed poetic—and not the naive expression of a peculiarly simple people. In fact, they are a strangely self-conscious and intertextual reproduction of an old and already highly conventionalized cultural genre based in a poetics of intensification. In these songs the poetic is further accentuated or carried to excess in the process of re-presenting it.[2]

The conventionality and stylistic excess that makes country seem at once contrived and naive to some are among the features of a cultural poetic Northrup Frye calls "romance," opposing it to "realism." The "romantic" mode, Frye argues, is the structural core of all fiction—a vision of life as a quest. Or I would say it is the essential narrative function—that is, to hold open a space of

Revised version of a paper presented at the American Anthropological Association Annual Meeting, Phoenix, November 1988.

suspense or desire. In country's sad songs representations of this space of desire dominate the more temporal and linear narration of a sequence of events which would be the chosen mode of a realist narration. Instead, they represent life as a kind of maze where the hero finds himself in the midst of things and suspended in a dream world of floating extremes in which the narrative movement rises into wish fulfillment or sinks into anxiety and nightmare (Frye 53) in a world outside (or beyond) the "realities" figured by realism—the world of ordinary historical time, or "everyday life," or recognizable social causes.

If realism superimposes a map on the maze to provide a plan of action or a sequence of events that follow one another and can be sensibly followed, the country song on the other hand starts at that unmappable point where a person's sensibilities are overwhelmed. John Anderson's "Till I Get Used to the Pain," for instance, devotes itself to establishing a lyric image of pain so full and overwhelming that there is no room in the "story" for what then becomes extraneous actional detail. Or, in other words, narrative *action* comes to a full stop in the face of the lyric. Anderson then *represents* this movement of narrative as a state of mind: "You can find me lying here / just whisperin your name / til your memory goes away or I get used to the pain." All of what is ordinarily thought of as the stuff and essence of narrative is, in *this* kind of narrative, overwhelmed by a spatial, metonymic representation. What is more, the narrator seems to take note of the differences between the two narrative modes and fills his own mode with an aura of ultimate significance and the power of self-reflection. In "Hello Walls" Willie Nelson corresponds with desire by talking to the walls—a correspondence that apparently fills his days and nights, or has become his life: "Hello walls. How'd things go for you today?... I'll bet you dread to spend another lonely night with me..."

Three other points need noting: first, this is not the voice of an "individual" but the voice of a "type" of person formed by a particular situation and a mode of consciousness. Second, the mode marked in these songs is not an *absence* (e.g. of a love object or of happiness) but an *excess* of sensation that overwhelms "the senses" (or ordinary sensibilities); there is too much pain, too much longing, too many memories, unforgettable sights, inescapable hindsight, or terrible things overheard by accident. Things overwhelming are presented as overwhelming the narrator so that actions and events are narrated in the condensed form of lyric images or scenes in which the narrator finds himself; meaning appears as a figure on a horizon of feeling and adrift in the weighted excesses of memory, imagination, and myth. Third, the narrative movement here is not a horizontal movement, drawing us forward in the suspense of fulfilled actional sequences from one act to the one that follows, but a vertical movement up and down between poles of good and bad or high and low, and particularly a movement "down" to where the narrator speaks, as they say, "from the heart." It is the kind of story that begins at the end and at the end point of a referenced actional narration.

Country's own origin story begins at the end of things, with the event of the hero's downfall. A man suddenly finds himself dumped and turned around; ordinary life literally comes apart; like Alice in Wonderland, he falls out of life and finds himself alive in another register in a special place "below" that is filled to overflowing with desire, allegorically "afloat" in freely mixing beers and tears. For instance, John Conlee's "Back Side of Thirty" stories a man who was "making money at thirty with a wife and son, then a short five years later it all comes undone." His wife goes "back to mama" with his son, leaving him "wine-drunk and runnin'." The chorus, as is conventional in these songs, is a "high point" or excess that works through repetition of the ordinarily unspeakable: "On the back side a thirty the short side a time / back on the bottle with no where to climb."

The lowly "final resting place" of the song contains its own memorium; it is the setting for the realization of the ultimate significance of a sequence of events or a "life story." And that significance is here figured as a kind of perfect relationality realized too late and figured as a lost opportunity—a love lost but still and forever painfully visible on an ever deferred horizon. Put another way, it is a relationality which has only become perfect in its loss or one that *represents* desire itself; it is effected through the technique of deferral figured as a finished past. The song creates and then endlessly re-presents the space of desire by stripping thecountry boy of the trappings of social life and returning him to the heart of things. A male interiority suddenly and literally realizes itself in an unambiguous desire untempered by the strains of "reality" or by the biggest potential strain of all—the presence of the actual woman.

The song works its magic by repeatedly twanging the strings of this knowing, broken heart. Its tools are: first, his fetishes of the lost love—objects both reified and yet vibrant with life and figuring both loss and fulfillment such as old pictures of them together, a bouquet of roses for every time she broke his heart, or the sight of his closet all cleaned out. Second, it uses representations of highly mediated communications between him and his lost love such as old love letters saved, the act of showing her picture to strangers, rumors, lies, or long hoped for but never received phone calls. Third, the songs allegorize the desire imprisoned in his heart as an inventory of (or talk with) the walls of his lonely room or the bars of his prison cell, or the act of "walkin the floor over you" or watching from his grave over which she now walks sometimes at night, or the honky tonk vibrant with sad songs and flowing with tears and beers. Country music itself acts as an allegorical place where the story intensifies, as in the lyrics "I found a little place downtown where guys like me can go / and they got bright lights and country music" or "pour me a cold one and play me an old one and leave me to happily cry in my beer," or "guitars, cadillacs, and hillbilly music, the only thing that keeps me hangin on" or "just look for my name on the jukebox / when you're tired of bein alone."

And finally the image of the absent, or unrelentingly hard-hearted woman also confirms and intensifies the sad song poetic and its male space of desire. The image is actually given voice in female response songs (mostly written by men) which bespeak a "realist" counterattack on the sad song that aims to fragment the male romantic interpretation and then reinterpret events in the discourses of everyday life, social causes, and "real" responsibilities. Here we have songs like "Don't Come Home a Drinkin with Lovin on Your Mind." "It

Wasn't God Who Made Honky Tonk Angels," "I'm Gonna Hire a Wino" (to Decorate Our Home), "Pass Me By (if you're only passing through)," and "Don't Make Love to a Country Music Singer (Cause he'll tell the world about it in his country bedroom song)." Where the (male) romantic voice is center stage, even this sobering, belittling back talk from the hard hearted (female) realist adds to the poetics of intensification and provides yet more context for it and more proof of its meaningfulness.

In the saddest of sad songs these different techniques of intensification are combined and interwoven. So, for instance, John Conlee's "Miss Emily's Picture," narrates the life of a man around the act of him straightening her fetishized picture by his bed and on his office wall and showing it to the boys at the bar as he goes through his otherwise empty day. His life and the world are constituted scenically as a place surrounding the man with the picture and imbued with the single meaningfulness of that pair. Other songs start with the man with the picture and add representations of highly mediated, or "untrue" communications between him and the real her. Surrounding the man and his picture of her, then, is a world of missed meetings represented as rumors, insincere or futile phone calls, spoken denials of pain and lies. Ricky Van Shelton plays out this poetic line by line in "Could It Be Somebody Lied?", in which we hear the man's side of a telephone conversation. "You heard what?" he asks. "Well, it ain't true...I got over you the day you left..."

We don't hear her voice at all, but know from his half of the conversation (or his "side of the story") that she is calling because she has heard that he was heard calling her name, crying and showing her picture to strangers—the elements of a male abjection story. While his voice betrays the truth of this story his words deny it—"I bet somebody lied." After all, his story bespeaks a "deeper" truth (or other narrative)—the heart felt fact of her leaving and her being gone: "Don't worry, it wasn't me...just someone who looks a lot like me and loved someone like you."

The generalized reference to "someone who looks a lot like me" engenders the figure of abjection as male (i.e. a figure with an interiority and without boundary to mark it off from an "external" world) and the absent, hard figure (without interiority, fully bounded) as female. It also keeps her absent but close and so prevents a realist narrative closure on their "history" and instead enables its endless romantic reproduction. Often there is an ironic sensibility to this construction, as there is here in that Van Shelton's claim to have forgotten her is precisely the means he uses to remember her forever in his own private world filled with pain and perfect, though thwarted, love.

John Conlee reached new heights (or rather new depths) in the genre, with his song "I Don't Remember Lovin You" in which the hero has literally "lost his mind" and has been living for years in an mental institution when she finally comes to see him to confess and to apologize for having left him without a word. Her effort is to get him to comply with a move to bring their history into the realm of the ordinary and namable, though tragic. But he cannot be "brought to his senses."

Perhaps the best example of these saddest of sad songs is George Jones singing "He Stopped Lovin' Her Today"—an ultimate story of stories, the story of unrequited love carried to the grave. Jones introduces it with the words; "I cain't think of any other one that's more sadder than this one and it goes like this..." and then begins, on an already full voiced ecstatic twang, at the very heart of things—the original, rupturing dialogic: "He said, `I'll love you 'til I die.' She told him `you'll forget in time...'"

The fetishes of her pictures and letters fill his life and overwhelm any hope of an ordinary life story in the space of everyday life. He keeps her picture on his wall and her letters by his bed, in which he has underlined every "I love you" in red. The story is further intensified by being narrated by a friend who reads the signs of tragedy and desire in the free lyrical excess of imagining another's story; "I went to see him just today...all dressed up to go away..."

And of course death signals the giving over of that life to the memory and imagination of others. Then the single "chorus" (actually the whole song has the excess of chorus) breaks out with a wail: "He stopped lovin' her today, they placed a wreath upon his door...soon they'll carry him away..."

And finally, a last verse was added in a rewrite when the producer asked for an ending scene that would portray the woman at the funeral who came to see him "one last time..." we all wondered if she would.

So as is fitting in the romantic poetic, the woman's final return—too late and "over his dead body"—ends the song by starting the cycle of deferred desire all over again, with renewed spirit. Such a story as this always starts with the end of things...or rather, in the midst of things, in a place where story is culled to lyric and can only be narrated, they say, "from the heart," though it is not just one man's private heart, but more like "the heart of things."

Notes

[1] See Patterson; Cantwell.

[2] See Hartigan for a theoretical discussion of the interpretive practices involved.

Works Cited

Cantwell, Robert. *Bluegrass Breakdown*. Urbana, IL: U of Illinois P, 1984.

Frye, Northrup. *Secular Scripture: a study of the structure of Romance*. Harvard, 1976.

Hartigan, John. *It's That Same Old Lost Love Story; It's Sad, But It's True: Figuring Out Country Western Music*. MS, 1988.

Horstman, Dorothy. *Sing Your Heart Out, Country Boy*. Nashville: Country Music Foundation, 1986

Patterson, Tim. Notes on the Historical Application of Marxist Cultural Theory. *Science and Society* 39.3 (1975): 257-291.

Romantic Narcissism in "Outlaw" Cowboy Music

Michael Dunne

The predominating sentiment in American cowboy music has always been melancholy, an organically appropriate emotion given the scenic and narrative dimensions of the songs. Cowboys in traditional Western music, as well as in real life, performed strenuous and dangerous labor, usually alone, far from home and family, for small wages. Even a casual inspection of a collection of cowboy lyrics such as Jim Bob Tinsley's excellent *He Was Singin' This Song* will confirm this point.[1] A typical song, "The Cowboy," begins: "All day on the prairie in a saddle I ride / Not even a dog, boys, to trot by my side." In "Night Herding Song," the cowboy sadly sings to the cattle, "My horse is leg-weary and I'm awful tired / If you get away, I will be fired." The title of "The Dreary, Dreary Life" speaks for itself. It is clear in such songs that the lone prairie is an implicit wasteland that can appropriately function as an objective correlative for melancholy.

Moreover, both the recognized and the anonymous composers of traditional Western music have displayed an unusual fondness for sentimental extremity, permitting the dangers confronting the cowboy to prevail in order to produce the ultimate occasion for melancholy—violent death. The predilection is so pronounced, in fact, as to amaze even the cowboys themselves. In his autobiographical reminiscence *We Pointed Them North*, "Teddy Blue" Abbot tells Helena Huntington Smith that "cowboys used to love to sing about people dying," and he adds, "I don't know why" (223). Whatever the reason, the fondness is apparent. Surely the greatest source of unhappiness for the cowboy of traditional song should have been his very fragile hold on life. If a stampede didn't crush him, as it does in "Little Joe the Wrangler"; and if a wild bronco didn't mash his head, as it does in "Blood on the Saddle," then a shootout would probably cut him down in his prime, as it does in "The Cowboy's Lament," sometimes called "The Streets of Laredo." However gothic such sentiments might be, traditional cowboy songs of the sort usually contain within their lyrics the circumstances to justify their emotional extremity. They are, in short, organically consistent.

During the decade 1975-1985 cowboy music experienced a sort of renascence, brought about by the country music "outlaws." Through their

Reprinted from *Studies in Popular Culture*, 1989, 22-39 with permission of the author and the journal. A different version of this essay appears in Michael Dunne, *METAPOP: Self-Referentiality In American Popular Culture*. U of Mississippi P, Spring 1992. Reprinted with permission of University of Mississippi Press.

writing and/or performing, "Willie, Waylon and the boys" brought the cowboy to popular attention again and along with him the conventional properties of traditional Western music: ranges, cattle, horses, saddles, boots, guns, and—of course—melancholy. "Blue Eyes Crying in the Rain" from Willie Nelson's *Red Headed Stranger* album (1975) went to number one on the charts. *Wanted: The Outlaws* (1976), featuring Willie Nelson, Waylon Jennings, Jessi Colter and Tompall Glaser, shocked the more staid members of the Nashville music establishment by going gold despite its unconventional arrangements and lyrics. Willie's picture appeared on the cover of *Newsweek* in 1978. Willie and Ol' Waylon dominated the Grammy awards in 1979. Two feature films, *Honeysuckle* (1980) and *Songwriter* (1984) were released, based on the exploits of musicians who dressed like cowboys. A herd of imitators sought to tag along on the trail drive, as is epitomized most clearly perhaps in David Allan Coe's title "Willie and Waylon and Me" (1978). Even as late as 1985, the *Highwayman* album by Waylon, Willie, Johnny Cash and Kris Kristofferson contained "The Last Cowboy Song," "Jim, I Wore a Tie Today" and "Desperados Waiting for a Train." A few of the songs appearing during the period could, in fact, have easily been written in earlier days. Several cuts from Willie Nelson's *Red Headed Stranger* , for example, carried very traditional resonances. Especially in the interconnected narratives of "Time of the Preacher," "Blue Rock Montana" and "Red Headed Stranger" we can recognize the isolation, violence and inconsolable sorrow habitually associated with the genre. Similarly, Mike Burton's song, "Night Rider's Lament," performed by Jerry Jeff Walker, displayed a number of traditional elements. Consider the chorus:

> Why does he ride for his money
> Why does he rope for short pay?
> He ain't gettin' nowhere,
> And he's losin' his share.
> He must've gone crazy out there.

Loneliness, social alienation, poverty and the strain of arduous physical labor are all suggested. Furthermore, although this wrangler's life is lamentable in several respects, he does not seem particularly dissatisfied with his circumstances. After all, he is admittedly the one who chose them in the first place. To this respect also the Burton/Walker cowboy had a claim to authenticity. Jim Bob Tinsley argues that this sort of wide acceptance is characteristic of most traditional Western music. In fact, Tinsley dismisses a social-protest version of "I Ride Old Paint" as "conspicuously out of character for the cowboy who rarely complained of his work and was not known for his protest songs" (129). Paradoxically, then, melancholy and stories may be combined in cowboy music, both in its traditional sense and in its modern revival.

Most songs by the latter-day cowboys would surely have failed to win Tinsley's approval, however, or that of "Teddy Blue" Abbott, or of serious collectors of Western music such as John and Alan Lomax or N. Howard "Jack"

Thorp because the largest percentage of contemporary outlaw music represented a significant thematic departure from the authentic traditional to the admittedly sentimental but objectively grounded narrative to the Western ballad, these writers and performers substituted equally sentimental but merely self-reflexive form of romantic expressivism. In the process, the organic relation of conclusion and sentiment which characterized traditional Western music was replaced by a melancholy narcissism, a modern version of the poetic mode mordantly identified by the English romantic poet John Keats in a letter of 1818 as the "egotistical subliminal" (349). As a result of this development, the cowboy of song became merely a persona, a rhetorical device by which the songwriter and performer sought to exploit the listener's habitual sympathetic disposition toward the genre of the cowboy. In place of the cowboy's plausibly occasioned physical and emotional suffering, these outlaw songs offered thinly disguised accounts of the supposed rigors of the country music business. Instead of blood on the saddle, these songs offered frustration on Music Row. Instead of the prospect of premature and violent death, they recounted the agonies of unrecognized musical genius. Instead of Western stoicism, they professed pathetic whining.

First of all, we should observe that these songs usually emerge from the lips of a cowboy who refers to himself directly as "I." This in itself is not unusual. Tinsley explains about "The Old Chisholm Trail" that although many anonymous hands added verses to the song during its long evolutionary development, "The first person pronoun was always used regardless of who sang the song or made up the verses" (25). That is to say, many voices were absorbed into one cowboy who spoke as "I" for all. A distinction to be observed about the outlaws' contribution to the genre is that no matter what the "I" claimed, he was not a cowboy at all, but rather a show business performer pretending to be a cowboy. Often, the displacement in these songs was so slight as to erase the line between the biography of the performer and the fiction of Western life—the work of Waylon Jennings and Willie Nelson serving as the most obvious illustrations of the trend. Whatever the purported Western subject, the actual subject was the same: the life and hard times of the country singer.

In this respect especially these outlaw songs resembled not the externally grounded lyrics of anonymous trail hands, but a form of self-referential verse often written in the early nineteenth century by highly sophisticated English romantic poets. Even in its most accomplished expressions—Percy B. Shelley's "To a Skylark," for example, or John Keats's "Ode to a Nightingale"—this poetic mode called as much attention to the artistic struggles of the creators as to the subject, perhaps more. During the romantic period, William Hazlitt objected that lyrics of this sort attempted to reduce the entire external world to an opportunity for self-reflexion. In annoyance, Hazlitt observed about the more self-involved efforts of his contemporaries, "Their minds reject, with a convulsive effort and intolerable loathing, the very idea that there was, or was thought to be, anything superior to themselves" ("On Shakespeare..." 310). To Hazlitt, such poems erroneously focused on poets writing poetry rather than on human beings inhabiting a recognizable world. Some poems in this mode written by Shelley, for example, so thoroughly advertised their author's presence that, in the judgment of T.S. Eliot, it was "difficult to read the poetry without remembering the man." Eliot saw this as a serious difficulty because "the man was humorless, pedantic, self-centered and sometimes almost a blackguard" (89). As a result, Eliot felt, the reader could not concentrate on the putative subject, whether skylark or west wind, but only on Shelley. Though separated by a century, then Hazlitt and Eliot both protested against lyric writers' converting the natural world from a subject for realistic presentation into an occasion for autobiographical expression, an expression usually couched in a tone of complaint. A similar protest could be brought against outlaw music. It requires only the slightest flight of fancy to imagine an outlaw from the prairies of Austin or Nashville declaiming a variant of the often-ridiculed lines from Shelley's "Ode to the West Wind": "I fall upon the cacti of life! I bleed!"

Another revealing element of outlaw music was an obligatory association of cowboy and performer, the presumption that all cowboys are musical, as in this lyric by Ed and Patsy Bruce: "Mamas, don't let your babies grow up to be cowboys / Don't let them pick guitars and drive them old trucks...." That trucks have replaced horses need not necessarily invalidate the authenticity of this song, but the equation of playing guitar and punching cows might. Western historians disagree concerning the function of music in the traditional cowboy's working life, but probably none would disagree with the general remark by an actual cowboy, "Jack" Thorp: "I never did hear a cowboy with a real good voice; if he had one to start with, he lost it bawling at cattle, or sleeping in the open, or tellin' the judge he didn't steal that horse" (16). Real cowboys probably did little more than hum, definitely without guitar accompaniment. Humming repetitiously and perhaps tunelessly, whether to distract a nervous herd or to inform other riders of the cowboy's location, is one thing; playing the guitar while singing is another. Surely, then, when Willie Nelson and Waylon Jennings sang the Bruces' lyrics on their very successful recording of "Mamas, Don't Let Your Babies," they were referring to something other than actual work on the range.

This discrepancy between language and meaning emerged even more clearly in another outlaw song, this one performed by Jennings and written by Nashville composer, producer, performer and entrepreneur "Cowboy" Jack Clement. In "Let's All Help the Cowboys Sing the Blues," the melancholy verse makes only passing reference to the supposedly Western locale: "Cowboys have to fall in love, get hurt, and all that bit / Let their hearts hang out so they can write you all a hit." As in traditional Western music, the sad tone is contrived to enlist the listener's sympathy for the song's central character, the cowboy, but the grounds of this character's suffering have surely shifted. The cowboy created by Clement and portrayed by Jennings feels compelled to suffer so that he may write a song; he is not reduced to misery by natural circumstances beyond his control. Even if we accept as ironic the conjunction of the traditional term "cowboy" and the contemporary show business slang suggested in "sing the blues" and "all that bit," we must recognize the effort to transfer the melancholy associated with traditional

Western songs to the contemporary circumstances of the country music scene.

No occasion was too unlikely to convert into a symbolic episode in the lives of such cowboys. In Sharon Vaughn's song "My Heroes Have Always Been Cowboys," once again performed by Waylon Jennings, the cowboy sings dolefully, "Picking up hookers instead of my pen / I let the words of my youth slip away." Here a failed emotional life is translated simply into lost songwriting opportunities and trivialized in consequence. As was the case with more self-reflexive poems written during the early nineteenth century, every event could be transformed through what Hazlitt acerbically called "the morbid feelings and devouring egotism of the writers' own minds" ("On Shakespeare" 310). Some of William Wordsworth's poems, for example, attempted, in Hazlitt's words, to "persuade you that the most insignificant objects are interesting in themselves because he is interested in them" ("On the Character" 300). By the same token, the outlaw writers simply presupposed that every circumstance surrounding the life of the country music cowboy was potentially interesting material for a song, and they felt compelled to write it all down because of the imperative to "write you all a hit."

Most vulnerable to objection in such music is the strain of self-pity running through all these egotistical reflections. Like their English predecessors, each of the outlaws chose the unconventional path of the artist and then lyrically lamented the culture's unsupportive response. The utilitarian disposition against which the romantic poet defined his aesthetic personality was perhaps best articulated by Shelley's associate Thomas Love Peacock when he wrote in "The Four Ages of Poetry":

> The highest inspirations of poetry are resolvable into three ingredients: the rant of unregulated passion, the whine of exaggerated feeling, and the cant of factitious sentiment: and can therefore serve only to ripen a splendid lunatic like Alexander, a puling driveller like Werther, or a morbid dreamer like Wordsworth. It can never make a philosopher, nor a statesman, nor in any class of life an useful or rational man.(21)

Unsympathetic views of this sort did not deter self-reflexive lyricists from taking the road less traveled, however. They chose to write verse instead of studying law or pharmacy, and they thereby enacted the romantic model to be later adopted by their American epigones, who would decisively reject the opportunity to join the "doctors and lawyers and such" of the Bruces' song and then demand the listener's sympathy precisely because this refusal entailed unhappy consequences.

This analogy is not so contrived as it might at first seem. In the highly self-indulgent film *Songwriter*, the Willie Nelson character, Doc Jenkins, is assured by his estranged wife that all his financial and emotional reverses in the country music business are attributable to one source: "You're not a businessman," she tells him. "You're a poet." Thus, his melancholy is translated into his aesthetic virtue. Like Doc Jenkins, the outlaws deliberately excluded themselves from conventional society, the security of a regular income and the emotional comforts of family life; and then complained of their sufferings in the music business.

The potential illustrations are myriad, but a few should suffice to establish this point. Again, "Mamas, Don't Let Your Babies" supplies an example. One reason to avoid the life of a cowboy, the song says, is that "they never stay home and they're always alone / Even with someone they love." Listening to this, one might imagine Lord Byron in bluejeans and a Stetson, or Percy Shelley nobly suffering alone in a motel somewhere in Nebraska in the middle of a six-week road tour. This isolated romantic artist was glorified too in Clement's "Let's All Help the Cowboys":

> A cowboy takes his lonely pen in hand
> And tries to make somebody understand,
> But she has ears to hear a different tune,
> And that's what makes the cowboy sing the blues.

The social and emotional isolation played upon here was a given of outlaw music, as was the conviction that the cowboy's suffering deserved not only sympathy but also applause, because this alienation had been deliberately chosen.

The Bruces' outlaw anthem again provides a wonderful example of this pose:

> Them that don't know him won't like him,
> And them that do sometimes won't know how to take him,
>
> He ain't wrong, he's just different,
> But his pride won't let him do things to make you think he's right.

Here the cowboy is lonely not because he rides the range alone without even a dog to trot by his side, but because he refuses to accommodate his behavior to the norms of society. In his very interesting study, *The Cowboy Hero: His Image in American History and Culture*, William W. Savage, Jr., says about the lyric, "To say that Bruce's [sic] cowboy is merely an individual is to be nothing less than charitable; to say that he is an insensitive sociopath is to fall nearer the mark. He is egocentric, dissipated, and alienated, and he is a hero because of it, for Bruce's song is a paean to this neo-cowboy, a paean in the negative mode" (91). There is great insight in Savage's remarks, but we cannot avoid the feeling that this cowboy's defiance is less social than musical, aimed less at the materialistic culture from which a working cowboy—contemporary or traditional—might withdraw and more at conventional modes of thinking that might withhold complete approval of the outlaw's musical career.

This sort of emotional self-indulgence sometimes grew so extreme as to preclude the possibility of distinct utterance, as in "My Heroes Have Always Been Cowboys." Having equated the vocation of the modern cowboy with the anti-social role of a drifter, the lyric seems to totter under the burden of its sentiment:

> Cowboys are special, with their own brand of misery
> From being alone too long.
> You could die from the cold in the arms of a nightmare
> Knowing well your best days are gone.

One sign of the non-traditional sentimentality at work here is the contemporary psychobabble term "special." Another is the shift in pronoun from "their" to "your," a clear indication that the pretense of presenting a narrative ballad has been abandoned in favor of sheer romantic expression. Something here is almost too sad for words, and it has more to do with the singer than with any working cowboy. One must recognize an excess of melancholy here, a sadness unexplained by the details of the song's lyrics. The explanation lies, of course, in a recognition that this song is not really about cowboys at all, but about composers and singers, specifically in this case, about Vaughn and Jennings, who ask to be both pitied and applauded for being different or "special."

The artists' private concerns shaped these songs so insistently that there was little serious effort at the sort of displacement usually considered essential for fictional verisimilitude. The paraphernalia of Western life thus became a matter of mere "gesture," a convention on which the composer lavished little creative attention. In "Mamas, Don't Let Your Babies," for example, the cowboy's mode of dress involves "Lone Star belt buckles and old faded Levis," the latter conceivably the product of hard riding, but the former clearly a sign of trendy consumerism. In the song "Luckenbach, Texas," by Chips Moman and Bobby Emmons, when a cowboy and his gal seek to flee the strains of modern urban life for a simple West Texas Town, they first decide to "buy some boots and faded jeans." The prospect of buying new jeans and breaking them in apparently does not please, and the possibility of having already-faded jeans somewhere in the attic does not even occur. These musical cowboys could be easily envisioned doing their shopping in places like the Alamo in Nashville or Loretta Lynn's Western Clothing Stores as so many of their listeners might do. There, the racks are crammed with jeans in all stages of fadedness, as well as with suits embroidered all over with rhinestone wagonwheels or sixshooters if that should be the consumer's desire. Such clothing can operate only as an attendant circumstance of the professional entertainer's contrived "image" and not as a significant symbol of anyone's condition as a true cowboy.

Moreover, the list of the cowboy's "likes" composed by the Bruces—"smoky old poolrooms and clear mountain mornings / Little warm puppies and children and girls of the night"—derives more from the tradition of romantic primitivism, an urban mode of sentimentality, than from any experience of the wide-open spaces. In consequence of this transparent conventionality, it is insincere and foolish for the persona of such a song to pretend that his suffering has been produced by natural forces outside his control. A cowboy defined by what can only be called his "lifestyle" has repudiated his kinship with the cowboys depicted in traditional Western music.

Of course, as we have seen, these outlaws were not cowboys in any real sense, merely country music personalities, or as Shel Silverstein called them in a song performed by Waylon Jennings, "Whistlers and Jugglers and Singers of Songs." Thus, unlike traditional cowboys, they were seldom depicted on horseback. Even when in motion, these musical cowboys failed to exemplify the traditional Western mode. If they were not driving semi's down the highway, listening to country music on a tape player, they were probably riding in lavishly appointed tour busses they were probably one concert date to the next. The source and setting of this grand misery were thus ultimately the same: "the road," not the lone prairie. Consider this plaintive and representative testimony composed and performed by Waylon Jennings:

> Ten years on the road making one-night stands,
> Speeding my young life away.
> Tell me one more time just so's I'll understand,
> Are you sure Hank done it this way?

Although Jennings makes no direct references to cowboys in this song, a listener cannot help recalling images of Tex Ritter, Gene Autry and Roy Rogers—perhaps even of Porter Wagoner—when Waylon lists "rhinestone suits and new shiny cars" as elements of the country music scene that need to be changed by the new wave that he represents. Furthermore, the presiding spirit in this song, Hank Williams, was most often pictured wearing a cowboy hat, however urbanized the rest of his outfit. More significant than anyone's clothing, however, is the familiar melancholy tone of the lyric and its unabashed sentimentality. An emotional complex of self-pity and Byronic self-congratulation resonates through the phrase "speeding my young life away," for example. One hears suggestions of fragile health and still-more-fragile youth in these words, a covert—and probably unconscious—conjuring of John Keats' spirit. One also hears a perverse pride in the singer's self-destructive use of amphetamines, or "speed," an overt—and surely conscious—conjuring of Hank Williams' hard-rolling ghost. In his book *The Outlaws: Revolution in Country Music*, Michael Bane argues that such echoes are representative of the whole outlaw movement: "The legacy of Ole Hank remains a two-edged sword. For all the good that he and his music did, he did give country music a *tragic* figure to revere and follow. He provided a prototype for the hard-living, hard-drinking, got-no-future-but-I'm-sure-as-hell-on-my-way hillbilly singer..." (18-19). One recognizes the true ancestor here.

"Are Your Sure Hank Done It this Way" typifies the emotional complexion of these songs: an open admission that the singer freely chose this way of life and a simultaneous call on the listener's sympathy because of the attendant negative consequences. This attitude is clear as the lyric continues: "Lord! I've seen the world with a five-piece band / Looking at the back side of me." Seeing the world, or even large sections of the United States, might possibly be conceived as a benefit of the performer's mobile life, but "the road" is actually the source of this outlaw's distress. As in the analogous rock and pop songs popularized by performers as various as Kiss, Leo Sayer, Paul Simon and Bob Seger, the precise nature of this suffering remains indefinite. Tedium perhaps; the need to perform irrespective of personal feelings; the exposure of one's human frailties to an inquiring audience—any or all of these factors may be operating, but the effect is clearly represented by the weary ejaculation "Lord!"

The same attitudes operate more schematically in another song performed by Jennings, Bob McDill's "Amanda." In the first stanza the melancholy romantic theme of fading youth receives the principal focus:

> But it's an awful awakening in a country boy's life,
> To look in the mirror in total surprise
> At the hair on my shoulders and the age in my eyes.

Perhaps it is pressing the issue too closely to attribute much self-congratulation to the long hair mentioned in this last line, but the hair is at least a sign of deliberate social unconventionality. The second stanza of this song concentrates more obviously on the theme of self-satisfaction, however, and thus gives equal attention to both sides of the emotional complex:

> It's a measure of people who don't understand
> The pleasures of life in a hillbilly band.

One should note, in addition to the omnipresent bluejeans, mentioned in the second verse, the singer's sense of belonging to an elect of taste, those who understand the pleasures of a performer's life. However—as Keats, the composer of the "Ode on Melancholy," would surely agree—only one who can experience this pleasure can appreciate the equally delightful sadness of discovering that he is speeding his young life away and whining about it.

Another crucial issue raised by this song is the rhetorical implication that the listener is also one of the privileged group of initiates. In a very important sense, this sort of music was addressed to a closed community. Note the lyric specificity required to establish the fact of Jennings' fronting a five-piece band. Note too the adventurous use of the derogatory term "hillbilly," converted by its context into an ironic joke intended for the initiated. Just how initiated the listener might need to be grows apparent in Michael Bane's chapter in *The Outlaws* on Tompall Glaser and his recording studio nicknamed "Hillbilly Central." There Jennings recorded "Are You Sure Hank Done It This Way," "Let's All Help The Cowboys Sing The Blues" and "Bob Wills is Still the King" under the supervision of producer "Cowboy" Jack Clement. Along the way, Bane explains, "The unorthodox took on a strange kind of orthodoxy all its own, and the word "hillbilly" became both a statement of identity and a war-cry against the middle-of-the-road monster that was eating Nashville's talent alive" (38). Bane's remarks suggest a double form of self-referentiality often at work in these songs. Frequently, the outlaw performer defines himself not only counter to the straight world of "doctors and lawyers and such," as any artist whether romantic poet or rock singer might do, but also counter to the dominant modes of contemporary country music.

The case of Willie Nelson can be taken as exemplary, as Al Reinert makes clear in a feature story written for the *New York Times Magazine* during 1978, the *annus mirabilis*. According to Reinert, Nelson's struggle for self-definition took place in the context of a country music milieu best characterized as "background music, shallow vocals adrift in vanilla arrangements, daytime music for complacent people." When singers such as Perry Como could be, and were, marketed as country singers, Reinert adds, "The harmonies got richer as the studios did, the rhythms slackened, and, by the mid-60s, it was all strings and no sting" (26). In these circumstances, the outlaw could conceive a two-fold alienation and consequently a two-fold call for sympathy. Since the outlaws acted on the assumption that all of this professional information was widely known and fully accepted, their listeners could be simultaneously flattered as privileged insiders and suborned into endorsing some outrageous emotional self-indulgence, a practice sometimes called in more political times "co-option."

This co-option was most successfully practiced by Willie Nelson who, in a campaign to engage his listeners directly in his romantic agony, deliberately equated his private life and his professional image in song and on the motion picture screen. In *Honeysuckle Rose*, for example, the initiated viewer was encouraged to recognize in Buck Bonner's fictional band Willie's actual band members: Mickey Raphael, Jody Payne, Bee Spears and so forth. This viewer could also associate the huge outdoor performance that concludes the film with Willie's then-annual Fourth of July picnic, down to the guest appearances by Nelson cronies such as Hank Cochran and Johnny Gimble. That is, elements of Nelson's biography were deliberately portrayed in the film as fiction. At the same time, fictional events deriving from the film's source, *Intermezzo* (1939), were given some sort of biographical authority. The co-opted viewer might thus find himself asking, "Did Willie really have an affair with a young female singer? Are there really all-night Nelson family reunions with music and dancing for all? Is Willie's sister Bobbie as taciturn in real life as she seems on stage and in this movie?" Such questions, suggestive of soap- rather than horse-operas, point to both the completeness of Nelson's self-promotion and to the distance of all this from the stoicism of traditional Western music.

Because Willie Nelson usually wrote his own songs, moreover, he could combine biography and fiction on record as well as on the screen. In the process he could produce an illusion of authentic personal testimony calculated to elicit his listeners' sympathies with great immediacy. The lyrics aimed toward this end often manifested the properties identified in other outlaw music: a melancholy usually in excess of that justified by internal evidence; a social outcast's pride in resisting the lure of a safe conventionality; an acute attention to the specific details of the performer's professional life; and a consequent invitation to the listeners to share in this community as a reward for recognizing the insider's references. Furthermore, with the exception of the narrative sections of *Red Headed Stranger* , the title song of *Poncho and Lefty* (1982) and the narrative sections of *Tougher than Leather* (1983), Nelson's songs conformed to the contemporary mode in suggesting, rather than delineating, the cowboy's ethos. In the first line of "Me and Paul," for example, Nelson sings, "It's been rough and rocky traveling," suggesting, perhaps, hard riding by a Texas cowpuncher. The subsequent lyrics make clear, however, that this traveling has taken place on "the road" in quest of stardom rather than on the trail in quest of stray dogies.

"Me and Paul" represents the self-reflexive extreme of Nelson's work. After discarding the pretense of being a cowboy's story in the first stanza, the lyrics go on to recount loneliness, police harassment, lack of appreciation and social ostracism in Nashville, Laredo, Milwaukee and Buffalo. "The road" clearly functions as the source and symbol of Nelson's melancholy. All this *angst* culminates in a sad episode obviously rooted in the specific details of Nelson's professional experience:

> Well, we drank a lot of whiskey, so I don't know
> > if we went on that night at all,
> But I don't think they even missed us, I guess
> > Buffalo ain't geared for me and Paul.

As in "Are You Sure Hank Done It This Way," Byronic excess is mixed with pathos in an attempt to win the listener's admiration as well as his tears. An additional thrill awaited the listener who could recognize the names of the other performers and vicariously experience the frustration of a long backstage wait—in Buffalo, of all places! This listener could join the brotherhood of the initiated: you and me and Paul (English—Nelson's drummer and longtime friend).

By the time outlaw music developed such intricate levels of self-referentiality, the movement probably had attained some sort of critical mass. Because the symbolic equation of performer and cowboy had become even more than complete, there was very likely nowhere else to go in that direction. As early as 1978, Waylon Jennings posed the musical questions, "Don't You Think This Outlaw Bit's Got Out of Hand?" After nearly a decade of development, an affirmative answer must have seemed increasingly necessary.

Several signs confirm this conjecture. On Willie Nelson's 1983 album *Tougher Than Leather*, for example, the title song is not about a performer, but a gunslinger who shoots people without any reference to their possible connections to the Nashville music scene. "Somewhere in Texas" on the same album presents a cowboy who drives an old pickup truck, but he does not play the guitar or sing, and he has little obviously in common with Willie Nelson. Most importantly, this cowboy is referred to throughout as "he," not "I." *The Highwayman* (1985), the album that closed the outlaws' decade, showed a similar turning away from the farther extremes of narcissism. The significant cut "The Last Cowboy Song" focuses neither on the composers, Ed Bruce and R. Peterson, nor on the outlaws who performed the song on the album: Willie, Waylon, Johnny Cash and Kris Kristofferson. Although the song affirms the attraction that the cowboy figure continues to exercise for a considerable segment of the American male population, it also sadly recognizes the historical distance separating the open range and the recording studio.

The following lyric particularly illustrates how these final stages of the outlaw movement differed from its more exclusively egocentric stages:

Remington showed us how he looked on canvas,
And Louis Lamour has told us his tale.
Me and Johnny and Waylon and Kris sing about him,
And wish to God we could have ridden his trail.

Self-reflexion surfaces in the third line here but in a much less pronounced form than might have occurred some years earlier. There is at least one "I" in this song, and this "I" is a country singer, as was true, for example, in "Let's All Help the Cowboys Sing the Blues." There is a crucial distinction, however, in the fact that this singer is not the suffering hero of the song. A cowboy's melancholy life is the subject, but he is a real cowboy, a "he," not a singing outlaw.

In this sense also the outlaw music movement of the 1970s and 1980s resembled its nineteenth-century English romantic ancestor. When a crippling narcissism seemed about to engulf the whole romantic movement, Keats proposed "negative capability" and Hazlitt called for "sympathetic imagination" as more "objective" forms of fictionality (Keats 346; Hazlitt, "On Shakespeare" (307-311). The purpose of both was to allow the artist to escape the narrow confines of his own sensibility into the world that artist and audience inhabited together. In response to these and similar correctives, nineteenth-century English verse was able to continue—T.L. Peacock notwithstanding—and to continue in modes probably enriched by the excesses of romantic expressivism deplored by the earlier critics. The same might be said of the final stages of the outlaw movement. By the time of the *Highwayman* album, the battle against the Nashville establishment had been won. Willie Nelson and Waylon Jennings in particular had become commercial successes on a scale undreamed of by the Music City moguls of the early 1970s, and they had done so by proclaiming their antagonism to the establishment. Since there was no arguing with success, there was no Nashville authority left to oppress them and to legitimize that form of alienation. The larger conflict between the outlaw performer and American culture in general naturally continued, as was probably
inevitable in this post-romantic era. As in the case of nineteenth-century English verse, the later stages of the outlaw movement were clearly modified by the excesses of the earlier ones. "The Last Cowboy Song" epitomized the shift in showing that however imperfect the lives and careers of the composers and performers might have been, they were finally willing to admit, first of all, that they were musicians not cowboys; and second, that their lives consisted of "making music with their friends." Though the cacti of life continued to bristle, the outlaws finally stopped pretending that country singers were the only ones to fall on them.

Notes

[1]See also John A. Lomax and Alan Lomax, *Cowboy Songs and Other Frontier Ballads* , revised and enlarged. (New York: Macmillan, 1938).

Works Cited

Abbott, E.C. "Teddy Blue" and Helena Huntington Smith. *We Pointed Them North: Collections of a Cowpuncher* . 1939. Norman: U of Oklahoma P, 1955.

Bane, Michael. *The Outlaws: Revolution in Country Music.* New York: Doubleday Dolphin, 1978.

Eliot, T.S. *The Use of Poetry and the Use of Criticism* . London: Faber & Faber, 1933.

Hazlitt, William. "On Shakespeare and Milton." *Criticism: The Major Texts.* Ed. Walter Jackson Bate. New York: Harcourt, 1970.

"On the Character of Rousseau." *Criticism: The Major Texts* . Ed. Walter Jackson Bate. New York: Harcourt, 1970.

Keats, John. "To Richard Woodhouse (27 October 1818)" *Criticism: The Major Texts* . Ed.Walter Jackson Bate. New York: Harcourt, 1970.

Peacock, Thomas Love. "The Four Ages of Poetry." *Works* 10 vols. 1924-1934. Eds.H.F.B. Brett-Smith and C.E. Jones. New York: AMS Press, 1967. Vol. 8.

Reinert, Al. "King of Country." *The New York Times Magazine* 26 March 1978: 26.

Savage, William W., Jr. *The Cowboy Hero: His Image in American History and Culture* Norman: U of Oklahoma P, 1979.

Thorp, N. Howard "Jack." *Songs of the Cowboys Variants, commentary, notes and lexicon by Austin E. and Alta S. Fife.* New York: Clarkson N. Potter, 1966.

Tinsley, Jim Bob. *He Was Singin' This Song: A Collection of Forty-Eight Songs of the American Cowboy, With Words, Music, Pictures, and Stories.* Orlando: UP of Florida, 1938.

The Streets of Bakersfield
(The Lights of Baltimore):
Personal, Political and Social Issues

Country music has always been "up close and personal" in its treatment of both the everyday concerns and cares of life and the impact of larger social issues and institutions on its audience, whether these take the naively romantic form of Lee Greenwood's "God Bless the USA," the liberating anger of Johnny Paycheck's "Take This Job And Shove It," or that ultimate cry of rural frustration, "I Got The Interstate Runnin' Through My Outhouse."

On the interpersonal level, a major concern in country songs is the relationship between a man and a woman. What are appropriate gender roles? And what happens if a man or a woman steps outside these socially approved roles (an issue touched upon previously in "Tension, Conflict and Contradiction")? In "Image of Women and Men in Country Music" Karen Saucier takes this analysis further in her gender specific study of country music lyrics. She concludes that, although the lyrics of country songs may serve as one way of expressing discontent with the restrictions of traditional gender roles, "clearly the symbolic world offered by country music lyrics represents a rather bleak, limited world for both men and women in regard to status, role and power. (Politically) the only aspect of their lives that is somewhat under their control is the relationship between themselves and their lover."

This relationship can be a special one that, itself, strains the boundaries of conventional morality and can become a political issue—a situation Stephen Thompson investigates in "Forbidden Fruit," a look at the treatment of interracial love affairs in country music. For the most part, these affairs end tragically. But, as Thompson notes, there are a "handful of exceptions" to this— and these exceptions are, ultimately, "more intriguing than the regularities."

At the institutional level, organized religion plays an important part in the lives of members of the country music audience, even though they are ambivalent about the "organized" aspect of it, as Jimmie Rogers and Stephen Smith show in their essay. They conclude that "a strong sense of individualism dominates the typical Southerner's world view with regard to religion, just as it does in politics, justice and other social and economic relationships...Glen Campbell voiced the feelings of many in the country music audience when he sang, 'I Knew Jesus (Before He Was A Star),' and this distinction remains consistent between entertainment by public spectacle and religion as a personal and private affair."

These sentiments are echoed in Jock MacKay's "Populist Ideology and Country Music," in which he examines American (and Canadian) country music

239

and its audiences. MacKay asserts that, in both countries, the largest portion of the audience is "located in the same socio-economic interstices as the traditional following of populist movements" and that country music reflects a view of the ideal society that is very similar to that articulated by populist movements. MacKay describes this as a view that values "simplicity, self-reliance, trustworthy family, friends and neighbors in a viable community network." Yet, perhaps because of the position of helplessness many of those in the audience find themselves in, in modern capitalist society, country music (and populism) also contain what MacKay calls an "ambiguous tension" between a vision of peoples' power and a careless life of drunkenness, promiscuity and redneck violence, to cite the extremes this position can take.

PLAYLIST

Kathy Mattea	Willow In The Wind	Polydor
Dolly Parton and		
Porter Wagoner	Just Between Me and You	RCA
Marty Robbins	El Paso	Columbia
Emmylou Harris	Sally Rose	Warner Bros.
Merle Haggard	Songs I'll Always Sing	Capitol
Tom T. Hall	Jesus On The Radio	RCA
Simani	Salt Water Cowboys	Quay
Stompin' Tom Connors	The Northland's Own	Dominion

Images of Women and Men in Country Music

Karen A. Saucier

Mass media have been acknowledged by social scientists to be one of the most powerful socializing agents (Tuchman, Daniles and Benet; Goffman; McLuhan) and yet their impact on social behavior has been difficult to gauge. However, since socialization occurs throughout the life span and since the mass media in industrial society permeates virtually every aspect of a person's life, the media's effect on our concepts of self, although impossible to determine precisely, are probably underestimated.

Since the creation of television and movies, the medium of radio and popular music has received less attention in social research as a shaper and/or reflector of social behavior. Popular music as transmitted by audio (records, radio in car and/or home, jukebox) is perhaps even more pervasive in our daily lives than the other forms of media because of its constant presence. Radio music should then be of importance to sociologists as an element of culture which can provide some insights about values of the members of a society.

As a mechanism which transmits social norms, popular music is a significant socializing element. Moreover, socialization plays a critical role in determining what members of a society believe to be acceptable behavior for members of their sex. How one becomes a male or female through socialization has been studied extensively in recent years. Influences such as the family, education, peer groups and the mass media help form our conceptions of maleness/femaleness (Chafetz; Weitz; Sternglanz and Serbin). Gender roles exhibited by men and women have been explored extensively in television, movies, books and advertising, but radio and music have been virtually neglected.

Significant attention has, however, been paid in recent years to life in rural areas where country music is often identified as being the main or only music choice. Researchers in rural areas have investigated sociological significance of the changing roles of men and women in different community structures (Moen et al; Joyce and Leadley).

Lyrical analysis has suggested that popular song lyrics may serve as stereotypical models (Riesman), but country music as a medium has rarely been studied as an influence in gender role socialization. It has long been viewed as an "artistic and intellectual wasteland" (Buckley 293) in the field of social

Reprinted with permission from the *Journal of Popular Culture* 20.3 (Winter 1986): 147-65.

research and thus has received little theoretical or empirical attention.

The roles that men and women have been expected to play have been changing in recent years and research in the media has indicated that these changes have been reflected very slowly in television, advertising and in the printed media. In rural areas changes happen even slower. Country music has long been characterized by traditional male/female images. Though often described as being a "a persuasive medium for the transmission of rural conservatism" (Buckley 294), country music in recent years has become popular outside of the "rural country." In the last ten years country music has become increasingly popular with the non-rural working class. Country songs are also enjoying popularity outside of the rural areas and/or working class, drawing listeners from all strata of societies (Buckley). So not only are roles of men and women experiencing change, but the type of music listened to is no longer confined to one stratum or regional area. But even though country music has become increasingly popular outside rural areas, it still remains the most common musical genre found in rural areas (Thaxton and Jaret).

It has been suggested that even with the changes occurring in men's and women's roles in rural areas that differences between rural and urban areas are inevitable (Fischer). Contention is that rural areas will always be the last to change as a result of what Fischer calls the "trickle down" effect in which cultural innovations are continuously being created in subcultures of large urban centers from which they spread to other social worlds in these centers and eventually to smaller outlying communities.

Thus, there is a need in social research not only to explore the roles of men and women in music—specifically country music—but also to explore its theoretical application to gender role theory. In this study those gender roles presented in country music are identified and linked to theoretical perspectives on gender stratification generally and to the concepts of status, role and power. Content analysis is used to identify themes in country music songs and the images of men and women as depicted in the music is explored. The theoretical perspective of gender stratification is thus utilized to link empirical findings with theoretical explanations. This study will explore the question: To what degree does an analysis of country music lyrics support sociological theory regarding gender stratification, roles, status and power?

Social scientists have, however, demonstrated some interest in the analysis of song lyrics because of the belief that the lyrics provide some insight into societal values. Adorno offered the first serious social investigation into popular music when he described the fundamental character of popular songs as well as showing how music companies standardized certain themes in controlling the music market. Peatman utilized content analysis to differentiate themes in popular songs of the mid-1940s centered around the theme of male/female relationships. Mooney documented that music in the 1920s and 1930s reflected a higher incidence of romantic love imagery when compared to the later decades of 1949-55. He suggested that this might reflect the values of romantic love in the 1920s and 1930s contrasted with the more practical aspects of love relationships in the latter period.

Since these early studies, social scientists have continued to find an emphasis in musical lyrics on male/female love relationships. In the 1950s, Horton explored the courtship patterns of young men and women as expressed in popular song lyrics. A decade later, Carey used a similar approach when he compared courtship patterns in popular song lyrics with those observed by Horton. Carey found that courtship patterns, as reflected in lyrical content, had changed to emphasize more of the physical aspects of love.

Most studies of song lyrics have been done with popular music; few inquiries have examined country music and lyrics. Music historian Bill Malone traced the development of country music from Anglo-Celtic ballads to hillbilly and eventually to contemporary country music. He analyzed lyrical content and showed that songs in particular time periods reflect the degree and quality of cultural change. Di Maggio, Peterson and Esco examined popular country music lyrics and identified four distinctive themes: love, liquor, work and the passing of the good old ways.

Lund went further and examined the religious, racial and political themes which have been expressed in country music during this century. In a significant comparative study Freudiger and Almquist analyzed country, easy listening and soul music to detect male and female stereotypical images. The study concluded that males (in the songs) conform more to stereotypical male traits in all three types of music more often than women (in the songs) conform to stereotypical female traits.

After reviewing the research which has been done in the area of country music and gender roles, it is apparent that sociological inquiry has been less than complete. The research has largely neglected to connect theoretical knowledge on gender role socialization and the significance of all themes in country music as related to male and female roles in society. Moreover, the research on the socialization of gender roles has concentrated in the areas of the family, education, employment and the media. However, popular music and other media influences have tended to be studied in isolation from the other institutions in our society and consequently there has been little integration of theory.

Methods

Data for the study were collected from the top 40 country songs of 1981 as ranked by *Billboard* magazine. The top 40 country songs were chosen for the sample because they are the ones most frequently heard and consequently, reflect at least some degree of public acceptance. Each year *Billboard* magazine names the single records that have received the most air play and have sold the most in retail sales. The records are ranked weekly throughout the year and are compiled at the end of the year. There are other factors besides public acceptance which accounts for records being played. The reasons include domination or control of specific record companies at certain periods of time (Peterson and Berger). However, the significance of the music being played is not so much whether it is the best of all records made or whether it is the choice of the listener, but that it is *heard* most frequently by listeners. As Freudiger and

Almquist contend: "popular songs drum a subliminal litany into the collective consciousness of the mass of Americans" (51).

As a method suggested by Hirsch for analyzing popular songs, each song has been analyzed at the lyrical level in order to determine the theme as it relates to gender roles. Most songs contain several themes, but the pattern is for one to dominate, while the others are secondary (Buckley). Therefore, the central theme of a song determined its classification.

Content analysis of the lyrics was utilized for the identification of themes. The analysis was limited to the lyrics for three reasons. First, country music lyrics are meant to be listened to (Buckley). Unlike other forms of music where melody is equally important, the essence of country music song is its story (Lewis, "Country"). Second, country music lyrics are unambiguous. Without double meanings, the listener has no difficulty in identifying the meaning of a country song (Buckley). Third, the lyrics of a country song attempt to tell a complete story in a "three-minute soap opera" (Thaxton and Jaret 309). In this story the lyrics are often an attempt to represent reality. The people and situations in country music are intended to be "realistic reproduction of life," thus eliciting universally shared emotions (Buckley 294).

The categories were created by first transcribing the lyrics of the 40 songs from the recordings. After listening to each song, initial themes were identified. The lyrics were then reanalyzed and a dominant theme was identified for each song. After the dominant themes emerged, mutually exclusive and exhaustive categories were constructed. The songs were then placed in each category and the frequency recorded. Independent coders were also utilized in the establishment of reliability. The coders generally agreed on the coding schemes as defined, and the boundaries of the categories were found to be mutually exhaustive and exclusive[1]

Theoretical Background

Gender Stratification

Gender stratification is defined as "the hierarchical distribution by gender of economic and social resources in a society" (Anderson 77). Since stratification implies a process whereby groups or persons have unequal access to social and economic resources, men and women then have different opportunities in society (Anderson).

Gender as a primary determinant that stratifies social groups exists in most societies (Yorburg). Cross-cultural evidence suggests that women's access to social and economic opportunities is largely influenced by the degree to which they control the means of social and economic production (Leghorn and Parker). Women's work has been either invisible or devalued in virtually all societies though this work sustains the society. Specifically, as industrialization has developed in society, economic production has shifted from the home to factories and other sources outside of the home. In American history the result has been the devaluation of women's work at home (Anderson).

Gender stratification occurs because once control over resources is gained, efforts to retain the power and status that accompany control comes into play.

Gender stratification then results from men's acquiring dominance and finding ways to keep it, i.e., control of the social institutions, law, social practices, beliefs and the like (Nielson).

Status

Because of the economic and social devaluation of women's work, statuses of men and women have different values. Status is thus the social value attached to one's position in the stratification system (Anderson) and is usually determined by a person's occupation and/or income. Therefore, status can also be viewed as the amount of honor and prestige that a person receives from members of the community and from the larger society (Chafetz).

Moen et al have identified two dimensions of status in an attempt to define a women's status. Status is not only an individual characteristic (i.e., personal status) but is also reflected on an aggregate level within the culture of the community. The latter is what she terms *contextual* status. In the community, a woman's personal status is derived from what prestige and power she possesses herself, as well as that which she shares with her family. In the home, however, personal status is determined on the basis of the characteristics of each person.

Contextual status can be further defined as the "balance of constraints and opportunities in a society that helps or hinders the acquisition of personal status" (Moen et al 10). Examples are job discrimination practices and stereotypical images in the media. The portrayals of men and women in country music are part of contextual status.

Role

A role is a part a person plays in society as a result of the particular status. "A person's role in any situation is defined by a set of expectations (i.e., norms) held by others and the person him/herself" (Nielson 171). Gender roles then are both expected and actual behaviors and characteristics that differentiate females from males in a specific society. Thus, "there is a behavior (actual) as well as a normative (expected) component" to gender roles (Nielson 3).

Several researchers (Yorburg; Bernard, "The Paradox"; Parsons and Bales, 1955) have characterized gender roles as either expressive or instrumental. Women's roles have centered around the family and are described as being emotionally expressive—ministering to the needs of others. The expressive role involves enhancing others' emotional satisfaction (Chafetz). The instrumental role which is more associated with men is more task oriented—getting the job done with businesslike efficiency. Men and women, however, can play both expressive and instrumental roles, but there is evidence that the above dominant role patterns are widely expressed (Bernard, "The Paradox").

Power as Related to Status and Role

Power is defined as the "ability to acquire one's ends in life even against opposition" (Tumin 12). When examining power in male/female statuses, it is important to differentiate between informal and formal power. Formal power is legitimate power and is often referred to as authority. Informal power is unassigned power and is referred to as influence (Scott). Men's power resulting from their status is usually formal power; women's power is usually informal (Nielson).

As a result, women who lack formal power (or legitimate authority) often resort to informal power methods to meet needs. Nielson (145) believes that the traditional female role (i.e., deference, submissive, ignorance, cajoling, smiling) "is an adaptive technique in a gender stratified society." In other words, expected female role characteristics, such as manipulation and sexual bargaining, are viewed as the only available techniques available to those who are legitimately powerless (Chafetz). Nielson views these behaviors as conscious, calculated, rational mechanisms developed "primarily for successful interaction with members of the dominant group—men" (145).

Power, then, as a function of status, is a measure of opportunity and of how much control people have over their lives (autonomy) and the lives of others (power). Differences in status then are the manifestations of inequality in a society (Moen et al).

Media and the Maintenance of Gender Roles/Gender Stratification

In addition to exploring the origins of gender roles and status in the social structure, another equally important consideration is how and why these systems are maintained. Weitz contends that the symbolic realm of a society is critical in understanding gender role and status maintenance in a society.

By symbolic, she means those social representations of the relationship between the sexes that tend to reflect existing social conditions as well as to assist in affirming and maintaining them. She does, however, stress that along with the reflective-maintaining character of symbolic representation comes the need to consider simultaneously psychological and sociological factors in the understanding of such representation. She includes among many general symbolic images the media and its specific symbolic role models (i.e., the context in which men and women develop their own gender role norms and which influences perception). Further, according to Gerbner, the ideals of the population are incorporated into symbolic representation. The reflection hypothesis acknowledges that while media images exist as make-believe, they do encapsulate dominant social beliefs and images (Anderson). It has been found that these stereotypical images serve as potential role models and seem to encourage both men and women to define men in terms of men or in the context of the family (Tuchman).

In conclusion, the theoretical perspective used in the analysis of the data is derived from gender stratification theory. Three concepts—status, role and power—have been identified for study. The maintenance of this system is explored through male and female images in country music.

Findings

General Findings

In the songs selected for analysis, 95 percent presented a male/female theme. The male/female relationship in these songs displayed three phases in the live relationship: the anticipation of the love relationship, which constituted 5 percent of the sample: the establishment of the relationship which made up 38 percent of the sample; and the disintegration of the relationship, which made up 38 percent of the sample. In addition to the three stages identified, two other themes emerged which also related to the male/female relationship. One dealt with male sexual prowess and another theme focused on a social commentary/advice theme. Each of these made up 8 percent of the total sample. Two songs had themes that were not related to male/female relationships; one was about nature and the other was about the South and going home. These were not included in the analysis (see Table 1).

As can be seen in Table 1, the majority of the songs in this sample dealt with both the establishment and the disintegration of the love relationship. This finding is consistent with other analyses of country music where romantic involvement is a common theme (Nietzeke; Freudiger and Almquist; DiMaggio, Peterson and Esco).

Identified in the category of the establishment of the love relationship were two subcategories: 1) celebration; and 2) ambivalence.

Six subcategories of the major theme of disintegration of the male/female relationship were identified: 1) mourning; 2) alcohol use; 3) reversibility of decision; 4) bargaining; 5) confidence in ex-lover's mistake; and 6) rationalization that break-up was inevitable and due to fate. The prevailing mood after analyzing these songs is one of despair resulting from a disastrous love affair. The listening audience not only knows that the singer is unhappy, but why in detail. One or more of the partners have been unfaithful, weak, or inattentive and this has led to disintegration, repentance and/or regrets.

Application of Gender Stratification, Status, and Role to Findings

The degree to which the country music lyrics analyzed support sociological theory regarding gender stratification, roles, status and power is explored in this section. Indicators for each concept are examined for theoretical relevancy.

Status

The statuses presented in the lyrics reflected traditional values. Since status in American society is usually determined by income and/or occupation, the women presented in country music have little prestige. In none of the songs studied was work, occupation, career, or education referred to. Since the woman's domestic work was also never mentioned, these lyrics support the theoretical position of Blumberg and Leacock concerning the invisibility of women's work. The country song's view of women's personal status then

Table 1

Analysis of Themes in Sample

n=40

Category/Themes	Frequency	Illustrated Content
I. Male-Female Relationship	38 (95%)	
A. Establishment of Love Relationship	15 (38%)	Relationship is confirmed, consummated, commitment has been made
1. Celebration		Affection, euphoria, enthusiasm over physical aspects of relationship
2. Ambivalence		Feelings of celebration and fear of loss co-exist; feelings expressed over being consumed and weakened by desire
B. Disintegration of Love Relationship	15 (38%)	Relationship is dying or is already dead
1. Mourning		Anguish, sadness, reminiscing, celebration of virtues of lost love
2. Alcohol use as consolation		Excessive use of alcohol to forget
3. Reversibility of decision		Postition that ex-lover can come back "no matter what
4. Bargaining		Pleading, begging to be given another chance
5. Confidence in ex-lover's mistake		Ex-lover will regret decision to leave
6. Rationalization of break-up		Break-up attributed to "fate"
C. Anticipation of love relationship	2 (5%)	The pursuit of a relationship, seeking a lover/desiring a lover
D. Male's prowess in love relationship	3 (8%)	Macho, virility, experience with women; knows how to "please" women
E. Social commentary on love	3 (8%)	Advice is given based on experience relationship about the nature of men and women
II. Other		
A. Home - Nature		

Total percentages may not add up to 100% because of rounding.

eliminates a woman's access to the opportunity structure through her own efforts.

When a man's work was mentioned in the lyrics it was as a "job," not an occupation or a career. The jobs described in country music lyrics tended to be routine, monotonous blue-collar positions, where the only reward is money: "Well, it's eighteen wheels rolling heavy through the desert night / I been driving all day but I won't shut her down tonight./ 'cause the Midnight Hauler is cannon ballin' her home." And in another song: "I work 10 hours on a John Deere tractor / Just thinkin' of you all day."

This reflection of contextual status in the community provides limited resources from which to gain rewards. Neither men nor women in country songs seem to gain satisfaction from their work.

A woman's personal status is often defined in terms of "her man" since she evidently, according to country music lyrics, has little else to increase her status. She is portrayed as having virtually no status as related to property or economic structure in the community or work place. This finding concurs with Blumberg's argument that the relative status of women is determined by economic power. Since women portrayed in country music are never identified with the economic structure, their status is evidently derived from their ability to get and keep a man.

Thus, the man derives his status primarily from his work and how well he provides for his family and functions to satisfy his woman (or women); the woman derives her status from how well she takes care of her man.

Roles

The only really acceptable role for women in country music is of housewife, mother and lover. Women are viewed as lovers, best friends, wives and mothers but never as co-workers or career persons.

These roles represent stereotypes and are considered the norm as expressed in country music. The gender roles that are most depicted in the songs for women were clearly expressive: the woman acts as the "emotional fixer." When a woman's love (and consequently her role as emotional supporter) is pulled out the effect on the man is devastating:

But I couldn't see
That when the flame burned out
It would leave a cold, dark cloud
Rainin' down on me.

In another song:

I had a good thing
That I never thought I'd lose
Now all those precious memories
Are pulling me in two.

The Woman expresses disappointment in the loss of a love, even though there doesn't seem to be quite as much intensity: "You said you'd never go / Believing in you, babe / that was my greatest heartache." The grief that men express over the disintegration tends to cause the man much anguish, because the stabilizing part of his life is gone. Because of the central focus on the male/female relationship, when it disintegrates both men and women have lost the essence of their existence. There are several references to alcohol use in the sample and these are a result of this grief and anguish.

Liquor is often the only consolation to losing a lover that a man uses. The liquor apparently works to anesthetize emotional despair, at least temporarily: "Since love ain't here I don't feel a thing / I think I'll just stay here and drink." In another song: "It shouldn't take us very long / Another sip or two and you'll be gone." Lyrics such as these reflect the despair. Another example is:

If the whiskey doesn't get me
I know the memories will
Cause you left a hole in my heart too deep to fill.

Chalfant and Beckley confirmed that men in country music most commonly use alcohol to assuage problems. The use of alcohol by the man in order to "deaden" the loss of a love lends evidence of the emotional support and social buffering that the woman provides in the home.

Moen et al found in their research of boom town women that women traditionally have been the main equilibrators of the family and in the community. This reflects this dominant expressive role pattern as women act to enhance others' emotional satisfaction and abilities (Moen et al). When that support is withdrawn and the woman no longer provides that stabilizing function, the man turns to alcohol as a substitute.

A significant finding in the analysis dealt with the gender of the singer when alcohol was mentioned in the song. Alcohol use is entirely limited to men as an appropriate way of dealing with grief. Drinking alcohol is associated with a machismo type of behavior and does not seem to be acceptable in any form for a woman in the country song. This lack of reference to women's use of alcohol again supports the stereotypical roles of traditional males and females portrayed in country music.

In contrast, when the woman is grief-stricken over the loss of a lover she doesn't quite allow herself to completely shatter. She only needs her man to stay with her temporarily until she can regain her footing:

The taxi cab is waiting for you to go
But tell him that you've changed your mind and stay until tomorrow
Cause I know tonight that I'll need someone to hold me when I cry.

However, she still reminds the man, "Don't worry 'bout me darling / cause I'll get by." An attempt on her part to remain composed and to show that she will pull herself together is an attitude that further reflects the view that women as the stabilizers in the home bear much of the responsibility of holding the household together.

Another woman describes her willingness to take the ex-lover back at any cost:

And if you ever change your mind
Oh, give it one more try
Some magic place and time.

Again the man doesn't need to be "strong" because the woman will always be there to provide emotional support in case the other woman doesn't. The burden of emotional strength relies almost entirely on the woman because the man needs to be free, as described by this female singer: "Drifter, I'll be waiting / Should you ever drift back in."

Thus, the role portrayals in country music tend to be expressive when women are depicted. This norm supports the concept of females as being emotionally expressive. The expressive role involves enhancing others' emotional satisfaction and in a modern, industrial society "the economic-opportunity system bestows its rewards *not* on those who perform expressively but on those who perform instrumentally" (Scanzoni and Scanzoni 27).

The male's role in country music does not as clearly illustrate an instrumental orientation. Quite often the man portrayed in country music displays an ineptness rather than efficiency:

I was born to stumble
Searching for something I never will find
　　　* * *
You were always there to pick me up
After love let me down.

Perhaps because successful instrumental roles imply "getting the job done," the man expresses somehow this failure in relation to his intimate relationship—he has let himself and his woman down. Consequently, since work for both men and women seems to be meaningless and unsuccessful, they turn to the only thing of importance in their lives for fulfillment—each other.

The woman is always there for support when the man stumbles but is not as clearly reciprocated, as this male singer laments: "You're bound to love your hard-luck boy / When I let you down you don't show it."

Power

Informal power or influence is probably the best illustrated of all the concepts related to gender stratification. The woman depicted in country music clearly has minimal formal or legitimate power. Nielson argues that people with little formal power must be "extremely sensitive to the likes and dislikes of the dominant group" in order to acquire personal and material rewards (145). This use of informal power is illustrated by one female singer:

So sit down here beside me
After you say good-bye
Cause I'll need someone to hold me when I cry
And stay until tomorrow

This song suggests that women use sexuality as a bargaining tool. Specifically, the woman is attempting to buy time in hopes that if the man stays the night he will be convinced to stay with her more permanently. This supports Collins' belief that gender stratification is related to the potential resource of sexual attractiveness. He argues that people struggle for as much dominance as their resources permit; changes in resources lead to changes in the ability to dominate in specific situations.

"Drifter, I thought my kiss stopped all your restlessness / But you proved again / No one ropes the wind." The woman again attempts to use her sexuality as a resource. The woman in country music recognizes what a valuable commodity her sexual attractiveness is and attempts to use it in order to secure rewards. As a man describes his inability to resist a woman's charms, he confirms her informal power:

Might as well admit it
Your love had got the best of me
You can take one night
And turn it into a lifetime.

There is a definite ambivalence between the celebration of the relationship and the fear of the loss of freedom in country music lyrics. The man expresses anxiety over being dependent and vulnerable to a woman's spell; he fears being consumed and weakened with desire:

I keep coming back
Even though I know it's more than I can take
I'm standing at your door
Cause I keep coming back for more.

In another song: "Why lady why can't I leave you alone / I try lady try but the feeling's too strong." This reflects the position offered by Chafetz that men fear the power of a woman, even in her utilization of emotional support and sexuality as resources. Therefore, men try to resist this weakness in order to maintain their higher status, no matter how powerless they might actually be.

The confidence that the ex-lover will regret the decision that he/she made is also described in country music. This is illustrated by the Ronnie Milsap song "There's No Getting Over Me":

So you can walk out on me tonight

If you think that it ain't feelin' right
But darlin' there ain't no getting over me.

The song reflects a very confident attitude by the man that he is the best thing that had happened to her. This knowledge seems to provide some sort of inflation for the man's ego in viewing himself as irreplaceable. This song describes an attempt by the man to give the appearance of being confident in his ability to be an adequate lover. He may be well trying to convince the woman that she holds no resources which he needs. Yet from all other portrayals in the lyrics of the male, it seems that this confidence may well be a facade.

Other Findings

Willie Nelson sings:

I knew someday you'd fly away
For love's the greatest healer to be found
So leave me if you need to
I will still remember Angel flying too close to the ground.

Breakups are often viewed as inevitable and due to fate. Fatalism was found to be a dominant attitude in a study of rural residents by Moen et al where energy development was viewed as inevitable. This generalized notion that things happen the way they are supposed to happen has long been associated with the lower and working classes (Ryan; Lewis, "The Culture"). This could contribute to the acceptance by women of their men's weaknesses, lack of emotional responsibility, excessive drinking and occasional infidelity. As pointed out by Moen et al, this fatalistic attitude of men and women in rural boom towns most affects women. The lack of autonomy could further reduce women's ability to act as family and community integrators and stabilizers.

Another theme which emerged is related to the anticipation of the love relationship and the active pursuit by the male. "Step by Step" instructs the male pursuer how to win a "lady's love." "You take the first step / Ask her out and treat her like a lady." The male is expected to play the active role by "asking" the woman out, which reflects the dominant behavior acceptable for traditional male and female relationships. This further suggests that country music lyrics identify with stereotypical (expected) behaviors of men and women. The stereotype is further portrayed by the theme of male sexual prowess illustrated in the following:

I've been around some
And I have discovered
That older women know
Just how to please a man.

And by:

254 All That Glitters

Here's to the ladies
In saloons and living rooms
Summer nights that lasted until dawn
Here's to the memories

And by:

I'm no stranger to loving arms
I'm accustomed to ladies' charms
You know I didn't just ride into town
You might say I've been around.

This kind of sexual behavior presented in a boastful manner would be totally unacceptable for the woman in the country music genre as indicated by no references in the lyrics to female sexual prowess as a value. This restrictive view of men and women in country music led Nietzeke to the conclusion that country music represents a "working class world of diminished personhood" (114). These findings further suggest that roles for men and women in country music are highly constricted.

A major theme in the lyrics was identified as the establishment of the love relationship. By far the most common expression of this theme was in the celebration of the relationship. These songs expressed affection, romance and euphoria over the relationship with great emphasis placed on the physical relationship. Examples include:

And keep me warm tonight
So hold me close and love me
Give my heart a smile.

And:

Lovers live longer
Lovers live right
So let's stay together
Cause the way that we're going.

And: "I came alive when you came along / You brought life into me." This celebration with the romantic intensity of the love relationship reflects how important the male/female love relationship is for fulfillment of a person's life. It has been suggested through research on the working class that the family is the focus of their lives. In contrast to the upper and middle class where the emphasis is on the career and work interests, the working and lower class is more often concerned with family interests (Rubin; LeMasters; Komarovsky).

Both men and women in country lyrics express the devastating effects of a lost love with much greater intensity than other forms of music (Coker). This could be an indication of the strong value placed on the male/female dyad in more traditional families. The women and men portrayed in themes related to the dying stage of love tend to view love as being their social buffer, a haven from the world that provides security. Without that security there is nothing but despair and hopelessness. This reflects the significance of the family in the traditionally held values of the rural community.

Even the songs in the sample which did not fall into any stage of the relationship—those that gave social advice—focused on the "nature" of men and women: "Everywhere you look / You can write a book on / The trouble between a woman and a man." And:

You gotta keep an eye open all the time
Or you'll get your heart broke all the time
Too many lovers
Not enough love these days.

And:

Picking up strangers
Let me tell you bout the dangers
Some are just common thieves they say
The next thing you know
One'll steal your heart away.

Again, these examples provide some evidence of the importance of the male/female love relationship in country music lyrics. This emphasis on the male/female dyad may further explain in part the other three concepts related to gender stratification. Because the dyad is the focus for both the men and women as portrayed in country music other sources of status such as occupation become secondary at best. Children and/or other family members are not mentioned in the lyrics nor are other female friends. The male friends of the men are occasionally mentioned as "drinking or partying" companions. Therefore, the resources for power are limited for both men and women

Conclusions

The results of this research offer support for the belief that country music creates a symbolic world where status limits men and women's acquisition of resources. It has been demonstrated through a content analysis of the lyrics of 40 country music songs that a woman's status is derived from her ability to get and keep a man. A man's status is derived from his ability to provide for his woman and family as well as his ability to satisfy his woman. For each, the love relationship clearly is the most important element in their lives. A woman's role is demonstrated to be primarily expressive—she is primarily responsible for holding the man together emotionally. This finding supported the theoretical notion of informal power as well. The woman in country music, at least on the surface, appears to make maximum use out of her only resources—emotional support and her sexuality.

The only appropriate roles identified in country music lyrics for women were those of lover, wife and mother—never as worker or career woman. The man's roles were less clearly defined but when mentioned were those as lover and provider. For both, work is secondary and unsatisfactory, leaving primarily the love relationship as the most intense and consequently the most powerful aspect of their lives. When the love relationship is threatened or is failing the effects are crippling.

Clearly the symbolic world offered by country music lyrics represents a rather bleak, limited world for both men and women in regard to status, role and power. The only aspect of their lives that is somewhat under their control is the relationship between themselves and their lover.

The sample of songs used in the study was small and for that reason is considered a limitation on the derivation of themes. However, the data are suggestive that country music contributes to contextual status by these limited roles. The lyrics in the country songs analyzed perhaps serve as one way of expressing the discontent of these restricted roles. The presentation of traditional gender roles in country music lyrics serves to reinforce the images of men as dominant and controlling and women as submissive and supportive even in the face of discontented suffering. This is important in the maintenance of gender stratification in society because as Bernard contends, men and women learn who they are from what they tell each other (*The Sex Game*).

Notes

This study was funded in part by Health & Human Services Grant #MH 33524, U.S. Government.
¹Transcribed song lyrics and coding scheme available on request.

Works Cited

Adorno, T.W. "On Radio Music." *Studies in Philosophy and Social Science*. New York: Institute of Social Research, 1941. 17-48.

Anderson, Margaret L. *Thinking About Women: Sociological and Feminist Perspectives*. New York: MacMillan, 1983.

Bernard, Jessie. "The Paradox of the Happy Marriage." *Woman in Sexist Society*. Ed. V. Gornick and B. Moran. New York: New American Library, 1971. 145-162.

_____.*The Sex Game*. Englewood Cliffs, NJ: Prentice Hall, 1968.

Blumberg, R. *Stratification: Socioeconomic and Sex Equality*. Dubuque, IA: William C. Brown, 1978.

Buckley, John. "Country Music and American Values." *Popular Music and Society* 6 (1979): 293-306.

Carey, James T. "Changing Courtship Patterns in the Popular Song." *American Journal of Sociology* 74 (1969): 720-731.

Chafetz, Janet S. *Masculine, Feminine, or Human: An Overview of the Sociology of*

Gender Roles. Itasca, IL: F.E. Peacock, 1978.

Chalfant, Paul and Robert E. Beckley. "Beguiling and Betrayal: The Image of Alcohol Use in Country Music." *Journal of Studies on Alcohol* 38 (1977): 1428-1433.

Coker, Wilson. *Music and Meaning*. New York: Free P, 1971.

Collins, Randell. "A Conflict Theory of Sexual Stratification." *Social Problems* 19 (1971): 3-21.

Denizen, Norman K. "Problems in Analyzing Elements of Mass Culture: Notes on the Popular Song and Other Artistic Productions." *American Journal of Sociology* 75 (1970): 1035-1040.

DiMaggio, Paul, Richard A. Peterson and Jack Esco, Jr. "Country Music: Ballad of the Silent Majority." *The Sounds of Social Change*. Ed. R. Denisoff and R. Peterson. Chicago: Rand McNally, 1972. 38-56.

Fischer, Claude S. "Urban-to-Rural Diffusion of.Opinions in Contemporary America." *American Journal of Sociology* 84 (1978): 151-159.

Freudiger, Patricia and Elizabeth M Almquist. "Male and Female Roles in the Lyrics of Three Genres of Contemporary Music." *Sex Roles* 41 (1978), 51-69.

Gerbner, George. "The Dynamics of Cultural Resistance." *Hearth and Home: Images of Women in the Mass Media*. Ed. G. Tuchman, A.K. Daniels and J. Benet. New York: Oxford UP, 1978. 46-50.

Goffman, Irving. *Gender Advertisements*. New York: Harper and Row, 1976.

Hirsch, P.N. "Sociological Approaches to the Pop Music Phenomenon." *American Behavioral Scientists* 14 (1971): 389-399.

Horton, Donald. "The Dialogue of Courtship in Popular Songs." *American Journal of Sociology* 62 (1957): 569-578.

Joyce, L.M. and S.M. Leadley. *An Assessment of Research Needs of Women in Rural United States*. University Park: Pennsylvania State University Agricultural Experiment Station, 1977.

Komarovsky, Mirra. *Blue Collar Marriage*. New York: Vintage, 1962

Leacock, E. "Women's Status in Egalitarian Society." *Contemporary Anthropology* 19 (1978): 247-275.

Leghorn, L. and K. Parker. *Women's Worth: Sexual Economics and the World of Women*. Boston: Routledge and Kagan Paul, 1981.

LeMasters, E.E. *Blue Collar Aristocrats: Life Styles at a Working Class Tavern*. Madison, WI: U of Wisconsin P, 1975.

Lewis, George H. "Country Music Lyrics." *Journal of Communication* 26 (1976): 37.

Lewis, Oscar. "The Culture of Poverty." *Scientific American* 215 (1966): 19-25

Lund, Jens. "Fundamentalism, Racism, and Political Reaction in Country Music." *The Sounds of Social Change*. Ed. S. Denisoff and R. Peterson. Chicago: Rand McNally, 1972. 79- 91.

Malone, Bill C. *Country Music, U.S.A*. Austin: U of Texas P, 1968.

McLuhan, Marshall.*The Medium is the Message*. New York: Bantam, 1967.

Moen, Elizabeth, Elise Boulding, Jane Lillydahl and Risa Palm. *Women and the Social Costs of Economic Development: Two Colorado Case Studies*. Boulder, CO: Westview P, 1981

Mooney, H.F. "Popular Music Since the 1920s: The Significance of Shifting Taste." *Sounds of Social Change*. Ed. R. Denisoff and R.   Peterson. Chicago: Rand

McNally, 1972. 181-197.

Nielson, Joyce M. *Sex In Society: Perspectives on Stratification*. Belmont, CA:Wadsworth Publishing, 1978.

Nietzke, Ann. "Doin' Somebody Wrong." *Mass Media and Society*. 3rd ed. Ed. M. DeFleur, S. Ball-Rokeach and A. Wells. Palo Alto, CA: Mayfield Publishing, 1979. 111-116.

Parsons, Talcott and Robert F. Bales. *Family, Socialization and the Interaction Process*. Glencoe, IL: Free P, 1955

Peatman, J. "Radio and Popular Music." *Radio Research: 1942-43*. Ed. P. Lazarsfield and F. Stanton. New York: Duell, Sloan and Pearce, 1944. 335-393.

Peterson, R.A. and Berger, D.G. "Cycles in Symbolic Production: The Case of Popular Music." *American Sociological Review* 40 (1975): 158-173.

Riesman, David. "Listening to Popular Music." *Mass Culture: The Popular Arts in America*. Ed. B. Rosenberg and D.M. White. Glencoe, IL: Free P, 1957. 40-60.

Rubin, Lillian. *Worlds of Pain: Life in the Working Class Family*. New York: Basic Books, 1976.

Ryan, William. *Blaming the Victim*. New York: Random House, 1972.

Scanzoni, L. and John Scanzoni. *Men, Women and Change*. New York: McGraw-Hill,1976.

Scott, W. Richard. *Organizations: Rational, Natural and Open Systems*. New Jersey: Prentice-Hall, 1981.

Sternglanz, S. and L. Serbin. "Sex-role Stereotyping in Children's Television Programs." *Developmental Psychology* 10 (1974): 710-715.

Thaxton, Lyn and Charles Jaret. "Country Music and Its City Cousin: A Comparative Analysis of Urban and Rural Country Music." *Popular Music and Society* 6 (1979): 307-313.

Tuchman, Gayle, A. Daniels and J. Benet. *Hearth and Home: Images of Women in the Mass Media*. New York: Oxford UP, 1978.

Weitz, Shirley. *Sex Roles: Biological, Psychological, and Social Foundations*. New York: Oxford UP, 1977.

Yorburg, Betty. *Sexual Identity: Sex Roles and Social Change*. New York: John Wiley and Sons, 1974.

Forbidden Fruit:
Interracial Love Affairs in Country Music

Stephen I. Thompson

On June 12, 1967, the United States Supreme Court issued a unanimous decision in the case of Loving vs. Virginia. The plaintiffs, Richard P. Loving, a white male and his wife, Mildred, a woman of part black and part Indian descent, were both natives of Caroline County, Virginia who had been married in the District of Columbia in 1958. Upon returning to their home state they were arrested and prosecuted for violation of Virginia's anti-miscegenation law. Thirty-eight states have had such laws on the books at one time or another and thirty-one remained in force at the end of the Second World War. However, by 1967 fifteen of these had either been repealed or overturned in state and federal courts. At the time of the Loving decision, there were only sixteen still in effect—in Alabama, Arkansas, Delaware, Florida, Georgia, Kentucky, Louisiana, Mississippi, Missouri, North Carolina, Oklahoma, South Carolina, Tennessee, Texas, Virginia and West Virginia (Sickels 64).

Only once previously had a challenge to an anti-miscegenation statute reached the Supreme Court: in 1883 the tribunal upheld an Alabama law prohibiting interracial marriage on the grounds that, since it applied to whites as well as blacks, it was not discriminatory. However, the Loving vs. Virginia decision repudiated that reasoning; writing on behalf of a unanimous panel, Chief Justice Warren appears deliberately to have worded his decision broadly enough to invalidate not merely the Virginia statute, but all of the sixteen surviving anti-miscegenation laws on the grounds that they violated the equal protection clause of the fourteenth amendment (*New York Times 28*).

Whatever one's position may be with regard to the Warren court in general, it seems clear that in this case the difference between the 1883 and 1967 rulings reflects a major shift in American opinions and attitudes over the intervening eighty-four year period. Moreover, it comes as no surprise that the sixteen states that still had anti-miscegenation laws in force in 1967 were the eleven states of

Reprinted with permission from *Popular Music and Society* 13.2 (Summer 1989): 23-37. Edited Version.

the old Confederacy, the border states of Delaware, Kentucky, Missouri and West Virginia; and Oklahoma, not yet officially opened to white settlement at the time of the Civil War but subsequently peopled largely by southerners. This was, of course, the area of the country where Jim Crow laws persisted the longest and in which school desegregation was resisted most bitterly. It was also, coincidentally, the heartland of country music.

Although a plausible case can be made for a heavy black influence on early country music,[1] and although a handful of black performers, notably Charley Pride and O.B. McClinton, have recently achieved prominence in the genre, country is overwhelmingly perceived, both by its fans and by its detractors, as white people's music—music performed by white musicians for a white, predominantly rural, predominantly southern audience. It is also perceived, with considerable accuracy, as being essentially apolitical, and when overt political content does creep into a country song—as in Merle Haggard's "Okie from Muskogee," for example, or Guy Drake's "Welfare Cadillac" (sic)—it is usually a staunch conservatism. It is therefore somewhat surprising to discover that a fairly large number of country songs, most of them predating the Loving vs. Virginia decision, have dealt with interracial love affairs and that many have treated the topic with considerable sympathy. This paper will examine some of these, attempt to identify what, if anything, they have in common and consider the question of whether changing racial attitudes in the nation as a whole have been reflected in the content of country music.

From a cursory examination of country songs with miscegenation as a theme, three generalizations emerge. First, the non-white partner is invariably American Indian, Hispanic, Asian, or even Eskimo, but not black; second, it is nearly always the male protagonist who is white and the female who is non-white; third, the affair usually ends tragically, in the death of one or both of the lovers or in the desertion of one of them. There is a handful of exceptions to each of these, which will be discussed presently; in many ways, the exceptions are more interesting than the regularities.

Songs depicting love affairs between white men and Indian women long antedate the emergence of country music as a distinctive genre. Fife and Redden (1954) discuss a dozen or so of these which are either authentic folksongs or early popular songs that have passed into the folk tradition; the best known of their examples are "Shenandoah," "Fallen Leaf" and "Little Mohee." Invariably, as in all three of these cases, the heroine is a chief's daughter, the proverbial Indian Princess. The affairs seldom end in marriage; either the girl's father rejects the match, as in "Shenandoah" (although in one version the couple subsequently elope), the girl herself spurns her suitor ("Chippewa Girl"), or the white lover simply disappears mysteriously, as he does in "Fallen Leaf." "Little Mohee" is an exception. In this song, originally a British broadside ballad, the heroine may either be Hawaiian or Indian. She makes the initial advance but is reluctantly refused by the man, who has his "own sweetheart in (his) own country." Upon returning home, however, he finds that his first love has proved unfaithful during his absence, and the final verse has him again crossing the ocean to the arms of his Little Mohee.

Another well known example which may fall into this category is the familiar "Red River Valley." Sigmund Spaeth (357) traces the origin of this to an 1896 James J. Kerrigan composition, "In the Bright Mohawk Valley," which was later transplanted further west, but Bill Malone suggests (personal communication, 8/31/87) that it may have originally referred to the Red River of the North and have depicted a love affair between a Canadian Indian girl and a British soldier. This theory is supported by Lax and Smith's *Great Song Thesaurus*, which states that Kerrigan's 1896 work was ^"based on a traditional Canadian folksong" (832) and by the version of "Red River Valley" presented by Carl Sandburg in *The American Songbag* The last verse of that begins: "And the dark maiden's prayer for her lover, To the Spirit that rules over the world" (131), a fairly clear indication of Indian ethnicity.

Considering the prevalent stereotypes of Indians in early American literature and mythology, it is hardly surprising that there are few songs dealing with Indian males and white females. As Richard Slotkin points out (205), the Indian was associated by the Puritans with "the forces of the unconscious, the suppressed drives and desires that undergulf the intellect" and was therefore enormously threatening. Slotkin provides an exhaustive analysis of the captivity narratives which constituted a staple of colonial literature, largely because of the moral lessons they were believed to impart. The most popular of these detailed the purported tribulations of female captives, who were subjected to horrible ordeals but who emerged morally unscathed and sexually unsullied because of their faith in the benevolence of the Christian God. Mary Rowlandson, the minister's wife whose 1682 account was the first published captivity narrative, spoke of her captors as "atheistical, proud, wild, cruel, barbarous, (in one word) diabolical creatures" (Berkhofer 84).

In view of this general Puritan tendency to equate the Indian with the forces of Satan, it was particularly irritating to them that the numerous incidences of white men voluntarily joining the Indians and "going native" on the early colonial frontier were matched by no cases of Indians doing the reverse. In the words of Leslie Fiedler, "The Male imagination, for better or worse, tends to transform the tale of captivity into one of adoption, to substitute the male dream of joining the Indians for the female fantasy of being dragged off by them" (90). If the heroines of captivity narratives were expected to preserve their virtue or die in the attempt, males who fantasized about joining the Indians, in colonial times and later, seldom envisioned a life of celibacy.

The Indian princess motif which recurs so frequently in these ballads reflects an American cultural tradition that dates back at least as far as the semi-legendary figure of Pocahontas and perhaps even further. Rayna Green points out that Pocahontas' well-known rescue of John Smith, celebrated in song and story and the subject of poems by Walt Whitman, Carl Sandburg, Vachel Lindsay and Hart Crane, among others (Fiedler 85), was foreshadowed, in a remarkable example of life imitating art, by a sixteenth- century Scottish song, "Young Beichan" (Child Ballad #40), in which the hero is miraculously saved from certain death at the hands of the Turks by the last minute intervention of the "Turkish king's" daughter, with whom he promptly falls in love. Historians still debate the authenticity of the Pocahontas-John Smith story, but it is significant that it is that episode, rather than her subsequent marriage to John Rolfe, that is learned and remembered by every American school child. The young girl who saved Smith's life was a virgin Princess who, not coincidentally, lived in Virginia, the colony named after a supposedly virgin queen. The mature women who married Rolfe became a wife and a mother, but in the process she relinquished her virginity, and her status degenerated from that of Indian Princess to Squaw.

This princess/squaw dichotomy has been explored at length by Fiedler, Green and Mary Dearborn. Green states it succinctly: "The Princess is sacrosanct; her sexuality can be hinted at but never realized. The Princess' darker twin, the Squaw, must serve this side of the image" (710-11). Until the sexual revolution of the 1960s, writers of songs depicting Indian-white romances were usually circumspect concerning the consummation of these affairs, but, consummated or not, none of them that I know of (with the possible exception of "Shenandoah") ends in marriage. In "Cherokee Maiden," for example, a popular Bob Wills number from the 1930s, there is a fleeting reference to "one night of love," but the lovers are then separated, and, although the hero vows in the last verse to return to his paramour, one senses that the vow will remain unfulfilled.

"Eskimo Pie," a 1976 George Jones novelty piece, has a similar denouement. Here, the male protagonist is trapped in an Alaskan blizzard. On the brink of death, he is rescued by a beautiful Eskimo woman^ldla scene that evokes images both of Pocahontas saving Smith and of a sort of human St. Bernard. She takes him to her igloo to recuperate. It is not clear whether sexual hanky-panky is part of the therapy, but once again the final verse finds the lovers separated with the hero vowing to return.

Green sees Pocahontas as a mother symbol, an interpretation supported by the succoring heroine of "Eskimo Pie," but it is a sexually pristine mother, an American Virgin Mary, as it were: "Indian woman began her symbolic, many-faceted life as a Mother figure—exotic, powerful, dangerous and beautiful—and as a representative of American liberty and European classical virtue translated into New World terms" (Green 703). A sexual encounter with such a figure is an act of symbolic incest, debasing the woman from virgin Princess to squaw and polluting the man; small wonder that there are few happy endings in songs about such relationships.

I have been able to identify only two songs which reverse the standard picture and deal with romances between Indian men and white women. Both are of fairly recent vintage. Peter Lafarge's "White Girl" is, strictly speaking, a 1960s protest song which is admitted to the country canon here only by virtue of having been recorded by Johnny Cash. The author was the son of Oliver Lafarge, the noted anthropologist/novelist and a Navaho mother. The "White Girl" of the title is a blonde 1960s civil rights activist who comes to the reservation to better the lot of its inhabitants and assuage some of her liberal guilt, flings herself into an affair with the Indian hero which he clearly takes much more seriously than she does and then recoils in horror when he proposes marriage. Having been taught by her to drink whiskey, he takes refuge in the bottle. The song is written explicitly from the Indian point of view, a rarity in this genre, and is remarkably bitter but quite eloquent. "Bitter Tear," the album of Indian protest songs on which it appears, is well known among Indians and forms part of the record collection of many anthropologists, this writer included, but among country music fans in general it probably ranks as Johnny Cash's most obscure release.

Emmylou Harris' "Ballad of Sally Rose," from the album of the same name, is similarly unusual in being written from the point of view of the woman. Sally Rose, the eponymous heroine, is the offspring of a brief affair between a white female hitch-hiker and the Sioux driver who picks her up on a South Dakota road. The title song describes this relationship, ending with the departure of the now pregnant woman; the rest of the theme album deals with Sally Rose as an adult, tracing her passionate relationship with a white rock singer which in turn ends with his death in a highway accident. Ethnicity is explicit only in the title number, and one must listen carefully to the lyrics or read the liner notes to be aware of it even there; one suspects that most listeners grasped it only subliminally if at all. Again, this is one of the more obscure of the artist's album releases. The only number to receive any significant air play as a single was "White Line," the song in which Sally's lover is killed, and the radio audience was presumably completely oblivious to her ethnic background in that.

In summary, then, out of a dozen or so songs treating Indian-white romances, most of them predating the emergence of commercial country music, in only two ("Little Mohee" and one version of "Shenandoah") is there any indication of marriage or probable marriage, and in only another two, both very recent, is the Indian partner male and the white partner female. One could perhaps argue that happy endings, because they are undramatic, are rare in any sort of music. Unrequited love seems to lend itself to song more readily than successful marriage; where would opera be without it? Nevertheless, the suspicion lingers that, in the eyes of American society, American songwriters and the American musical audience, one who falls in love with an Indian does so at his or her peril; social disapproval and perhaps even Divine retribution lie in wait.

The same generalization seems to apply even more consistently to Anglo/Hispanic romances. Strictly speaking, songs about such love affairs should probably not be classified as interracial, but since the Hispanic partner is invariably Mexican, since most white Americans consider Mexicans to be non-white and since a majority of the Mexican population has some Indian ancestry, it seems legitimate to deal with them here. The frequency of violent death of one or both parties in such songs is even higher than among American Indian and white lovers.

This pattern was apparently already established as early as the nineteenth century. Fife and Redden (384) discuss a ballad of that era called "Juanita" (not to be confused with the better known C. Norton composition of the same name) which, though they treat it as an Indian song, clearly depicts an Anglo/Mexican romance. In the first verse the American partner bids farewell to his Mexican lover. "Senor," she replies, "if you loved me you would never, never leave." He answers with a remarkably lame excuse:

I did not think that my flirtations
Would leave an impress on your heart.
When I return to wed a maiden
Of my country, we must part.

Retribution is swift and sure, as revealed by the seventh and eighth verses:

In the morning two vaqueros
Chanced to rest beneath the shade
For siesta's softest shelter
Close beside the foliage made.

`Por Dios', cried un vaquero
As he pulled the vines apart.
Here lies un Americano^
With a dagger in his heart.

Similar violence pervades almost all country songs dealing with Anglo/Hispanic romances, beginning with "El Paso," an enormous hit for Marty Robbins in 1959 which has since become a standard. Here, the hero falls in love with Felina, a bar girl and/or prostitute who frequents a spot called Rosa's cantina. One night another American customer makes advances to Felina. In a fit of jealousy, the singer shoots his rival and then flees for his life from the law. Alas, however, his love for Felina is too strong to permit his successful escape. Drawn inexorably back to El Paso, he is overtaken by a posse, shot many times and dies on Rosa's doorstep in Felina's arms.

"Tequila, Sheila," a 1979 Shel Silverstein novelty number recorded by Bobby Bare (Silverstein, a successful cartoonist, is the author of such other country novelty tunes as Johnny Cash's "A Boy Named Sue,") ends in the death of the woman rather than the man. This time the hero is an American outlaw who is holed up in a Juarez brothel with another Mexican maiden of easy virtue, Sheila—admittedly an unlikely name for a Hispanic, but Silverstein was presumably more interested in rhyme than in ethnic verisimilitude. Suddenly he becomes aware that the place is surrounded by *federales* (Mexican national police), to whom Sheila has betrayed him. Yankee ingenuity triumphs over Latin treachery, however; he forces Sheila to dress in his clothing while he dons her "red satin dress" and shoves her out the door to be shot down while he makes his getaway through the window.

Ethnicity is less explicit in "Seven Spanish Angels," the 1984 T. Seals and E. Selser song which was a major hit for Ray Charles and Willie Nelson, but again it seems to describe a romance between an American cowboy, once more a wanted man and his Mexican lover. In the first verse the couple are already cornered by the law in the "Valley of the Gun"; since there is a reference to taking him back to Texas dead rather than alive, the locale is apparently somewhere in Mexico. The hero fights off his pursuers until he runs out of ammunition and is then killed. Proclaiming her inability to live without her man, his lover then picks up the empty gun and is herself immediately slain.

Although it may be stretching the point, it is even possible that Townes Van Zandt's "Pancho and Lefty" (1973) depicts a homosexual Anglo/Hispanic affair. Pancho is a Mexican bandit and Lefty his gringo sidekick. Pancho is ultimately taken by the federales, evidently as a result of Lefty's treachery^ldlthe symbolism is heavy here and much interpretation is necessary. Lefty returns to Ohio, full of remorse, to live out his days in guilt. My imputation of homosexuality to their relationship may well be far off the mark. A colleague whose opinion I value on such matters insists that "Pancho" is in fact Pancho Villa and that it is preposterous to imagine that the quintessence of Mexican machismo might be gay, even in a song; if he is correct, then perhaps "Lefty" is intended to be John Reed and the name symbolizes his politics. In any case, whether or not there is any sexual dimension to this relationship there is certainly a close male bond, and once again it is severed by death.

The only happy ending in Anglo/Hispanic country love songs occurs in the most recent, Hank DeVito and Danny Flower's 1986 "Señorita," recorded by Don Williams. This number is essentially a recitative, describing the love of a cowboy for a Mexican girl whom he is reluctant to approach. Significantly, his reluctance stems not from their differing ethnicity, but from a combination of natural shyness and the fear of family opposition, the latter a result of the two families having been on opposing sides of old range wars. Ultimately he declares his love, the couple marry and, presumably, live happily ever after.

It is tempting to conclude that the contrast between the placid resolution of "Señorita" and the death and destruction that marks most of its predecessors is a reflection of changing racial attitudes in American society, and that conclusion may well be at least partially valid. Reinforcement comes from the recent emergence of Johnny Rodriguez and "Freddy Fender" (Baldemar Huerta) as major Mexican-American country vocalists. On the other hand, although both Rodriguez and Fender have recorded many love songs, none to my knowledge mentions the blonde hair or blue eyes of the female object of adoration; it is still invariably the male partner who is Anglo in these mixed romances.

The Second World War and the subsequent overseas posting of thousands of American servicemen generated a large number of songs concerning love affairs with foreign women. The best known of these, Lawton Williams' 1957 "Fraulein," deals with an international but not interracial romance, but others— "Geisha Girl" (mispronounced "Gesha"), "Filipino Baby," "Filipino Rose"— crosscut racial lines. Again, it is always the male partner who is white in these songs, understandably in this case since only a relative handful of female military personnel were ever afforded the opportunity to fraternize with the natives at an overseas base. Typically, in the last verse the American has come back to the U.S., left the military and is pining for his lost love. "Filipino Baby" is an interesting exception to this generalization, with the hero returning to the

Philippines at the end of the song and marrying his "little Filipino baby." It was copyrighted in 1940 by Billy Cox and Clark Van Ness and was a major postwar hit for Cowboy Copas. However, Van Ness revealed to Dorothy Horstman that the original version was written by Charles K. Harris at the time of the Spanish-American War and was about a "colored sailor with a face as black as jet" (Horstman 272-73).

Along with the 1898 annexation of Hawaii, the American acquisition of Puerto Rico and the Philippines after the war with Spain represented our first venture into overseas colonialism. Rudyard Kipling vigorously exhorted his American cousins to "Take up the White Man's burden" and civilize the brown heathens. Many Filipinos, however, were unenthusiastic about exchanging Spanish imperialism for American, and the ensuing suppression of Emilio Aguinaldo's insurrection generated numerous atrocities on both sides and an outpouring of racist rhetoric from the editorial columns of American newspapers (Wolff; Miller). The racial climate of the time would not have tolerated a happy marriage between a white American and a Filipina, even in song, but a black American was, to put it crudely, a horse of a different color.

The most recent example of this genre, attesting to the continuing overseas American military presence, is Mack Vickery's 1985 "Tokyo, Oklahoma," recorded by John Anderson. Its premise is a transpacific phone call from a lovesick Tulsan to his Japanese sweetheart. Like most of its earlier counterparts, the song makes only a feeble pretense at ethnic authenticity. "Geisha" is again mispronounced in the lyrics, and the heroine has the distinctly un-Japanese name "Su Lin-fu." It is significant, however, that in the 1980s racial liberalization has proceeded to the point that the song ends with the hero's return to Japan to marry his lover.

It is also perhaps worthy of note that there have apparently been no country songs depicting love affairs between American GIs and Korean or Vietnamese women, in spite of a substantial number of such romances in real life, a fair proportion of which ended in marriage. It may be that love songs are incongruous with actual military combat. Both the Korean and Vietnamese conflicts were basically civil wars in which the opponents as well as the allies of the American forces were Koreans and Vietnamese. Racial epithets such as "slope" and "gook"[2] were in widespread use and were sometimes extended to the entire native populations, friends as well as enemies. Such situations do not lend themselves readily to romanticization.

Given the history of race relations in the United States, it is not particularly remarkable that country songs about romances between blacks and whites are extremely rare; indeed, I have been able to identify only two. What *is* somewhat surprising, however, is that the first of these,

Pretty Quadroon," dates at least from the 1930s and is perhaps substantially earlier than that. It was recorded by a California duo called the Happy Chappies (Nat Vincent and Fred Howard) who were best known for such Western standards as "Strawberry Roan" and "When the Bloom is on the Sage" (Malone 150). The origins of "My Pretty Quadroon" are uncertain, but its title constitutes the only overt racial reference. Bill Malone's response to my inquiry about it is illuminating:

> "My Pretty Quadroon" used to be performed quite often by country and cowboy singers, and I'm not sure that the singers always knew what "quadroon" meant. It is a sort of sentimental, minstrel-type song. Cora, the heroine of the piece, dies, and the narrator opines that his heart is "like the strings" of his banjo—"all broke for my pretty quadroon." Except for the use of the racial word, there is really nothing racial about the song. Although white singers sang it all the time, it does not seem to have been about an interracial love affair. I suspect that the song may long predate the Happy Chappies. (Malone, personal communication 8/31/87)

The other example, Merle Haggard's "Irma Jackson," is considerably more recent and much more overtly racial. Haggard introduces the recorded concert version by remarking that he wrote the song some time previously but delayed its release because the time did not seem to be right. It depicts a love affair between a white male, the singer, and the titular heroine, a black female. The two grow up together, fall in love, but realize that society will never accept their relationship. Recognizing this, Irma Jackson leaves forever. In the refrain, the singer vows that he will love her till he dies.

This is a remarkable song for many reasons, not the least of them being that it stems from the pen of Merle Haggard. Because of the phenomenal success of his "Okie from Muskogee" and its hawkish sequel, "The Fighting Side of Me," Haggard has acquired the reputation of an extreme right winger, and his very name is anathema to many liberals. His personal history has become the stuff of country music legend. A second generation Dust Bowl refugee born in Bakersfield, California, he was in and out of reform schools until being sent to San Quentin prison in 1956 at the age of nineteen. It was during his prison term that he became serious about music. His professional career began with various local gigs after his release in 1960, and by the late 1960s he was one of the top singer/songwriters in the country field (Malone 292-98).

The political content of Haggard's music has always been ambiguous. "Okie from Muskogee" earned him an invitation to Richard Nixon's White House, and he is, according to Malone (374), Ronald Reagan's favorite country singer, but, as Malone goes on to point out, several of his songs (e.g. "Big City"), express criticisms of Reagan's economic policies. Overall, his work reflects a combination of chauvinistic patriotism with social and economic liberalism, a blend which is somewhat unusual but not entirely unheard of in an era when political pundits are telling us that many of Jesse Jackson's white supporters are former adherents of George Wallace. In fact, in the last decade or so an anti-establishment neopopulism has arisen in country music, represented by such songs as Johnny Paycheck's "Take This Job and Shove It" (written by David Allan Coe), Alabama's "Forty Hour Week" and numerous other lamentations of the plight of the working man, as well as by Willie Nelson's much publicized Farm Aid concerts. Haggard's work as a whole falls squarely within this tradition. Unfortunately, he appears to have been unduly optimistic in his conclusion that the time had become ripe for the release of "Irma

Jackson." In spite of its considerable musical merit, the song was never, to my knowledge, released as a single and seems to have sunk without a trace. Nevertheless, its very existence, ephemeral though it may have been, is testimony to a very different racial climate in country music from that of twenty or thirty years ago.

Notes

[1]According to Bill C. Malone, "...Of all the southern ethnic groups, none has played a more important role in providing songs and styles for the white country musician than that forced migrant from Africa, the black. Nowhere is the peculiar love-hate relationship that has prevailed among the southern races more evidenced than in country music. Country music—seemingly the most "pure white" of all American musical forms^ldlhas borrowed heavily from the black. White Southerners who would be horrified at the idea of mixing socially with blacks have nonetheless enthusiastically accepted their musical offerings: the spirituals, the blues, ragtime, jazz, rhythm-and-blues and a whole host of dance steps, vocal shadings and instrumental techniques. (4-5)

[2]John A. Dower traces the etymology of "gook" to "goo-goo," a pejorative ethnic label applied to Filipinos at the turn of the century (162).

Acknowledgements

...The original idea for this paper stemmed from a series of conversations several years ago with Rebecca Bateman, who shared many of the insights derived from her extensive collection of sheet music of popular songs dealing with American Indians. Bill C. Malone, preeminent historian of country music, provided useful guidance to a neophyte in the field. My colleagues and fellow fans Bob Brooks, Danielle Langholtz, Bill Savage, Jack Hofman and Don Wyckoff helped me to identify relevant songs. Ronnie Pugh, chief research librarian at the Country Music Foundation library in Nashville, was extremely helpful in tracing and providing tapes of several relatively obscure numbers.

Works Cited

Berkhofer, Robert F., Jr.*The White Man's Indian: Images of the American Indian from Columbus to the Present* New York: Alfred A. Knopf, 1978.

Dearborn, Mary V. *Pocahontas's Daughters: Gender and Ethnicity in American Culture.* New York: Oxford UP, 1986.

Dower, John W. *War Without Mercy: Race and Power in the Pacific War.* New York: Pantheon, 1986.^

Fiedler, Leslie. *The Return of the Vanishing American.* New York: Stein and Day, 1968.Fife, Austin and Francesca Redden. "The Pseudo-Indian Folk Songs of the Anglo-Americans and French-Canadians." *Journal of American Folklore* 67 (1954): 239-51, 379-94.

Green, Rayna. "The Pocahontas Perplex: The Image of Indian Women in American Culture,." *Massachusetts Review* 16 (1975): 698-714.

Horstman, Dorothy.*Sing Your Heart Out, Country Boy* New York: Pocket Books, 1975.

Lax, Roger and Frederick Smith.*The Great Song Thesaurus* New York: Oxford UP, 1984.

Malone, Bill C. *Country Music U.S.A.* Revised Ed. Austin: U of Texas P, 1985.

Miller, Stewart Creighton. *Benevolent Assimilation: The American Conquest of the Philippines, 1899-1903^* New Haven: Yale UP, 1982.

Sandburg, Carl. *American Songbag* New York: Harcourt, Brace and World, 1927.

Sickels, Robert J. *Race, Marriage and the Law* Albuquerque: U of New Mexico P, 1972.

Slotkin, Richard. *Regeneration through Violence: The Mythology of the American Frontier, 1600-1860.* Middletown, CN: Wesleyan UP, 1973.

Spaeth, Sigmund. *A History of Popular music in America.* New York: Random House, 1948.

Country Music and Organized Religion

Jimmie N. Rogers
and
Stephen A. Smith

In the early years of this century, before the emergence of radio, television and mass mediated culture, H.L. Mencken surveyed the Southern scene and pronounced it the "Sahara of the Bozarts." Among the targets of his scorn were the region's music and religion. "In all that gargantuan paradise of the fourth rate there is not," he said, "a single orchestra capable of playing the nine symphonies of Beethoven, or a single opera house...," and when it comes to music composers "there is not even a bad one between the Potomac mud-flats and the Gulf." He was equally unsympathetic to the religiosity of the period, calling the South the "bunghole of the United States, a cesspool of Baptists, a miasma of Methodism, snakecharmers...and syphilitic evangelists" (Mencken 138-9; Angoff 126).[1]

Had Mencken been writing at a later date, he probably would have focused his attention upon commercial country music and the haranguing homilies of big-time televangelism—two communication genres prominent in the south and generally dominated by Southerners.[2] In fact, when Tom Wolfe was stalled in traffic on his way to stock car races at North Wilkesboro Speedway in 1964, like Paul on the road to Damascus, he was struck with the realization that "all the conventional notions about the South are confined to...the Sunday radio. The South has preaching and shouting, the South has grits, the South has country songs, old mimosa traditions, clay dust, Old Bigots, New Liberals—and all of it, all of that old mental cholesterol, is confined to the Sunday radio" (106). Today the preaching and shouting and the country songs share the satellite spectrum to reach their audiences, often over their own satellite television networks, such as "The Nashville Network," "Country Music Television" and Pat Robertson's CBN "Family Channel."

Religion and country music also remain prominent symbiotic cultural institutions in the South. For example, as a part of its mediated ministry, the Radio-Television Commission of the Southern Baptist Convention produces a weekly radio program called "Country Crossroads." This country music show, featuring interviews and music, is aired on more than 1500 stations to spotlight "the strong, religious heritage of this nation [and] to inform people that Christianity is relevant, that Christ can make a permanent difference in our lives." Although the theme of the program is "taking the Cross of Christ to the

Crossroads of the world," that message is particularly strong in the South where it is carried by an average of more than sixty stations per state in the old confederacy—compared to an average of twenty-one per state outside the region[3]

The relationship between music and ministry is not, however, always one of mutual support. There is considerable evidence in the lyrics of commercial country music that this cultural communication institution often critiques the value and values of another indigenous institution, organized religion and its messengers who utilize the public forum and the media of mass communication. Despite the suggestion by at least one scholar that the country music message is a prime medium for religious fundamentalism, country songwriters have sometimes been less than kind to the messengers and the mediated messages of organized religion (Lund). Likewise, Southern televangelist Jimmy Swaggart, who has inveighed against the messages of rock lyrics, said of country music, "In a more subtle way, it is just as bad" (Podesta).

Perhaps we can unravel these intertwined symbolic strands to provide a better understanding of the composite social and cultural fabric which they comprise. Scholars of religion, at a recent conference on "theomusicology" at Duke University, emphasized the need for a better understanding of "the secular theology being propagated by the priests and liturgists of popular music" and suggested that such sources as the lyrics of Patsy Cline could be productively mined for nuggets of insight (Coughlin). The recognition of the power of popular music to shape cultural beliefs and attitudes is not, however, a recent phenomenon. Plato knew that lyrics and music could either reinforce or undermine respect for the gods and the quest for *telos* in his *Republic* (Jowett); James Madison understood the power of popular songs to influence political behavior in the new American republic; Zelda Fitzgerald believed that "people live their lives by the philosophies of popular songs" (Milford); and these same arguments inform contemporary communication scholarship as well (Goodall xvi).

In this study, we embrace the above assumptions and further ground our analysis on Clifford Geertz's position that the "culture of a people is an ensemble of texts, themselves ensembles, which...[can be]...read over the shoulders of those to whom they properly belong." A close reading of cultural texts, Geertz says, can "open up the possibility of an analysis which attends to their substance rather than to reductive formulas professing to account for them." Such an approach would seem especially appropriate when one ensemble of texts (country music) appears to critique another institution (religion) within the same culture. Societies, Geertz contends, "contain their own interpretations. One has only to learn how to gain access to them" (452-453).

To discover the reasons for the apparent ambivalence in some country lyrics toward the nature of organized religion and mediated religious communication in the South, this study reviewed the lyrics of commercially popular country songs and isolated those which contained assertions about organized religion, religious communication and the agents who delivered religious messages in public and mass mediated contexts.[4] Several questions were posed in this investigation. First, what attitudes were expressed toward the messengers and messages presented through the mass media? Second, what attitudes were expressed toward organized religion? Third, what type of religious communication seemed to receive the most support in the lyrics? Fourth, what attitudes were expressed about religion in general? And finally, what do the answers to the above questions reveal about the nature of contemporary Southern culture vis-a-vis these two important regional communication genres?

"I'd Like To See Jesus (On the Midnight Special)"

Television, the latest mass medium for channeling the religious message, has received notice from the country songwriters and singers. Some see the benefit of delivering the message through the medium and note the impact that television can and does have on an audience. Tammy Wynette, back when a certain television show was popular, expressed this desire: "I'd like to see Jesus on the Midnight Special"[5] She wanted to see Wolfman bring Him on stage, but ignored the effect such an event would have on both Wolfman and the "worldly" performers who used to appear on that spectacle. She was only interested in the forum such a program would provide for Jesus to deliver a message to the masses.

Although Wynette's wish does indicate an understanding of the major use of the channel, her song expresses a view held by a minority of songwriters and singers. More common are the observations that those who employ television to send a religious message are more interested in collecting and storing up treasures on earth than in advancing any religious teaching. The effect on one audience member after he confused the message and the messenger is found in a song recorded by Bobby Bare. The lyrics describe an unfortunate response that occurred when a listener became disoriented after being exposed to a common appeal made by people utilizing the electronic church. As the man in the song relates the story, he dozed off on the couch while watching *Colombo* and was awakened at a quarter past three in the morning by the voice of a preacher on television exhorting listeners to "praise the Lord and send me the money." Thinking it was a vision and "trembling with guilt," the man wrote a check for $10,000 and mailed it to the preacher who insisted that Jesus desperately needed the money. The next day he realized he had written a hot check to Jesus. Rather than let the check bounce, he took a second job in a gasoline station in order to pay the debt and attempt to be as happy as the man on the television.[6]

The reactions of other country observers are more critical and perceptive. Charlie Daniels, when articulating his view of individualism (a major theme in country music), identified television ministers as one group seeking to mold the free thinking and free living person he wished to be into someone he found distasteful. In "Long Haired Country Boy," Daniels attacked what he and several other songwriters consider to be the major flaw in television evangelism: hypocrisy. The man in this song also describes a "preacher man" on television who was seeking a donation "cause he's worried about my soul."

While acknowledging the truth in the preacher's observation that Jesus walked on water, the man in the lyrics also believed that the "preacher man" would like to "do a little walking, too."[7]

In 1982, seven years after Charlie Daniels gave his views, Hank Williams, Jr., covered some more specific points and once again attacked the money-raising aspect of the electronic ministry in "The American Dream." Williams was not only critical of the preachers' hidden motives, but displeased with their personal appearance and persuasive appeals used to secure money. He also described the key to their approach when he said: "They want you to send your money to the Lord, but they give you their address."[8]

Daniels and Williams openly question the television evangelists who appear to be more interested in earthly treasures than in souls and although the audience may certainly perceive humor in the lyrics, laughter is not the primary goal of the songwriters or the singers. There are, however, examples of more deliberate attempts at humor in this genre of commercial country music. For instance, Bobby Bare recorded a song in which a particular lifestyle is highlighted. "Drinkin', Druggin' and Watchin' TV" is more accurately directed toward the hypocrisy embedded in some people's way of living rather than the hypocrisy of a television preacher, but it demonstrates the almost casual consumption of the medium and suggests that the preacher does hold some unstated power over non-believers. In the song, Bare first describes how people who know the couple would be surprised if they really knew what they were doing in the privacy of their room. She brings the chemicals, he brings the wine; and drunk and drugged they fall on the floor naturally performing unnatural acts. Then the source observes that they are going to hell "making love with the sound off the P.T.L."[9]

"Would Jesus Wear a Rolex?"

The above discussions of television ministries all preceded and anticipated the fall of the mighty in 1987. The $6 million evangelical extortion of holy hostage Oral Roberts, the PTL financial felonies and the sexual sleaziness of televangelists Jim Bakker and Jimmy Swaggart undermined public support among the formerly faithful viewers and contributors that spring ("The Gallup..." 18A). Nowhere was the impact greater or more noticeable than in the South, and Jerry Falwell lamented, "I don't ever remember a time when people driving trucks, talking on CBs, and sitting in restaurants were having such a heyday ridiculing all that is Christian." An equally perverse and pervasive message was dominating the country format radio stations across the South. Van Mac, of WOKK in Meridian, Mississippi, said that about a dozen country songs on the theme had been produced in Nashville, including such titles as "The PTL Has Gone to Hell, So Where Do I Send the Money?" by Rev. Needmore and the Almighty Bucks and "Poverty-Stricken TV Christian" by Bobby Goodman (Schmidt 1, 32).

The most requested song on many country stations was Ray Stevens' "Would Jesus Wear a Rolex?" Although the song was written (by Chet Atkins and Margaret Archer) and produced for an album before the scandals became public, the single was released early to take advantage of the public interest in the news stories; the record sold 500,000 copies in the first three weeks, and it dominated radio request lines and airplay (Edwards 4B). Stevens' narrative seems to have given voice to the thinking of many Southerners, as he sang:

> Would He wear a pinkie ring? Would He drive a fancy car?
> Would His wife wear furs and diamonds? Would His dressing room have a
> star?
> If He came back tomorrow, there's something I'd like to know.
> Can you tell me, would Jesus wear a Rolex on His television show?

Stevens, reared a Southern Baptist, said of the song, "I'm not a preacher. It asks a question, and I'm not answering it. That's for you to do" (Edwards 4B). Joe Gatlin, station manager at country station WKNZ in Collins, Mississippi, seemed to think that most of his audience had already answered that question, and his station responded to overwhelming requests by playing it every hour and a half. "What's funny is this is the Southern Baptist Belt, yet I think people love this song," he said. "I think a lot have come to realize over the years that what the song says is true" (Schmidt 32). The persuasive power of the enthymeme works because the audience already holds the premise.

"Turn Your Radio On"

Radio, as a delivery system for the religious message, seems more acceptable to the country singer/songwriter than does television. As Tom Wolfe noted, the mediated reality of the rural South was, for longer than the rest of the nation, constructed by radio rather than television. This experience is discussed in "I Watched It All (On My Radio)," by Lionel Cartwright, wherein he remembers his childhood being formed and informed by radio baseball games, the Grand Ole Opry, a preacher "to tell me what's right, to tell me what's wrong." He fondly recalls, "Over the airwaves the world came to me," and that world included both country music and religious messages.[11]

The majority of songs mentioning the use and impact of radio support the observations found in a classic song "Turn Your Radio On," written in 1937 by Albert E. Brumley. Brumley ignored the reality of the secular purpose of this medium and told the audience to "listen to the Master's radio / Get in touch with God, turn your radio on."[12] When the song was written, most of the radio gospel message was being delivered in the songs or by local ministers the listener already knew. Radio in rural areas was still a local source (as far as the music and religious message were concerned), and there was little difficulty in extending loyalties to a local preacher speaking on the new medium while still delivering an accepted religious message.[13]

Although radio preachers are viewed more favorably than their counterparts on television, the preachers on that medium are not exempt from all blame for problems created either by the delivery system or the message itself. Tom T. Hall, who frequently gets to the core of many flaws in our society, has described the mental and emotional conflicts enhanced by a gospel message on radio. In "Jesus On The Radio (Daddy On The Phone)" a young man tells of his mother listening to the "Grand Old Gospel Times" on radio while her husband entreats her by telephone to join him for a few drinks at a bar. To resolve the conflict between the messages the woman retreats into a world where she feels more secure. Hall describes the mother's solution and final condition in the last verse:

> I came home one evening there was Mama on her knees
> Big old tears of gospel joy a-running down her cheeks.
> She said, "You don't have to worry son, we are not alone
> I got Jesus on the radio and Jesus on the phone.["14]

Hall has another fine song ("The Little Lady Preacher") which describes a more understandable frailty than those Williams and Daniels found in the television preachers. It is one of the few songs that provides a view of those sending rather than receiving the message and reinforces an assumption contained in many of these songs—that the self-anointed representatives of the Lord are no better qualified than the listeners to interpret the religious message. The man in the song is a member of the band which plays for a woman preacher, a woman who not only exudes a religious message to the radio audience but a worldly message to the picker. He noted that "She was nineteen years of age and developed to a fault" and "was down on booze and cigarettes and high on days to come / And she would punctuate the prophecy with movements of her hips." The lady was in love with Luther, another member of the band with more than lust in his heart, who sometimes "showed up at the studio half tight / And smoking was a thing he liked to do." The little lady preacher tried to send her views of the Bible to the radio audience, but could not cast out the devil in her own life. She finally succumbed to a more basic "call" and deserted her station with Luther, leaving a void in the picker's life and perhaps in the life of the listeners. The lyrics also contain one of the truly religious tenets found in any of these songs when the singer says, "Lord, if I judge 'em let me give 'em lots of room."[15]

"Air Mail To Heaven"

Although television and radio predominate as the channels for the religious message in commercial country music, they are not alone. Jim Nesbitt has a recitation called "Phone Call From The Devil" in which another "good old boy" receives a call from hell when the devil checks out his new "hot" line. This is a novelty song, but Nesbitt observes that the preacher has been "talking trash" about the devil and says he is confident the preacher knows the devil quite well.[16] Mass circulation magazines and books are seen as culprits in one song, "Dust On The Bible," when the lyrics point out that the Good Book is not receiving the proper amount of attention because people are spending too much time reading about worldly matters.[17] Finally, the familiar billboards that are often used to threaten travellers are mentioned in another song by Tom T. Hall. In "Trip To Hyden" the singer describes the desolate and forbidding environment of a coal mining town and observes: "Every hundred yards a sign proclaimed that Christ was coming soon / And I thought, 'Well, man, he'd sure be disappointed if He did'."[18]

"Me And Jesus"

Singers and songwriters of commercial country music are following a well established tradition when they debunk the messengers and channels rather than the religious message. One of the prevailing characteristics of commercial country music is the lack of faith in institutions—whether political, social, or religious (Smith and Rogers). Not only are the institutions generally mistrusted, but those who act as spokespersons for those institutions are also held in low esteem. This is not to say that the country music message rejects the philosophies that supposedly guide those institutions, just that people in the music are more apt to support the principles than they are the practitioners. Most of the songs describe a personal relationship with a superior being, but few express much support for the agencies or agents that purport to act as intermediaries between God and believer. Theirs is a retail religion that cuts out the middleman.

Many songs contain a plea for help to survive this world ("One Day At A Time," for instance) or to insure a better or more pleasant place after death. Others voice contentment with their lot in life ("Richest Man On Earth," recorded by Paul Overstreet), or express reliance on the Bible as a guide in daily life ("Doing It By the Book," recorded by The Whites). Some songs are celebrations of the religious experience of singing spirituals that warm the heart of the singer and the listener. Often desires are as simple as a wish to be in a different place on earth—such as "Texas (When I Die)"—but most have higher aspirations and expectations.[19]

Although most of the lyrics generally celebrate the religious experience, there are many that question the traditional delivery system for the religious message just as critically as they do the modern electronic media. The objections usually center around the innate hypocrisy and the failure to meet their own ideals. Johnny Paycheck's "The Outlaw's Prayer" describes how a picker is ushered out of church for wearing a big black hat, long hair and a beard. Sitting on the curb outside the inhospitable church, he talks directly to God and questions the actions and attitudes of the congregation of that particular church. For instance, he observes a wino across the street and laments that money spent on one stained glass window in their building could feed that man's family for years and also speculates that John the Baptist and Jesus would be unwelcome due to this group's dress code. Paycheck concludes his prayer by observing that if God plans to take these people to His kingdom, then he was not particularly interested in going along.[20] As Don Williams sings in "I Believe in You," most Southerners "don't believe that heaven waits for only those who congregate."[21]

Among the particular targets of country critics are those members of congregation who are quick to judge those whom they believe less worthy. Ray Stevens' "Mississippi Squirrel Revival" relates the antics of a crazy rodent turned loose in the "First Self-Righteous Church" of Pascagoula, Mississippi, stripping the facade of piety from "Sister Bertha Better-Than-You" and others among the flock.[22] A Sunday school teacher is attacked in Cal Smith's "The Lord Knows I'm Drinking" when a man sitting in a bar with a drink and a young woman (who is not his wife) is accosted by a woman member of the church. He calls the intruder, among other things, a "self-righteous biddy" and tells her that if she is not too offensive he will put in a good word for her later on that night when he talks personally with God.[23]

The validity of the institutions are questioned in some songs. Larry Gatlin describes the "success" of a rescue mission and observes that some of the "rescued" who frequent the place are saved three times a week in order to get something to eat in his song, "Midnight Choir."[24] The so-called Christians, who make a great effort and demonstration on the Sabbath and turn their backs on the religious precepts during the reminder of the week, are chastised in "Sunday Morning Christian" and warned in "Your Credit Card Won't Get You Into Heaven."[25]

The real heroes in these narratives are more likely to be the "lower sort," marginalized individuals who enact Christian principles in their daily lives. For example, in Skip Ewing's "The Gospel According to Luke," a down-and-outer says, "give to your brother if he is in need" and then demonstrates his faith by sharing the change he had collected with those less resourceful[26] In Kenny Price's recording of "Northeast Arkansas Mississippi County Bootlegger," the "deacons and their ladies" scorn the bootlegger's family, that is until they need money for a new sanctuary and find their manna comes from mash.[27] Under such circumstances, it is easy to see why self-aggrandizing religious institutions are built upon sand in the South. As one scholar concluded, "Anyone who wished to be liberated from worldly standards which demeaned him or her would obviously be susceptible to a movement which honored the individual member" (Matthews 240).

The effectiveness of the criticism of organized religion and its agents in country music lyrics owes much to the narrative format of the lyrics and the skillful use of ironic humor. Storytelling and humor have traditionally been used to flank confrontation among friends on the social battlefields of the South, and the adaptation of those techniques in this genre allows the points to be made with a rhetorical rapier rather than a broadsword (Smith, *Myth...* 104-05, 144-54). Even the songs which support the acceptable religious message are filled with humor. For instance, Bobby Bare's "Dropkick Me, Jesus" carries the football metaphor to a greater extreme than any politician ever has.[28] John Prine, who masterfully uses the play on words for which country songwriters are widely known, does not retreat from what some might call a semi-sacrilegious treatment of a personal encounter with a superior being. In "Everybody," a man is out in his boat when Jesus appears and starts a conversation. The man says, "Jesus, you look tired," and his savior replies, "Jesus, you do too!"[29]

From the focus and the manner in which the criticism is stated, we are able to see that the electronic ministry does not receive much support in the lyrics of commercial country music. This approach is a continuation of the attitudes expressed toward religious institutions and those who speak for them in early country music. If there is any messenger or channel they prefer, it is one that is closest to the people. The "old time" preachers and religious practices are favored, although they are not exempt from all criticism. "Preaching Up A Storm" contains a description of an old time outdoor baptism in running water from the view of a young man who speaks of the fear the event can create.[30] "Preacher Berry," by Donna Fargo, tells of the foibles and weaknesses of a preacher who was killed when drinking and driving, but she thinks he will do better in heaven.[31] A preacher who was more successful in an earthly pursuit is described in Barbi Benton's "The Reverend Bob." The woman in this song was relating her experiences as a sixteen year-old member of the choir in her father's church when Bob served as a visiting pastor during a yearly revival. She said, "I could tell when Reverend Bob looked at me, the Devil wasn't all he was after." The handsome preacher saved a number of souls and also succeeded in his quest for heaven on earth according to the singer for "what he said and what we did made a woman out of me."[32]

Those people who speak in the songs seem to prefer an interpersonal relationship with their God and do not see the need for any electronic mediation or any organized group. They seem to agree with the message as delivered by the son of a Baptist minister, Tom T. Hall.

> Me and Jesus got our own thing going
> Me and Jesus got it all worked out
> Me and Jesus got our own thing going
> We don't need anybody to tell us what it's all about.[33]

These folks are generally traditional in their approach to religious practices; however, that tradition is one of Moses going to the mountain to talk personally with God, rather than having a preacher on radio or television giving them "The Top Ten Commandments" and asking for pious payola.

Cultural Implications

Despite the sometimes cynical assessments of organized religion and its agents, the message in the country music lyrics should not necessarily be interpreted as anti-religious. Shenandoah sings of "Sunday in the South," noting the local congregation's integral role in the regional culture, and even Charlie Daniels, caustic critic of television preachers, sings that many of the world's ills can be attributed to the fact that "people done gone and put their Bibles away."[34] These messages are, in fact, indicative of many of the social attitudes and cultural values prevalent in the contemporary South. Like other mediated narratives, those of country music both reflect and reinforce the sociocultural myths or world views of the primary audiences. What, then, can we conclude from this textual study of country music lyrics, and what can we infer about the nature and attitudes of the country music audiences in the South?

First, we believe this analysis demonstrates that a strong sense of individualism dominates the typical Southerner's world view with regard to religion, just as it does in politics, justice and other social and economic relationships. The popular theology—both from the pulpit and from the juke box—supports that rhetorical mythology of individual responsibility for the here-and-now as well as for the hereafter. Studies of Southern religious practices have consistently concluded that "the primary presuppositions and concerns of popular religion are individualistic, centering on the salvation of each soul.... Whether the issue is social responsibility, the nature of the church, basic theology, or the meaning of salvation, Southern Protestants think dominantly in individualistic terms" (Eighmy 201). As John Shelton Reed suggested, "the South is refining and beginning to exemplify a world view that puts individual responsibility at the heart of things and insists that individuals should—and, by and large, do—get what they deserve" (175).

The view of individual theological autonomy has considerable historical support in the region's cultural experience, and it is a force which sometimes operates against membership in any group beyond the family. In a contemporary survey of religion in the South, Samuel Hill argued convincingly that "a religion of salvation...does not present a theology of community" (396). Consequently, it is not surprising that Jack Weller observed of the typical Southern mountaineer, "that even if he does join a group (a union, a PTA, or even a church) his intention, however unconscious, is that the organization shall serve his own personal interests and needs. If it does not, even though it may be serving a worthwhile goal, he will not continue in the group" (Weller 31).[35]

Second, the fact that the individualistic Southern religious heritage is consonant with the larger regional world view may be one of the reasons that low-church Protestantism has flourished in the South. It is certainly a factor contributing to the relatively large number of small congregations, which in turn has supported the public perception of religiosity in the region. Such churches, said Reed, "emphasize the individual's salvation and his role in accepting it.... Nobody else can walk the lonesome valley, as the old song has it. You've got to walk it by yourself. Others can and do help, but ultimately you're on your own" (172-73). The resulting religious climate, notes one study, is one typified by "religious individualism,...little distinction between clergy and laity, sectarian concepts of the church and its mission, revivalism, informality in public worship, and opposition to central authority of state or church." Under such circumstances, noted Weller, "The Baptist form of government, which set up the local church as the only authority and allowed no interference from regional or national bodies, was most compatible with the leveling philosophy" of folks in southern Appalachia (Brewer 201; Weller 121).

Third, as evidenced in many of the lyrics cited in this study, the religious heritage and the cultural individualism lead Southerners to establish direct personal relationships with God and to discount the necessity for ordained intermediaries. Historically, noted Donald Matthews, "Among the religious themselves, isolated, uneducated, and relatively powerless whites would often complain about the aloofness of denominational authorities and resist as best they could the professionalization of the clergy." If they had to have any minister, he says, they "preferred to have leaders who could identify with them and evoke the cathartic and healing ritual of self-discovery and forgiveness, rather than clergymen who would preach careful sermons of correct understanding and refined sentiments" (Matthews 241). As a result of this stance, said Weller, each individual could be his or her "own highest authority" in matters of religion, and Reed supported this view, suggesting that even local congregations are merely "convenient gatherings of voluntarily associated individuals, each of whom maintains his own unmediated personal relations with transcendent Deity" (Weller 123; Reed 173). Therefore, it is not surprising to find so little adoration and adulation in the lyrics for the electronic brokers of religion.

Fourth, consistent with the lyrical criticism of piety and pomp in organized religion, those Southerners who do prefer to congregate do so only on their own terms, and the propensity to relocate with alacrity has traditionally resulted in the proliferation of new splinter churches. Reed explained that the "proposition 'Love it or leave it' seems perfectly reasonable to many Southern churchmen. From time to time, groups do leave to set up their own congregations or to found entirely new denominations" (Reed 173). Likewise observed Weller, who spent several years as a Presbyterian minister in West Virginia and Kentucky, "If a church does not suit the mountaineer by preaching what he wants to hear in the way he wants to hear it or does not give him an opportunity to assert himself and be heard, he will quit and go elsewhere. If he is a strong personality, he may even form his own church, where he is minister and 'boss', perhaps erecting a building in his front yard and naming the church after his family" (Weller 126).

In summary, the influence of individualism evident in the religious world view discovered in this study permeates and reinforces other aspects of Southern culture and society. For example, the Southern religious heritage and the Southern political tradition both appear to be manifestations of the same social forces. In both cases, the audience is frequently moved by fear appeals and motivated by visions of a promised land. In both instances, the audience demands a personally-oriented messenger who will promise and deliver goods and services of some value to the individual and who will do so at very little personal cost, beyond faith, to the recipient. The demand for local autonomy for religious congregations finds obvious parallels in the nineteenth-century Nullifiers and twentieth century States Righters who advocated local option on the Constitution and federal statutes, while the Southern penchant for leaving one church and starting a new one seems analogous to Southern "fire breathers" who seceded from the Union and started their own country. Today, both big government and big religion find underwhelming support in country music lyrics and the South generally.

In preaching, politics and popular country music, Southerners seem to prefer good storytellers in the best tradition of the region's oral cultural heritage; they like showmanship and enjoy a good fight, whether the context is a local bar, a football game, a "rasslin' " match, a political campaign, or a pulpit. Jimmy Swaggart puts on a good show, and Billy Graham can fill a football stadium as easily as early rural evangelists could draw a crowd to their canvas tents. Such observations, however, are not necessarily contradictory to the findings in our analysis of assertions about organized religion, religious messengers, or religious messages. Exposure to such messages is often more recreational than theological, and in most instances the listener can change the channel or remain anonymous in the crowd; such an experience does not require any continuing commitment to participation, nor formal membership, nor even a cash contribution. Glen Campbell voiced the feelings of many in the country music audience when he sang, "I Knew Jesus (Before He Was a Star)," and this distinction remains consistent between entertainment by public spectacle and religion as a personal and private affair.[36] That is the argument collectively made in the country music message, and it offers unique insights into this aspect of the Southern cultural heritage.

Notes

[1] The best discussion of Mencken's charges and the Southern response is Fred C. Hobson, Jr., *Serpent in Eden: H.L. Mencken and the South* (Chapel Hill: U of North Carolina P, 1974).

[2] An increasing popularity of country music seems to indicate that it is more of a national rather than a regional phenomenon; however, for a view of the music's Southern roots see Bill C. Malone, *Southern Music/American Music* (Lexington: UP of Kentucky, 1979). For further amplification of this thesis see Bill C. Malone, *Country Music, U.S.A.*, rev. ed. (Austin: U of Texas P, 1985); Douglas B. Green, *Country Roots: The Origins of Country Music* (New York: Hawthorn, 1976); Charles K. Wolfe, "The Birth of an Industry," *The Illustrated History of Country Music*, ed. Patrick Carr (Garden City, NY: Country Music Magazine Press/Doubleday, 1979), 30-101; Richard A. Peterson and Russell David, Jr., "The Fertile Crescent of Country Music," *Journal of Country Music* 6 (1975): 19-27; Ben Marsh, "A Rose-Colored Map," *Harper's* July 1977: 80-82; and Stephen A. Smith, "Sounds of the South: The Rhetorical Saga of Country Music Lyrics," *Southern Speech Communication Journal* 45 (1980): 164-72. For a view of how the nation may be becoming more Southern rather than the music becoming national see James C. Cobb, "From Muskogee to Luckenbach: Country Music and the "Southernization' of America," *Journal of Popular Culture* 16 (1982): 81-91.

[3] Data supplied by the Southern Baptist Radio-Television Commission, 6350 West Freeway, Fort Worth, TX.

[4] The primary songs used in this analysis are those which appeared on the most popular lists as compiled by *Billboard* magazine and reported by Joel Whitburn's Record Research organization. Whitburn's publications list all singles appearing on *Billboard*'s most popular charts since their origin on June 17, 1949. No recordings classified as "gospel" or from country recordings sold "under the counter" were included in this study

[5] Tammy Wynette, "I'd Like to See Jesus (On the Midnight Special)," Epic, 35442, 1978.

[6] Bobby Bare, "Praise the Lord and Send Me the Money," Columbia, 03334, 1982.

[7]Charlie Daniels Band, "Long Haired Country Boy," *The South's Greatest Hits Volume II*, Capricorn, CPN 0209, 1978. This recording had an interesting life. Although it appears on the anthology just cited, the single (Epic, 5084-5) received considerable airplay in early 1980. It reached the 27th position on the *Billboard* chart for February 23, 1980 and appeared on the charts for a total of ten weeks. Joel Whitburn, *Top Country Singles and LPs 1980* (Menomonee Falls, WI: Record Research, Inc., 1981), 10. The lyrics can be found in Frye Gaillard, *Watermelon Wine: The Spirit of Country Music* (New York: St. Martins, 1978), 232-33.

[8]Hank Williams, Jr., "The American Dream," Electra, 7-69960-C, 1982.

[9]Bobby Bare, "Drinkin' and Druggin' and Watchin' TV," *Drunk and Crazy*, Columbia, JC 36785, 1980.

[10]Ray Stevens, "Would Jesus Wear a Rolex," MCA, 53101, 1987.

[11]Lionel Cartwright, "I Watched It All (On My Radio)," MCA, 53779, 1990.

[12]This song has been recorded by several artists; however, the lyrics and a brief explanation of how Brumley came to write the song can be found in Dorothy Horstman, *Sing Your Heart Out, Country Boy*, rev. ed. (Nashville, TN: Country Music Foundation P, 1986), 65-66.

[13]The religious radio stations have been a part of the medium since the early days, and it was estimated that 700 to 800 stations were owned and operated by religious organizations in 1983. Samuel Becker, *Discovering Mass Communication* (Glenview, IL: Scott, Foresman, 1983), 280-81. For an example of the appeals used in early religious radio, see William C. Martin, "The God-Hucksters of Radio," *Side-Saddle on the Golden Calf: Social Structures and Popular Culture in America*, ed. George H. Lewis (Pacific Palisades, CA: Goodyear, 1972), 49-55.

[14]Tom T. Hall, "Jesus On the Radio (Daddy On the Phone)," RCA, AHL 1-3495, 1979.

[15]Tom T. Hall, "The Little Lady Preacher," *In Search of a Song*, Mercury, SR 61350, 1971.

[16]Jim Nesbitt, "Phone Call From the Devil," *Phone Call From the Devil and Other Funny Things*, Scorpion, SCS-0001, 1975.

[17]The lyrics of "Dust On the Bible" can be found in Horstman, 42.

[18]Tom T. Hall, "Trip To Hyden," *In Search Of a Song*, Mercury, SR 61350, 1971.

[19]For more examples of songs in this genre, see Jimmie N. Rogers, *The Country Music Message: Revisited* (Fayetteville: U of Arkansas P, 1989), 206-208; Horstman, 32-69; and Carol Offen, *Country Music: The Poetry* (New York: Ballantine, 1977), 110-120.

[20]Johnny Paycheck, "The Outlaw's Prayer," Epic, 8-50655, 1978.

[21]Don Williams, "I Believe In You," MCA, 41303, 1980.

[22]Ray Stevens, "Mississippi Squirrel Revival," MCA, 52492, 1984.

[23]Cal Smith, "The Lord Knows I'm Drinking," Decca, 33040, 1972.

[24]Larry Gatlin, "Midnight Choir (Mogen David)," Columbia, 11169, 1979.

[25]Cal Smith, "Sunday Morning Christian," *Jason's Farm*, MCA, MCA-2172, 1976; and Bobby Bare, "Your Credit Card Won't Get You Into Heaven," *Drunk and Crazy*, Columbia, JC 36785, 1980. For another type of religious warning, see John Prine, "Your Flag Decal Won't Get You Into Heaven Anymore," *John Prine*, Atlantic, SD 8296, 1971.

[26]Skip Ewing, "The Gospel According to Luke," MCA, 53481, 1989.

[27]Kenny Price, "Northeast Arkansas Mississippi County Bootlegger," RCA, 9787, 1969.

[28]Bobby Bare, "Dropkick Me, Jesus," RCA, 10790, 1976.

[29]John Prine, "Everybody," *Diamonds In the Rough*, Atlantic, SD 7240, 1972.

[30]Mel McDaniel, "Preaching Up a Storm," Capitol, P-A-5059, 1981.

[31]Donna Fargo, "Preacher Berry," Warner Brothers, WBS 49093, 1979.

[32]Barbi Benton, "Reverend Bob," Playboy, P 6056-A, 1975.

[33]Tom T. Hall, "Me and Jesus," Mercury, 73278, 1972. In this context, it is interesting to note that the vocal accompaniment on this recording is provided by the Mt. Pisgah United Methodist Church choir. The lyrics can be found in Rogers 207-08; and Offen 117-18.

[34]Shenandoah, "Sunday in the South," Columbia, 38-68892, 1989; Charlie Daniels Band, "Simple Man," Epic, 73030, 1989.

[35]See also, Harry Caudill, *Night Comes to the Cumberland* (Boston: Little, Brown and Company, 1963), 349.

[36]Glenn Campbell, "I Knew Jesus (Before He Was a Star)," Capitol, 3548, 1973. See also, Bob Arnold, "Billy Graham, Superstar," *Southern Exposure* 4 (1976): 76-82.

Works Cited

Brewer, Earl D.C. "Religion and the Churches." *The Southern Appalachian Region* Lexington: UP of Kentucky, 1962.

Coughlin Ellen K., "Religion Scholars Mine Popular Music for Intimations of the Divine." *The Chronicle of Highter Education*, 19 April 1989: A4, A9

Edwards, Joe. "Satirical' Tune Asks Questions: Stevens Says Message Relevant," *Arkansas Gazette* 30 May 1987.

Eighmy, John Lee. *Churches in Cultural Captivity: A History of the Social Attitudes of Southern Baptists*. Rev. ed. Knoxville: U of Tennessee P, 1987.

"The Gallup Poll: Public Loses Faith in Televangelists." *Arknasas Gazette* 23 May 1987.

Geertz, Clifford. *The Interpretation of Cultures*. New York: Basic Books, 1973.

Goodall, H. Lloyd, Jr. *Living in the Rock 'N' Roll Mystery: Reading Context, Self, and Others as Clues*. Carbondale: Southern Illinois UP, 1991.

Hill, Samuel S., ed. *Religion in the Southern States*. Macon, GA: Mercer UP, 1983.

Jowett, Benjamin, trans. *The Works of Plato*. New York: Tudor, 1937. 84-111.

Lund, Jens. "Fundamentalism, Racism, and Political Reaction in Country Music." *The Sounds of Social Change*. Ed. R. Serge Denisoff and Richard A. Peterson. Chicago: Rand McNally, 1972. 79-91.

Madison, James. Letter to William T. Berry. 28 Aug. 1828. James Madison Papers, Library of Congress.

Matthews, Donald G. *Religion in the Old South*. Chicago: U of Chicago P, 1977.

Milford, Nancy. *Zelda*. New York: Harper and Row, 1970.

Podesta, Anthony T. "Campaign Against Rock 'N' Roll is Censorship." *Houston Post*. 16 Oct. 1986.

Reed, John Shelton. *One South: An Ethnic Approach to Regional Culture*. Baton Rouge:

Louisiana State UP, 1982.

Schmidt, William E. "TV Ministry Scandals Lampooned in South." *The New York Times* 2 May 1987.

Smith, Stephen A. *Myth, Media, and the Southern Mind.* Fayetteville: U of Arkansas P, 1985.

Smith, Stephen A. and Jimmie N. Rogers. "Political Culture and the Rhetoric of Country Music: A Revisionist Interpretation." *Politics in Familiar Contexts: Projecting Politics Through Popular Media.* Eds. Robert L. Savage and Dan Nimmo. Norwood, NJ: Ablex Publishing, 1990. 185-98.

Weller, Jack E. *Yesterday's People: Life in Contemporary Appalachia.* Lexington: UP of Kentucky, 1965.

Wolfe, Tom. *The Kandy-Kolored Tangerine-Flake Streamline Baby.* New York: Pocket Books, 1966.

Populist Ideology and Country Music

Jock Mackay

Country music has always been the self-conscious vehicle of hinterland and under-class sentiment. Unlike blues, jazz and various folk musics, country music is seen by outsiders as in laughably bad taste (somewhat like soap operas, Bingo, or professional wrestling), one of the unfortunate trappings with which the masses are burdened. The adherents of the country music ethic and sensibility, however, view it as the only real music, one which engages them in an ongoing down-to-earth dialogue (Buckley; Rogers). Country music entertainers are of and for the common people: there is hardly an example of a country music performer who does not come from hinterland or working-class origins, and most are from both. The music responds to and interprets today's hinterland and working-class lifestyles more directly, and with a larger and more committed following, than any other single musical genre.

The participatory musical heritage of an identifiable people could be called communal music (as for instance in Blues, Celtic, Reggae, Cajun and Conjunto). The country music idiom can similarly be seen as a communal music—the property and expression of the white North American rural and industrial working class. Unlike other communal musics, country crosses geographic and ethnic lines with relative ease. In its dominant form, it is most popular among middle-aged blue-collar workers almost anywhere on the continent, and its commercial variant occupies a huge portion of the mainstream musical landscape. Indeed, its broadest influence continues to be as a force in the shaping of currents in popular music, from Western Swing through Rock 'n Roll to Cowpunk. Elvis Presley once played the Louisiana Hayride, as had Hank Williams; his is only one immense example of the impact of country music roots on popular music forms. But in the raw form of country music, as Hank Williams pointed out:

When a hillbilly sings...what he is singing is the hopes and prayers and dreams of what some call the common people. (Williams 272)

This paper was originally prepared for presentation at the Political Economy sessions of the Canadian Political Science Association at Montreal in 1985, and a variation of it for the Popular Culture Association at Toronto in 1990. Thanks are due Vanier College for a mini-grant in aid of its original writing. For encouragement and comments, I thank Hugh Armstrong, Pat Armstrong, Andrew Lawless, Terry Ross, Marc Raboy, Neil Rosenberg, Peter Narvaez, Melissa Ladenheim, Gerald Pocius, Carolyn Dellah, Padraig O. Laighin, Bud Davidge; and for a Herculean editing job, Karen Tennenhous

In contrast to many other commercial forms, the words of country music can always be heard and are meant to be listened to. Where other popular music producers look for a commercial "lick," country music producers look for a commercial lyric; a good "hook" is primarily in the words (DiMaggio, Peterson and Esco 41). But what is being said? What is "the message"?

Some analysts select from the tradition certain well-known songs, such as Merle Haggard's "Okie from Muskogee" or Tammy Wynette's "Stand by Your Man," to show that country music is a retrograde force espousing racism, sexism, imperialism, fundamentalism, even fascism. Others emphasize such progressive and pro-labour figures as Woody Guthrie, Utah Phillips, Anne Romaine or the Weavers to make the opposite argument (Brunton, Overton and Sacouman). Yet others concentrate on the theme of common folks dealing ingenuously with perennial subjects such as love, marriage, death, the country way of life, the passing of the good old ways, railroads, love of mother, tragic events and so on. As with all purist conceptions, each of these approaches ignores the contrary examples.

One must be careful of easy or programmatic interpretations of a broadly popular cultural form. The dynamics of rural and working class culture must be approached in their real dimensions, not merely viewed deterministically as adjuncts to political, economic or moral processes (Harker). Country music is hardly the cutting edge of an avant-garde ideological critique. But the living tradition of country music is *historical* and contains the frustrations and possibilities of people in time—working people in our time.

Populism

In both Canada and the United States populist ideology has intermittently served political movements of various stripes since the late nineteenth century. In particular, the American Populist movement and People's Party of the 1880s and 1890s are cited as the most successful of these movements (Hicks; Goodwyn). So are such Canadian political parties as the right-leaning Social Credit of Alberta (Macpherson; Pinard) and the Cooperative Commonwealth Federation or CCF (nicknamed the Crazy Communist Farmers in the 1930s) of Saskatchewan (Lipset). Less successful fragments include the United Farmers in several Canadian provinces and the Progressive Party of Canada (Clark, Grayson and Grayson). All of these formations, as populist movements, reached their zenith before the mid-point of this century. Recent years have seen a renewal of populist impulses in such formations as the Reform Party in Canada, the Rainbow Coalition and the Populist Party itself in the U.S. One can argue that these movements have been fuelled by political discontent with the endemic and selective nature of economic recession, especially its exacerbation of regional differences (Brym and Sacouman; Fairley, Leys and Sacouman) and with the ineptitude of elected representatives and corporate bosses. Movements of regional and nationalist resentment or independence, such as in Quebec, Newfoundland, or Texas, invariably have a strong populist flavor as well.

How to make sense of such a wide variety of political stances, incorporating such an array of class forces, under the common rubric of populism? At the risk of simplification, it can be said that populist moods and movements share certain characteristics of demographic composition, ideological content and political role.

The demographic and class makeup of such formations is broad, but the core participants in such alliances are small enterprisers and segments of the working class. Most populist movements have a base of farmers and other primary producers and a leadership of town-based small businessmen and professionals. Wage-workers and their unions may be part of the movement and leadership. The extent and nature of labour's participation can be critical to the direction of the movement (Brym). In their own terms, populist movements are composed of the common people whose control of societal forces has been usurped by a metropolitan elite.

On the ideological plane, though some have argued that the term "populism" has so diffuse a meaning that it is a useless concept, the term continues to be widely used. Marxists generally view populist movements as vehicles through which class politics are articulated when a mass movement is led by the petite-bourgeoisie (Laclau). As such, movements of popular resistance are seen to be tainted by their affiliation with the petite-bourgeoisie, diverted by their own diffuse populist rhetoric, or merely anachronistic contenders in a fight that has long since been lost (Johnson). Political pundits refer to populist forces in a pejorative fashion, belittling the approach as naive and simplistic, having little to do with political life "here in the real world."

But what is the content of populism? Populism asserts:

a) the primacy of independent activity unencumbered by bureaucracy or interference, based primarily on "human" concerns rather than political or economic ones;

b) the sanctity of a family and community life that is familiar, informal, and beyond question—a community life whose viability is threatened by concentrated interests from away, particularly big business, impersonal government and a bureaucratized labour movement;

c) a fundamental pride in one's homeland, usually defined in regional or linguistic terms, and in its local popular culture; and

d) a reverence for a casually natural environment which is not plundered by corporate interests.

Despite its association with political movements, the populist mood is only reluctantly political. Those who find themselves in populist movements would in general rather avoid politics, but the incursion of external threats has forced politics upon them.

Populist sentiment has underscored most North American movements of broad resistance, especially those with regional or rural bases. The tone of any opposition party must incorporate elements of this sentiment when it is virulently critical of entrenched power in government. The ideology of such a movement must reflect elements of the ordinary lived experience of its adherents and do so in a fashion which draws symbolically on emotionally charged referents from the culture of ordinary rural and working people

(Richards). But the populist rhetoric and style generally diminishes rapidly upon the assumption of power; such as it remains, a populist appeal by an incumbent government becomes a pale shadow of itself, an incantation rather than a content. In short, populist style is invoked by the most dynamic but less powerful sectors of formal politics in order to remain relevant to people's perceived needs; it is characteristically a politics of the marginalized.

When populist sentiment is appropriated by an aspiring class or fragment, the resulting political analysis or programme may express the "progressive" or the "reactionary" elements of that sentiment (Margolis). For example, the idea of a "golden age" that is shared by most populists may lead to strikingly different political conclusions. They range from a heavy-handed right-wing extremism, through a gentle and co-operative "people first" stance, to an almost anarchic primitive communism (Pollack 1967).

Populist movements differ widely in their modes of functioning, the interests which they concretely serve and the breadth of their spirit. For example, a populist movement may promote participatory democracy, plebiscites, constitutional structure, demagoguery, or vigilante justice. It may support policies which actually augment the power of rural and working people, or merely galvanize the specific interests of opportunistic sub-groups. It may be inclusive of ethnic and cultural differences or be narrowly xenophobic. Thus we see that under the rubric of populism are contained a myriad of interests and assumptions which are often contradictory.

The Populist Impulse in Country Music

In an early study of the messages in country music, DiMaggio, Peterson and Esco submitted that the lyrics expressed an odd combination of fatalism and "primitive rebellion":

Country music expresses a modern version of the *populist* world in which God's promise of freedom is land for the homesteader and his descendants. (Hofstadter; Nugent) But the agrarian way of life is no more, few jobs are really heroic, liquor becomes a way of retreatist escape, and love more often brings new pain rather than shelter of fulfilment. The music which underscores these realities might help develop revolutionary discontent (Greenway) but country music not only depicts the promise-and-denial tragedy, it also provides several means of rationalizing failure short of questioning the American dream itself. (51)

They go on to cite five accommodations to these forces that are found in the lyrics: 1) verbalize the problems in hopes of thus transcending them; 2) identify a malevolent force such as big business or big government; 3) underline a fatalism which declares "what will be, will be"; 4) promote escapist quests toward the freedom of a frontier or "the road; 5) boast a perseverance and pride in getting by. The authors conclude that the message of country music could best be described as "populism in retreat" in that it shares the aims and ideals of populism, but is pessimistic about the possibility of attaining them.

Within this general perspective, I suggest that connections between populist sentiment and country music may fruitfully be explored along the following lines:

1. The mass of participants in the world of country music (including fans) are located in the same socio-economic interstices as the traditional following of populist movements.

2. The two arenas share a common vision of the ideal society.

3. The lyrical message of country music shares the tensions and complexity expressed within populism, for example between `people's power' and reactionary redneck conservatism. An important special case is seen in songs about work and livelihood, where the polar attitudes are accommodation versus resistance to existing conditions

4. As with many populist spokespersons, the country music industry has consistently attempted to broaden its audience and influence, often at the expense of purity of message.

Let me examine each of these in more depth:

1. *The mass of participants in the world of country music (including fans) are located in the same socio-economic interstices as the traditional following of populist movements.*

The message of country music lyrics is one that, much like many populist movements themselves, accedes grudgingly to forces beyond the apparent control of those whose lives are profoundly affected by them. Rural and working class movements have an uncanny capacity to look out for their own, "covering their ass" and "hedging their bets" when the political odds are severe, leaving individuals to carve out a piece of the remaining pie, rather than putting all eggs in a long-shot basket. The bitterness toward economic forces which seem beyond people's control is real both for members of populist movements and for country music participants (Malone, *Country Music* 130). The exact fragments of the population which align themselves with populist forces may differ from those in country music circles, but they share an origin and a demographic location in a general way—the same political and economic forces drive their life conditions and their imaginations. I do not argue that country music expresses a militant populist sentiment, rather that the two are "responsive cousins."

Of course, country music began in the country and is still massively popular among rural and small-town people. Commensurate with the relative impoverishment and depopulation of the rural hinterland, what began as folk music went through several changes in its commercialization and move "uptown" with the migrating populace. It became successively "hillbilly" (in the early commercial period of the 1920s through early 1940s), "country and western" (from the late 1940s through the 1960s) and then simply "country" (since the 1970s). From its primarily Anglo-Celtic roots (Malone, 1985:1) within a threatened rural population, country music has become the most important and popular musical idiom for the white indigenous industrial proletariat. However "laundered" its present variants may be, this music was part of the cultural baggage which was carried to North American cities during the massive urbanization of this century.

It should be no surprise, then, that a disproportionate influence on the Canadian country music scene has come from underdeveloped areas enduring the kind of mixed economy which is imposed by the down side of uneven development. The international popularity of Wilf Carter (Montana Slim), Hank Snow, Carroll Baker and Anne Murray in commercial country music attests to the input from Nova Scotia alone. One could speculate that the creative nudge necessary for the most popular and relevant music comes from precisely those areas where the structural dislocation is profound and remains dynamic. One could think of this process as the soul/power exchange (Rosenberg, "Whose Music" 237), wherein the metropolis runs the political and economic show, but spiritual power, quaintness, friendly people, good music and tourist meccas are found in the periphery.

From data on radio listeners in selected U.S. centres, DiMaggio, Peterson and Esco found the country music audience to be middle-aged (25-49), less educated than the average radio listener and disproportionately blue-collar workers:

They are generally over-represented among unskilled and service workers and are *predominant* in the skilled and semi-skilled blue-collar occupations. (49)

They are concentrated in the lower-middle income level. DiMaggio, Peterson and Esco point out that country music fans tend to be sociologically "status inconsistent" in that they have low education and low-prestige jobs while enjoying relatively higher incomes." Otherwise stated, country music fans tend to be members of the classical industrial proletariat, their productive lives dependent on wage-labour, with very little hope of entering any other "career," they being under-equipped to compete in the employment market elsewhere. The authors conclude

Framing a composite, country music fans are urban-living, white adults with rural roots who are established in home, family, and job, but are content with none of these. (50)

This portrait, incidentally, is precisely that which Porter and others paint of the "surplus" rural population which has migrated to Canadian cities.

Country music fans are, so to speak, the "underbelly of populism," the casualties of what farmers' organizations refer to as the "cost-price squeeze," which drove them from their hinterland origins of small-plot farming, small-boat fishing, woods work, cottage crafts and other semi-independent livelihoods, into urban wage labour. Their lives reflect the very demographics which North American populist movements have tried to combat. The recent Farm-Aid benefit concerts, spearheaded by Willie Nelson, made explicit public links with the struggle to survive on the land, as have many other local performances.

In country music, the metaphors for the dislocation or its refusal are typically intensely personal and heroic, so that when the forces of capitalist "progress" threaten the rural lifestyle, resistance to them is admired. John Anderson sings of the "Disappearing Farmer" with imagery from the "Great" Depression:

> Grandpa saw it comin', of that there ain't no doubt
> With the bankers on his doorstep and a cotton-killing drought

The resistance is not that of a hot-headed or impatient person, but expresses a stern resolve:

> Well, he was a kind and he was a gentle man until the bitter end
> He was smilin' on his deathbed, glad he hadn't sold out to them.

In reality it was the rare "petty" producer who resisted these forces successfully, i.e. in a manner which provided a secure livelihood. The characteristic story was of "goin' down the road" to look for work or "goin' up and down the road" when semi-proletarianized (Sacouman); that is, made to drift in and out of wage-labour either seasonally or according to the demands of the wage market.

Usually this employment (or under-employment) was available in a centre larger than one's community of origin. Economic success was to obtain a steady job in such a centre, be it Saint John, Toronto, or Calgary; Memphis, Chicago, or Bakersfield. But this "success" included a bitterly felt compromise, a cultural and personal one. Such migrants became "marginal" persons, "in" but not "of" the city they moved to. It is not surprising that country music lyrics reflect this alienation, framing a kind of echo of the politics of the marginalized.

Emotionally, the temptation to "throw in the towel" was strong. When Merle Haggard sings of the "Big City," it is not only big, but dirty, frustrating and ultimately not worth the trouble:

> I'm tired of too much work and never enough play
> And I'm tired of these dirty old sidewalks
> Think I'll walk off my steady job today.

I know of a family, originally from Cape Breton, Nova Scotia, who moved to Sudbury, Ontario, some 1300 miles distant, where the father worked at International Nickel for most of his productive life. Every summer the family went "back east" for the whole of the father's vacation. The very day after he retired from Inco, they loaded up all their belongings and moved back to Cape Breton. Much as with other populations, such as migrant workers from southern Europe and northern Africa "camping" on jobs in the high-wage areas of northern Europe (Berger and Mohr) they had, in a very real sense, never left home.

Of course, many don't last until retirement. In "Big City," Merle Haggard ṣings:

> ...keep your retirement
> And your so-called social security
> Big city, turn me loose and set me free.

Feeling a bit like a "John Deere tractor in a half-acre field," many will fantasize or decide to return to the country. After all, as Red Taylor's classic song put it

> I can't pay the rent
> Lord, I'm not completely broke
> But brother, I'm badly bent.

Being "badly bent" here is a typical tongue-in-cheek pun, suggesting both near-desperate financial straits and a state of drunkenness—conditions which often go together in country music circles.

2. *The lyrics of country music and the worldview of its adherents share a vision of the ideal society with that articulated by most North American populist movements.*

The very name "country" suggests a preference for (what is seen to be) the rural and small-town way of life: simplicity, self-reliance, trustworthy family, friends and neighbours in a viable community network. As a genre, country music paints the idealized life as uncomplicated, humane, rural and natural. While many urbanites find life in the "boonies," far from urban amenities and anonymity, to be an intolerable combination of isolation, "fish-bowl" visibility, meddling intrusion and narrow-minded ignorance (Furay), country music sings its praises. Singing of "Liverpool," a small coastal town in Nova Scotia, Jim and Don Haggart boast

> ...mostly it's the people there
> That make this little town so fair

Leaving aside for the moment songs about the "love cycle," which constitute the vast majority of country and other popular songs, the message that is most enthusiastically received draws from the lodestone of origin and uniqueness, a reminder of an "old home place" that had provided a particularistic integrity. There are countless songs in this mould, harkening to a thinly protected or already lost way of life:

> Then the coal company came with the world's largest shovel
> And they tortured the timber and they stripped all the land.

With typical irony, John Prine suggests in "Paradise" that this pillage is chalked up to the "progress of man."

Though often romanticized, the country that is being sought is one's place of origin, which serves as both a source of pride and a utopia. Listen to Eddie Legere of Nova Scotia:

> I'm just a bluenose hillbilly
> And I'm longing for the land

Nova Scotians are colloquially known as "bluenosers," after the famous racing schooner. Here he makes his homeland sound not only paradisical but specifically so in a touched and path-worn way

> From the Tantramar Marshes
> To the wild Cape Breton hills

Such pride of place is a constant in country music circles. A first acquaintance at a country music gathering is more likely to ask "'Where ya from?" than "What do you do?" Invariably, the members of a performing band will be introduced first by name, then by place of origin. (Buck Owens used to jest with this tradition by introducing one of his band members as coming from "the state of shock.") Not uncommonly, the band leader will also ask "How many people here are from _____?", to which there is always either a scattered applause or a thunderous ovation. The degree of response seems to depend primarily on the severity of dislocation and unemployment in the place that is named. Commonly such identity of origin is followed by regional jokes based on the ethnic stereotype mould.

Hank Snow's "Nova Scotia Home," Dolly Parton's "My Tennessee Mountain Home," Utah Phillips' "Green Rolling Hills," Alistair MacGillivary's "Song for the Mira" or John Denver's "Take Me Home, Country Roads" are only some of the better known of the many thousands of songs about a hinterland home. The country music heart lies somewhere between "Sonny's Dream" (about a young man's desire to leave Newfoundland in order to see the world) and "Eastbound 401" (the main highway leading to and from Toronto), depositing the indecisive at a mid-point somewhere around Moncton, New Brunswick, I guess.

This lyrical emphasis on an idealized rural life is a highly eco-rhythmic one, but politically ambiguous. Some malevolent force is identified as the enemy, but its concrete designation is rare. C.W. McCall, of "Breaker, Breaker 1—9" trucking songs fame, paints a grim picture of landfill sites filled with beer-cans wearing ecological warnings and of water-skiing across reservoirs where there used to be favourite rivers:

> And them supersonic ships is gonna take you 'cross a sea of pavement
> To one more faceless brickyard on the shore...

His apocalyptic vision is filled with junkyards, fire and smog, and the collapse is rapid:

Yea, it's only gonna take a minute or so
Till the factories block the sun out

The ultimate insult to our natural bounty is that:

...the whole damn world's gonna be made of styrene.

The party responsible for destruction in the above song quite apparently refers to corporate capitalists, though examples just as stark could be found for a government threat.

As with the rural-based adherents of populist movements, concern for the land is emphasized: its integrity, usefulness and beauty to the people who work and live on it. Human beings are seen as guardians rather than exploiters of the earth. "America's poet of the working man," Merle Haggard, sums it up in his rather whimsical song, "Rainbow Stew." After reminding listeners that "the countryside's a sin," he recites a litany of economic and ecological challenges—from eliminating inflation, war and pollution, through to using sunlight and water as energy sources and tossing out the automobile—and then he suggests there could be a bright future

One of these days when the air cleans up
And the sun comes shining through
We'll all be drinkin' that free bub-a-lub
And eatin' that rainbow stew.

In these broad country music themes of family and community, place of origin and a concern for land and nature, we see direct parallels with populist thinking.

3. *The lyrical message of country music shares the tensions and complexity expressed within populism, for example between "people's power" and reactionary redneck conservatism. An important special case is seen in songs about work and livelihood, where the polar attitudes are accommodation versus resistance to existing conditions.*
The country music audience and all but the most successful of its performers have a tough row to hoe. By the standards of our society they are moderately successful at best. The rural-urban drift and the "push" factors from the hinterland economy have been detailed in popular folk and country songs for decades. Over and above the romanticization of life on the land and the criticism of an urban lifestyle, there are references to the backward economic priorities that can allow food production to be strangled by profit, greed and short-term needs, stories about the human consequences of being forced off the land and sea and about the class injustice suffered by the people who must earn a livelihood from childhood on, move to a strange place to do it and be culturally shunned in the process. Little is offered by way of programmatic

solutions, and precise causes of the dislocation are hazy, but the bitterness is clear. George Jones sings:

> I woke up this morning aching with pain
> Don't think I can work, but I'll try...

After a day when he loses his last two dollars on "the ponies," his car breaks down and he gets laid off his job, it is little wonder that Jones sings:

> Oh, these days I barely get by.

They feel, for good reason, that their backs are against the wall and that life is an uphill struggle. Because this struggle is normally an individual one (or seen to be), the resulting tension can lead to a resentment of all forces which curtail success and fulfilment. Sociologists would argue that their "status inconsistency," resulting from moderate income and low prestige, could lead to personal instability or extremisms of a political or social nature. Both these tendencies are expressed in the music, and it is not only difficult but inappropriate to label the ideology (Frith).

The most pointedly critical songs are of industrial work and the plight of working people. The heavy hand attached to the long arm of the job undermines the economic security of the family as well as its spirit and resilience. In "If We Make it Through December," Merle Haggard sings of his young daughter's disappointment in the frugal Christmas that is foisted on his family. The song begins

> Got laid off down at the factory
> And their timing's not the greatest in the world

Probably the best known song suggesting spiritual defeat as a result of work experience in a far away city is Mel Tillis' *Detroit City:*

> By day I make the cars
> By night I make the bars
> ...
> I wanna go home

With respect to industrial work, there is some confusion in the songs, as there is in the population at large, about the relative fault of the industrial process itself, as against the ownership pattern. There is a strong dose of Luddism in country music, as there is in populism. The story of John Henry, perhaps the best known musical legend of a worker at work, tells of a "steel-drivin' man" who challenged a steam-driven hammer to a contest and won, though he died of exhaustion. There is a genuine admiration for the strong and able worker (such as in Jimmie Dean's "Big John") and a pride in making do in life as a manual labourer, though its expression is sometimes defensive. Hank

Snow sings:

> These hands aren't the hands of a gentleman
> These hands are calloused...

Jimmie Rodgers was known as the singing brakeman, Loretta Lynn is the coal miner's daughter, Tom T. Hall sings story after story from the lives of working people. There are countless references to assembly lines, auto plants, cotton mills, mines and other worksites, with never a positive word about the work conditions.

Many songs express alienation from the work process and a sense of injustice at disparity in wealth and privilege. And they portray the authoritarian structure in the workplace as inefficient and soul-destroying.

The solutions or alternatives posed are commonly of two sorts. The first and most common is an escapist idealization of certain types of mobile lifestyle, particularly of free-lance and classical petit-bourgeois occupations that are romantically appealing, or of no occupation at all. The cowboy, the trucker, the hobo and the troubadour are released fully from the time-clock and the precise obligation which wage-labour entails (Cornfield). He can enjoy the low life and the natural life in any given day. As expressed in Ed Bruce's hugely successful "Mamas, Don't Let Your Babies Grow up to be Cowboys":

> Cowboys like smoky old poolrooms and clear
> mountain mornings,
> Little warm puppies and children and girls of the night.

In populist rhetoric, a similar independence of spirit and pride in being unfettered is often attributed to the life of the small enterpriser, especially the farmer.

There is a second and perhaps more important alternative to accepting the pattern of industrial work as given. That is to resist it directly, rebelliously, by thwarting authority, sabotaging the production process, or dramatically and symbolically "giving two shits," thus undermining the predictability of the worker to the employer. This "war at the workplace" (Rinehart 143-56) has many colourful variations in reality, from Monday cars to water fights to nicknames for foremen and supervisors. Johnny Cash's "Oney" and "One Piece at a Time" are excellent examples of this rather primitive but rewarding politics, and the songs of this sort are extremely popular. Structural solutions are rarely even hinted at, but the lyrics in the music reflect a daily reality, one in which collectivist visions of the control of the production process are not ideologically entrenched. The music will reflect the development of such visions as it happens, but only rarely engender them consciously.

Most commonly in the English North American musical tradition, in Blues as well as country, the war is turned inward, as a feeling of personal defeat, a certain ambiguous disgust with oneself and one's conditions (usually seen as inseparable). There is a contemptuous air (as in David Allan Coe's

"Take This Job and Shove It") and the internalization of frustration often results in abuse of various inebriants, especially alcohol. Interestingly enough, however, the musical expression is in a sense collective, first simply by being a song in the public world and also by everyone hoping together that "the sun gon' shine in my door someday."

The "crazy" life of the "hell-raiser" is often romanticized, framing a justificatory rhetoric for drunkenness, violence, promiscuity and careless gambling. This "wild side of life" is recognized as the precise opposite of what would be preferred if only the level of frustration were diminished. The lifestyle is considered quite contrary to the homespun values within which country music "folks" were reared. In the time-worn homily which Jimmie Rodgers attributed to his mother

Son, don't start drinking and gambling
Promise you'll always go straight.

But "temptation" strikes deep, and in a kind of obverse fundamentalism, when one yields to such worldly pleasure, one undercuts the potential for revelation that fundamentalism promises and instead a self-reviling attitude emerges:

Hey, I'm goin' off the deep end
I'm slowly losin', losin' my mind

Even Johnny Paycheck's own personal life, from his alcoholism to his recent term in jail, serves as testimony to the veracity of the song:

Well, I don't like me
And the way that I'm livin'
But I can't hold myself in line.

This attitude toward insanity and social incapacity is akin to that of the school of anti-psychiatry espoused by people such as R.D. Laing and Thomas Szasz. As Waylon Jennings sings:

I've always been crazy
But it keeps me from going insane.

Yet in a somewhat stammering defence of the common people, John Conlee sings of his mongrel dog and his ordinary vehicle and the peace of mind which such commonness affords:

If I have my say, gonna stay that way
Cause high-browed people lose their sanity
And a common man is what I'll be.

Small wonder that no clear political position emerges, and that, just as in populist ideology, country music embodies tension and contradiction along several dimensions. Apparent political dissonance is common. Thus Merle Haggard can sing "Working Man Blues" and "A Working Man Can't Get Nowhere Today," then show up for a cameo appearance at Nixon's White House. Jerry Reed sings "Lord, Mr. Ford," then says that what America needs is a good war. Manitoba's Stew Clayton sings:

> Oh, Strike! Strike! Strike!
> Everywhere you turn
> Everybody's striking
> No matter what they earn

Despite galloping inflation, Clayton says the strikers carelessly press on, threatening to ruin the country. In the next verse he counters with an equally caustic view of the politicians. When people appeal to the federal government for action to break the strike, they discover: that it is just a waste of time because these in Ottawa have been on strike for years.

Good examples of politically progressive lyrics are rare. In part this reflects the relative impotence of working people's organization. Caught between a rock and a hard place, rural and working people like to keep a few eggs in each of several baskets. Even the more self-conscious "organic intellectuals" (Patterson; Gramsci) among country music writers and performers are more likely to work their vision through story and metaphor than through didactic or analytic engagement

4. The country music industry has always sought to reach and influence larger markets. Most often this has entailed softening the lyric message and sweetening the raw sound; in their larger political ambitions, populist movements have engaged in the same process. But there are also exciting examples of translation and syncretism across regional and ethnic barriers, creating locally meaningful patterns.

The country music tradition has always walked a thin line between a traditionally accepted style/message and "selling out" to commercial innovations. Those in the industry and the more ambitious performers have augmented their appeal as carefully and in as self-interested a fashion as possible. The more successful of these have crossed over to the popular charts. The term "crossover" gained a broad currency in the 1970s, especially through artists such as Linda Ronstadt, Kenny Rogers, Olivia Newton-John, Crystal Gayle, Anne Murray, Willie Nelson and even Canada's Stompin' Tom Connors. But the desire to broaden market appeal has fuelled recorded country music since its inception in the 1920s.

Just as, within populist movements, aspirants to formal power have tried to soften the message so as to widen receptivity, so have commercial forces within country music continuously attempted to reduce the "rejection quotient" resulting from the raw sound of the hillbilly and honky-tonk traditions (Malone,

"Honky Tonk"; Ives). All of mass culture responds in some fashion to the lowest common denominator of popular taste, thereby simultaneously becoming successful and reducing the "punch" of the art.

This purist/commercial contradiction has many manifestations. Certain sectors of the country music world, both in the metropolis and in outlying regions, are most comfortable with top-40 American pop-country music, preferring a polished repetitive sound to the variety and occasional harshness of hard-core country and lesser known local performers. As many casual listeners say, "I like country music as long as the singers don't sing through their nose and wail on about heartbreak." Some performances are slavish imitations of the commercial mainstream, often losing context and assuming a kind of surreal air (Lehr). Such "cultural grey-out" (Nettl 345-54) is a concern not only to loyal and serious fans, but also to ethnomusicologists, and not incidentally, the cultural programme of many populist movements.

There are thousands of examples of tension between the commercial demands of the industry and the aesthetic priorities of artist and audience. The most profitable investments by recording companies tap the energy and inventiveness of untutored musicians, who often have a naive view of the industry. Just as in "pop" music the sound of Motown or Reggae are incorporated (in a watered-down form) into hugely popular "covers" and imitations, so are the various "sources" of country music commercially exploited, turning tradition-based forms into "country-politan" hits. Many country performers become so disillusioned by the demands of agents, promoters, "a & r" people and producers that they return to their "day-jobs."

The process is somewhat like the experience of those rural and working-class adherents of populist movements who find their raw sense of outrage over injustice usurped by an opportunistic urban petite-bourgeoisie. Their dissatisfaction, energy and imagination serve as a kind of legitimizing patina for the more urbane, ambitious and enterprising members of a rising leadership.

But transformation of country music to reach new listeners is not always a matter of diluting or perverting its fundamental message. In other cases, particularly where other communal musics have a solid and continuing foundation, the musical syncretism is profound (Narvaez; Nettl 353), and country music takes root as a working idiom in quite a different way. Similar demographic niches adopt forms of the country music style and message despite important differences of particular regional identity, ethnicity, or language. Rather than a uniformity of style and repertoire, each region of the continent is found to have its own particular kind of country music. Selecting from the media-disseminated mainstream, adding from local tradition, mixing styles eclectically and maintaining musical forms that have roots in past generations, each area weaves its own pattern of country music (Bronner; Leary). As folklorist Neil Rosenberg has pointed out in a model based on the case of country music in New Brunswick, the mix of favoured artists, songs and styles is comprised both of the top commercial music excerpted in a regionally meaningful fashion and of local material that is solidly built on ethnic and familiar foundations/traditions.

· The simplest of such localizations is the insertion of local place names, or even personal names, into a song that has broad currency. A more complex way to do the same thing is to invent parodies, either humorous or serious (Narvaez, "The Folk"). This is a common formula in much North American folksong: a parody simply puts new words to an old air, as was done in the rich broadside tradition and by many hymn writers and union troubadours. Almost anywhere that middle-aged rural and working class people gather, a mix of commercial country and local tradition makes up a large part of the musical diet. The music may have an Irish hors d'oeuvre, a Ukrainian side dish, or a French salad, but the meat and potatoes is always country music, whatever that might mean locally.

One Newfoundland duo, Simani, have sold more than 100,000 copies of their record *Saltwater Cowboy* privately and by word of mouth. They have had little or no radio airplay in major markets and no professional promotion or distribution:

> How are ya doin'
> Ya son of a b____?
> You can't fool your old man by dressin' like that
> You're still just a Newfie in a Calgary hat.

In Toronto's Country Music Store, whose clientele is largely those displaced from the Atlantic provinces, the owners feel obliged to tape handwritten signs on those new releases which are "down-east music," to distinguish them from "country" records, i.e. those with the commercial "Nashville Sound."

Perhaps the most profound example of this process is that of Quebec "Western" music, or "musique de la compagne." On AM radio in Quebec, American top-40 country is played back to back with "Quebecois" songs, many of them lyrical translations or adaptations of English-language country music. Johnny Cash's "Folsom Prison Blues" becomes Willie Lamothe's "Le Mur d'Acier" (Steel Wall). "The Battle of New Orleans," itself based on an older tune, "The Eighth of January," was a huge hit for Johnny Horton in 1959. The song remains a perennial favourite in Quebec "Western" circles, in part, I would posit, because of the lines about fighting the "bloody British." The traditional American country-folk murder ballad "Banks of the Ohio" was once recorded by Joan Baez and is a bluegrass standard. When sung by Richard Huet in Quebec it becomes "La Baie James," the lament of a migrant construction worker.

Conclusion

Country music, like any massively popular music in a market society, has no single consistent programme or political position. Nonetheless, the conditions which have led to populist responses are those which the core of the country music audience have also experienced. The lyrical portrayal of those conditions, and of the lifestyle and ideals of those who lived through them, is abundant.

The reaction is convoluted, much as anyone's would be in novel and uncontrollable life circumstances. Such convolution, both in country music and in populism, is sometimes characterized as political or thematic ambiguity. But it is more than that; the contradictions should be recognized as reflecting the multiple complexities and tensions which must be present in arenas so dynamically bound up with the lives of working people.

Perhaps the tension between a "resistant" and an "accommodationist" attitude, as well as the "escapist" middle ground, needs more investigation. Many examples of their co-existence are revealed only during times of extreme societal tension, wherein the possibility of successful resistance becomes a catalyst for the expression of deeply held resentments which normally lie below the surface (Gaventa). Until an avenue for effective resistance is apparent, the psychologically safer route is to accept large abstract forces as given, and accommodate them with a pragmatic attitude that borders on fatalism. As Anton Zijderveld has put it:

> Homo duplex is neither rebel nor conformist, but moves between consensus and discontent. He therefore shares the uncertainties and tensions of democracy. (122)

In the words of *New Left Review* editors shortly after the events in France of May, 1968:

> We need a theory of dual consciousness, a theory which can take account of abrupt and unexpected alternations and switches. Just as history shows uneven and combined development, so too does consciousness.

Country music messages are paradoxical in much the same way as working class ideology in general must be in a capitalist society.

In this context, we should note that much of the lyrical message is a revolving door of romantic love: sought, gained, disillusioned, lost, or unrequited. But the devolution of the social relations in community and family onto an attachment to the "one" other, the "loved one," has forced allegories of love into romantic ones, and nowhere is this more profoundly expressed than in the various forms of popular music. As Cornfield has claimed of country music themes:

> It seems as though the anger and the disappointment are stronger than any that could be caused by the specific soap-opera situations of the songs. Real discontent is expressed with the whole of life—with your job and the government, the unclear social structure, unfulfilled ambitions, unfulfilled American dreams, constant insecurity, bitterness that you aren't among the winners. Put these feelings into a song, and the song turns out to be about spurned love. (27)

Any explicit message songs must be couched in metaphors that have a folksy flavour. In the main, the lyrics of country music songs reflect changing attitudes rather than promote that change. Country music will not leap, as one body, onto a new and unlikely politics or morality, as do certain musicians in other fields. As with any popular format, it sometimes accepts (apparently) easy solutions to complex problems, or no solution at all. As a widely popular idiom, its primary focus must reflect the reigning tenets of the dominant ideology. Yet there is a changeable and often resistant vein which has always run rich in the country tradition.

Works Cited

Berger, John and Jean Mohr. *A Seventh Man: A Book of Images and Words about the Experience of Migrant Workers in Europe*. London: Penguin, 1975.

Bronner, Simon J. *Old-Time Music Makers of New York State*. Syracuse, NY: Syracuse UP, 1987.

Brunton, R., J. Overton and J. Sacouman. "Uneven Underdevelopment and Song: Culture and Development in the Maritimes." *Communication Studies in Canada*. Ed. Liora Salter. Toronto: Butterworths, 1981. 105-32.

Brym, Robert J. "Regional Social Structure andAgrarian Radicalism in Canada:Alberta Saskatchewan, and New Brunswick." *Canadian Review of Sociology and Anthropology* 15.3 (1978).

Brym, Robert J. and James R. Sacouman, eds. *Underdevelopment and Social Movements in Atlantic Canada*. Toronto: New Hogtown, 1979.

Buckley, John. "Country Music and American Values." *American Popular Music: Readings from the Popular Press Volume II: The Age of Rock*. Ed. Timothy E. Scheurer. Bowling Green, OH: Bowling Green State U Popular P, 1989.

Clark, Samuel D., J. Paul Grayson and Linda M.Grayson, eds. *Prophecy and Protest: Social Movements in Twentieth-Century Canada*. Toronto: Gage Educational Publishing, 1975.

Cornfield, Robert. *Just Country*. New York: McGraw-Hill, 1976.

DiMaggio, Paul, Richard A. Peterson and Jack Esco, Jr. "Country Music: Ballad of the Silent Majority." *The Sounds of Social Change: Studies in Popular Culture*. Ed. R. Serge Denisoff and Richard A. Peterson. Chicago: Rand McNally, 1972. 38-55.

Fairley, Bryant, Colin Leys, and James Sacouman, eds. *Restructuring and Resistance: Perspectives from Atlantic Canada*. Toronto: Garamond, 1990.

Frith, Simon. "Introduction." *Pop Goes the Culture*. Craig McGregor. London: Pluto, 1984.

Furay, Conal. "The Small Town Mind." *The Popular Culture Reader: Third Edition*. Eds. Christopher D. Geist and Jack Nachbar. Bowling Green, OH: Bowling Green U Popular P, 1983.

Gaventa, John. *Power and Powerlessness: Quiescence and Rebellion in an Appalachian Valley*. Urbana: U of Illinois P, 1980.

Goodwyn, Lawrence. *The Populist Moment: A Short History of the Agrarian Revolt in America*. Oxford: Oxford UP, 1978

Gramsci, Antonio. *Selections from the Prison Notebooks*. London: Lawrence and Wishart, 1971.

Harker, Dave. *One for the Money: Politics and Popular Song*. London: Hutchinson,

1980.

Hicks, John D. *The Populist Revolt: A History of the Farmers' Alliance and the People's Party.* 1931. U of Nebraska P, 1961.

Ivey, William. "Commercialization and Tradition in the Nashville Sound." *Folk Music and Modern Sound.* Eds. William Ferris and Mary L. Hart. Jackson: UP of Mississippi, 1982. 129-38.

Johnson, Leo. "The Development of Class in Canada in the Twentieth Century." *Capitalism and the National Question in Canada.* Ed. Gary Teeple. Toronto: U of Toronto P, 1972. 141-83.

Laclau, Ernesto. *Politics and Ideology in Marxist heory.* London: New Left Books, 1977.

Leary, James P. "Ethnic Country Music on Superior's South Shore." *John Edwards Memorial Foundation* 19 (1983): 219-30.

Lehr, John. "'Texas When I Die': National Identity and Images of Place in Canadian Country Music Broadcasts." *Canadian Geographer* 27.4 (1983): 361-70.

Lipset, Seymour Martin. *Agrarian Socialism: The Cooperative Commonwealth Federation in Saskatchewan.* Berkeley: U of California P, 1950.

Macpherson, C. B. *Democracy in Alberta: Social Credit and the Party System.* 2nd ed. Toronto: U of Toronto P, 1962.

Malone, Bill C. *Country Music U.S.A.* Rev. ed. Austin: U of Texas P, 1985.

_____. "Honky Tonk: The Music of the Southern Working Class." *Folk Music and Modern Sound.* Ed. Ferris and Hart. 119-28.

Margolis, Richard J. "The Two Faces of Populism." *The New Leader* (April 1983).

Narvaez, Peter. "Country and Western in Diffusion: Juxtaposition and Syncretism in the Popular Music of Newfoundland." *Culture and Tradition* 2 (1977): 91-105.

_____. "The Folk Parodist." Canadian Folk Music Journal 5.

Nettl, Bruno. *The Study of Ethnomusicology: Twenty-nine Issues and Concepts.* Urbana: U of Illinois P, 1983.

New Left Review (Nov.-Dec. 1968). Editorial.

Pinard, Maurice. *The Rise of A Third Party: A Study in Crisis Politics.* Englewood Cliffs: Prentice-Hall, 1971.

Pollack, Norman, ed. *The Populist Mind.* Indianapolis: Bobbs-Merrill, 1967.

Porter, John. *The Vertical Mosaic.* Toronto: U of Toronto P, 1965.

Richards. John. "Populism: A Qualified Defence." *Studies in Political Economy* 5 (1981).

Rinehart, James W. *The Tyranny of Work: Alienation and the Labour Process.* 2nd ed. Toronto: Harcourt, Brace, Jovanovich, 1987.

Rogers, Jimmie N. *The Country Music Message: Revisited.* Fayetteville: U of Arkansas P, 1989.

Rosenberg, Neil V. "Folk and Country Music in the Canadian Maritimes: A Regional Model." *The Journal of Country Music* 5 (1974): 76-83. Rpt. Memorial University of Newfoundland Department of Folklore Reprint Series, no. 2.

_____. "Whose Music is Canadian Country Music?: A Precis." *Ethnomusicology in Canada.* Ed. Robert Witmer. Toronto: Institute for Canadian Music, 1990.

Sacouman, R. James. "Semi- Proletarianization and Rural Underdevelopment in the Maritimes." *Canadian Review of Sociology and Anthropology* 17.3 (1980)232-245.

Williams, Roger M. "Hank Williams." *The Stars of Country Music: Uncle Dave Macon to Johnny Rodriguez*. Ed. Bill C. Malone and Judith McCullogh. Urbana: U of Illinois P, 1975.

Zijderveld, Anton C. *The Abstract Society: A Cultural Analysis of Our Time*. Garden City, NY: Doubleday, 1970.

If Wishes Were Changes:
Country at the Crossroads

On September 20, 1973, friends of Gram Parsons hijacked his body and burned it in the high desert outside of Joshua Trees, California, an event memorialized by Emmylou Harris in her song "From Boulder To Birmingham." The particular crossroads that country music stands at today can be traced back to that artist, date and time.

Writer and musician Gram Parsons died at age 27 of a drug overdose in his California motel room. Like Hank Williams before him, who was dead at 29, Parsons led an emotionally turbulent and tragically short life. Also, like Hank Williams, he left a legacy (in Parsons' case, a fusion of traditional and country/rock) that has become central to present day country music. Parsons' early work with Cris Hillman (in the Byrds and Burrito Brothers) defined the term country rock—a type of music best represented today by country groups like Alabama, Highway 101 and Hillman's own Desert Rose Band.

Parsons also discovered Emmylou Harris in a Washington D.C. folk club and persuaded her to join his band and sing country with him. His posthumously released album, "Grievous Angel," with Harris singing backups and duets, is considered by many critics and musicians to be one of the landmark albums of country music—virtually defining the rock-traditional fusion that was to become so hugely important in the industry. Yet, at the time of its release, this album was largely overlooked by both pop and country audiences.

"Gram was a real pioneer," Emmylou Harris told Irwin Stambler. "He cut straight through the middle with no compromises. He was never afraid to write from the heart, and perhaps that's why he was never really accepted. It's like the light was too strong and bright and people just had to turn away...not many people can take music that real."

Harris could, and in the past two decades, has pushed on with what Parsons began, in her stunning and influential career. Her backup group, the "Hot Band," reads like a "who's who" of modern country, anticipating both the strong country/rock sound of today and the reactive return to tradition taken by other contemporary artists. James Burton (Elvis' legendary guitarist) worked with both Parsons and Harris, was in the Hot Band and continues to produce original and tasteful guitar work on albums such as Carlene Carter's 1990 chart buster, "I Fell In Love." Rodney Crowell, multi-talented songwriter, recording star and producer, began his career in the Hot Band, as did contemporary producer Tony Brown, who has worked with country artists as diverse as Lyle Lovett, Nanci Griffith, Kelly Willis and Wynonna Judd. Finally, Ricky Scaggs, who has gone on to lead what is known as the neo-traditionalist movement in

305

modern country, started out in Harris' band.

In all these cases, the musical roots trace back through Emmylou Harris to Gram Parsons who, in his short career, attempted to bring more of a rock sound to country, yet—at the same time—root his music in the rural tradition of the past. This is a tough balancing act, and few accomplish it with the grace and skill of Emmylou Harris or, more recently, Rosanne Cash (who, herself, is plugged into this same network, as her first albums were produced by her ex-husband, Rodney Crowell).

The tensions between these two impulses—continuing a fusion of country and rock, on the one hand, and connecting this fusion to country's own rural traditions, on the other—lies at the creative heart of modern country music and defines much of the controversy in the field today. As critic David Gates puts it, going too far in the traditional direction risks "aesthetic suicide," by freezing the music in a narrow and time-bound regional backwater. But going too far in the other direction risks "generic suicide," by crossbreeding the music out of existence, as many felt was happening in the 1980s.

In a way, this dilemma is similar to the one country artists faced in the early 1950s. Hank Williams and Patsy Cline borrowed from other musical traditions to create their own distinctive music. Elvis delved deeply into black musical forms and styles and merged them with country. Bill Monroe found a way to bring dignity back to the traditional sound and popularize it as "blue-grass" in the process. Each, in their own time, stood at a crossroads. And each forged a path that helped define what modern country music was to become.

Today, with music as traditional as that of Randy Travis and as rock-oriented as that of Hank Williams, Jr., both active on the charts, country has come to another crossroads. In "The Old Sound Of New Country," Ken Tucker examines the contradictions that exist within the "neo-traditionalist" movement of the late 1980s and early 1990s—contradictions that have allowed Ricky Scaggs to view his music "as an essentially conservative medium, one that will revitalize all of the traditional values he prizes," while at the same time, Reba McEntire sees it as "a clarion call to freedom, a way for women to express progressive, even radical notions."

David Gates has a different view of this neo-traditionalist music, pointing out that it is more of an "emulation of distant figures out of a legendary past" and may even suggest a "rejection of the here and now." As Gates says in "Are You Sure Hank Done It This Way," Hank Williams lived in his own present and borrowed from other pop traditions. He did not advance the music and become a superstar by becoming just like past country masters—"he was too busy trying to outsell Roy Acuff."

The contemporary-traditional conflict is present today in bluegrass, as well as in mainstream country music. Mark Fenster in "Alison Krauss and the Contemporary Traditional Conflict in Modern Bluegrass" examines the reactions of the bluegrass (and the pop) communities to the music of Alison Krauss, as, in the early 1990s, she tried to infuse her music with non-traditional elements, yet stay close in touch with bluegrass traditions. Fenster sees Krauss as not exploiting bluegrass, but "pushing the music in a positive direction and helping to promote the genre." However, for many in the traditional bluegrass audience, Krauss's newer sound is an "example of the intrusion of commerce into the precarious traditions and culture of bluegrass," about which they are both angry and bitter.

Finally, in Jan Hoffman's "Rosanne Cash Walks Her Own Line," the conflict within an artist herself who, raised deep in the country tradition, has broken free and borrowed many musical ideas from the most current forms of popular music, is sketched. In albums such as "Interiors," Cash has created a new music, as she walks the tightrope between contemporary and traditional—a process she calls "dancing with the tiger." She sings, affirming that she is "a real woman, changing every day," and "if you want to find out what I've got on my mind, you better hold on."

This attitude, and new music of such change and hope, strikes a brilliant chord at the crossroads of pop forms and tradition. For those in the industry in Nashville, not knowing who will strike such ringing chords (nor when they do, what the chords will sound like) makes the business of modern country music a nerve-wracking one. But for the artists and the fans, it's exactly this characteristic that makes for excitement and involvement—the "Touch" that makes country music, and with it, all that glitters, a vital force in American popular music today.

Playlist

Gram Parsons	Grievous Angel	Reprise
Ricky Skaggs	Waitin' For the Sun To Shine	Epic
Reba McEntire	My Kind Of Country	MCA
George Strait	Chill Of an Early Fall	MCA
Randy Travis	Heroes and Friends	Columbia
Alison Krauss	That Old Feelin	Rounder
Rosanne Cash	Interiors	Columbia

The Old Sound Of New Country

Ken Tucker

I just got tired of hearing all these songs about drinkin' and cheatin'; I figured I could sing about something else that would interest people. Whether you call it traditional country, or hard country, or whatever, it's the music I like best.

Ricky Skaggs

It's still pretty unusual to hear a woman sing a song about having an affair or standing up for herself in this world. To me, that's one of the things that hard country music is all about—the freedom to say things that you can't say in the other, more pop-oriented kinds of country music.

Reba McEntire

Any worthwhile artistic movement has the ability to contain within itself extreme, even contradictory, points of view, and the so-called "hard country" movement is no exception. Consider, for example, the quotations above from recent interviews with two of the most popular performers in the country music industry these days. Ricky Skaggs views hard country as an essentially conservative medium, one that will revitalize all of the traditional values he prizes as both a musician and a man. Reba McEntire hears hard country as a clarion call to freedom, a way for women to express progressive, even radical, notions within a pleasing, entertaining context.

This is just one reason why hard country—the stripped-down, back-to-basics country music currently played by artists such as Skaggs, McEntire, George Strait, the Whites, the Judds and others—is the most interesting and exciting thing to happen to the country music industry in years. Hard country stands in implicit—and sometimes explicit—defiance of the esthetically exhausted "countrypolitan" sound developed by Chet Atkins and other members of the Nashville establishment three decades ago. With its renewed emphasis on keening pedal steel guitars and baleful fiddles, its palpable enjoyment of Southern accents and lyrical realism, hard country harks back to the honky-tonk music of Lefty Frizzell, Webb Pierce and George Jones, to the plaintive eloquence of Patsy Cline and the tart forthrightness of Kitty Wells.

Hard country stands as a blunt rebuke to the watery pop-country of such best-selling acts as the Oak Ridge Boys, Alabama and Exile. Whereas these gold-chained businessmen make the most superficial, one-dimensional kind of

Reprinted from *The Journal of Country Music*, 11.1 (1986) 3-8 by permission of The Country Music Foundation and the author.

country music, hard country can be used by its practitioners for varying purposes—for Ricky Skaggs, it illuminates an essentially conservative world-view; for Reba McEntire or Gail Davies, it exposes a progressive one. Whatever point of view it expresses, however, hard country offers glowing proof of traditional country music's ongoing richness and vitality.

The ostensible superstars have inspired a deluge of imitators releasing records that are little more than third-rate versions of rock 'n' roll's singer-songwriter movement a decade ago. In this atmosphere, failed-pop-singer-gone-country Marie Osmond has as much claim to the country charts as failed-country-singer-gone-pop Charly McClain. Much has been made of the economic slump within the country music industry; one need only listen to the half-baked pop songs passing for country on supposedly country music radio stations to understand why the country music audience would rather get its entertainment from television.

That country music audience is a large and diverse one, and the current commercial success of artists such as Skaggs, Strait and McEntire demonstrates that there is obviously a sizable public for the efforts of a forward-looking country music that has roots in a vividly remembered history. In the midst of country music's version of the Depression, hard country singers are being seized upon as the saviors of the industry, but it is important to make a distinction here: hard country is patently not a mere marketing strategy, the latest scheme of the Nashville crowd to boost record sales. The proof is easy to summon up: Skaggs, Strait, McEntire and virtually all the other hard country artists were making this kind of music years ago, to small audiences and industry indifference. Industry bigwigs view the current hard country boom as the inevitable swing of the music biz pendulum—one trend giving way to its opposite—but that sort of facile analysis demeans the lifework of a family like the Whites, or the painstaking western swing scholarship of George Strait.

With his gleaming white cowboy hat and his gleaming white teeth, George Strait is almost too good to be true. He is the only country music star I've ever seen whose idea of a stage costume includes a Brooks Brothers button-down-collar shirt. Strait could start a new genre: yuppie-billy. He's so pristinely handsome that you figure he must be a doof, a nerd, or at best a sly put-on. But when he opens his mouth to sing, you realize that this is one Dudley Do-Right who knows how to honky-tonk. Strait has taken one of country music's most admired star traits—gulping, aw-shucks humility—and turned it into a reason to get excited about country music again.

Strait courted instant self-parody by entitling his 1981 MCA debut album *Strait Country*, but upon listening to the album's first big hit, "Unwound," you knew this was something different: music whose transcendent quality was that it sounded so guileless, so straightforward. (In fact, I figured that would be the title of his follow-up: *Strait-Forward*. To be followed, of course, by the inevitable *Strait-Laced*.) "Unwound" was, at first, merely a nice ballad, calm and stately, a song whose strong emotions were subtly underplayed in Strait's crisp, unmannered phrasing. But after repeated listenings, the song's charms became even more inveigling. Most beguiling was the title image, the notion of a love affair becoming unwound—slack and lifeless. It was a beautifully simple yet vivid metaphor, one that Strait worked out carefully over the course of this Dean Dillon-Frank Dycus composition.

Since then, Strait's popularity has grown steadily; there seems to be a substantial audience for his cool, no-nonsense synthesis of western swing and honky-tonk. On *Does Fort Worth Ever Cross Your Mind* (1984), Strait recorded a handful of Sanger D. Shafer songs, including the album's title tune, "Honky Tonk Saturday Night" and "I Need Someone Like Me," that luminously depicted Strait's essential point of view: melancholy and rather pessimistic, but fundamentally decent and, when the occasion permitted, good-natured. Shafer's idiosyncratic combination of lugubriousness and wordplay—a style that probably reached its peak in the hits he wrote for Moe Bandy in the early 1970s—was well-suited to Strait's earnest but never dour demeanor.

Strait's recent album, *Something Special*, is the singer's most confident release to date, bursting with an insouciant swing that is usually the province of an older musician. Unlike Ricky Skaggs, for whom the recording studio is the most comfortable area of artistic expression, Strait seems most at home in front of an audience that is eager to dance. It is this quality that comes through most enjoyably on *Something Special*, in songs such as "Dance Time in Texas," "You're Something Special to Me" and "You Sure Got This Ol'Redneck Feelin' Blue." Here, with Johnny Gimble fiddling merrily in the background, Strait is harking back to the barnstorming days of Bob Wills and all the other western swing players who gave Strait his basic rhythm. This only makes Strait's commercial success more impressive, for if five years ago you'd told the average country music a&r man that the next country sex symbol would be a fellow who idolized Wills and mumbled like Merle Haggard, you'd probably have been greeted with raucous laughter and a swat upside your head with a Barbara Mandrell album.

In the matter of becoming popular by locating one's own style, the example of McEntire is particularly instructive. In recent years, the young vocalist had been marketed as your usual female country singer—i.e., a malleable tool for whatever all-seeing, all-knowing producer happened to be free to grind out ten tracks on her this week. Stuck with performing bland, at times pseudo-pop songs, McEntire made the best of it, curtailing her twang in the service of subtle expressiveness. The result was a modestly successful commercial career that had not, esthetically speaking, yielded a record that even bore mention in John Morthland's definitive survey of the genre, 1984s *The Best of Country Music*.

"I was feeling frustrated by my career" is McEntire's own analysis. "I felt I could be singing music that was more country than what I was recording.... It was a big chance to take, but I decided I had to insist on producing myself. And it paid off, didn't it?"

It certainly did. Upon taking control of her own career and having the temerity to sing country music to the country music audience, McEntire allowed her twang to bloom: her clear, friendly, powerful contralto voice created hits bigger than any she'd had before, and suddenly every country performer on every televised awards show in the United States wanted to tell you just how much he/she loved/admired Reba.

The finest result to date of this country music Marxism—singer seizing control of the means of production—is *Have I Got a Deal for You*, co-produced by McEntire and Jimmy Bowen, the latter the perspicacious industry executive who granted McEntire her creative freedom in the first place. *Have I Got a Deal for You* deftly intersperses the heartbroken-in-love ballads that made McEntire a worthy successor to Patsy Cline with prickly, nudging compositions like Michael P. Heeney and Jackson Leap's "The Great Divide," a romantic tune couched in odd, striking metaphors and McEntire's own "Only in My Mind," a closely observed song about a woman's inner torment.

Aided by the astringent fiddle of Johnny Gimble and pulsing bass guitar of Emory Gordy, Jr., *Have I Got a Deal for You* boldly expresses feelings that Tammy Wynette had to sneak into the edges of her hits—anger and vindictiveness as well as suffering and pain, wit and craziness as well as devotion and common sense.

For all this, McEntire has neatly avoided that much-feared quality that sends chills down the spines of male record executives: she hasn't alienated her audience by being "too aggressive" or "uppity." She has merely claimed her own piece of what men have been singing about in country music for years—feelings of yearning, lust and guilt.

By contrast, Ricky Skaggs is country music's reigning neoconservative. Where Reba McEntire looks at the sexist, prudish country industry and sees fences that need to be torn down, Skaggs gazes balefully at the moral and commercial chaos all around him and seeks to put a few fences back up again. How interesting, therefore, that the music made by these two profoundly contrasting musicians is so similar in its stripped-down eloquence and let's-hear-it-for-regionalism twanginess.

For such a young artist, Skaggs has spent his career seeking out areas for inventive traditionalism. Unlike McEntire, he has never suffered at the hands of unsympathetic producers; he hasn't had to choke back disgust at being handed bland pop material to sing. That's because, early on, Skaggs found a way to make a living in the country music industry that did not compromise his tastes. Instead of submitting himself to the tortures of the commercial country field, he established his reputation within its sub-genres, bluegrass and honky-tonk. Working as a guitarist, mandolinist and fiddler for Ralph Stanley, the Country Gentlemen and Emmylou Harris, Skaggs polished his professionalism while figuring out the most sensible strategy for his solo career.

The result was that, by the time he made his major-label debut in 1981 with *Waitin' for the Sun to Shine*, Skaggs had already acquired a certain amount of creative control based on the trust and good will he had accrued from his earlier associations. For example, Skaggs was permitted to produce *Waitin' for the Sun to Shine* himself, a rare privilege for a first-time solo performer, but an ironclad condition of Skaggs' recording contract with Epic Records. For all his apparently genuine humility, Skaggs is no bashful dunderhead when it comes to dealing with the industry; his forthright hard-headedness has enabled him to go his own way from the start. Fortunately for Skaggs—call it luck, call it just-rewards—*Waitin' for the Sun to Shine* found a sizable audience. Skaggs' career was launched, and his creative freedom was confirmed by the balance sheet.

The albums that have followed *Waitin' for the Sun to Shine* have further defined Skaggs' intentions. Producing himself to achieve a ringingly clear, crisp, uncluttered sound, Skaggs sings about true love, strong marriages and the soul-cleansing pleasures of rural life. Occasionally, a doubt creeps into his voice—in 1984, on *Country Boy*, he employed the George Jones hit "Window Up Above" to express the sort of intense romantic/sexual yearning that he too often banishes from the rest of his music.

For ultimately, there is something about Ricky Skaggs that is unsatisfying—at his weakest, you get the feeling that his avoidance of sensuousness, both as subject and technique in his music, amounts to a prudishness about, or even an abhorrence of, the juicy side of life. Skaggs has attracted a lot of praise for the cleverness of the video he made to illustrate "Country Boy." Plunking Skaggs and one of his heroes, Bill Monroe, down in New York's Times Square, the "Country Boy" video was indeed a much more imaginative and humorous project than the vast majority of country music videos. But even here, Skaggs' standoffish quality comes through in an unpleasant way, as black teenagers breakdancing in the subway are used as if they were aliens from another planet. Skaggs' message to Nashville here is, "I may be a little bit of an upstart to you guys, but I'm basically just a good ole boy who can't make heads or tails of this kind of thing." The "Country Boy" video, which was probably seen by many more people than will ever tune in a country radio station, only confirms the worst image of country artists: corny rubes who have no connection to the rest of the country.

For all this, however, Skaggs is undeniably the most important figure in the hard country movement just now: he sells the most records, he commands the most respect, and he is, in matters of technique, hard country's most impressive musician. He reminds both the country industry and his audience of its invaluable but all too often disparaged heritage by covering compositions by the Stanley Brothers and Lester Flatt and by updating their styles. And there is no getting away from the pleasures of his music: when his plaintive sweet-and-sour voice howls the lyric of "Patiently Waiting" or "Heartbroke," you realize what you've been missing from country radio for lo these many years.

Oddly—or perhaps appropriately—enough, Skaggs' noble sentiments and sensible ideas about returning country music to its roots are more unself-consciously presented on his recent production work with the Whites. Even aside from Skaggs's personal stake in the matter—Buck, Sharon and Cheryl White are, respectively, his father-in-law, his wife and his sister-in-law—Skaggs has helped the Whites achieve a lusty spiritedness that is sometimes missing on his own impeccable but rather dry albums. On two recent Whites albums, *Old Familiar Feeling* (1983) and *Whole New World* (1985) (the latter co-produced with Marshall Morgan), Skaggs has made the Whites' essential appeal clearer than it's ever been on record. Whereas on his own records Skaggs' intersection of country generations—1950s bluegrass and honky-tonk meets 1980s rock technology and revisionism—is metaphorical, with the Whites it's actually there in their harmonies: Buck White, contemporary of revisionist heroes George Jones and Buck Owens, vocalizing with Sharon and Cheryl, whose singing has been influenced as much by Emmylou Harris as it is by Kitty Wells.

What are the implications of the hard country singers? Does their success signal a return to the verities and an industry rejection of pop crossover? Not hardly. Having tasted the profits from the *Urban Cowboy* era, the country industry will never tire of trying to find a way to attract that pop audience—in other words, there'll always be an Exile. And it bears saying that industry acceptance of hard country has been grudging at best; sure, everyone professes to admire Ricky and Reba and George, but as I write this, a middle-aged hard-country crazy like Carmol Taylor is cutting excellent records in comparative obscurity. Which is to say, Skaggs and Company haven't been so successful that they've started a trend in which anyone with a twang and pedal steel accompaniment can get signed for a couple of albums. In Nashville, it's still much better to be an Alabama rip-off than a smart whippersnapper developing original variations on Webb Pierce and Faron Young. (Say a prayer for whippersnapper Dwight Yoakam, who is mixing Webb and Faron with rock 'n' roll and is now the owner of a freshly signed contract with Warner Bros. Records.)

The problem, it would seem, boils down to this: the country music industry persists in thinking that it can compete in audience size and pop-cultural outreach with the rock industry. A more realistic and healthy assessment might be that country music's audience is more similar to the ones that appreciate jazz, the blues, or rap music: smaller than rock's, but in some ways even more passionate, more knowledgeable, more committed. It is to these people that Ricky and Reba and George appeal. Far from being throwback reactionaries, or representing the last gasp of a dying industry, they suggest the enduring appeal of country music.

Are You Sure Hank Done It This Way?

David Gates

What I'm about to say has to be prefaced by a couple of Don't Get Me Wrongs. Don't Get me wrong: country music for me is *hard* country, by which I mean not just Hank, Haggard and Jones, but a whole tradition that includes Roscoe Holcomb, Ralph Stanley and North Carolina fiddler Tommy Jarrell. Don't get me wrong: I love all these new records by Ricky Skaggs, George Strait, Reba McEntire, the Whites, the Judds and the rest of the Nashville neoconservatives. And don't get me wrong: I loathe most crossover country, from softcore Millsappery to the dreary peppiness of Alabama, Exile, and the other undistinguishables. Yet today's neotraditional country music still makes me uncomfortable. And I think I know why.

The Skaggs-Strait-McEntire movement is hardly the first time a back-to-basics impulse has been felt in country music. Song lyrics have always romanticized (or de-romanticized) the Tennessee Mountain Home, and the barnyard iconography of mules, haybales and bib overalls has always been embarrassingly ubiquitous. And certain performers have deliberately suppressed their progressive urges in order to develop—or in order not to alienate—a popular following. Earl Scruggs cranked out "Foggy Mountain Breakdown" and "Flint Hill Special" for years before he ventured into country-rock, and Doc Watson was playing electric guitar in a country-western band when he discovered there was more money in taking his D-28 on the college circuit.

But while country music purism, or at least quasi-purism, is nothing new, it's never before been promoted so vigorously by the music industry, and it's never before been associated with so many young performers. Older singers like Kitty Wells continue to do the songs that made them famous in the musical style that was current when they were young. There's nothing unusual about this: they have a loyal and conservative audience to please. But Skaggs, Strait, McEntire and company are rediscovering, recreating and reworking music that doesn't really belong to their era and implicitly criticizing their contemporaries and immediate predecessors for going too far.

This is something new. The country music demigods who are revered by today's Nashville neocons—Ernest Tubb, Bob Wills, Hank Williams—were not purifiers or reactionaries. In fact, they were progressives, even iconoclasts, who adulterated country music to suit their own imperatives. Ernest Tubb armed his sidemen with electric guitars so they could be heard over the noisy crowds in honky-tonks; Bob Wills introduced hot choruses and horn sections because he

Reprinted from *The Journal of Country Music* 11.1 (1986), 9-11 by permission of The Country Music Foundation and the author.

thought they sounded good. Certainly they were betrayers of what was currently country music tradition, and they were resisted as such by the Grand Ole Opry, which held out against electric guitars and drums long past the point where it was silly to do so.

Satisfying as today's neocon country music is, there's something offputtingly didactic about it, too. When Skaggs puts Bill Monroe in his video, or when Strait includes a Hank Williams song in his concert set, we're being lectured at even as we're being entertained: attention is being called to a neglected master. Hank, needless to say, never done it that way—he was too busy trying to outsell Roy Acuff. This is partly a question of temperament, of course. But it's also a sign of the times: people don't start to value tradition unless that tradition is imperiled.

This heightened awareness of tradition has fostered a heightened self-consciousness, as if today's performers had always wanted to be country music stars and are now watching themselves impersonate them. Of course there's always been a note of unreality about country stardom: a scene in which the fledgling star is astonished to find himself singing on the same stage as a onetime idol is obligatory in country music autobiographies. But among the country neocons, the unreality is aggravated by their remoteness from the cultural mainstream. Earlier singers came from environments where county music was the norm and they essentially ratified the esthetic values of the communities in which they grew up. (Their often-rebellious choice of music as a career, of course, is something else again.) But nowhere is country music the norm anymore: even in the deepest South, rock 'n' roll is more fashionable, thanks to television, radio and records. Like everybody else their age, Skaggs, Strait and McEntire grew up listening to the Beatles. For them to have become country singers—especially *purist* country singers—was less a matter of role-modeling than of role-playing. When Loretta Lynn dreamed of being the next Kitty Wells, she was dreaming of supplanting a popular contemporary. When George Strait dreams of being the new Tommy Duncan, or Ricky Skaggs the new Bill Monroe, it's a more rarefied fantasy. Their emulation of distant figures out of a legendary past suggest a rejection of the here-and-now.

And musically, what choice do they have? That is, if they're going to play country music at all. The history of country music has come to a point at which its very identity is threatened. In the early days of country music, it was possible to tell a Kentucky fiddler from a Mississippi fiddler from a Texas fiddler. By the 1940s such regional distinctions had become meaningless; by the early 1960s, the center of hard country music wasn't Nashville but Bakersfield, California. The next step was predictable: just as country music became one big nonregional music, country and rock and pop began to meld into one generalized American music. (Eventually American music itself may be a regional component in some form of world pop music. It's already hard to tell African pop from Jamaican pop from American new-wave dance music, and country fans should check out the steel guitar on King Sunny Ade's records.)

What this suggests to me is that hard country, and its currently popular successor, the neotraditional country of Skaggs, Strait and McEntire, is a historical musical form which will continue to have its devotees—including me—but can never grow and change except within narrow limits and, like Gregorian chant or revival string-band music, can never again be at the cutting edge. And hence my discomfort. The Nashville neocons are making it clear that the limits of country music have been defined and that forward progress has stopped. Delightful as it is to hear the steel guitar once again on the radio, the Skaggses, Straits and McEntires can only do their music by willfully closing their ears, limiting their influences and circumscribing the bounds of the permissible. And that's not the way Hank done it.

Alison Krauss and the Contemporary-Traditional Conflict in Modern Bluegrass

Mark Fenster

Bluegrass was developed as a style of commercial country music in the early and mid-1940s by Bill Monroe and the Bluegrass Boys[1] and was initially produced and distributed by the same media institutions as the best selling country artists of the day. As Neil Rosenberg describes, the rise of the "bluegrass community," the belief that bluegrass was a special form of acoustic country music that needed to be preserved, and even the name "bluegrass" itself were the result of a number of developments, including the withdrawal of support for bluegrass by mainstream country music record labels and radio programmers, as well as various periods of (relatively limited) public interest in bluegrass due to its association with the urban folk revival, the use of bluegrass for film and television soundtracks (e.g. *Deliverance* and *The Beverly Hillbillies*) and the success of outdoor bluegrass festivals.

The current position of bluegrass as a "specialty" or "niche" music with a highly organized community of support places bluegrass artists in the middle of two overlapping conflicts. First, bluegrass musicians must follow the recognized and somewhat rigid conventions of the genre, which dictate the kinds of instruments that can be played and, within a certain range, the ways in which they can be played, in order for their music to be considered bluegrass by the genre's very knowledgeable and vocal fans. At times this conflicts with an artist's or band's desire to construct an individual style and to set themselves apart from other artists in the marketplace, whether through vocal style, musicianship, or songwriting. Thus at specific points in the history of the genre—most obviously in the rise of "progressive" and "new grass" bluegrass that incorporated jazz and rock instruments and sounds—deviation from accepted conventions was considered controversial within the bluegrass community, and a number of arguments ensued over what "was" and "wasn't" bluegrass. Second, bluegrass is constructed around a number of revered musical and cultural traditions that at times conflict with artists who attempt to be more contemporary in sound, lyrics and physical appearance. In other words, to be contemporary sometimes means being in conflict with the strong traditions of bluegrass.

For musicians to reach and please the bluegrass audience, they must remain faithful to bluegrass as a genre and "traditional" form; for bluegrass artists to reach a wider audience and increase record sales and their ability to earn a living as professional musicians, they must also attempt to become

317

contemporary stars who can both live within and move beyond the conventions and traditions of bluegrass. Given the limited size of the bluegrass market, expanding the base of support for bluegrass is an important goal of most successful bluegrass artists, businesses and the relatively new bluegrass trade organization, the International Bluegrass Music Association. Yet for many bluegrass fans the attempt by artists to broaden the music and reach new audiences often brings with it the risk of sacrificing the genre and its traditions. The problem for bluegrass artists and bands who want to expand their audience base is to resolve these conflicts by becoming a star who can master and transcend bluegrass conventions in order to become both a traditional and contemporary performer.

It is within this context that Alison Krauss' rise to the top of the national bluegrass scene has occurred, and her success displays these conflicts and their resolutions. Krauss, a 19 year-old fiddler, vocalist and leader of the band Union Station have become a major attraction both on the bluegrass festival circuit and in the showcase clubs and folk festivals that draw non-bluegrass fans. Her recent solo album, *I've Got That Old Feeling*, has become one of the top-selling bluegrass albums of the past few years. For some members of the bluegrass community, her success with non-bluegrass audiences, the fact that she is not from a "normal" bluegrass background, the promotion and attention that she has received from the bluegrass industry and the mainstream media and the instrumental arrangements on her third album—which include piano and drums and exclude or downplay the use of the banjo—mark her as challenging the traditions of bluegrass in order to sell more records. In addition, the acceptance of women as bluegrass musicians, particularly vocalists, is a relatively new phenomenon. There were few if any women in bluegrass before the mid-1960s, and it is only in the past few years that female musicians/band leaders/singers like Krauss, Laurie Lewis and Lynn Morris have been able to establish themselves in the national bluegrass scene. Krauss is the first *female* bluegrass star, and the female voice represents a deviation from bluegrass conventions and traditions.

However, her avowed devotion to the music, her recognition as a top bluegrass vocalist and fiddler who is able to carry on and innovate within the music's traditions and her very public attempt to promote bluegrass in interviews has helped to gain her acceptance within the bluegrass mainstream and also construct her as a public figure who is attempting to protect bluegrass as a "traditional" form of music. Thus Krauss and her record company's very public attempts to resolve the tension between her position as a bluegrass artist who is able to reach non-bluegrass audiences represent an important example of the development of a contemporary bluegrass star who does not abandon or betray the crucial notion of bluegrass as a traditional form of music.

The Rise of Alison Krauss and Union Station

Like many contemporary bluegrass performers, Alison Krauss was not brought up in a family from the southern part of the United States that played bluegrass, old-time, or country music. Raised in the college town of

Champaign, Illinois, the daughter of a real estate agent and rental property owner, Krauss' background is not a "natural" one for a bluegrass musician; in fact, her first exposure to bluegrass and old-time music was from her mother trying to learn banjo from an instruction book.[2] Her parents noticed her musical talent early in her childhood as she was learning classical violin. As a young girl she began to take up old-time fiddle playing, competing in local, regional and finally national contests from the time she was eight years-old. Because she was not from a family or an area where old-time music was prevalent, her main method of learning was from books and records, as well as from watching others playing at contests.

At thirteen, Krauss won her first major contest, the fiddle championship at Winfield, Kansas. She began to play in bluegrass bands in the Midwest and was at one point a member of two bands simultaneously: one, based in Indianapolis, was a progressive, New Grass Revival-type band called Classified Grass, and the other, based in Champaign and called Silver Rail, leaned more towards the traditional and contemporary. The latter band, which would ultimately become Union Station, included songwriter/musician John Pennell, who would make audio cassettes for Krauss. These included both the founders and newer artists of bluegrass so that she could learn more about the genre, its traditions and its various singing and instrumental styles.

In 1985, with a 14-year old Alison Krauss singing and playing fiddle, Union Station was beginning to play dates throughout the Midwest. It won the Best New Bluegrass Band contest at the 1986 Kentucky Fried Chicken Bluegrass Music Festival in Louisville, Kentucky, enabling it to secure a spot at the prestigious Newport Folk Festival that year and ultimately helping lead to a contract for Krauss with Rounder Records. The first record released by Rounder was an Alison Krauss solo album, recorded in Nashville with many of the best-known young bluegrass musicians, including Sam Bush and Bela Fleck from New Grass Revival. The record was warmly received within the bluegrass community, and the band was able to tour more extensively around the country, including a return to Newport and an invitation to play at the Vancouver Folk Festival. In addition, Krauss was asked to play on the Masters of the Folk Violin tour sponsored by the National Council for the Traditional Arts. As Union Station became established performers on the bluegrass circuit, it was signed in 1987 by Keith Case and Associates, one of the most prestigious bluegrass and folk booking agents in Nashville.

The second album on Rounder, *Two Highways*, featured Krauss and Union Station and was more of a bluegrass band album than the initial solo record. The album included a few up-tempo instrumentals and a version of a classic bluegrass song. It also featured another lead vocalist, in addition to Krauss, and had a more traditional bluegrass sound. Meanwhile, as Union Station became a full-time touring act and Alison Krauss increasingly became its central focus, the band went through a series of line-up changes. Presently, Krauss is the only member of the band who played on the *Two Highways* album. In addition to Krauss, the current Union Station line-up includes Alison Brown, a banjo player from California who had played with the progressive/contemporary New England bluegrass band Northern Lights and three former members of the more traditional East Tennessee band Dusty Miller.

Krauss' second solo record, *I've Got That Old Feeling*, was released in 1990 and has been phenomenally successful, selling far more copies than the previous two albums, indeed, more than most bluegrass records, and winning a Grammy award for Best Bluegrass Performance. Prior to that album, Krauss had received a good deal of attention from non-bluegrass media due to her age and gender as well as her talent, but in 1990 she was written about twice in *Billboard* and once each in *Musician, Rolling Stone, Newsweek,* as well as in other mainstream publications. In addition, the record has been well supported by Rounder, who hired an independent promoter to help Krauss and the album received media attention. The promoter featured the album in its major bluegrass retail promotion, produced two music videos from it and pitched it to commercial country radio stations as well. Krauss became recognized not only as one of the top figures in bluegrass, but also as one of its younger, contemporary artists; one who is able to make the music appeal to a wider audience. As Ken Irwin of Rounder has said, in her ability to reach new audiences Alison Krauss may be able to do more to promote bluegrass than all of the efforts of the International Bluegrass Music Association.[3]

The Recordings of Alison Krauss

Alison Krauss' three albums on Rounder Records have included two solo records and one album with Union Station. While the first two records worked within the conventions of contemporary bluegrass albums, the most recent album stretches those conventions in its arrangements and prevalence of slow ballads. Krauss' first album, *Too Late to Cry*, was recorded in Nashville with some of the best-known contemporary and progressive bluegrass musicians. It is part of what Neil Rosenberg has called the trend towards "studio-star albums" in bluegrass; albums which feature a relatively small group of established musicians who play on a number of other artists' recordings on a regular basis. The presence of some of the most respected names in the business on her debut album gave Krauss a certain degree of credibility as both a musician (keeping up and playing along with some of the "hottest" bluegrass musicians) and artist (she was able to get these "big stars" to play on her album). Since their playing is so recognizable for many bluegrass fans—Jerry Douglas' Dobro playing is easily distinguishable, as is Sam Bush's mandolin style—her first record seemed less a debut than it did a recording that fit into mainstream trends and sounds of contemporary bluegrass. In addition, the fact that the album is mainly composed of new songs rather than traditional songs or "classic" bluegrass compositions—eight of the eleven songs were written by young bluegrass songwriters and six of them by then-Union Station bassist John Pennell—also marks the record as a relatively "mature," professional album rather than the work of a young amateur.

Too Late to Cry mixes a number of different styles and arrangements that work within the conventions of contemporary bluegrass. The dominant instruments taking lead and playing the melody are Krauss' fiddle, the banjo, mandolin, Dobro and, with less frequency, guitar. There are two classic up-tempo bluegrass songs kicked off by the banjo,[4] and three somewhat slower, mid-tempo songs which also feature the banjo as well as the fiddle and mandolin.[5] Two fiddle songs, one the traditional song "Dusty Miller" and the other a contemporary song composed by banjo player Tony Trischka, feature Krauss' playing along with a banjo. Three slow-tempo ballads in waltz time include lead and melody playing by combinations of guitar, dobro, fiddle and mandolin and omit the banjo. These latter songs sound more like "folk" or acoustic country and work less within the conventions of bluegrass than the others on the album, both because of their rhythm and the absence of the banjo. In fact, one of the three ballads, "Song For Life," was written by country singer/songwriter Rodney Crowell and has been recorded by a number of folk and country performers. But despite these songs, the album still fit well within the conventions and parameters of a studio-star bluegrass album.

Two Highways, the first album with Alison Krauss and Union Station, places Krauss within a bluegrass band context. Four of the twelve songs are sung by Jeff White, who at that time was guitar player for the band, and, with two instrumentals, Krauss' lead vocals are limited to half of the album's songs. Again, most of the songs are contemporary-sounding bluegrass and three of them are by John Pennell. Like many bluegrass band albums, however, there is some variety to the material, including one gospel song (backed only by a guitar) and two up-tempo instrumental tunes (the traditional "Beaumont Rag" and "Windy City Rag," composed by Kenny Baker, one of Bill Monroe's most famous fiddlers) in swing rhythms. The album's mix of singers, arrangements, tempo and songs place it firmly within the conventions of the bluegrass band album in which each member of the band is highlighted on different songs and the album provides a wide variety of repertoire for the band to perform live.

However, Krauss' third album, *I've Got That Old Feeling*, represents a departure from the studio-star album and the bluegrass band album formats, although it is close enough to the former that it remains identifiable, for some bluegrass fans, as a bluegrass album. Like *Too Late to Cry*, the album features a number of well-known bluegrass musicians playing with Krauss, including Jerry Douglas (who co-produced the album with engineer Bill VornDick, who had produced *Two Highways*), Sam Bush and Stuart Duncan *Old Feeling* also includes new songs by younger songwriters, including three by John Pennell and four by Sidney Cox (a member of the Cox Family, a bluegrass band from Louisiana). However, this album, unlike the previous ones, has far less banjo, fewer up-and mid-tempo songs with standard bluegrass arrangements and includes a piano on four songs and drums on three. Neither the piano nor the drums—which are not part of the accepted instrumentation of bluegrass—dominate the arrangements or mix of the recording; the drums lay back with the rhythm guitar and bass, while the piano provides some fill-in phrases between vocal lines and song introductions in ways similar to the fiddle and other instruments on the album. In addition, the album has a much larger number of ballads than either of the two previous records. At least half of the twelve songs are either slow waltzes or feature slow tempos in duple meter (2/4 or 4/4). None of these aspects of the record are new or radical departures; instead, they mark the record as a bluegrass record blended with elements of folk and acoustic country.

I've Got That Old Feeling has been both Krauss' most successful record to date, garnering critical praise in mainstream periodicals and very high sales levels for a bluegrass album. It has also been her most controversial album, causing much debate within the bluegrass community. The elements that separate this album from the previous two—the arrangements that include piano and drums, the prevalence of ballads, the absence of banjo except on a few tracks—may have made the album more acceptable outside bluegrass, but within it they constitute (for some within the bluegrass community) a challenge to the genre's accepted musical practices.

Constructions of Alison Krauss
Within the Bluegrass and Mainstream Media

Reviews of her records and feature articles about her career in mainstream periodicals consistently construct Krauss' music as lying on the borders between the traditional and contemporary and between the conventions of the genre and the innovations of the creative artist. In rock-oriented *Musician* and *Rolling Stone* , for example, she is described as making "traditional bluegrass seem utterly contemporary—a rare accomplishment at any age" (Macnie), and she and Union Station "may have that old feeling, but it definitely has a few new twists" (Wild 48). Given the marginality of bluegrass within the mainstream record industry, the appearance of even short articles about a bluegrass performer in these magazines is rather extraordinary, and it certainly makes sense that the writers describe Krauss' music or draw comparisons in ways that would be recognizable for their readership. (For example, she is described as having "old-time country soul" and her "haunting vocals recall the early Dolly Parton.") In a sense, these articles articulate the tension in bluegrass between the creative star and the conventions and ensemble unit of bluegrass, as well as the tension between bluegrass as "traditional" and bluegrass as a contemporary commercial form of music. The writers imply that Krauss is an individual creator representing a traditional form of folk music, while simultaneously working within and transcending the genre within which she works.[6]

The sense of her music as operating on the borders between traditional and contemporary is replicated in interviews she gives as well as in press kits and press releases distributed by the band, its publicist and the record company. One interview, in the important "Artist Developments" section of *Billboard* , explicitly deals with this issue. Krauss states that, "We [Union Station] try to stay in the circle of traditional bluegrass. When we do new stuff it's done tastefully, so that nobody says, 'Why did they do that? Why did they play that lick, or end that song like that?'...There's definitely room for new music in bluegrass, so long as it's played in the circle" (Bessman). The circle thus serves as a metaphor for the genre and for tradition. Krauss constructs herself, within an article that notes her "loyalty to tradition" and her "faithful[ness] to bluegrass' structural roots," as playing new material within this circle—in other words, remaining a bluegrass musician while retaining a degree of personal style and artistry.

The band's press kit and a record company press release promoting Krauss' second solo album replicate this sense of her as working creatively within the "circle." The press kit, a very professional twelve-page booklet intended for concert and festival promoters as well as for media outlets, features a group picture and description of the band's accomplishments, as well as portraits and biographies of the individual band members. The band is constructed as new, young and accomplished. Each of the band members' biographies lists awards that they have won individually and as a group, as well as the other groups and bluegrass stars with whom they have performed. The group biography describes them as combining the traditional with the contemporary: "Together these five musicians create a sound which combines the drive and feeling of the best traditional bluegrass with the acoustic textures of contemporary country music."

The Rounder Records press release for *I've Got That Old Feeling*[1] makes this combination at once more explicit and more problematic:

> Bluegrass, Alison's idiom of choice, is a difficult one to work in given the traditional nature of its parameters. The sound of Appalachia has never been the most cosmopolitan, and therefore there's an inherent nostalgia to it, stemming from its old-timey acoustic instrumentation. Yet under Krauss' adept and gentle touch, these songs live and breathe and are as "cutting edge" as any form of music. The vitality she breathes into the songs gives them a passion and a sense of belonging to the here and now.

Like the band press kit, this description of Krauss and her music places her within the practices of bluegrass in order to promote her as a bluegrass performer. It goes further, however, by setting up an opposition between bluegrass—difficult, traditional, nostalgic and old-timey (used here to refer to both the musical genre and the adjective)—and Krauss—one who autonomously "chooses" bluegrass, who is adept, "cutting edge," vital and working in the "here and now"—the latter term encompasses and appropriates the former into a new, independent creation. Within this construction, Krauss' music (as well as that of her band) transcends the duality between traditional and contemporary in representing a new, individual musical entity.

This is not the only such construction at work; interviews with and articles about Krauss in bluegrass and mainstream music publications often note her faithfulness and devotion to bluegrass. An article from the *Associated Press* wire notes that, "Though still a teenager, she has firm views about bluegrass music and what she will and won't do.... Although she has a recording contract with an independent label, she's not ready to jump to a more prestigious label. 'We want to play bluegrass music and if somebody signed us, it would be totally something else,' she said" (Edwards). A number of interviews and articles continue this theme: in the *Musician* article she is quoted as having said,

"I'm not striving for a hit. We just want to play bluegrass" (Macnie). An article in one of the Nashville, Tennessee daily newspapers, which describes the interest that major country music labels have shown in her, states that, "Krauss remains more interested in continuing to grow musically than in pursuing the brass ring of stardom. 'We just want to play what we play and try to do it better all the time' " (Goldsmith). And, in a bluegrass publication, she describes her respect for the music and its tradition, saying, "A lot of people spend much of their lives in bluegrass, and have given up a lot for the music. I would like to be able to give back as much to it as I've gotten out of it" (Neill). In fact, her respect for bluegrass leads her to take on the role of missionary in some interviews. "I just want people to get a chance to hear bluegrass music. I think the only reason it isn't more popular is just that people haven't been lucky enough to hear it" (Wild).

I am not arguing that this is some marketing ploy used to sell records. Krauss' love of bluegrass and her desire to reach new listeners and get them interested in it is quite sincere. Rather, it is crucial to note that these public constructions of Krauss continually work within and further illustrate both the notion of bluegrass as a traditional form of alternative music with a relatively small audience and the conflicts faced by a younger artist who must balance both the "traditional" and the "contemporary" while trying to reach new listeners. The same *Associated Press* feature that noted her faithfulness to bluegrass, represents this tension well, describing how Krauss "refuses to play such bluegrass standards as 'Orange Blossom Special,' 'Rocky Top' and 'Fox on the Run.' 'Our goal is to play our own music,' she said. 'Haven't people heard those song enough yet'?" (Edwards).

Within bluegrass, these tensions between traditional and contemporary and between the genre and the innovative artist are often the source of public arguments concerning how performers can and should expand the musical and commercial limits of bluegrass. Through her first two albums, *Bluegrass Unlimited* had given unwavering support for Krauss' work. The review of her first record was highlighted and described the album as "one of the most important new releases of the last few years....The performances are flawless and surrounded by a first-rate production effort that has definite crossover possibilities that could return bluegrass to the country music mainstream" (Martin). A profile of Union Station seven months later introduces the band in similarly glowing terms, describing them as possessing "superb musicianship and a love for the style" (Kubetz). As Krauss and the band gained in stature within the bluegrass community, the magazine noted both her commitment to the genre and her ability as a musician and singer.

However, *Bluegrass Unlimited's* review of *I've Got That Old Feeling* (Kleinke 51) was overwhelmingly negative and was followed, two issues later, by a number of published letters in response.[8] Significantly, both the original review and the responses to it discuss not only the album's music but its position within the bluegrass industry and the music industry as a whole. The review, by J.D. Kleinke, describes how the author had been a vocal supporter of Krauss through her first two records. ("When [her] first record hit the airwaves a few years back, the unfamiliar voice was so fresh, evocative and exciting, I used to pull off the road to listen.") The reviewer was thus "surprised" that he found the new record instantly forgettable. For Kleinke, Krauss' singing on the album "betrays her youth"—(her "overuse of vibrato" makes her sound "like a teenager singing about grown-up stuff"). The "new tunes are softer core and seem to be holding her back." The album is "overproduced," and its "edges are rounded off." He concludes that, "Rounder is trying to capture a larger audience, but is afraid to take decisive action in any particular direction," either towards a folk or country instrumentation and audience. The review ends on this note:

> I recognize that many people prefer silky-edged, presweetened, pop-type music and they very well may love this album. Who knows? If Rounder finds its way in enough of the right offices in commercial radioland, maybe it will win a lot of people over to acoustic music.
>
> But for this loyal fan of Ms. Krauss' work, this album is a disappointment, a squandering of her tremendous musical gift.

The implications here are clear. Krauss' record, which fails to adequately follow the conventions of bluegrass, represents the intrusion of commercial aspirations in an effort to transcend the limits of the bluegrass audience. Rounder is the active agent attempting to carry this work, that it has tainted, into non-bluegrass institutions ("commercial radioland"). This scenario suggests the opposite of the ideal; that the bluegrass industry, as a non-intrusive commercial structure, can resolve the tension between commerce and tradition. For Kleinke, commerce has proven victorious, and bluegrass has lost the talents of a rising young star, at least for this record.

BU published eight letters that responded directly to Kleinke's review in its February 1991 issue,[9] seven of which defended the record. Many of the seven letters touched on the same arguments, the most frequent of which was that Krauss has the potential to appeal to a wider audience and can help to popularize bluegrass like other former bluegrass stars who had crossed over into country music. Phil Leadbetter of Hendersonville, Tennessee wrote that, "I'm glad to see artists like Alison Krauss release music to large medias [sic]. We need to support these artists, instead of slur their CDs." Sarah Wasson of Clay City, Kentucky, argued that, "Alison is doing for bluegrass now what needs to be done. She is helping bluegrass to be heard by the world and [the reviewer] recommends not listening to the album. Therefore, I can't see where he wants much for bluegrass." Gene Howell of Louisville, Kentucky, stated that Kleinke "probably took the same tone when Ricky Skaggs, Keith Whitley, the Whites, Vince Gill, etc. achieved success on country radio." For these letter writers, Krauss' music is helping to expand the bluegrass audience by reaching new listeners without utterly sacrificing the genre. Therefore, what she is doing is ultimately a benefit for bluegrass, and it is the reviewer whose slurs and criticisms are most harmful to the music.

Another recurring theme within the letters is an objection to Kleinke's implicit definition of bluegrass which excludes Krauss' album. Sarah Wasson asserted that Krauss' album *is* a bluegrass record and that Kleinke only seems to like "highly strict traditional bluegrass music" which few bands and no woman can successfully emulate. Brian Hall of Missoula, Montana, stated that while he too felt some of the "softer-edged" songs were a bit weak, the record as a whole was quite good and Kleinke was apparently suffering from "hardening of the categories"—too strict a sense of what constitutes bluegrass. These arguments concerning definitions of what is and is not bluegrass simultaneously attempt to construct a definition and use it to place Krauss and her record within or outside the genre.

Significantly, a number of letter-writers also defended Rounder Records and Krauss' relationship with the label. For example, Lou Martin of Albany, New York (who had written the very favorable *BU* review of Krauss' first album), asserted that Rounder, rather than trying to manipulate its artists in order to make a hit record, works with their artists to make both popular records and records that are "directionally positive for the future of the music." In addition, Martin argued that Krauss is not a pliable youth manipulated by a greedy label but instead is a "powerfully charismatic band leader who points the way for other musicians by towering personal example." This is a much different construction than that of the reviewer. For this letter-writer, this album does not represent a selling out of the traditions of bluegrass for commercial gain, but rather represents an artistic statement by a great performer, released on a record label that allows such artists to challenge themselves and their music.

While only one letter in the February 1991 issue of *BU* directly defends Kleinke's review (applauding the magazine for writing a critical review, rather than agreeing with the position taken by the review), another letter written on a somewhat different subject directly agreed with Kleinke. Richard Dale of Wellsboro, Pennsylvania, in a letter that was not grouped together with those responding to the initial review, wrote to criticize what he saw as the "insidious presence" of "money, greed, commercialism, [and] big business" creeping into bluegrass through the "few, rich, powerful types who control everything and everyone they touch" in the bluegrass music industry. Significantly, Dale associated Alison Krauss with this presence, arguing that *I've Got That Old Feeling* , because it adds drums and piano and eliminates the banjo on a number of songs (particularly the title cut and first music video), represents a "cop out" and an insult to "those of us who love bluegrass the way it is." Krauss, Dale argued, should be "satisfied" with her career (he plays banjo for a band which is frustrated with its lack of success in obtaining a record contract) in bluegrass and should not be "bowing to the masses" in order to make more money. For Dale, Krauss has surrendered her music and the traditions of bluegrass to commerce and the rich, powerful figures lurking within the exploitative bluegrass industry.

At stake within these various constructions is both the placement of Alison Krauss within the bluegrass community and the operations of the artists and institutions that must resolve the tension between their roles in the commercial context of the music industry and the expected musical and social practices of the community. Whether Krauss and her record label have "softened" the edges of bluegrass or abandoned it all together in an effort to cross over to larger audiences is not simply a musical issue—it also challenges the "integrity" of the business institutions which produce and distribute bluegrass music as well as of the bluegrass community as a whole. For those who defend her, as well as for those mainstream media outlets that celebrate her, Krauss represents the potential for bluegrass to reach a wider audience and draw more people into the ranks of bluegrass fandom. Her album is not a crass commercial "sell out," but music that can please listeners who had been previously unaware of or who disliked bluegrass. Rounder is not exploiting Krauss or bluegrass but is pushing the music in a positive direction and helping to promote the genre. For those who criticize her, however, she and the institutions which produce and distribute her represent a further example of the intrusion of commerce into the precarious traditions and culture of bluegrass. As her career progresses, this tension will undoubtedly continue. The decision made by Krauss and Union Station to record their forthcoming album in a more traditional style will certainly appease critics within the bluegrass community (Krauss). But it may or may not be so well received by her newer listeners and the mainstream media—again, the recurring problem of tradition and commerce that bluegrass artists like Krauss must continually attempt to resolve.

Notes

[1]See Cantwell, this volume.

[2]This profile is based upon interviews with Fred and Louise Krauss (8 Nov. 1990) Alison Krauss (10 Feb. 1991), Ken Irwin (20 Nov. 1990) and Keith Case (20 Nov. 1990); Logan B. Neill, "Alison Krauss and Union Station," *Southern Bluegrass News* May-June 1990: 15-16; Rebecca Mabry, "The Queen of Bluegrass," *Champaign-Urbana News-Gazette*: 15 Feb. 1991, Weekend section, 6; and Rick Kubetz, "Union Station: Traditional, Progressive & Original," *Bluegrass Unlimited* Oct. 1988: 56-59.

[3]Irwin interview. When I told a number of other people in the bluegrass industry about this scenario, many of them agreed.

[4]"Too Late to Cry" and "Don't Follow Me."

[5]"Foolish Heart," "In Your Eyes" and "On the Borderline."

[6]Interestingly, this is the same kind of argument that has been at the core of rock criticism and ideology for more than two decades.

[7]Most of the press release was culled from the liner notes to *I've Got That Old Feeling*, which were written by Holly Gleason, a music critic and journalist based in Nashville.

[8]Krauss told me (Alison Krauss interview) that she had heard that the magazine received more mail in response to the review than it ever had received for anything that it had published.

[9]The eight letters responding to the review comprised the bulk of the letters section that month and constituted a large number of letters for any single topic in issue of the magazine—in fact, eight letters is the average number of total letters published in a

month.

Works Cited

Bessman, Jim. "New Bluegrass Feeling." *Billboard* 27 Oct. 1990.

Edwards, Joe. "Music's Gain Is Roller Skating's Loss." *Cleveland Plain Dealer* 7 Dec.1990.

Goldsmith, Thomas. "Alison Krauss Plays Second Fiddle to No One in Bluegrass." *Tennessean* 15 Sept. 1990.

Kleinke, J. D. Rev. of *I've Got That Old Feeling*, by Alison Krauss. *Bluegrass Unlimited* Dec. 1990.

Krauss, Alison. Interview. 10 Feb. 1991.

Kubetz, Rick. "Union Station: Traditional, Progressive and Original." *Bluegrass Unlimited* Oct. 1988: 56-59.

Macnie, Jim. "Alison Krauss: A 19-Year-Old's Old-Time Country Soul." *Musician* Feb. 1991.

Martin, Lou. Rev. of *Too Late to Cry* , by Alison Krauss. *Bluegrass Unlimited* March 1988.

Neill, Logan B. "Alison Krauss and Union Station." *Southern Bluegrass News* May-June 1990.

Rosenberg, Neil. *Bluegrass: A History* Urbana: U of Illinois P, 1985.

Wild, David. "New Faces: Alison Krauss." *Rolling Stone* 15 Nov. 1990.

Rosanne Cash Walks Her Own Line

Jan Hoffman

Trouble when you're searching and you ain't so very young
Can't fit into table talk but you can't hold back your tongue
You have what they all desire so you must want it too
Looking for a corner to back my heart into.

"Looking for a Corner," Rosanne Cash, 1982

She doesn't look at all like the sultry gamine on her album covers. Her hair, once a purple bob, then an orange bristle, is back to its original inky shade and scatters wild at her shoulders. Her exotic features, now makeup free, look nearly ordinary tonight; her tidy figure is swollen from the 10-plus pounds of the first trimester of pregnancy.

Over lunch she had gotten through the part about the father who was famous, absent, a drug addict and an occasional pyromaniac. Now it's after 10 p.m., and the tumble of children, guitar players, business associates, dogs, cats and a family assistant has finally slowed for the night. Into the bedroom, she beckons, for another installment of this perambulating interview.

Rosanne Cash is in full bloom, having just finished a 60-date tour for her fifth album, *King's Record Shop*, a choice grab bag of pop ballads, rockers and country tunes. This time round, she finally got it right: first the record, next the tour, then the baby. Usually she screws it up and tries to sabotage her career. Well. She had her reasons. Now all she's going to do for the next few months is lie back, get fat, send her daughters off to camp every day, maybe work on her short stories and, along with everyone else in Nashville, watch her album sales go gold.

Nashville is blooming again, too. The slump of the early 1980s is over: the city's showcase clubs are jammed every night, record sales are climbing and acts are being signed regularly. Rosanne Cash is not the only woman among the new crew who are crowding onto the charts. There's K.T. Oslin, Sweethearts of the Rodeo, k.d. lang and, of course, the Judds. Like so many of the guys who are making a stir—George Strait, Ricky Skaggs, Dwight Yoakam, Randy Travis, Ricky Van Shelton, the O'Kanes—they have rejected the bloated sound of the superstars who dominated country music for almost 20 years. While these

Reprinted from the *Village Voice Rock and Roll Quarterly* Summer 1988: 18-21, by permission of the Village Voice and the author.

so-called New Traditionalists have turned towards a kicky, cleaner mix of "authentic" country styles, their music often ends up sounding conventional, even conservative—the New Mainstreamers.

But within the same generation, another group of musicians have shaken country loose by owning up to their rock and blues roots: they play raucous, with lyrics that are rude and witty. Within Nashville's hip songwriting community, it is these artists—John Hiatt, Lyle Lovett, Steve Earle, John Prine, Steve Forbert, Guy Clark, Rodney Crowell—who enjoy a luminous, cult-worship status. Rosanne Cash is not only one of the first in this crowd—certainly she's the most successful—but she's still the only woman who's managed to stay on the rockin' rebel-country bus.

She's talking now about the making of her debut album, *Right or Wrong*, nine years ago. Like four of her albums, it was produced by her husband, singer-songwriter Rodney Crowell, who's just come into the bedroom.

"We were both pretty insecure and we were fighting a lot over stupid things in the studio," continues Rosanne. "I used to study engineering manuals at night and try to take over the boards. And we were doing a lot of cocaine."

Right or Wrong was the right album at the wrong time. Charming but tart, country with a snarl, a tight drummer and a rock 'n' roll guitarist, it featured many of the musicians who would wake Nashville up six years later—Rodney's former boss Emmylou Harris, Crowell himself, Ricky Skaggs, Cheryl and Sharon White and Tony Brown, now a senior vice-president at MCA Records. But 1979, in the words of Music Row's chief pest, *Tennessean* music critic Robert Oermann, "was the height of the Barbara Mandrell period." And *Right or Wrong* tendered no rhinestones, no demure girl-next-door: the front photo shows Rosanne in heels and jeans, a drink by her side; on the back, she's barefoot and dressed in a clinging black sheath, her mouth a carmine pout, her heavy-lidded stare both a come-on and a stop sign.

Rodney sits up on the pillows, leaning on his elbow, "I didn't say much then, but I was kind of resentful of you. I thought that you were given a chance to make records because you were Johnny Cash's daughter." Crowell, who's written and produced many hits for others, has just had his first number-one single ever.

Rosanne looks at him, steady and dead-on. "So you didn't think I was talented?"

Rodney doesn't back down. "I thought you were talented but I didn't think you had paid your dues enough to make a record. You had never slugged it out. And if your closest friend and lover was judging you that way, just imagine how other people were."

A grim exhaustion, as much from the stirred-up memories as the demands of the day, settles into her eyes. "People don't always pay dues in the same way," Rosanne replies. "There's no formal schedule of dues-paying, either. I just paid them in other ways. And I paid them later, believe me." Then she changes the subject.

She's feeling every new sensation
Giving in to each temptation
I know she'll pay after a while.

"Rosanna's Going Wild," Johnny Cash, 1968

The old man's crying tonight
'Cause it all happened so fast
He's frightened by the future
Embarrassed by the past.

"My Old Man," Rosanne Cash, 1984

Country Music fans consider themselves on a first-name basis with their stars, and stars are expected to grant them every consideration. After Rosanne's concerts, fans surge backstage to gape and tell her how beautiful she is, to fling meaty arms around her small shoulders and be photographed with her. They pat her belly and knowing, of course, that she has two daughters and a step-daughter, ask, "Hoping for a boy, right?" "Hoping for a baby," she replies cheerfully. Then somebody always needs to know, "So where's your dad, huh?" Her shoulders stiffen as it all rushes up again—the comparisons, the ambivalence, the danger zone. And she turns on them, smiling tightly, and says, "Hey, I'm a 33-year-old woman. I don't know how old you are, but do you still bring your dad with you wherever you go?"

There was a time when being known as Johnny Cash's kid, says Rosanne, "was definitely not cool." During the late 1950s and 1960s, in Southern California, where Rosanne and her three younger sisters were raised, country music was a joke, and her dad was considered a hick. But that was the least of it. There were all those mornings when she'd walk into her nice little Catholic girls' school and somebody would start in with the chant: "Hey, I heard your dad got arrested again."

On this sunny afternoon in Nashville, Rosanne's inhaling a generous, pregnant-lady lunch at an unprepossessing restaurant, where she sits almost unrecognized. That's the way she likes it, too, half-threatening to make a poster saying "Fame Kills." Throughout the lunch, waiters glance at her sideways, puzzled. She has the same tough set to her chin as her father, and like him, she can't help looking like Someone.

"That celebrity shit was with us all the time—the TV cameras in the living room, interviewing us. We all hated it. My mother is a really shy person, so it was really painful for her. I mean, the fucking Ku Klux Klan burned a cross on our front yard when I was six or seven years old. They hated my dad because he spoke out in favor of Indian rights and they said that my mom was black. And that hurt my mother so much.

"She's Italian, from San Antonio. Yeah, Italian Texans: grits marinara. That Italian passion and loyalty, that familial bond, mixed with that Southern nosiness, you know? She was incredibly overprotective when I was growing up. But she gave me a strong sense of how passionate motherhood can be. And also she went through a lot of shit and came out intact. Or, she was broken apart, and then put herself back together."

John Cash came from a large family of Scottish dirt farmers from Arkansas; Vivian Liberto was convent-school trained, the naive daughter of a prosperous insurance agent. They met while he was in the air force, married in 1954 and settled in Memphis. By the time Rosanne was born a year later, Cash had signed with Sun Records and was doing guest appearances with Elvis Presley, Carl Perkins, Jerry Lee Lewis, Johnny Horton and George Jones. By 1957, "I Walk the Line" was a national hit, he'd toured the States, Europe and the Far East, and had been on *American Bandstand* and *The Ed Sullivan Show*. He had also discovered Benzedrine, Dexamyl and Dexedrine. Within a few years he was well into a hefty amphetamine-barbiturate habit that lasted nearly a decade, during which he crashed, overturned and sank innumerable vehicles, trashed the stage of the Grand Ole Opry and nearly savaged his family. In 1959 he moved them to southern California.

"Once he moved us to Casitas Springs, northeast of Ventura. There was a great-looking mountain behind it that he really liked, so he just carved out the side, and so we sat in this nice big new house looking over this really poor community, population 400. And then he was gone all the time—whenever he was home, he upset the routine, things didn't feel normal. There were no children to play with. The people down below looked at us, like, who the fuck is this? At Christmastime he'd put giant speakers on the side of the mountain and blast Christmas carols down to the little community below. Then once he was up there on his tractor, and it sparked, he just fucked up, and set the whole fucking mountain on fire.

"In 1969 he won six CMA awards in one night," continues Rosanne, "and I went to school the next day and people said, 'Wow, your dad really cleaned up last night,' and I thought"—she sighs—"this is really nice. I finally didn't have to apologize for him."

Rosanne doesn't tell these stories easily—as if she's picking shards of glass out of her memory—and worries that the traumatic episodes will translate in print as "interview fodder." These days, she pursues the most aggressively normal lifestyle of any country music star in Nashville. She and Rodney live on a rural spread way out in the opposite direction from suburban Hendersonville, the turf prized by the *Homes of the Country Music Stars* guidebook, which includes Barbara Mandrell Boulevard, Porter Wagoner's Wife's House and House of Cash (a museum of sorts, distinct from Johnny Cash's Home, Johnny Cash Parkway, the Cash Game Preserve and Johnny Cash's Parents' Former Home).

"My dad definitely had heroic proportions. He wasn't a man you could sit down and talk to about like, what's going on in math class. He's sort of frightening. Incomprehensible. But he's also extremely literate and intelligent—that didn't come with his upbringing.

"My mom is not an artist. She likes to talk about details and she likes things small. She's not comfortable with things she doesn't understand, whereas he was seeking things he couldn't understand. She might have been able to go there, too. But instead, his addiction made her want to be more controlling

"My parents fought a lot at first," she said, "and then it went beyond fighting, and emotionally it got deadly." In 1966, when Rosanne was 11, her parents divorced. Johnny Cash married June Carter, the singer whose own troubled, talented clan are the Kennedys of country music.

Rosanne was a plump, lonely, angry kid who spent a lot of time in her room, listening to music: the Beatles, Tom Rush, Fleetwood Mac, Joni Mitchell, Traffic, the Band; Marty Robbins and Ray Charles, whom her mother played. But mostly she read and began writing "bad, mushy poetry." She refused to sing. "I learned piano, but I wouldn't learn guitar. It would have been like courting my dad's whole thing, the celebrity and the pain."

When Rosanne was 14 she started smoking pot and quickly stepped up to mescaline and acid, turning into a champion bad-Catholic-girl troublemaker. Her rage turned on her mother, who had remarried and was struggling to bridle her daughters. The day after Rosanne graduated from high school in 1973, she accepted her father's invitation and left California to travel with the Johnny Cash Show as laundress. Soon after, with her stepsister Rosey Carter, she sang backup. For three years they toured almost constantly. "Once my father pulled me aside and said, 'Here's a list of 100 essential country songs—you have to know them if you want to be my daughter'."

She fought it, ducked it, denied it. Went to London for a year, worked for CBS Records, who introduced her round as their "authority on country" (she'd snicker). Ate, cried and partied 30 pounds on, then headed home to Nashville and double-majored in English and drama at Vanderbilt University. Left and went to southern California to study acting at the Lee Strasberg Theatre Institute. When Ariola Records in Germany suggested Johnny Cash's daughter send them a demo of her songs, she relented; so far from the Nashville shadow, it would be a safe way to test her talent.

Needing a producer for the demo, she hired a married songwriter who was a friend of her stepsister, the singer Carlene Carter. Ariola fell in love with the songs and called her; Rosanne fell in love with the married producer and called her mother. Right on cue Vivian Cash said, "Give him up, honey, it'll never work" and kept sending her daughter rape whistles, mace and toilet seat covers for Christmas.

Rosanne flew to Germany to make the album. On arriving, she plunged into a paralyzing depression. "I had thought of myself as a songwriter, and I had no confidence in my voice. I couldn't get out of bed, couldn't talk. I wanted to die." Certain she was inviting in her father's troubles, "I kept thinking: 'If you really want to do this, there's no turning back'."

It took months to eke out the album and the experience only further "chipped away at my confidence." For solace, she wrote careful letters home to the producer, who was separating from his wife.

Rosanne got back to the States on the night of Carlene's debut-album party. The producer had mentioned he might show up. Her flight to L.A. was delayed and then customs took forever, so by the time she got into town, everyone had already left for Carlene's. She was nervous and late, but she knew she looked like hell, so she broke into Rosey's apartment and took a shower. He was at the party, waiting near the door for her. Within a few weeks, Rosanne Cash and Rodney Crowell moved in and started recording, performing, and doing drugs together.

To her secret relief, Ariola never released that first Rosanne Cash album. CBS, Johnny Cash's long-time label, also rejected it, but offered his daughter the chance to cut a new one. The company okayed Rodney as producer, which restored some of her confidence.

When *Right or Wrong* came out, it received a lot of attention from both pop and country critics and spun out two hit singles. Rosanne was 23—the same age as her father when he had his first hit—and was feeling more than a bit over-whelmed: She had a new husband, a two-year-old stepdaughter, her own infant, rising celebrity and an accelerating drug problem. CBS told her it was time to tour and promote her album. She respectfully declined, pleading motherhood, thinking failure.

> If you think you need a woman like me, you better hold on
> If you want to find out what I've got on my mind
> Baby, hold on.
>
> *"Hold On ,"Rosanne Cash, 1984*

It's a Big Time, nervous making, stars all-over-the-damn-place, country music scene; the barbecue before the evening taping of a Cinemax special at the chapel of Nashville's Fisk University. The concert honors two generations of country musicians—most of whom happen to be in the rebel rather than the mainstream tradition. It's also a celebration that country music has been brought back from the land of the dead.

Some of country's stalwarts are here—Bill Monroe, Waylon Jennings, Carl Perkins—standing apart like national monuments, signing autographs and suffering adulations loftily. (Merle Haggard's still back at the Shoney's Inn, resting.) Minnie Pearl swoops in for a shrill look-see. The mother-and-daughter Judds sweep through with glassy smiles for all, on stage even when they're not, makeup queens costumed in casual rehearsal-wear.

And here is the Man in Black's outlaw daughter, in a slapdash black T-shirt, black leggings, cowboy boots, her hair a raggedy mess, sunglasses, not even a faint dusting of the pouty star face she paints on for concerts and album covers.

She's not acting at all like the Country Music Hall of Fame's most recent inductee, but everyone, it seems, waves or stops by to pay her homage. John Hiatt, the rock 'n' roller who moved to Nashville and has written several songs for Rosanne (including "The Way We Make a Broken Heart") gives her a bear hug. Newcomer k.d. lang plops her plate of greens next to Rosanne, and they start gabbing about acupuncture, ginseng, papaya enzymes and deadly nightshades. At the next picnic table the Jordanaires, Elvis' backup boys turned gospel singers, with thinning blow-dried hair, pinky rings and matching lime-green blazers, salute Rosanne with barbecued drumsticks.

Nashville still doesn't know what to make of her. In concert, dressed like a smoky pop princess in New York-hip black outfits, backed by a band that—doesn't include a fiddler but does boast a skinhead drummer, she'll sing her latest number-one country single, the light-footed "Tennessee Flat Top Box" (written by her father in 1961). In the same evening she'll roar into Hiatt's "Pink Bedroom" ("She thinks all her boyfriends are so dumb / She drinks Coca-Cola with Valium") and play air guitar.

Bolstered by accumulating prizes (she won the 1985 Grammy for Best Female Country Vocalist and a 1987 BMI writing award), she sings her own ballads with a small, fierce smile of pleasure on her lips. She is not one of the great country interpreters, but she has a tenacious and sweet soprano. "When Rose talks in another room, you can hear this real pleasing quality to her voice," says Rodney, who calls himself her co-conspirator. "And when she laughs, it goes up an octave and it's even more pleasing—and that's her gift as a singer."

She just doesn't do stupid or false songs—what distinguishes her music is its meticulous, upending, direct language: "I'll play the victim for you, honey / But not for free" ("Blue Moon With Heartache"); "Numbness overcomes me now, like alcohol and fear" ("The Real Me"). "Most country songs go something like,'Oh honey / you left me / And now I'm so sad," says Rosanne. "I'm more interested in the hidden agenda: 'Oh honey / You left me / And why did I want to get you to do that?'" Although she is ambivalent about recording and performing them, her songs have an urgent explicitness—her fourth album, *Rhythm & Romance*, chronicles the adulteries, drug-taking and emotional dueling of two anguished, intelligent people. Taken together, her five albums—especially *King's Record Shop*—have the quality of a charged conversation between close friends: unsparing, intimate, self-doubting, excited.

Rosanne Cash became country music's first modern woman. "It was also her image that was so different," says Tony Brown, now a senior vice-president at MCA Records. "Ten years ago, there was nobody around in country music that the audience wanted to emulate: most artists were overweight, ugly, uncool and corny. And then came Rose." She was sexy but in a smoldering, understated manner—not a Tanya Tucker. "Rose was as fashionable as a rock star but she came from a blue-blood country heritage. Like, you can drop by her house and even if she's in her housecoat she still looks like she's in style. I mean, Rose is so cool."

Her second album, *Seven Year Ache*, was her commercial breakthrough and pressed what *Right or Wrong* had started. Rodney had whistled up his buddies from Emmylou Harris' Hot Band—including Ricky Skaggs, Hank Devito, Albert Lee and Tony Brown—and reconvened them as the Cherry Bombs, who hit weekend juke joints up and down California. "We sounded different, more raw, with more of a rock 'n' roll attitude. We were making such a stir in country music that being associated with Rodney and Rose was seriously raising my hip factor in this town," says Tony Brown. Nearly 10 years later, members of the Cherry Bombs, who are among Nashville's top studio musicians, still record and tour with Cash and Crowell (Brown just co-produced Rodney's album, *Diamonds & Dirt*).

But this was all cresting too early, 1980, 1981, 1982. "No one else jumped in because they didn't know how to get that sound, find those songs." By 1983, Rosanne was a mess, had stopped touring and writing. Tony Brown went to MCA. Within two years, Nashville was ready to hear more of Rosanne and Rodney's kind of music: Tony Brown, asked to revive MCA's country division, signed and recorded Steve Earle, Lyle Lovett, Nanci Griffith and Patty Loveless. The rough spareness of Earle's *Guitar Town*, says Brown, was influenced by Rodney; Patty Loveless reminds him of Rosanne when she was getting started.

When it finally got under way, the Cinemax concert was uneven. But there's a soaring middle section that's pretty damn wonderful, ruled in succession by Carl Perkins, Rosanne, John Hiatt and k.d. lang. Rosanne, her features heightened by makeup and wearing high-laced black boots, a capacious but thigh-high black blouse and low-slung belt, trips quickly onto the stage, crashing a red tambourine. Pointing to her belly and warning about hit-and-run guys, she swings into the rocking "My Baby Thinks He's a Train." Then Rodney joins her in the duet "No Memories Hangin' Round." They stand hip-to-hip, mouth-to-mouth at the mike; on this warm spring night in a church in a Bible Belt city, it's a blatantly erotic performance, undisguised and unrepentant.

> I don't think you know how bad you treat me
> But I can't live like a whore
> She thinks she's got the key to your heart
> Now I've got to wait by the door.
>
> *"Second to No One," Rosanne Cash, 1984*

Rosanne and Rodney moved to Nashville in 1981 from Los Angeles to get away from drugs and to raise their girls in a saner place. But the drugs followed them. After the success of *Seven Year Ache*, Rosanne suffered from incapacitating anxiety attacks and nightmares. While Rodney spent more and more time in town, producing records, she was alone, without housekeeping help, with the babies.

She couldn't meet her album-a-year contract and CBS kept putting her on probation. Pregnant with Chelsea, she unwillingly recorded *Somewhere in the Stars*, a respectable enough work with at least one stunner, "Looking for a Corner." But she did not care much for the album, scarcely promoted it, and slid into a severe six-month-long postpartum depression. She was feeling isolated, like a fraud, a songwriter who couldn't write. Her marriage was cracking up. She was doing a lot of drugs.

She entered a program in Atlanta. "I didn't want to leave my children in the dark about my problem, like I had been about my dad, so I told Caitlin why I was going away. She was about four and her attitude was one of like"— imitating her freckle-faced daughter, her expression regretful and mourning— " 'Oh Mom, what took you so long to figure this out?' She accepted it with relief. That was so painful."

"Rodney cleaned up on his own, but it took a really long time for me and him to get it right with each other again. You have to work to be in love. You think we're happy, right? Well, we earned it."

Within six weeks of finishing treatment, Rosanne, determined to reclaim herself as a musician, returned to the studio. It took a year to record, but she finally emerged with *Rhythm and Romance* . " I really came out on that album. I dyed my hair orange—it had been purple before so this was a big change, you understand. I felt like I had written some good songs, I was straight, it was a new world, and I was really liking it."

As she speaks, stray phrases of acoustic guitar music float through the windows; Rodney's out back with some of the guys, sitting around, trying to write a new song. "I don't much care for formal religion except that I'm interested in ritual as an art form," she says. "I do believe absolutely that there's a God, but there are many ways to find out about him or her. I pray a lot, mainly because I feel that gratitude is a real state of grace. And I really feel a lot of gratitude."

> This is the real me
> Breaking down at last
> Hey it's the real me
> Crawling out of my past
>
> *"The Real Me," Rosanne Cash, 1986*

"C'mon Rose, look sultry!"

She breaks up, and the photo opportunity is momentarily lost. On another afternoon, friends and record company people are hanging out at the house, shooting possible covers for the next album before Rosanne gets enormous. She keeps pulling antique clothing from her closet and poses luxuriantly on today's prop, a white linen couch set out on her rolling, spring-green yard. Unseen: two giggling little girls, ducking behind the couch, who make off with their mother's Kenneth Cole black high heels as soon as she takes a break.

Rodney, who's toting a six-string; Stewart Smith, their young speed-of-light lead guitarist; and Rosanne flop on the grass, eating strawberries and casually harmonizing on some Ry Cooder and T Bone Burnett songs, while the girls gobble their rations of Goo-Goo Clusters, the Official Candy of the Grand Ole Opry.

After *Rhythm and Romance*, Rosanne was fried and just wanted to work on her short stories. The next album was supposed to be a simple best-hits collection. "I was driving home one night," begins Rodney, with a tall-tale look in his eyes, "and all of a sudden, out of the sky, a thunderbolt flashed into my mind and I said to myself—God, here comes that word again—Rose is an artist!'"

"Ar-*tiste*," corrects Rosanne, who's laughing.

"Yeah, well. Rose is a *thang*. And really good thangs don't put out greatest hits records. So I came home, and after about three hours of 'I Will Not Be Denied,' she started leading *me* around and we began to conceive what turned into *King's Record Shop*."

The album was done in six weeks. Imitating a TV game-show host,

Rodney quizzes Rosanne. "For 15 points, why do you think we work together better now? Tick, tick, tick..."

"Uh, because we're more secure?"

"Wrong! Bzzzz!"

"Uh, because we're more mature?"

"Bzzzz! Rose, ya' only got one more choice."

"Because we're dumber!"

He applauds. "Yeah, we just keep getting dumber and dumber!"

Lolling on the grass, Rosanne places her hands on her belly and gives a deep contented sigh. "Do you have to suffer deeply to be a good artist?" she asks. "We talk about that a lot. Think about Renoir: happily married, three children, idyllic country life. Not to draw comparisons between me and Renoir but—"

"—You'd look like a Renoir painting if we took your clothes off," says Rodney.

"You're so sweet to me."

"Well, I have to keep her spirits up."

"Wait, there's a thread of thought I don't want to lose here, oh yeah. I think if you've had the emotional experience, you can always reach back and draw on it. You just don't have to keep living it." She twirls a ripe strawberry between her finger tips. "I often feel like putting a code on the back of my albums saying, 'P.S. I don't feel like this anymore'."

Contributors

John H. Buckley has written about country music lyrics for several academic publications.

Robert Cantwell lives in Chapel Hill, North Carolina and has written extensively on bluegrass.

James C. Cobb teaches Southern Studies and History at the University of Tennessee.

Michael Dunne, author of *META-POP: Self-Referentiality in Contemporary American Popular Culture*, is with the English Department, Middle Tennessee State University.

Mark Fenster is with the Department of Telecommunications, Indiana University, and has written on country music videos.

Aaron Fox, author of "The Jukebox of History," is a graduate student in the Anthropology Department, University of Texas.

Paul Fryer has written in the areas of cultural geography and music.

David Gates is a music and culture critic for *Newsweek* magazine.

Jan Hoffman, a free lance writer, has appeared in the pages of the *Village Voice* and other publications.

Charles Jaret is with the Sociology Department, Georgia State University.

Joli Jensen, author of *Redeeming Modernity: Contradictions in Media Criticism* is with the Faculty of Communication, University of Tulsa.

Richard Leppert teaches in the Humanities Department, University of Minnesota.

George H. Lewis, editor of this volume, teaches in the Sociology/Anthropology Department, University of the Pacific.

George Lipsitz, author of *Time Passages*, is with the Ethnic Studies Department, University of California at San Diego.

Jock MacKay teaches in Social and Cultural Studies at Vanier College, St. Laurent, Quebec.

Bill C. Malone is author of *Country Music, U.S.A.* and numerous other publications in the field of country music.

Karl Neuenfeldt has an advanced degree from Simon Fraser University and is a musician and former record producer.

John H. Planer is Professor of Music at Manchester College.

Jimmie N. Rogers, author of *The Country Music Message*, is Chair of the Department of Communication, University of Arkansas.

Neil V. Rosenberg, author of *Bluegrass: A History* is with the Folklore Department, Memorial University of Newfoundland.

Karen Saucier writes on gender roles from a social science perspective.

Stephen A. Smith, who has written extensively in the area of country music and popular culture, is with the Department of Communication, University of Arkansas.

Nicholas Spitzer is with the Office of Folklife Programs of the Smithsonian Institution.

Katie Stewart teaches in the Department of Anthropology, University of Texas.

Ken Thompson is television critic for *Time* magazine's *Entertainment Weekly*.

Stephen Thompson is with the Department of Anthropology, University of Oklahoma.